D1483624

THE HOUSE OF
TUDOR

THE HOUSE OF
TUDOR

ALISON PLOWDEN

SUTTON PUBLISHING

First published in 1976 by Weidenfeld & Nicolson

First published in this revised edition in 1998 by
Sutton Publishing Limited · Phoenix Mill
Thrupp · Stroud · Gloucestershire · GL5 2BU

Copyright © Alison Plowden, 1976, 1998

All rights reserved. No part of this publication may be reproduced, stored in a
retrieval system, or transmitted, in any form, or by any means, electronic,
mechanical, photocopying, recording or otherwise, without the prior permission
of the publisher and copyright holder.

The author has asserted the moral right to be identified as the author of
this work.

British Library Cataloguing in Publication Data

A catalogue record for this book is available from the British Library

ISBN 0 7509 1890 X

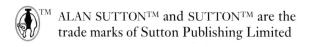ᵀᴹ ALAN SUTTONᵀᴹ and SUTTONᵀᴹ are the
trade marks of Sutton Publishing Limited

Typeset in 11/12pt Ehrhardt.
Typesetting and origination by
Sutton Publishing Limited.
Printed in Great Britain by
Butler and Tanner, Frome, Somerset.

Contents

Picture Credits

The author and publisher wish to thank the following for supplying prints and granting permission to reproduce illustrations:

Ashmolean Museum, Oxford: 54, 73
The Bodleian Library, Oxford: MS Douce 365, fol. 115r: 32 (top)
Bridgeman Art Library: 255
British Library: 112
© The British Museum: 21, 68, 76, 83 (bottom), 104, 109, 149, 179 (top), 204 (bottom)
The College of Arms: 233
By permission of the Dean and Canons of Windsor: 23
By courtesy of the Collection of the Duke of Northumberland: 241
Foto Biblioteca Vaticana: 107
Getty Images: 32 (bottom)
Guildhall Library: 200 (bottom)
Kunsthistorisches Museum, Vienna: 38, 119, 215
The President and Fellows of Magdalen College: 43
Mansell Collection, Time Inc., Katz Picture Agency: 211
By courtesy of the Marquess of Salisbury (print supplied by the National Portrait Gallery, London): 257
By kind permission of the Marquess of Tavistock and the Trustees of the Bedford Estate: 94

The Methuen Collection, Corsham Court: photograph Courtauld Institute of Art: 262
Musée du Louvre, © Photo RMN: Holbein, INV1348 Louvre: 133 (left)
National Gallery of Art, New York: 130 (top)
National Museum of Wales: 230
By courtesy of the National Portrait Gallery, London: 26, 83 (top left), 98, 133 (right), 135, 138, 155, 190, 200 (top), 204 (top), 219, 225, 231, 235, 258
Private Collection: 170
Public Record Office: 192
Queen's College, Cambridge: 11 (right)
RCHME © Crown Copyright: 13 (right), 216
Royal Academy of Art: 179 (bottom)
The Royal Armouries: 64
The Royal Collection © 1998 Her Majesty The Queen: 42 (left), 60, 100, 101, 121, 130 (bottom), 140–1, 151, 162, 260
St John's College, University of Cambridge: 13 (left)
Scottish National Portrait Gallery: 83 (top right), 250
Society of Antiquaries: 11 (left), 18, 55, 153
Victoria & Albert Museum, London: 246
Weidenfeld & Nicolson Archive: 6
Westminster Cathedral Library: 228

Chronology

1429?	Marriage of Owen Tudor and Queen Katherine Valois
1430–1436	Births of Edmund and Jasper Tudor and two other children
1437	
3 January	Death of Katherine Valois
July	Arrest of Owen Tudor
1439	
November	Owen Tudor released and granted a general pardon
1452	
23 November	Edmund Tudor created Earl of Richmond
1455	Marriage of Edmund Tudor and Margaret Beaufort
1456	
1 November	Death of Edmund Tudor
1457	
28 January	Birth of Henry Tudor, later King Henry VII
1461	
3 February	Battle of Mortimer's Cross
	Execution of Owen Tudor
1471	
4 May	Battle of Tewkesbury
21 May	Death of Henry VI
September	Henry and Jasper Tudor escape to Brittany
1483	
9 April	Death of Edward IV
26 June	Richard, Duke of Gloucester proclaimed King
July	Disappearance of the little Princes in the Tower
September	Unsuccessful conspiracy against Richard III

1483

25 December   Henry Tudor swears an oath to marry Elizabeth of York 'so soon
               as he should be king'

1485

22 August   Battle of Bosworth
               Death of Richard III
               Henry Tudor proclaimed King

1486

16 January   Marriage of Henry VII and Elizabeth of York
20 September   Birth of Prince Arthur

1487

16 June   Battle of Stoke
               Capture of Lambert Simnel

1495/96   Perkin Warbeck conspiracy

1497

October   Defeat and capture of Perkin Warbeck

1501

14 November   Marriage of Prince Arthur and Catherine of Aragon

1502

2 April   Death of Arthur

1503

11 February   Death of Elizabeth of York
8 August   Marriage of Margaret Tudor and James IV of Scotland

1509

21 April   Death of Henry VII
3 June   Marriage of Henry VIII and Catherine of Aragon

1513

9 September   Battle of Flodden
               Death of James IV

1514

August   Marriage of Margaret Tudor and the Earl of Angus
9 October   Marriage of Mary Tudor and Louis XII of France

1515

1 January	Death of Louis XII
February	Marriage of Mary Tudor and Charles Brandon, Duke of Suffolk

1516

18 February	Birth of Princess Mary, later Queen Mary I

1519

June	Birth of Henry Fitzroy, Henry VIII's bastard son

1527

May	Henry VIII takes first steps towards his divorce from Catherine of Aragon

1529

June	Hearing of the King's divorce case opens at Blackfriars before Cardinals Campeggio and Thomas Wolsey
July	Pope transfers hearing of the case to Rome

1530

29 November	Death of Cardinal Wolsey

1531

July	Henry separates from Catherine of Aragon

1533

25 January	Marriage of Henry VIII and Anne Boleyn
10 May	Archbishop Thomas Cranmer pronounces Henry's first marriage null and void and his second good and lawful
24 June	Death of Mary Tudor, Duchess of Suffolk
7 September	Birth of Princess Elizabeth, later Queen Elizabeth I

1534

March	Pope gives judgement on the divorce in Catherine's favour

1535

15 January	Henry VIII assumes title of Supreme Head of the Church
6 July	Execution of Sir Thomas More

1536

7 January	Death of Catherine of Aragon
19 May	Execution of Anne Boleyn
30 May	Marriage of Henry VIII and Jane Seymour
June	Princess Mary acknowledges her parents' marriage to have been unlawful and repudiates the Pope
22 July	Death of Henry Fitzroy, Duke of Richmond

1537

12 October	Birth of Prince Edward, later King Edward VI
	Death of Jane Seymour

1538

December	Henry VIII excommunicated

1540

6 January	Marriage of Henry VIII and Anne of Cleves
July	Henry divorces Anne of Cleves
28 July	Marriage of Henry VIII and Catherine Howard

1542

13 February	Execution of Catherine Howard
23 November	Battle of Solway Moss
8 December	Birth of Mary Queen of Scots
14 December	Death of James V of Scotland

1543

12 July	Marriage of Henry VIII and Catherine Parr

1547

28 January	Death of Henry VIII
	Edward Seymour, Duke of Somerset, becomes Lord Protector
May	Marriage of Queen Catherine Parr and Thomas Seymour

1548

7 September	Death of Catherine Parr

1549

20 March	Execution of Thomas Seymour

1550

4 June	Marriage of Robert Dudley and Amy Robsart

1552

22 January	Execution of Duke of Somerset

1553

21 May	Marriage of Lady Jane Grey and Guildford Dudley
6 July	Death of Edward VI followed by Duke of Northumberland's attempted coup and brief reign of 'Queen Jane'
19 July	Mary Tudor proclaimed Queen in London
22 August	Execution of Duke of Northumberland

1554

January	Wyatt Rebellion
12 February	Execution of Jane Grey
18 March	Princess Elizabeth taken to the Tower
25 July	Marriage of Queen Mary and Philip of Spain
November	England reconciled to Rome

1555

	Mary believes herself pregnant
April	Elizabeth released from house arrest at Woodstock

1556

21 March	Thomas Cranmer burnt as a heretic

1558

7 January	Loss of Calais
17 November	Death of Queen Mary

1559

January/ May	Elizabethan Settlement of Religion

1560

8 September	Death of Amy Dudley
December	Marriage of Lady Katherine Grey and Earl of Hertford

1561

August	Mary Queen of Scots returns to Scotland from France

1564

29 September	Robert Dudley created Earl of Leicester

1565

29 July	Marriage of Mary Queen of Scots and Lord Darnley

1566

19 June	Birth of Prince James, later King James I

1567

10 February	Murder of Darnley

1568

27 January	Death of Lady Katherine Grey
16 May	Flight of Mary Queen of Scots into England

1587

8 February   Execution of Mary Queen of Scots

1588

July/August Defeat of the Spanish Armada
4 September   Death of Earl of Leicester

1601

February   Essex Rebellion
25 February   Execution of Earl of Essex

1603

24 March   Death of Queen Elizabeth

CHAPTER 1
A Bull of Anglesey

A Bull of Anglesey demanding satisfaction
He is the hope of our race.

When the bull comes from the far land to battle with his great ashen spear,
To be an earl again in the land of Llewelyn,
Let the far-splitting spear shed the blood of the Saxon on the stubble . . .
When the long yellow summer comes and victory comes to us
And the spreading of the sails of Brittany,
And when the heat comes and when the fever is kindled,
There are portents that victory will be given to us . . .

sang the bards in the 'long yellow summer' of 1485, as they waited for the fleet which would carry 'the one who will strike', Henry Earl of Richmond, the black bull of Anglesey, the peacock of Tudor, back to the land of his fathers. There was longing for Harry, they sang, whose name 'comes down from the mountains as a two-edged sword', for *mab y darogan*, the long promised hero who would fulfil the prophecy of Myrddin the wizard, who would deliver his people from the Saxon oppressor and bring content to the blessed land of Gwynedd.

'The most wise and fortunate Henry VII is a Welshman', remarked the Italian author of *A Relation of the Island of Britain*, and although the Welshness of the first Henry Tudor can easily be (and often is) exaggerated, Henry himself was fully aware of the importance which should be attached to the fulfilment of bardic prophecies. He was also conscious of the political advantages to be gained by polishing his image as 'a high-born Briton of the stock of Maelgwyn' – prince of the line of Cadwaladr of the beautiful spear. At any rate, David Powel, writing in 1584, says that the King appointed a three-man commission to enquire into the matter of his pedigree and that these seekers after knowledge, having consulted the bards and other appropriate authorities, 'drew his perfect genelogie from the ancient Kings of Brytaine and Princes of Wales'.

It must be admitted that the actual origins of the House of Tudor do not quite match the imaginative flights of the Abbot of Valle Crucis, Dr Poole, canon of Hereford and John King, herald. At the same time, the historical story of the family's rise, untidy and incomplete though it is, should be romantic enough for most people.

The earliest Tudors were landowners in a small way from North Wales, farming the country round Colwyn Bay to the east of the River Conwy, and their fortunes were founded by Ednyfed Fychan (Ednyfed the Younger) who flourished during the first half of the thirteenth century. Ednyfed enjoyed a long and successful career in the service of Llywelyn the Great, Prince of Gwynedd, and was rewarded with grants of land in Anglesey and Caernarvon, as well as estates in West Wales. He married, as his second wife, Gwenllian, daughter of Rhys, Prince of South Wales, and his sons, Goronwy and Tudur, inherited both his office of seneschal or steward to the rulers of Gwynedd and his considerable property.

The final subjugation of Wales by England in the early 1280s does not seem to have seriously affected the family's status. Like a good many other native magnates, Ednyfed's grandson, Tudur Hen ap Goronwy, probably supported the English Crown – at least he is recorded as having done homage to Edward of Caernarvon, the first English Prince of Wales, in 1301 – and by the middle of the century this Tudur's grandson, another Tudur ap Goronwy, was established as an influential member of the new gentry class that had begun to emerge out of the decay of the old Welsh tribal society.

But unfortunately for the descendants of Ednyfed Fychan, the old Welsh tribal loyalties were not yet dead. Tudur ap Goronwy the Second had married an aunt of Owain Glyndwr, and when Glyndwr rose in revolt against Henry IV at the beginning of the 1400s, Tudur's surviving sons came out for their cousin. In fact, in a highly complicated political situation, the loyalties involved may well have been as much English as Welsh. Glyndwr is said to have served in Richard II's army, and three of the Tudur brothers had at one time been members of Richard's retinue. But whatever their motives in joining the revolt, it was to have disastrous results for the whole clan.

Harsh reprisals were taken against the rebels and, according to the chronicler Adam of Usk, Rhys ap Tudur was executed at Chester in 1412. All the Tudur estates were confiscated, although one property, Penmynydd in Anglesey, was eventually recovered by the heirs of the eldest brother, Goronwy. This branch of the family, which took to spelling their name Theodor, remained at Penmynydd, obscure country squires taking a modest part in local affairs, until the line petered out towards the end of the seventeenth century, leaving nothing behind but some monuments in the parish church. And that might very well have been the whole story, were it not for the quirk of fate that brought Owain, son of the youngest brother, Maredudd, into the English royal household.

No one knows exactly where or when Owain ap Maredudd ap Tudur, more conveniently Owen Tudor, was born, but it must have been some time around 1400. Nor does anyone know exactly how or when he entered the royal service, although he may have followed Glyndwr's son, who was officially pardoned in 1417 and became a Squire of the Body to Henry V. There is no evidence to support the tradition that he was present at Agincourt, but he may have been in France in 1421 on the staff of the distinguished soldier and diplomat Sir Walter Hungerford. Sir Walter was one of the executors of Henry V's will, and in 1424 became steward to the infant Henry VI. It is at least possible that he was the means of introducing the promising young Welshman to the notice of the Queen

Dowager, Katherine of Valois. All we know for certain is that at some point in the 1420s Owen Tudor became Clerk of the Wardrobe to Henry V's widow and that in 1429, or it may have been in 1432, he and the Queen were married.

The traditional story goes that Owen and Katherine concealed their relationship from the world until, one day, their secret was betrayed to Humphrey, Duke of Gloucester, Protector of the Realm, who promptly incarcerated the Queen in a nunnery, where she died of a broken heart, and threw Owen into prison. From the known facts, scanty though they are, it is possible to reconstruct a rather more prosaic, if no less remarkable sequence of events.

Although so many of the circumstances surrounding the romance of the French princess and the 'gentleman of Wales' which was to have such far-reaching consequences for England remain shrouded in mystery, it seems reasonable to assume tradition is right in saying that Owen and Katherine fell in love. At least, it seems reasonable to assume that Katherine fell in love. Shakespeare regardless, her short-lived marriage to Henry V had been a matter of high politics. She was barely twenty when she became a widow and her son, 'Harry born at Windsor' and destined to lose all the glory his famous father had won, became King at the age of nine months. As Queen Dowager, Katherine's position was not a happy one. She had no say in the government and none to speak of in the upbringing of her little son. Bored, lonely and with nothing to look forward to but the prospect of a lifetime of barren exile, she would naturally be susceptible to the attentions of an attractive man – 'following more her appetite than friendly counsel and regarding more her private affections than her open honour', as the chronicler Edward Hall was to put it.

There are no strictly contemporary descriptions of Owen Tudor, but Hall says he was 'a goodly gentleman and a beautiful person' and Polydore Vergil, who began his *History of England* in the reign of Owen's grandson, is enthusiastic about his 'wonderful gifts of body and mind'. An earlier chronicler, with no royal Tudor patrons to consider, is noticeably less complimentary in a passing reference to 'one Oweyn, no man of birth neither of livelihood'. All the same, Owen obviously had something to recommend him, and good looks and personal charm would seem to be the most likely attributes. We can only speculate – but the Queen and her Clerk of the Wardrobe would have been in daily contact, they were about the same age and both were strangers in a strange land. Perhaps it is not so surprising that they should have gravitated together.

The fact that the King's mother had 'privily wedded' one of her servants was not advertised. The earliest known reference to it occurs in one of the London chronicles in a brief entry under the year 1438, and says that the common people knew nothing of it until after the Queen was dead and buried. This may well be true, and it also seems possible that the young King was kept in ignorance of his mother's second marriage during her lifetime. But it must certainly have been common knowledge in court circles generally. At least, none of the traditional accounts explain how Katherine contrived to produce four Tudor babies – Edmund, born at the royal manor of Hadham in Hertfordshire, Jasper, born at Hatfield, another son, Owen, and a daughter – without anybody apparently noticing these interesting events. Everything, in fact, points to the conclusion that the Queen and her socially undesirable husband were left in peace to enjoy the all too brief period of their married life. When Katherine retired into the Abbey of Bermondsey some time in 1436 there is no evidence at all that this was due to anything but the 'long and grievous illness' which finally killed her on 3 January 1437.

After the Queen's death, her second family broke up. Edmund and Jasper were placed in the care of the Abbess of Barking, who looked after them for the next three years. The two younger children have no part in this story, but Owen later became a monk at Westminster, surviving into his nephew's reign, and the girl is said to have gone into a nunnery. As for their father, the remainder of his career has a distinct flavour of melodrama.

Now that he could no longer count on the protection of his wife's status, the adventurous gentleman of Wales seems to have thought it prudent to make himself scarce for a while. At any rate, he was as far away as Daventry in the Midlands when, shortly after Katherine's death a summons was issued by the Council requiring 'one Owen Tudor which dwelled with the said Queen Katherine' to come into the King's presence. Owen evidently suspected a trap, for he declined to accept the invitation unless he was first given an assurance, in the King's name, that he might 'freely come and freely go'. A verbal promise to this effect was duly delivered by one Myles Sculle, but Owen was not satisfied. He did, however, make his way secretly to London where he went into sanctuary at Westminster, resisting the persuasions of his friends to come and disport himself in the tavern at Westminster gate. After a period of time described as 'many days', days no doubt spent in reconnoitring the situation, Owen emerged from his lair to make a sudden appearance in the royal presence. He had heard, he said, that the King was 'heavily informed of him' and was anxious to declare his innocence and truth. But almost certainly Henry, now fifteen years old, had just wanted to take a look at his unknown stepfather and Owen was allowed to depart 'without any impeachment'. In fact, he had freely come and freely gone – but not for long.

Like so much else about him, the reason for Owen Tudor's arrest and committal to ward in Newgate gaol remains a mystery. Polydore Vergil says it was ordered by the Duke of Gloucester because Owen 'had been so presumptuous as by marriage with the Queen to intermix his blood with the noble race of kings', but there is absolutely no evidence to support this assertion. In two obscurely worded documents, one of which is dated 15 July 1437, the Council were at considerable pains to establish the legality of the arrest, having regard to the King's recent promise of safe conduct and also, it may be assumed, to the prisoner's royal connections. In neither of these documents is any specific charge mentioned, but from the very meagre information they do contain, it looks as if Owen was involved in a private quarrel – probably of a financial nature – with some person or persons unknown.

The next news of him appears in the Chronicle of London, which records that he 'brake out of Newgate against night at searching time, through help of his priest, and went his way, hurting foul his keeper; but at the last, blessed be God, he was taken again.' This exploit took place early in 1438, for in March of that year Lord Beaumont received twenty marks to cover his expenses in guarding the fugitives and bringing them before the Council. Owen, his priest and his servant were sent back to Newgate in disgrace, but a sum of eighty-nine pounds which was found on the priest was confiscated and handed over to the Treasury. Who this enterprising cleric was, where that quite sizeable amount of money came from, and why Owen had been so desperate to escape are three more unanswered questions. He was transferred from Newgate to Windsor Castle in July 1438, a move which is again unexplained but which seems to have marked the beginning of an improvement in his fortunes. In July of the following year he was conditionally released – one of the conditions being that he made no attempt to go to Wales or 'parts adjacent'. Presumably the authorities were remembering the old Tudor involvement with Glyn Dwr. At last, in November 1439, he was granted a general pardon for all offences committed before October, though there is still no indication as to what those offences had been.

Owen had spent two years in gaol without trial and a further four months on probation, but from then on he became respectable. The King, 'moved by special causes', provided him with a pension of forty pounds a year, paid out of the privy purse 'by especial favour' and his name crops up from time to time over the next twenty years in the Calendars of the Close and Patent Rolls as witness to a charter, as sharing in the grant of a holding at Lambeth, as receiving an annuity of a hundred pounds; but it is an entry of 1459 which is the most significant historically, for it was then that Owen ap Meredith ap Tudur seems to have finally become Owen Tudor esquire. Owen himself followed the normal Welsh custom of adding his father's name to his own – at least he referred to himself as Owen ap Meredith in his petition for letters of denizenship in 1432. In official documents he is variously described as Owen ap Meredith, Owen Meredith, Owen ap Meredith ap Tudur (or Tider) until 1459, when a hurrying clerk wrote him down as Owen Tuder and gave England a Tudor instead of a Meredith dynasty.

While their father was enduring his mysterious difficulties and gradually winning his way back into polite society, Edmund and Jasper Tudor were growing up. In November 1452 they were created Earls of Richmond and Pembroke respectively and thereafter were granted lands and offices by the Crown. In fact, the gentle, devout, ineffectual Henry VI showed both his half-brothers a remarkable degree of generosity, but never more so than when it came to choosing a wife for the new Earl of Richmond. In 1455 Edmund Tudor married Margaret Beaufort – an event which took him a giant step up the social ladder and which was to have an incalculable effect on the whole course of English history.

The Beaufort family was the result of a long-ago liaison between John of Gaunt, Duke of Lancaster, and his daughters' governess, Katherine Swynford, née de Roet. Their four children were indisputably born on the wrong side of the blanket, but after the death of his second wife John of Gaunt had made an honest woman of Katherine, and his Beaufort progeny (so called after the castle in France where they were born) had been legitimized by the Pope, by Letters Patent issued by Richard II and, for good measure, by Act of Parliament. The Beauforts grew rich and powerful – Cardinal Beaufort, last survivor of Katherine Swynford's brood, had governed England with the Duke of Gloucester during Henry VI's minority – and after the King and his heirs they represented the ruling family of Lancaster.

Pembroke Castle, birthplace of Henry Tudor.

The bestowal of Margaret Beaufort, a great-great-grand-daughter of Edward III, was a matter of State and what prompted the King to grant first the wardship and then the marriage of this important heiress of the blood royal to such a junior member of the peerage, son of an obscure Welsh esquire but with possibly complicating royal connections, is yet another mystery. Perhaps, at a time of increasing political instability, Henry simply felt that the Tudors at least could be trusted to remain loyal Lancastrians. If so, he was to be proved right.

Edmund's marriage coincided with the outbreak of that long-drawn-out dynastic struggle among the all too numerous descendants of Edward III, conveniently known as the Wars of the Roses. The roots of the quarrel went back to the *coup d'état* of 1399, when Henry Bolingbroke had wrested the crown from his cousin Richard, and, like most family quarrels, it became progressively more bitter and more complicated with the passage of time.

Edmund Tudor, Earl of Richmond, did not live to see its outcome. Nor did he live to see his son. He died at Carmarthen in November 1456, leaving his young wife six months pregnant. Jasper at once came to the rescue, taking his brother's widow under his protection, and Margaret Beaufort's child was born at Pembroke Castle on 28 January 1457. There is an interesting tradition that the baby was to have been christened Owen (which sounds like Jasper's choice), but that his mother insisted he should be given the royal and English name of Henry. Although the Countess of Richmond was herself little more than a child – she was probably only twelve years old at the time of her marriage – this sort of determination would have been perfectly in character. An intelligent, serious-minded, deeply religious girl, she later developed into a formidable personality, exercising a profound influence on the dynasty she had founded.

In the general turmoil of the 1450s the arrival of a fatherless infant in a wintry and uncertain world attracted no particular attention, and for the first five years of his life Henry Tudor stayed with his mother, snug in his uncle Jasper's stronghold of Pembroke. Not that he saw much of his uncle Jasper. The fortunes of the Tudor family were now inextricably involved with those of the Lancastrian cause and as the deadly power-game of York and Lancaster unfolded, the Earl of Pembroke was proving himself one of Henry VI's most useful supporters.

At first things went relatively well but early in 1461 came disaster, when the Lancastrians were heavily defeated at the battle of Mortimer's Cross. One casualty of this reversal was Owen Tudor, quite an old man by now but who had nevertheless been present fighting under Jasper's banner. Owen was among those captured by the Yorkists and taken to Hereford to be executed in the market place. It is ironical, but not untypical of his whole story, that it is not until the moment of his death that we get our only authentic personal glimpse of the man who sired a line of kings and whose remote descendants sit on the English throne today. It seems that the gentleman of Wales could not bring himself to believe that his luck had turned at last, for William Gregory's chronicle says that he trusted 'all away that he should not be headed till he saw the axe and the block, and when that he was in his doublet he trusted on pardon and grace till the collar of his red velvet doublet was ripped off. Then he said "that head shall lie on the stock that was wont to lie on Queen Katherine's lap" and put his heart and mind wholly unto God and full meekly took his death.' His head was displayed on the highest step of the market cross and there followed a gruesome incident when 'a mad woman combed his hair and washed away the blood of his face, and she got candles and set about him burning more than a hundred'.

Jasper, tough, energetic and resourceful, escaped from Mortimer's Cross with his life – though that was about all he escaped with. Some six weeks later the Yorkist Earl of March was proclaimed King as Edward IV and another Lancastrian defeat, at Towton, soon confirmed his position. Henry VI's indomitable Queen, Margaret of Anjou, managed to keep the fight alive for a time, but eventually she and her son were forced to take refuge in France. Henry himself, reduced to a wandering fugitive, was betrayed to his enemies and deposited in the Tower. The eclipse of the Lancastrians seemed complete.

It was not long, of course, before the misfortunes of his relatives rebounded on the little boy at Pembroke. Jasper Tudor, wanted for treason by the new regime and stripped of his lands and title, was reported 'flown and taken to the mountains'. With the best will in the world he no longer had any power to protect his nephew and his sister-in-law. Pembroke Castle surrendered to the Yorkists in November 1461, and Henry Tudor was separated from his mother and transferred to the custody of Lord Herbert of Raglan. It must have been a traumatic experience for a child of four-and-a-half, but his new guardian seems to have treated him kindly. In fact Lord Herbert planned to marry him to his daughter, Maud, so it is reasonable to assume that he was brought up as one of the family and given an education proper to his station in life. The names of two of his tutors are known, and he is said to have been an apt pupil.

Young Henry remained with the Herberts in Wales for the next nine years. The existence of this obscure sprig of the ruined Lancastrians did not cause the ruling Yorkist party to lose any sleep. Henry Tudor was being raised in a reliable Yorkist family – he would have plenty of opportunity to see where his own best interests lay. Then came a dramatic series of developments which temporarily altered the whole political situation, and permanently and drastically altered the status of Lord Herbert's ward.

In 1469 Edward IV fell out with his most powerful supporter, Richard Neville, Earl of Warwick, known as 'the Kingmaker'. Warwick went over to the other side and by the summer of 1470 he was in France, burying the hatchet with Queen Margaret, once his bitterest enemy, and canvassing the support of Louis XI for another *coup d'état*. By the autumn a remarkable triple alliance had been sealed. Edward, caught unawares, found it necessary to go abroad in a hurry and the brief 'Readeption' of Henry VI had begun.

Prominent among the returning exiles was Jasper Tudor, who had spent most of his years in the wilderness conducting a one-man guerrilla campaign against the Yorkist regime – moving from one safe house to another in Wales, then turning up in Ireland, then Scotland, making a descent on the Northumbrian coast, over to France (where King Louis recognized him as cousin), then landing in Wales again with fifty followers to make a commando-type raid on Denbigh Castle. 'Not always at his heart's ease, nor in security of life or surety of living' Jasper never gave up and missed no chance, however unpromising, of keeping a spark of resistance alight.

One of his first actions on arriving in England was to make the journey to Wales to retrieve his nephew, whom he found 'kept as a prisoner, but honourably brought up with the wife of William Herbert'. Jasper took the boy, now rising fourteen, back to London with him, and early in November Henry Tudor was presented to Henry VI. It is natural that Jasper should have been anxious to remind the newly restored King of the existence of his brother's son, but Polydore Vergil was probably improving on the occasion when he records that Henry VI, after gazing silently on the child for 'a pretty space', turned to his attendant lords and remarked: 'This truly, this is he unto whom both we and our adversaries must yield and give over the dominion.' Admittedly the King was widely regarded as a holy man and a mystic who might be expected to feel moved to prophecy, but very few Englishmen in that unsettled winter would have been prepared to commit themselves for more than a few days ahead, and to the practical men of affairs at Court Henry Tudor's future would have looked as precarious and uncertain as their own.

In spite of his signal services to the Lancastrian cause, there was no government appointment or seat on the Council for Jasper Tudor. He and his nephew were sent back to Wales with instructions to be ready to mobilize their people should the war be renewed, but Jasper did at least have the satisfaction of recovering his earldom from the Herbert family. Even this was short lived. Barely six months after his flight, Edward IV was back in England re-proclaiming himself King. On Easter Day 1471, he defeated Warwick's army at Barnet – a battle fought, appropriately enough, in thick fog. The Kingmaker was killed and Henry VI, 'a man amazed and utterly dulled with troubles and adversity', found himself back in the Tower.

On the day that Barnet was being lost and won, Queen Margaret and her son, Edward Prince of Wales, landed at Weymouth – too late to save the situation. Together with the Lancastrian lords who rallied to them, they marched up the Severn valley, hoping to join forces with Jasper Tudor and his Welshmen hurrying down from the north. But Edward IV, moving with his usual speed and tactical skill, intercepted the Queen at Tewkesbury – an encounter which ended in final and complete disaster for the Lancastrians. The last surviving male members of the Beaufort family lost their lives and the Prince of Wales, for whose sake his mother had striven so long and so gallantly, was killed as he tried to escape. On Tuesday, 21 May, King Edward returned to London in triumph and that same night, 'between eleven and twelve of the clock', King Henry was released from his earthly troubles by a Yorkist sword.

When Jasper heard the grim news that Queen Margaret 'was vanquished in a foughten field at Tewkesbury and that matters were past all hope of recovery', he retreated to Chepstow, where he narrowly escape capture and death. Again a hunted fugitive, Jasper had to move fast if he was to be able to perform one more vitally important service for the future of his party. After the horrifying events of the past few weeks, his young nephew had incredibly become the only surviving male of the Lancastrian line. At all costs Henry Tudor must be prevented from falling into Yorkist hands.

It is not entirely clear whether Henry was with his uncle's army – more likely he had been left behind at Pembroke. At any rate, Jasper made straight for Pembroke from Chepstow and was promptly besieged in the castle by Morgan Thomas, acting on instructions from Edward IV. But the Tudor luck held. Morgan Thomas's brother David was an old friend of Jasper's, and after about a week he succeeded in getting uncle and nephew through the 'ditch and trench' of the besiegers' lines. Jasper and Henry, with a small party of servants and followers, reached the coast at Tenby where they found a ship, helped it is said by Thomas White, mayor of the town. It would be fourteen years before they saw Wales again.

The refugees were making for France where they might reasonably expect to be granted political asylum. But, fortunately as it turned out, a storm blew them on to the coast of Brittany. According to Polydore Vergil, Duke Francis II 'received them willingly, and with such honour, courtesy and favour entertained them as though they had been his brothers, promising them upon his honour that within his dominion they should be from thenceforth far from injury, and pass at their pleasure to and fro without danger.'

Not surprisingly Edward IV had not been pleased by the Tudors' escape and attempted to bribe Duke Francis into giving them up – with the inevitable result of impressing the Duke with a sense of the value of his guests. He had promised them asylum, he told the English ambassador, and of course he could not break his word, but he would undertake to keep uncle and nephew 'so surely' that the King of England need not be afraid 'they should ever procure his harm any manner of way'. Edward was obliged to agree to this arrangement, which proved highly advantageous to Brittany. Jasper and Henry were separated, deprived of their English servants and guarded instead by Bretons, while in return Duke Francis collected a handsome pension from King Edward.

Four years later, in August 1475, England and France came to terms in the Treaty of Picquigny, and Edward made another determined effort to get his hands on Henry Tudor – 'the only impe now left of King Henry VI's blood'. He despatched another embassy, 'laden with great substance of gold', with instructions to tell the Duke of Brittany that he was anxious to arrange a marriage for Henry that would unite the rival factions of York and Lancaster. After some persuasion Duke Francis was convinced, either by the sight of that 'great substance of gold' or by the smooth-talking envoys, and he handed his prisoner over. 'Not supposing', says Polydore Vergil, 'that he had committed the sheep to the wolf, but the son to the father.'

The ambassadors set off with their prize towards the coast, while Henry, 'knowing that he was carried to his death, through agony of mind fell by the way into a fever' – or pretended that he did. Luckily, the Duke was warned in the nick of time that the young man 'was not so earnestly sought for to be coupled in marriage with King Edward's daughter, as to have his head parted from his body with an axe'. It seems that Francis had not been moved solely by financial considerations, for he reacted swiftly to the news of King Edward's treachery, sending his Treasurer, Peter Landois, hurrying to the rescue. Henry was snatched back at St Malo and removed to sanctuary in the town. After this, although he continued to pay for having Henry and Jasper kept in protective custody, Edward was apparently content to leave them where they were. He had sons of his own growing up by this time and any threat posed by the penniless exiles in Brittany could scarcely be regarded as pressing.

We know virtually nothing about how Henry and his uncle passed their years of confinement. Their material needs would have been provided for; they would have had books and music and been able to take exercise, but all the same – for Henry especially – it must have been a singularly cheerless existence. Time was passing and Henry Tudor was growing into a man helpless to defend himself, entirely dependent on the goodwill of a protector who might at any moment be subjected to irresistible pressure from outside. Fretting in his Breton captivity, he can have seen very little prospect of ever being able to lead a normal life, or indeed of ever being in a position to recover his father's earldom of Richmond.

Then suddenly, in April 1483, Edward IV was dead. His two young sons fell into the hands of their uncle Richard, Duke of Gloucester, and were lodged in the Tower of London, pending the coronation of the thirteen-year-old Edward V. But before this could take place, Gloucester made the interesting discovery that Edward IV's marriage to Queen Elizabeth Woodville had been invalid and that his children were therefore illegitimate. By the end of June, Richard of Gloucester had been proclaimed King and it was noticed that the princes were no longer to be seen shooting and playing in the Tower gardens. Yet another successful *coup*

Edward IV and his Queen, Elizabeth Woodville. Her marriage to Edward was declared invalid after his death and she gave her support to Henry's claim.

d'état appeared to have been accomplished. The Yorkists, though, were still in the saddle, and on the face of it there seemed no particular reason why the fortunes of the exiled Lancastrians should be affected one way or the other. Nevertheless, within three months there was to be a sensational improvement in their circumstances.

The precise origins of the conspiracy to replace Richard III by Henry Tudor remain somewhat obscure, as do the reasons that prompted Henry Stafford, Duke of Buckingham – who had played a prominent part in putting Richard on the throne – to come out that same year in favour of Henry. The obvious explanation, of course, is that by the end of the summer Buckingham had good reason to believe that Richard had had his nephews murdered. Controversy about the fate of 'the little Princes in the Tower' is still very much alive and, in the absence of any startling new evidence, it will probably remain so. Two facts, however, are not in dispute. After midsummer 1483 no one outside the Tower saw either of the boys again, and by early autumn rumours of their death by foul play were being freely circulated.

The date of the inception of the Tudor conspiracy is not known, but one thing seems pretty certain and that is that Henry Tudor's mother was one of the prime movers. Margaret Beaufort had married twice since her first widowhood and in

1483 was the wife of a prominent Yorkist, Thomas, Lord Stanley. She had borne no more children, and although she can scarcely have seen her son since he had been taken from her at Pembroke all those years ago, he had kept first place in her heart and thoughts. Margaret would, of course, be in a position to hear all the political gossip and the moment she realized that Edward IV's sons were being presumed dead, she began to devote all her considerable talents to the task of promoting the future 'well doing and glory' of her own offspring.

Her first step was to make contact with Edward IV's widow. Elizabeth Woodville had taken sanctuary at Westminster with her daughters but, by a fortunate coincidence, both she and Margaret Beaufort employed the services of a Welsh physician named Lewis, 'a grave man and of no small experience', well qualified to act as go-between. The plan he unfolded to the Queen Dowager was that if she and her numerous and ambitious relations would undertake to support Henry Tudor's claim to the throne, Henry, once he had unseated the usurper, would undertake to marry Edward IV's eldest daughter and thus unite the warring factions. The widow and her daughters proved agreeable – Elizabeth Woodville promising 'to do her endeavour' to persuade her late husband's friends to take Henry's part. Thus encouraged, Margaret Beaufort widened her net, entrusting her steward, Reginald Bray, with the delicate and dangerous task of enlisting the support of 'such noble and worshipful men as were wise, faithful and active' and ready to help her cause. In a surprisingly short space of time Bray had successfully interested quite a number of substantial gentlemen and Margaret was on the point of sending a courier to Brittany, when she learned that the Duke of Buckingham was also contemplating action.

The two happened to meet on the high road, so the story goes, as Margaret was travelling between Bridgnorth and Worcester. Until this moment Buckingham had apparently been thinking in terms of proposing himself as an alternative to King Richard – he was, after all, a Beaufort on his mother's side and doubly descended from Edward III. However, according to his own account, this casual meeting with Margaret Beaufort reminded him forcibly that she and her son stood as 'both bulwark and portcullis' between him and the getting of the Crown, so that he utterly relinquished 'all such phantasticall imaginations'. If we knew what really passed between Margaret and her 'cousin of Buks' in that convenient roadside encounter, we should probably know a good deal more about the complicated web of intrigue being spun in England that summer; but it seems that the Duke went on to have a serious talk with John Morton, Bishop of Ely, and as a result both men decided to commit themselves to supporting Henry Tudor.

Now that she was sure of these two important allies Margaret lost no more time in getting in touch with her son, and despatched one Hugh Conway with a large sum of money and instructions to urge Henry to return home at once. He was to make for Wales, where he would find help waiting. It is possible that Hugh Conway brought the first news of the astonishing change in his prospects; at any rate up to this time – about the middle of September – Henry had made no move on his own account. Not that he was in any position to do so. Although he had been free from actual physical restraint after Edward IV's death, he was still a

Left: *Margaret Beaufort as a young girl; an unauthenticated portrait by an unknown artist.*
Right: *Reginald Bray, steward to Margaret Beaufort, was entrusted with the task of enlisting support and raising money for Henry Tudor's cause.*

penniless refugee, dependent on his friends to set the ball rolling. But now this had been done it was up to Henry Tudor – still a completely unknown quantity – to show what he was made of, to justify his mother's faith in him and seize what might be the chance of a lifetime. With the advice and help of his uncle Jasper, an old hand at this sort of game, Henry responded bravely to the challenge. The Duke of Brittany was prepared to help with a loan of 10,000 crowns. The Tudors raised a small force of ships and mercenaries, and by the second week in October they were ready to go.

Meanwhile, in England, the worst was happening. King Richard had got wind of Buckingham's activities and a spontaneous rising in Kent seems to have erupted prematurely. The next sequence of events is uncertain, but by the time Henry made landfall off Poole harbour all element of surprise had gone. Swallowing his disappointment, Henry made the only wise decision – to cut his losses – and gave orders to hoist up sail.

He and Jasper were back in Brittany in time to hear the depressing news that the take-over bid had collapsed and that the Duke of Buckingham had been captured and executed. Margaret Beaufort herself only narrowly escaped the normal penalty for high treason – probably because Richard dared not risk alienating the powerful Stanley family. Some of the other conspirators escaped the King's wrath altogether. The Bishop of Ely, Thomas Grey, Marquis of Dorset and Elizabeth Woodville's eldest son by her first marriage, the Courtenays of Devonshire, the Brandon brothers, John Bourchier, John Cheyney and Thomas Arundel were among those who were able to cross the Channel and join the Tudors in exile. On Christmas Day 1483, at the cathedral of Rennes, Henry swore a solemn oath in the presence of his supporters that 'so soon as he should be King he would marry Elizabeth, King Edward's daughter'; after which they in turn swore homage 'as though he had been already created king'.

Anglo-Breton relations had naturally been somewhat strained after the previous autumn's fiasco but now Richard, who (according to Polydore Vergil) was leading a miserable life, tormented with fear of Henry's return, made up his mind to arrange another truce and rid himself of 'this inward grief'. His chance came early in June. Duke Francis was an elderly man, becoming feeble 'by reason of sore and daily sickness'. The reins of government passed temporarily into the hands of the Treasurer, Peter Landois, and it was Landois who received King Richard's ambassadors. They offered the annual revenues of the earldom of Richmond together with those of all the other English nobles who had taken refuge in Brittany in exchange for the surrender of Henry Tudor. Landois, 'a man of sharp wit and great authority' and consequently highly unpopular among his fellow-countrymen, saw an opportunity of gaining a useful foreign ally and it was apparently for this reason that he agreed to betray his master's protégé.

It was John Morton in Flanders who got to hear of this amiable scheme and sent a warning to Henry by Christopher Urswick, 'an honest, approved and serviceable priest', who had just come out from England. Henry was at Vannes when Morton's messenger reached him and he at once sent Urswick to France for permission to cross the border. As soon as this had been obtained, an escape plan organized on classic lines went smoothly into operation. It was arranged that Jasper should escort the English nobles to call on Duke Francis, whose retreat happened to be close to the frontier, their pretext being the need to discuss Henry's affairs. Instead, they were to turn aside and get themselves into France at the first opportunity. Henry himself left Vannes with only five attendants, saying that he was going to visit a friend who had a manor nearby. No immediate suspicion was aroused because of the large number of English left in the town, and the innocent-looking little party ambled peacefully out of Vannes unchallenged. But after they had covered about five miles, they left the road and Henry changed into 'serving man's apparel' in the shelter of a convenient wood. Thus disguised he rode the rest of the way behind one of his own servants, who guided him by the quickest route over the border into Anjou. They were only just in time, for Landois had been alerted and his men were riding hard in pursuit. Henry Tudor reached the safety of French soil with barely an hour's margin.

Thanks to John Morton and his own cool head, Henry had saved his own life by a whisker. He had also saved the most valuable of his supporters and was later able to salvage the rest. When Duke Francis recovered, he was much displeased with Peter Landois and gave orders that the English marooned in Vannes were to be allowed to leave for France with their travelling expenses paid.

The Tudor cause had suffered a serious set-back but on the whole the political situation in France was favourable. Louis XI had died the previous August, to be succeeded by his thirteen-year-old son, Charles, and the regency was disposed to be friendly to the exiles. At least, it was disposed to make use of them to embarrass King Richard and prevent him from sending military aid to Brittany – France was just then making preparations to swallow the last of her independent duchies. But it all meant delay, while the new government coped with more pressing matters, and Henry could not afford too much delay. Many of his followers were disgruntled Yorkists whose loyalty could not be relied on for ever – indeed the Marquis of Dorset did try to slip away – and his friends at home might lose heart, and interest, if they were left too long between hope and dread. Elizabeth of York was still unmarried, but there was no telling how much longer she and her sisters would be allowed to remain single and without the Yorkist marriage Henry's chances of uniting a chronically factious nobility would be minimal. In his ancestral Wales, where the forces of nationalism were working strongly in his favour, the bards were growing impatient:

> In what seas are thy anchors, and where art thou thyself?
> When wilt thou, Black Bull, come to land;
> How long shall we wait?
> On the feast of the Virgin fair Gwynedd, in her singing, watched the seas.

The letters being smuggled out of England brought messages of goodwill from Henry's stepfather Lord Stanley and his brother William Stanley, from Gilbert Talbot and 'others innumerable'. From Wales came word that Rhys ap Thomas and other 'men of power' in the principality were ready and waiting, and that the useful Reginald Bray had collected 'no small sum of money' to pay soldiers; but John Morgan, the lawyer, was urging haste. Then, in the spring of 1485, another message crossed the Channel – a rumour that King Richard, now a widower, had begun to cast his eye on his niece Elizabeth, and to desire her in marriage. Whether or not there was ever any foundation for this piece of gossip, the news, says Polydore Vergil, pinched Henry by the very stomach. At best his must be a desperate venture – further delay now might destroy any chance of success.

He borrowed money – 'a slender supply' from the French King and more where he could get it – and managed to find a few pieces of artillery and a force of between two and three thousand mercenaries from Normandy to supplement his five hundred or so Englishmen. The tiny armada, probably no more than a dozen ships, sailed from the mouth of the Seine on 1 August, with a soft south wind behind it, and set course for Wales. The 'long yellow summer' – the summer of the dragon, of the hero in a golden cloak, the summer of the 'Bull of Anglesey' had come round at last.

CHAPTER 2

The Rose of England

Our King he is the rose so red,
That now does flourish fresh and gay.
Confound his foes, Lord, we beseech,
And love his grace both night and day!

A little before sunset on Sunday, 7 August 1485, the fleet carrying Henry and Jasper Tudor nosed into the entrance of Milford Haven and dropped anchor in Mill Bay under St Anne's Head. The army disembarked without incident and marched over the headland in the summer twilight to make camp for the night at Dale. It was almost exactly fourteen years since uncle and nephew had fled from Tenby, just a few miles down the coast, and their situation now was very nearly as precarious as it had been then.

Next morning, at daybreak, the Tudors began to move inland, reaching Haverfordwest before noon, and it was here that the first news of their supporters reached them. This was Jasper's country and, as soon as they heard he was back, the men of Pembroke sent a deputation to their former earl bringing assurances of loyalty and service. But it seemed that Rhys ap Thomas, the most important and influential man of the region, whose support Henry had been promised, was publicly proclaiming his loyalty to King Richard. If this was true, it would be a very serious blow and was especially dismaying as being 'clean contrary' to the messages which had been reaching Henry in France.

Henry Tudor was not by nature a gambling man and he had learnt the lessons of caution and patience in a hard school – yet the venture he had now committed himself to was enough to terrify the most intrepid gambler. His retreat might be cut off at any moment and although he had sent couriers to his mother, to the Stanleys and to Gilbert Talbot, he could not hope to hear from them, or even to hear if they were still at liberty to help him, until he had passed the point of no return.

His route took him up the coast as far as the estuary of the River Dovey and here, about 11 August, he turned east. The passage through Wales had encountered no resistance and a number of gentlemen along the line of march had come in with their tenantry. But, despite the rousing calls of the bards, there had been no sign of any very wild enthusiasm for the Tudor cause. On Saturday, 13 August, the army had reached Welshpool, only a few miles from the border, and by this time reinforcements were arriving from the north – orderly bands of fighting men under their own leaders from Arfon and Mon, Eifionydd, Lleyn and Ardudwy. Rhys ap Thomas had also turned up at last with 'a great band of soldiers' and an assured promise of support.

Next day, just a week after landing at Milford, Henry Tudor set foot on English soil for the second time in his life. Late afternoon found him at the gates of Shrewsbury, where he was hoping for news of the Stanleys and their intentions; but, says the old ballad:

> At that time was bailiff in Shrewsbury
> One Master Mytton in the town.
> The gates were strong and he made them fast
> And the portcullis he let down.

One of Sir William Stanley's people had a quiet word with Master Mytton, and by Monday morning Henry was able to enter the town. The letters waiting for him there contained assurances that his friends would be ready to do their duty 'in time convenient' – a phrase which might mean anything or nothing. Gilbert Talbot came in with a force of five hundred man but, counting heads, Henry and Jasper knew they could not hope to win a major battle against a ruthless and determined enemy like Richard Plantagenet without far more substantial support than they had received so far. Everything now hung on the Stanley brothers, who between them controlled the whole of Cheshire and Lancashire.

After an overnight stop at Shrewsbury, the Tudors were on the march again, making for the Midlands and the rapidly approaching confrontation. By 17 August they were at Stafford, where Henry had a brief and apparently inconclusive meeting with William Stanley. The next night was spent at Rageley and on Friday the nineteenth the Tudor battalions camped outside the walls of Lichfield. King Richard had now left his headquarters at Nottingham and was moving south towards Leicester with 'an host innumerable'. The two armies must converge within a matter of days, and still no one knew for certain which way the Stanleys were going to jump.

A rather curious incident took place on the twentieth. Either by accident or design, Henry and a party of only twenty companions became separated from the main body of his forces. According to Polydore Vergil, he was so much exercised in his mind as to what would be his best course of action that he wanted peace and quiet to think. Is it just possible that he was contemplating cutting his losses once again and perhaps making a bolt for it back to Wales? As darkness fell, he realized that he had lost touch with his rearguard and was forced to spend the night in the open, afraid to ask for directions in case he was betrayed. When he rejoined the army at Tamworth 'in the gray of the morning', he found it in an understandable state of alarm and hastened to explain that he had withdrawn 'of set purpose to receive some good news of certain his secret friends'.

Later that day Henry had another meeting, with both the Stanleys this time, at the village of Atherstone. It seems to have been a satisfactory encounter and a number of useful men – Thomas Bourchier, Walter Hungerford, John Savage and several others – had now thrown in their lot with the Tudors. All the same, on that Sunday evening, when the opposing armies lay camped within striking distance of each other on rough moorland and scrub a couple of miles south of Market Bosworth, the balance of probabilities was still definitely weighted in Richard's favour.

We do not know what sort of a night Henry passed, but Richard slept badly, disturbed, so he said, by a terrible dream (the natural result of a bad conscience, thought Polydore Vergil), and woke before dawn on 22 August to find no breakfast ready and no chaplains about to say mass. After these deficiencies had been supplied, Richard proceeded to deploy his forces as impressively as possible along the crest of Ambien Hill, a horseshoe-shaped ridge dominating Redmore Plain where the battle would presently be joined. The Duke of Norfolk commanded a strong vanguard of archers, Richard himself, with a picked body of men, held the centre, while the Earl of Northumberland, at his own request, was in the rear.

Henry, positioned on the plain and separated from Ambien Hill by a patch of marshy ground, had no military experience to guide him. Bosworth, the most important battle of his life, was also his first battle. He was, of course, able to rely on the advice of his uncle Jasper and that veteran commander John Vere, Earl of Oxford, who had joined him in exile. But even at this zero hour the question remained – would he also be able to rely on the Stanleys? The Stanleys, Thomas

Richard III; this portrait, painted in Tudor times, depicts the defeated King as a hunchback with a broken sword.

and William, were certainly present with about three thousand men, stationed, according to Vergil, 'in the mid way betwixt the two battles' (that is, the two armies). Exactly where this was, is not clear. One thing, though, now became crystal clear – that they intended to be on the winning side. Henry, outnumbered by something like two to one, was naturally counting on them to join him before rather than after the issue had been decided, and first thing that morning he had sent a message to Thomas asking him 'to come with his forces to set the soldiers in array'. The reply, that Henry should set his own folks in order and Thomas would arrive in due course, must have come like a blow in the face. Henry indeed 'began to be somewhat appalled', but there was no time to argue the matter. The main body of the Tudor army, estimated at no more than a bare five thousand altogether, was deployed in a wedge formation, with a slender vanguard of archers in the centre, commanded by the Earl of Oxford. Gilbert Talbot led the left wing and John Savage the right, while Henry, still trusting to the aid of his stepfather Thomas Stanley, followed with one troop of horse and a few footmen. As they began to advance across the open ground towards Ambien Hill, keeping the marsh on their right, Richard, watching from above, gave the signal to attack.

Oxford was anxious to prevent his small force from being overwhelmed in the first onslaught and so had given orders that no man was to move further than ten paces from the standards. After an exchange of arrow shot and some hand-to-hand skirmishing there was a lull in the proceedings. The royal troops drew off and Oxford and his fellow commanders, thinking they could detect a certain lack of enthusiasm about the enemy, were encouraged to renew the attack. In the fierce fighting which followed the Duke of Norfolk and several other prominent Yorkists were killed and Norfolk's son, the Earl of Surrey, was taken prisoner.

Up to now only the two front-lines had been engaged. The Stanleys had still not moved; nor, significantly, had the Earl of Northumberland in the King's rear. In fact, it was beginning to look as though Henry Percy too was waiting to see what happened, and on Ambien Hill the smell of treachery hung heavy in the air. It is said that one of Richard's friends urged him to save himself while he could and even brought him swift horses for the purpose, but Richard would not hear of it – 'such great fierceness and such huge force of mind he had'.

> Give me my battle-axe in my hand,
>   And set my crown on my head so high,
> For by Him that made both sun and moon,
>   King of England this day will I die.

By this time, the King had been able to pick out his hated adversary from the general confusion on the battlefield, and the sight of that unknown Welshman, the impudent adventurer who, against all the odds, had reached the very heart of his kingdom, seemed to madden him. At any rate, he suddenly made up his mind to settle the issue – 'to make end either of war or life'. Surrounded by his household troops, he set spurs to his horse and launched himself straight for the spot where the red fiery dragon of Cadwaladr was being borne over Henry's head by his standard-bearer, William Brandon. It was the act of a berserker, and it came very close to success.

In the first fury of his attack, Richard personally overthrew the red dragon, killed William Brandon and, 'making way with weapon on every side', even managed to unhorse John Cheyney, a notable and outsize warrior, who attempted to check his progress. For a while it was touch and go, but Henry's guard closed round him and Henry himself stood his ground bravely. This, if ever, was the moment for a dramatic intervention and at this moment, right on cue, the Stanleys came thundering to the rescue. Richard was slain, fighting manfully in the midst of his enemies, and the Earl of Oxford, assisted by the arrival of massive Stanley reinforcements, was able to put the rest of the royal forces to flight without difficulty.

The Tudors and Stanleys were left in undisputed possession of the field and while Henry, 'replenished with joy incredible', was thanking God and his supporters and saying all the things proper to the occasion, the soldiers set up a spontaneous cry of 'King Harry'. To add the finishing touch, Richard's crown, or circlet, was picked up in the debris of the battle and handed to Thomas Stanley, who placed it solemnly on the victor's head, 'as though', wrote Polydore Vergil, 'he had been already by commandment of the people proclaimed king after the manner of his ancestors'. Thus the new dynasty, and with it the dawn of a new society, was ushered in by a scene which might have been taken straight out of some medieval romance.

As one story was beginning in clamour, confusion and a certain amount of over-excitement, another, old, heroic story was ending in shame. While the victorious army packed up its traps and prepared to ride off the field, the naked corpse of the last Plantagenet king, 'with not so much as a clout to cover his privy members', was being slung carelessly across the back of a horse and carried away, arms and legs dangling, for unregarded burial at the Franciscan church in Leicester. The 'beloved Bull' had ventured forth and slain the snarling boar – the dragon had taken vengeance on 'the Mole full of poison'. Bardic zoology might be somewhat eclectic, but the bardic prophecies had been triumphantly fulfilled in the angry end of the summer.

The new King of England was twenty-eight years old, of slender build and slightly above average height. His hair, according to the enthusiastic chronicler Edward Hall, was 'yellow like burnished gold', and his deep-set blue eyes 'shining and quick'. His face has been described as 'long and pale' and in repose it looks ascetic, rather melancholy. But Polydore Vergil, who knew Henry personally towards the end of his life, thought his countenance 'cheerful, especially when speaking', and his whole appearance 'remarkably attractive'.

To his new subjects, this slim, fair-haired man was a completely unknown quantity. It would probably be true to say that before Bosworth the great majority had never heard of him. To most English people the series of bitter contests which, over the past thirty years, had turned the crown into a trophy worn by the captain of the strongest team was not an issue which greatly affected the mainstream of daily life. These were 'King's games, as it were stage plays, and for the most part played upon scaffolds'. Ordinary men followed the fortunes of the

The young Henry Tudor; from the
Recueil d'Arras.

rival factions from a respectful distance, put up with the occasional inconvenience of a battle taking place in their midst, and on the whole successfully avoided involvement. To the crowds who came to the roadside to greet Henry Tudor and his retinue, he was simply another great lord who had come from somewhere beyond the seas to take a hand in the game. They were naturally curious to catch a glimpse of the new man who, it was said, had just won a victory which had put him at the top of the league, but public interest in his past history or the rights and wrongs of his cause was neither informed nor specially strong.

As for Henry, England and its people were almost as strange to him as he was to them, and this journey down Watling Street to London would be his first opportunity to have a good look at both. He saw a green, fertile, well-wooded, well-watered land growing all the wheat, barley and oats needed to support a population of around three million – a rich and beautiful land, abounding in what one visiting Italian described as 'comestible animals'. Huge tracts of what was still virtually primeval forest swarmed with game, and the damp, temperate climate produced lush pasturage for cattle and sheep. The islanders, surrounded by all this plenty, were a tall, sturdy, vigorous race and wherever their new King stopped by the way, he would have enjoyed lavish hospitality – sampling such delights as 'peerless' beef, excellent freshwater fish, venison, mutton and a wide variety of poultry.

Although the country possessed great natural mineral wealth, it was essentially an agrarian society. Apart from London, the only towns of any size were York, Norwich and Bristol; but London, the heart and the key of the kingdom, was something quite special in the way of cities. Visitors commented on the charm and convenience of its situation on the banks of a great tidal river. They admired London's handsome defensive walls, the strong fortress of the Tower, the fine stone-built bridge, the noble cathedral, the splendid mansions with their comfortable, prosperous inhabitants, the shops bursting with luxury goods of every kind; but the thing which chiefly struck every foreign visitor was the city's wealth and importance as an international commercial capital. 'Merchants from not only Venice but also Florence and Lucca, and many from Genoa and Pisa, from Spain, Germany, the Rhine valley and other countries meet here to handle business with the utmost keenness' wrote Andreas Franciscius in November 1497. The island's economy still depended chiefly on the export of raw wool and finished cloth – generally conceded to be the best in the world – but visitors, especially the Italians, were much impressed by the skill of the London metalworkers and by the quality of their products. In one street alone, Cheapside, there were, according to a Venetian diplomat, no fewer than fifty-two goldsmiths' shops. 'These great riches are not occasioned by its inhabitants being noblemen or gentlemen; being all, on the contrary, persons of low degree, and artificers who have congregated here from all parts of the island, and from Flanders and from every other place.'

Henry Tudor reached the outskirts of this thriving emporium of trade and industry on 3 September, twelve days after Bosworth. He was met at Shoreditch by the Lord Mayor and the aldermen and conducted with suitable ceremony, trumpeters going before him, to St Paul's. In the past London had been on the whole Yorkist in sympathy, but Richard III's forced loans had not made him popular with the mercantile community. Apart from that, the city fathers had a stronger interest than most in peace and stability. If Henry could put an end to the irritating, expensive and futile faction fighting which was not only bad for trade but was also beginning to breed undesirable habits of disrespect for law and order; if he could restore the authority and prestige of the Crown, and provide continuity and settled government, then he could count on the support of the business community and, indeed, of the population at large.

Not that the Yorkist cause was dead – far from it – and Henry, reviewing the serried ranks of his cousins, had no reason to feel complacent. Richard's son had, providentially, predeceased him, but there were too many Yorkist males still very much alive for the peace of mind of the only surviving Lancastrian. There was the ten-year-old Earl of Warwick, son of Edward IV's brother George; there were the de la Pole brothers, sons of Edward's sister Elizabeth, and there was also the young Duke of Buckingham, son of the Duke executed in 1483 and a four-times great-grandson of Edward III. Then there were the girls, whose marriages and progeny could (and did) provide further complications. Henry's fiancée, Elizabeth of York, had four sisters; the Earl of Warwick had a sister and so did the Duke of Buckingham.

Henry's awareness of the danger is demonstrated by the fact that within hours

The succession of the Kings of England; these painted wooden panels in St George's Chapel, Windsor, were commissioned by Henry VII to show the true line of succession. From right to left: Edward IV, the uncrowned Edward V and Henry VII.

of Bosworth a messenger was on his way from Leicester to the castle of Sheriff Hutton in Yorkshire, where both Warwick and Elizabeth had been lodged for safe-keeping by Richard. Both were now brought to London, the unhappy Warwick to the Tower and Elizabeth to be returned to her mother pending her marriage. Marriage, though, would have to wait a little – at any rate until the most pressing business of the new reign had been disposed of.

One thing which could not be postponed was the King's coronation. Preparations for making this a truly memorable occasion were put in hand at once, and Sir Robert Willoughby, Steward of the Household, sent his staff round

London to buy up all the scarlet cloth, crimson satin, purple velvet and cloth of gold they could lay hands on. Other items on Sir Robert's shopping list included silk fringe for trumpet banners, silk tassels for trimming caps, ribbon of Venice gold for the King's gloves, ostrich feathers and Spanish leather boots for the henchmen and footmen, seventy-one ounces of 'hangyng spangels of silver and double gilt' at eight shillings an ounce, quantities of powdered ermine and miniver for furred robes and mantles, harness and ceremonial trappings for the horses, four-and-three-quarter yards of fine russet cloth for the King's confessor, twelve coats of arms for the heralds, 'wrought in oyle colors with fyne gold' and costing thirty shillings each, two pairs of gilt spurs for the King and a considerable number of assorted cushions of red and blue damask and cloth of gold. It was all meticulously entered in the wardrobe accounts, down to the last quarter pound of thread, the yard of buckram for lining the collars of the henchmen's doublets and, fascinatingly, three-quarters of a yard of red velvet for dragons! It all cost a great deal of money, but Henry Tudor knew the value of putting on a good show – especially when it was a question of promoting public confidence.

The coronation date was set for the end of October and, while a small army of tailors and embroiderers, upholsterers and carpenters laboured to get everything ready, the King was quietly consolidating his position – appointing a Council from the hard core of his fellow exiles, reinforced by men like the Stanleys, Reginald Bray and, before the end of the year, John Morton; installing trusted supporters in strategic posts round the country; and issuing writs for the summoning of Parliament.

A few days before the coronation, the Court, following established practice, moved into the Tower and Henry marked the occasion by conferring the dukedom of Bedford on faithful uncle Jasper, without whom none of it would have been possible. Lord Stanley became Earl of Derby and William Courtenay, another of those stalwarts who had known exile with the Tudors, became Earl of Devonshire and was later further rewarded with a royal bride, the Yorkist princess Katherine. On 29 October came the traditional recognition procession through the city to Westminster, the King, wearing a long robe of purple velvet, riding bareheaded under a canopy of estate. The next day, Sunday, Henry Tudor was solemnly crowned in Westminster Abbey and 'after that solemnization was finished, a royal and excellent feast with all circumstances to such a feast appertaining was holden within Westminster Hall'.

A week later the first Tudor Parliament met to deal, among other things, with certain anomalies arising out of recent events. Henry had won his kingdom by right of conquest; he had been crowned and anointed by the Archbishop of Canterbury; yet in law, by an Act of his predecessor, he was still attainted of treason – a proscribed person without rights or property. Henry knew that his hereditary title would not stand up to close examination, but he also knew that the country was not so much interested in his legal right to wear the crown as in his ability to hold on to it. He had not summoned Parliament to recognize him as King – he was King already and, in any case, only a true King could summon Parliament. It was a splendidly illogical situation and Henry sensibly resolved the whole tangle by ignoring it, taking his stand on accomplished fact – on his 'just title by inheritance', on the judgement of God as delivered at Bosworth, and on the ruling of less exalted judges that his attainder had been automatically cancelled by his assumption of the throne. In order to regularize matters for the future and to satisfy the tidy-minded, a brief Act for the Confirmation of Henry VII was passed, declaring that 'the inheritance of the crowns of the realms of England and France . . . be, rest, remain and abide in the most royal person of our now sovereign lord king Harry VII and in the heirs of his body lawfully come, perpetually with the grace of God so to endure, and in none other.'

The King was not the only person whose affairs had to be sorted out by this Parliament. Elizabeth Woodville, Henry's prospective mother-in-law, had been stripped of her rank and dignity as Queen by Richard III and her children bastardized. These shameful injustices now had to be erased from the statute book and consigned to 'perpetual oblivion'. The King's own mother got back her estates which had been confiscated by Richard in 1483, and the Parliament of 1485 granted to Margaret Beaufort, Countess of Richmond and Derby, all the rights and privileges of a 'sole person, not wife nor covert of any husband'. She was, in fact, to have full and independent control over her very considerable property 'in as large a form as any woman now may do within this realm'. 'My lady the King's mother' was, therefore, not only an exceedingly rich woman – she also became an exceedingly important and influential woman. Indeed, to all intents and purposes she became honorary Queen Mother, thus receiving tacit recognition for the vital part, political as well as biological, which she had played in founding the new dynasty.

The House of Commons now turned its attention to the future of the new dynasty and on 11 December the Speaker presented a petition to the King, earnestly requesting him to take to wife Elizabeth, daughter of Edward IV, a request which was solemnly seconded by the lords spiritual and temporal. Henry is generally accused of deliberately delaying his marriage so that no one would have any excuse for saying he owed his throne to his wife. There is no question that Elizabeth's right to be Queen was a good deal stronger than Henry's to be King, but no one had ever suggested they should reign jointly. Henry's title, such as it was, could not be strengthened by his wife's – it was their children who would benefit from the union of 'the two bloodes of highe renowne'. So, while the marriage was obviously very desirable politically, it was even more important from the dynastic point of view and that made it all the more essential that it should be an indisputably valid marriage. It would have been unwise for Henry to claim his bride while she was still officially a bastard and, apart from this, the couple were closely enough related to need a papal dispensation. This had now been applied for but in the end Henry did not wait for Rome. He received an authority to proceed from the Bishop of Imola, papal legate in England, and on 16 January 1486, he redeemed the pledge given two years before at Rennes and married Elizabeth, King Edward's daughter.

Elizabeth of York was in her twenty-first year and generally agreed to be a pretty girl, with the silver-gilt fairness of the Plantagenets. Like her bridegroom, her childhood and adolescence had been disrupted by the civil war. She had twice been hurried into sanctuary with her mother and sisters, had suffered the grief of

Elizabeth of York by an unknown artist.

her brothers' disappearance, faced at least the possibility of marriage with her uncle Richard as well as the anxiety and insecurity attached to being her father's heiress. Tradition, as embodied in the epic ballad *The Most Pleasant Song of Lady Bessy*, credits Elizabeth with much of the under-cover work leading up to Bosworth, and describes how she sent for Lord Stanley, 'father Stanley', telling him she would rather die – 'with sharp swords I will me slay' – than become her uncle's leman, and begging his help for the exiled Henry.

> You may recover him of his care,
>   If your heart and mind to him will gree:
> Let him come home and claim his right,
>   And let us cry him King Henry!

Stanley had hesitated. He was afraid of Richard, and besides it would be a deadly sin to betray his King.

> . . . then should I lose my great renown!
> I should be called traitor through the same
>   Full soon in every market town!
> That were great shame to me and my name.

But Bessy persisted. She flung her head-dress on the ground and tore her hair, while tears 'fell from her eyes apace'. Stanley was touched by her distress, but still he hung back, protesting rather feebly about the difficulties of communicating with Henry. He himself cannot write and dare not confide in a secretary. But dauntless Lady Bessy overrode his objections. She can read and write, if necessary in French and Spanish as well as English, and she will act as scrivener. Much impressed by the talents of this 'proper wench', Stanley capitulated and late that night, alone in Bessy's chamber, they concocted a series of letters to Stanley's friends and to 'the Prince of England' in Brittany. It was Bessy who found a trusty messenger, Humphrey Brereton, and she was presently rewarded by a love letter from Henry, promising to travel over the sea for her sake and make her his queen.

The Song of Lady Bessy was probably written by Humphrey Brereton, a squire in the Stanleys' service, and contains some unmistakably authentic touches, as well as a good deal of poetic licence. It is, for example, highly unlikely that Elizabeth played an active part in the conspiracy, although she may have sent an encouraging message to Henry by one of the secret couriers going over to France. While she had never seen her future husband and can have known very little about him, the Yorkist heiress would certainly have been aware that marriage with Henry Tudor offered the best prospect of a secure and honourable future that she could reasonably expect.

The wedding should normally have been followed by the Queen's coronation, but this had to be put off for the best possible reason – the Queen was pregnant. The King spent the spring on a progress, going as far north as York to show himself to the people, but he was back in London by the beginning of June and not long afterwards set off with the Queen towards Winchester. It was there, at the ancient British capital, on 20 September 1486, that Elizabeth gave birth four weeks prematurely to a son – 'the rosebush of England' who would unite the warring factions. Winchester resounded to the pealing of bells and the singing of Te Deum Laudamus and as the 'comfortable and good tidings' spread round the country, bells were rung, bonfires lit in the streets and Te Deum sung in parish churches up and down the land as 'every true Englishman' rejoiced.

The infant prince was christened Arthur, a shrewd and imaginative choice, in Winchester Cathedral amid much pomp and ceremony, with three bishops officiating. The Earls of Oxford and Derby were godfathers, Queen Elizabeth Woodville godmother, and the baby was carried to and from the church by his aunt Cecily of York, supported by the Marquis of Dorset and the Earl of Lincoln, eldest of the de la Pole brothers. All the important relations from both sides of the family were present – although Lancastrians were heavily outnumbered by Yorkists. Everyone was on their best behaviour and in spite of the cold, rainy weather, the ceremony went off very smoothly. To an outsider it might have looked as if the ancient blood feud was over at last.

As soon as the Queen had been churched, the Court moved back to Greenwich to keep the solemn feast of All Hallows with more pomp and ceremony. Christmas was also spent at Greenwich. A quiet, family occasion this, at which, it is reasonable to assume, the new baby was the centre of attention. One way and another, the King could feel modestly pleased with his first sixteen months but, early in the New Year, the curious affair of Lambert Simnel provided an effective antidote to any incipient sense of false security.

Simnel, the son of an organ-maker from Oxford, turned up in Ireland, where he was being passed off as the Earl of Warwick, conveniently 'escaped' from the Tower. Henry took the obvious counter-measure of producing the real Warwick at High Mass in St Paul's, making sure that as many important people as possible saw him and spoke to him. Unfortunately, though, Ireland was a long way from St Paul's and the Irish chieftains had their own reasons for preferring to believe in Simnel.

A strong element of fantasy pervades the whole Simnel affair, but it soon became surprisingly dangerous – especially when it became clear that the unfortunate youth was being used as a stalking horse by more substantial personages. The Earl of Lincoln, who had absconded from his place at King Henry's council table, reappeared in Ireland early in May, accompanied by a business-like force of German mercenaries, paid for by his aunt Margaret, widowed Duchess of Burgundy and another of Edward IV's sisters. Thus encouraged, the Irish, with more enthusiasm than common-sense, proceeded to crown Lambert Simnel as Edward VI in Christ Church, Dublin, using a diadem borrowed from a handy statue of the Virgin. A month later, John de la Pole, his mercenaries reinforced by a hopeful contingent of 'wild Irishmen', landed at the Pile of Fouldry on the Lancashire coast.

Henry, meanwhile, had collected a sizeable army and set up his headquarters in the Midlands, just as Richard had done two years before. The confrontation came at Stoke on 16 June and the battle, which marked the real end of the Wars of the Roses, turned out to be an uncomfortably close-run thing. The Germans, conscientious professionals under their formidable commander Martin Schwartz, gave Margaret of Burgundy good value for her money. The half-naked Irish, too, 'foughte hardely and stuck to it valyauntly' – there would be much plunder for a victorious army in a rich country like England – but valour was no substitute for body-armour and they suffered heavy casualties.

There are unconfirmed reports that part of Henry's army – like Richard's at Bosworth – hung back and that rumours that 'the kyng was fled and the feeld lost' were deliberately circulated in the ranks by certain 'false Englisshemen'. Whatever the truth of these reports, the King could rely on two utterly loyal and experienced lieutenants in his uncle Jasper and John de Vere, Earl of Oxford, and after three anxious hours a vigorous charge by the first line of the royal troops finally settled the matter. John de la Pole was killed, but the capture of Lambert Simnel provided Henry with an opportunity to make a nicely calculated propaganda gesture by giving 'Edward VI' a job in the royal kitchens.

The House of Tudor had survived its first serious crisis, but the Simnel affair had demonstrated just how frighteningly thin was the crust it stood on – just how close to the surface lay the seething volcano of its rivals' vengeful ambition. But no hint of these anxieties was allowed to appear in public – especially not at the King's state entry into London on 3 November.

The city had made the appropriate preparations for this auspicious occasion. The streets through which the procession would pass were carefully swept and sanded, and representatives of the various craft guilds were lined up, 'in due order' and their best liveries, along the route from Bishopsgate to St Paul's. Meanwhile, the Mayor with his sheriffs and aldermen, 'all on horseback full well and honourably beseen', had ridden out to meet the royal party. 'And so at afternoon the King, as a comely and royal prince, apparelled accordingly, entered into his City well and honourably accompanied, as was fitting to his estate.' The citizens had turned out in strength to see the show and give the King a hero's welcome. 'All the houses, windows and streets as he passed by were hugely replenished with people in passing great number, that made great joy and exaltation to behold his most royal person so prosperously and princely coming into his city after his late triumph and victory against his enemies.'

Among the spectators were the Queen and the King's mother, who watched the procession from the window of a house beside St Mary Spital at Bishopsgate. The King went on to attend an official thanksgiving service at St Paul's, but the ladies went quietly back to Greenwich, 'to their beds'. Certainly Elizabeth of York had a heavy programme before her, since the date appointed for her much-postponed coronation was now less than three weeks away. This was to be another splendid state occasion, with no expense spared, no detail of pomp and ceremony omitted.

On 23 November the Queen left Greenwich by water for the Tower, accompanied, as usual, by her mother-in-law and by many other lords and ladies, all richly clad. The city fathers, too, were once more out in force in a flotilla of barges decorated with banners and streamers and the arms and badges of their crafts. One barge came in for special notice, as it contained 'a great red Dragon spowting Flamys of Fyer into the Temmys', and there were a number of other such gentlemanly pageants 'well and curiously devysed to do her Highness sport and pleasure with'. On arrival at the Tower, Elizabeth was greeted by her husband in a manner which the onlookers found 'right joyous and comfortable to behold' and that night eleven new Knights of the Bath were created in honour of the coronation.

Next day, after dinner, came the procession to Westminster. The Queen wore a kirtle of white cloth of gold under a matching mantle furred with ermines and fastened with 'a great lace curiously wrought of gold and silk' – an outfit which must have suited her pale prettiness perfectly. Her fair hair hung down her back and was topped by a golden circlet studded with precious stones. The royal litter, covered with cloth of gold and provided with large pillows of down, also covered with cloth of gold, was drawn through streets hung with tapestry and, in Cheapside, with gold velvet and silk. The craft guilds were out again in their liveries to line the route from the Tower to St Paul's, and children, 'some arrayed like angels and others like virgins', had been placed at strategic intervals ready 'to sing sweet songs as her Grace passed by'. The City always did this sort of thing very well.

The coronation ceremony in Westminster Abbey was performed by John Morton, the new Archbishop of Canterbury, and was watched by the King and his mother from a special platform erected between the pulpit and the high altar. The three days' festivity ended with the usual banquet and good old Jasper Tudor, 'the right high and mighty prince the Duke of Bedford', who had been appointed Great Steward of England for the duration of the feast was much in evidence, wearing a furred gown of cloth of gold and a rich chain of office about his neck. Under his supervision, trumpets blew, minstrels played and the newly crowned Queen and her guests were served with such delicacies as Shields of Brawn in Armour, Pike in Laytmer Sauce, Carp in Foile, Mutton Royal richly garnished, pheasant, partridge, peacock and swan, capons, quails, larks and venison pasties, baked quince, March Payne Royal and 'Castles of Jelly in Templewise made'. The torches had been lit by the time the Queen had washed and the Lord Mayor of London, Sir William Horne, had served her with hippocras and spices and received a covered cup of gold as his fee. And then, says the chronicler, 'the Queen departed with God's blessing and to the rejoicing of many a true Englishman's heart'.

Apart from her mother-in-law, Elizabeth of York had been supported by her sister Cecily, her aunt Elizabeth (mother of the de la Poles) and her cousin Margaret (sister of the imprisoned Warwick), but her own mother had been allowed no part in the proceedings. Elizabeth Woodville, in fact, was in disgrace. An incorrigible intriguante, she had somehow become mixed up in the plotting of the Lambert Simnel affair – or at any rate so the King believed – and as early as the previous February he had taken the precaution of transferring all her landed property to his wife and had installed the Queen Dowager as a boarder in the convent at Bermondsey, where she would have little opportunity of getting into mischief.

Christmas that year was again spent at Greenwich and was kept 'full honourably', the King going to Mass on Christmas Eve in a gown of purple velvet furred with sables, impressively escorted by his nobility. There was merrymaking as well as churchgoing, several plays were performed and on New Year's Day there was 'a goodly disguising'. Finally, on Twelfth Day, there was a state banquet with the King and Queen wearing their crowns, my lady the King's mother with a rich coronet on her head, and everybody who was anybody present in full panoply.

St George's Day was observed at Windsor with more displays of goldsmiths' work, of silk and velvet gowns, of cloth of gold and elaborate horse trappings.

> Here this day St George, patron of this place,
> Honored with the gartere cheefe of chevalrye;
> Chaplenes synging procession, keeping the same,
> With archbushopes and bushopes beseene nobly;
> Much people presente to see the King Henrye:
> Wherefore now, St George, all we pray to thee
> To keepe our soveraine in his dignetye.

It is noticeable how quickly the political significance of the Tudors' Welshness had receded. St George, the English champion, had taken over from such heroes of Celtic mythology as Cadwaladr of the beautiful spear, and by the end of the 1480s Henry Tudor, prince of the Welsh royal line, had become submerged in Henry Tudor the English King.

Henry VII's Court moved through the calendar of feasts and saints' days in a ritual dance of pageantry. It was all part of the great illusion – the illusion of stability and security skilfully concealing the extreme fragility of the structure which lay beneath it. From what we know of Henry's private character, he seems to have been a man of simple tastes who would probably have preferred to spend his free time quietly with his family. But this was a luxury he could not yet afford. He must continue to dress up in expensive, uncomfortable clothes and wear his crown in public, taking every opportunity of promoting an image of kingly splendour, of impressing the outside world with a sense of the power and confidence of the new dynasty, while behind the scenes he worked unremittingly at the task of turning illusion into reality.

It was just as well that he did, for at the beginning of the 1490s history began to repeat itself and Henry, as Francis Bacon put it, 'began again to be haunted with spirits'. Once again the apparition took the form of a good-looking youth, Perkin (or Peter) Warbeck (or Osbeck), a native of the city of Tournai in Flanders. Once again the first manifestation occurred in Ireland, and once again the origins of the affair are obscure. According to Perkin himself, in a confession made six years later, he landed in Cork with his master, a Breton silk merchant, in the autumn of 1491 and was immediately mobbed by the inhabitants, who insisted that this well-dressed young man (Perkin was advertising his master's wares on his person) was the same Earl of Warwick 'that was before time at Dublin' and would not accept his embarrassed denials.

Polydore Vergil, on the other hand, declares that it was all a deep-laid scheme instigated by Margaret of Burgundy, that inveterate enemy of the House of Tudor, who 'cherished such a deep hatred of King Henry, that it seemed she would be content with nothing short of his death'. Ever since the Lambert Simnel *débâcle*, says Vergil, Margaret had been biding her time, hoping to succeed by cunning and craft where force of arms had failed. She had come across Perkin by chance and, being impressed by his appearance and his sharp mind, had kept him secretly in her household while she coached him in the family history, 'so that afterwards he should . . . convince all by his performance that he sprang from the Yorkist line'. Margaret had then waited until Henry was embroiled in a dispute with France over the independence of Brittany before unleashing Perkin in Ireland, hoping that he would be successful in stirring up 'the barbarous natives who were always most ready for new rebellions'.

Whichever of these versions is correct, the latest 'Earl of Warwick' had little success among the Irish – even the most barbarous of the native chieftains proved disappointingly chary of making fools of themselves a second time. Perkin's next appearance was in France, where King Charles welcomed the 'feigned lad' with flattering attention, recognizing him not as Warwick but, more dramatically, as Richard Duke of York, the younger of the Princes in the Tower, miraculously saved from the murderers of his brother. The 'Duke of York' was made much of at the French Court, royally entertained and given a guard of honour, so that the young man from Tournai not surprisingly 'thought himself in heaven' – until the autumn of 1492, when a peace treaty was signed between France and England and the ploy had served its purpose. Charles would not go so far as to surrender

Margaret, Dowager Duchess of Burgundy and Henry's implacable enemy (above), *supported and financed the pretender Perkin Warbeck* (left) *who claimed to be Richard, Duke of York, one of the Princes in the Tower.*

Perkin to Henry, but he wasted no time in seeing his guest off the premises and Perkin returned, perforce, to Flanders, where he presented himself to his 'aunt' Margaret.

The Duchess at first appeared to doubt his claims, but after a careful interrogation she declared herself satisfied that this was indeed her nephew 'raised from the dead'. Margaret was in transports – 'so great was her pleasure that her happiness seemed to have disturbed the balance of her mind' – and Perkin once more received VIP treatment. He was installed in a fine house in Antwerp, given a guard of thirty archers who flaunted the white rose badge on their uniforms, and invited to state functions by Maximilian, King of the Romans.

Perkin was encouraged to tell the story of his adventures, of how he had escaped death by a ruse and of his subsequent wanderings round Europe. The news spread rapidly and created a considerable sensation – especially in England, where rumours that one of King Edward's sons might be alive after all 'came blazing and thundering' and, for a time, gained a good deal of credence, not only among the ordinary gullible public, but among some more important men 'who considered the matter as genuine'.

The trouble was that Perkin could just have been genuine. The fate of the little princes remained something of a mystery and the King, of course, was in no position to produce the real Duke of York – a point which had not escaped the notice of his adversaries. The most worrying thing from Henry's point of view was just how many important men did believe – or were ready to pretend to believe – in the impostor. He needed to know urgently if there was anyone in his immediate circle who was in the plot, and he made this his first priority. Fortunately his intelligence service was highly efficient and there were a number of arrests during 1494. But it was December before the King caught a really big fish in his net. This turned out to be no less a person than Sir William Stanley, who had helped to put the crown on Henry's head at Bosworth, the Earl of Derby's brother and his own mother's brother-in-law.

Stanley's somewhat inadequate motive for dabbling in treachery seems to have arisen largely out of resentment that he had not been given a peerage, and he also seems to have had some idea that the King would not dare to proceed against him. But although it undoubtedly came as a very unpleasant shock to find a traitor so close to home, once he was satisfied of Stanley's guilt, Henry never hesitated and Sir William was tried and executed in February 1495.

After this, the English end of the conspiracy (and there is no doubt that an active and dangerous Yorkist cell had existed) began to disintegrate. Perkin attracted no more native support of any consequence and, indeed, the rest of his story is soon told. Early in July he turned up off the coast of Kent with a small fleet and a few hundred assorted followers – 'human dregs' according to Polydore Vergil, but Margaret of Burgundy's resources were not inexhaustible. Perkin seems to have lacked the courage to go on shore, but some of his supporters did and were decimated by loyal Kentish men. He went on – poor wretch, he had little choice but to go on – and in November appeared in Scotland. Here he was welcomed by James IV, a brash young man looking for an opportunity to make a stir in the world and not at all reluctant to annoy his more powerful neighbour.

James took Perkin up, recognized him as Richard Plantagenet and even provided him with a wife, Lady Catherine Gordon, a distant kinswoman of his own. The Scottish king organized some Border raids for the pretender's benefit, but even the normally turbulent North showed not the slightest interest in his cause. Perkin stayed on in Scotland, half pensioner and half prisoner, for another two years, until James got tired of him and sent him packing. He ended his active career in the West Country, attempting to take advantage of some local disaffection in Cornwall, but he was now a lonely and discredited figure and although he managed to gather quite a large force, his followers had no armour, no artillery and few weapons and were cut to pieces assaulting Exeter. Perkin himself escaped, but was finally captured near Beaulieu early in October 1497.

Just enough doubt remains about Perkin Warbeck's origins to give him a faint aura of romantic mystery. Some people have felt that he would never have received so much royal recognition unless he was actually of royal blood, and have wondered if perhaps he might have been Richard Plantagenet back from the dead. It is possible that he was an illegitimate son of Margaret of Burgundy (this suggestion was current at the time), but it is much more likely that Perkin was, as he said in his confession, the son of respectable parents, John Osbeck and Catherine de Faro his wife, both convert Jews domiciled in Tournai.

He survived for another two years as Henry's prisoner and when his end came in November 1499 he took the Earl of Warwick with him. In Francis Bacon's vivid phrase, 'it was ordained that this winding-ivy of a Plantagenet should kill the true tree itself'. There had been another abortive attempt to impersonate Warwick at the beginning of the year, and Henry seems at last to have come to the conclusion that there would be no real security for himself or his children as long as the last Plantagenet in the direct male line remained alive. There is some evidence that Perkin was deliberately used as bait to trap Warwick into joining a plan for an escape to Flanders. Certainly, no sooner had this plot been hatched than it was conveniently 'discovered' and the conspirators brought to trial. Perkin, who was hanged on 23 November, probably got no more than he deserved but there was universal sympathy for poor young Warwick, beheaded five days later on Tower Hill, and little pretence that he had died for any other crime than that of being a Plantagenet, 'a race often dipped in their own blood'.

The first Henry Tudor, despite his reputation, was a humane man with no relish for shedding blood, guilty or innocent, and Warwick's death upset him – he became noticeably more devout and looked ill. All the same, once the sad corpse of Edward Plantagenet had been carried up-river to Bisham Abbey (at Henry's expense) to be buried among his Montague ancestors, the King could turn to planning the future of his own young family with a good deal more confidence.

The Tudor nursery had been filling up over the past ten years. In November 1489 Queen Elizabeth had given birth to her second child, a daughter christened Margaret after her grandmother who stood gossip, or godmother, and produced a useful present of a silver and gilt chest full of gold pieces. Eighteen months later, on 28 June 1491, came another son, Henry, born at Greenwich, and in 1492 another daughter, Elizabeth, who lived only three years. A third daughter, Mary, appeared in March 1495, and a third son, Edmund, in February 1499.

The younger members of the family spent a lot of their time at Eltham Palace in Kent, and in 1499 Desiderius Erasmus of Rotterdam records how he walked over from Lord Mountjoy's house with his friend Thomas More to see the royal children. While the company was at dinner Prince Henry, a self-confident eight-year-old who already had 'something of royalty in his demeanour', sent Erasmus a note 'to challenge something from his pen', and that renowned scholar was rather annoyed with More for not having warned him to come prepared.

As the year drew to a close, the House of Tudor faced the new century with confidence. It had survived some determined attempts to dislodge it and its enemies were in disarray – Margaret of Burgundy had been obliged to apologize to Henry. There would no more apparitions of ghostly Plantagenet princes and already the feuding of York and Lancaster was fading into history. The Tudor King could feel secure on his throne. A new generation was growing up, ready to take over his work. In only fifteen years it was an achievement of which to be proud.

CHAPTER 3

A Wonder for Wise Men

To speake againe of Henries praise,
His princely liberal hand
Gave gifts and graces many waies
Unto this famous land:
For which the Lord him blessings sent,
And multiplied his store;
In that he left more wealth to us
Than any king before.

The year 1500 brought sorrow to the royal family when, on 19 June, Prince Edmund died at Hatfield at the age of sixteen months. The pathetic little coffin was brought to London on the following Monday and given a state funeral in Westminster Abbey at a cost of £242 11s 8d with the Duke of Buckingham officiating as chief mourner.

Apart from the fact that it was terrifying, no one knows the exact rate of infant mortality among ordinary people in the early sixteenth century but even in families where the best care was available, parents could think themselves lucky if they reared three babies out of five. The Tudor nurseries were under the direct supervision of the King's mother, who had drawn up detailed instructions to be followed by the officials in charge. There was to be a Lady Governor to oversee the nursery nurse; the wet nurse's food and drink was to be carefully 'assayed' (that is, tasted) at all times while 'shee giveth the child sucke'; and there was to be a physician always on duty to stand over the nurse at every meal to make sure she was feeding the child properly.

In spite of these and other precautions, only four out of Queen Elizabeth's seven children (there had been another boy who died at birth) had survived their first, most perilous years. It was not a particularly good average, but neither was it unusually low. The King and Queen, like so many other bereaved parents, stoically accepted the will of God, and turned to the more cheerful business of preparing for the arrival of their first daughter-in-law.

Negotiations for a marriage between the King of England's eldest son and the Infanta Catalina, youngest daughter of the Catholic Kings of Spain – Ferdinand of Aragon and Isabella of Castile – had begun as long ago as the spring of 1488, when Arthur was eighteen months old and the Spanish princess Catherine was two and a bit. Ferdinand wanted an English alliance to secure his rear while he pursued a vendetta with France over the disputed territories of Italy – the Franco-Spanish power struggle was to dominate the international scene for more than half a century. Henry wanted friends abroad and a prestigious foreign bride for his son. Neither Henry nor Ferdinand wanted to pay more than he had to and being both, as Francis Bacon later wrote, 'princes of great policy and profound judgement, [they] stood a great time looking upon another's fortunes, how they would go'. But eventually, after a good deal of hard bargaining on both sides, satisfactory terms were hammered out and the marriage treaty was concluded in October 1496.

It had been agreed that the princess should come to England as soon as Arthur was fourteen, but at the last moment there were more delays and it was May 1501 before Catherine left the palace at Granada on the first stage of her long journey north, the end of September before she finally sailed from the port of Laredo on the Basque coast. It was not the best time of year to embark on a voyage across the Bay of Biscay, and the fleet ran into a succession of violent squalls which carried away spars and rigging and wrenched masts out of their sockets. The princess's soaked and seasick retinue huddled miserably below decks convinced that their last hour had come. It seemed the worst possible omen for the future. But after five hideous days the Spaniards limped into the shelter of Plymouth Sound and anchored safely off the Hoe on the afternoon of 2 October. The bruised and exhausted passengers were able to get into dry clothes. The sun came out and everybody cheered up.

The journey to London had been carefully planned in easy stages and all along the way the princess was given an enthusiastic welcome. At Plymouth the waterfront had been lined with cheering crowds and at Exeter there had been bells and banners and bonfires. At the West Country villages of Honiton and Crewkerne, the great abbeys of Sherborne and Shaftesbury, and the little market towns of Amesbury and Andover, housewives and shop-keepers and farm labourers gathered to wave and cry blessings from the roadside, while the local gentry – self-confident, well-fed country squires and their wives – came riding in to greet the new arrival and swell the ranks of her escort.

Apart from the fact that everyone enjoyed a break from routine and an excuse to dress up and have a party, everyone was pleased that prestigious foreign royalty had been willing to marry their daughter in England. More than anything else it was a sign that the troubles were over at last, and there would be no more tiresome squabbling over who should wear the crown. Catherine brought good royal blood that would add to the status of the new dynasty – was she not remotely descended from John of Gaunt? – and seemed a pretty, well-behaved child who would do the country credit. The English had an international reputation for being violently and unpredictably fickle, but during those first few weeks they took Catherine of Aragon to their hearts and they were to love and respect her to the end.

King Henry had originally intended to welcome his new daughter when she arrived at Lambeth on the southern outskirts of London, but early in November he suddenly became impatient and decided after all to go out and meet her. He left his smart new Thames-side residence at Richmond with a large company, stopping at the Berkshire village of Easthampstead to pick up Prince Arthur, who was coming south from Ludlow. Father and son then travelled on together.

News of their approach started something of a flutter in the Spanish dovecote, and before the two parties could converge an emissary arrived in the person of Don Pedro de Ayala, papal protonotary and Bishop of the Canaries. Don Pedro had the rather tricky assignment of explaining to the King of England that, according to Spanish etiquette, the princess could not receive her future father-in-law and could on no account be seen by her future husband until the marriage ceremony itself. Henry was not pleased to be instructed in his own kingdom by a parcel of foreigners and, turning his horse into a convenient field, he called an impromptu council meeting. After solemnly debating the point, the lords spiritual and temporal in his train gave it as their considered opinion that since the princess of Spain was now in England she had become the King's subject, and he had a perfect right to see her whenever he chose.

The King wasted no more time. Leaving Arthur to follow at a more decorous pace, he spurred on towards Dogmersfield, the small Hampshire village that Catherine and her entourage had reached a couple of hours earlier. When he arrived, at about half-past two in the afternoon, he was told that the princess was resting and could see no one – Catherine's duenna, the formidable Doña Elvira Manuel, was not giving in without a struggle. But Henry Tudor meant to be

Catherine of Aragon as a young girl; a portrait by Michel Sittow.

master in his own house. He had come to see the princess, he said bluntly, and he was going to see her even if she was in her bed. So the princess of Spain gave the King of England 'an honourable meeting in her third chamber' under Doña Elvira's disapproving eye. As Catherine spoke no English and Henry no Spanish, communication was effectively limited to smiles and bows, but when the King withdrew to change out of his muddy riding clothes he had seen all he wanted to see – a sturdy, well-grown, well-formed girl, with clear grey eyes, a fresh complexion and a quantity of auburn hair; a girl who, God willing, would be able to give him healthy grandchildren.

As soon as Arthur had ridden in, father and son paid the princess another visit. This time the occasion was more formal. The bridal couple were, of course, already legally contracted by proxy. Now they joined hands and went through a solemn betrothal ceremony in person before an impressive audience of bishops, both English and Spanish.

What the two young people thought of one another is not recorded, but when Catherine first set eyes on the Prince of Wales her spirits must surely have risen. The short November afternoon was drawing to a close and in the torchlight she saw a slender youth with a thatch of blond hair and skin as delicately pink and white as a girl's.

Next day the princess resumed her journey, going by way of Chertsey, Kingston and Croydon, while Henry and Arthur went back to Richmond to be ready to row down the river in state with the Queen. By the time Catherine had reached the archbishop's palace at Lambeth, the Court was installed at Baynard's Castle and London was packed to the rafters. All the world and his wife and his servants had come to town for the wedding; all the great nobles were keeping open house and every stable, every lodging, every spare room in the capital was full. The streets resounded with hammering as crush barriers were put up and carpenters added the finishing touches to triumphal arches and built stages for the elaborate tableaux and pageants which were to greet the bride's procession to St Paul's. Inside the cathedral a sort of cat-walk, the height of a man's head, had been erected, stretching the length of the nave from the west door to the choir and ending in a raised platform large enough to accommodate the King and the royal family on one side and the Lord Mayor and the city dignitaries on the other, with a space in the middle where the marriage ceremony would be performed – the whole complicated structure being lavishly draped in fine red worsted cloth. Henry was really splashing out on his son's wedding, and while it was no doubt in large part a gesture of calculated extravagance designed to proclaim to the outside world that the new English royal house must now be regarded as standing on fully equal terms with the other ruling families of Europe, perhaps Henry was also allowing himself a certain flourish of personal triumph and of pride in the handsome boy who was his heir.

On 12 November Catherine and her retinue left their quarters at Lambeth Palace and were met on the adjacent St George's Field by a glittering escort of English lords, both spiritual and temporal, with their attendant knights and squires. The procession formed up and moved off along the south bank of the river to Southwark. Here, at the entrance to London Bridge, the princess was welcomed to the city by St Katherine and St Ursula, who were surrounded with 'a great multitude of virgins right goodly dressed and arrayed' and seated in a two-storey 'tabernacle' surmounted by a picture of the Trinity and draped with red and blue curtains.

The Spanish marriage was especially popular among the business community. Spain was already a good customer for English wool and tin, and under the terms of the treaty of alliance English merchants trading in Spanish ports were to be accorded special privileges. So, encouraged by the prospect of increased profits, the city had gone out of its way to put on a really good show for the Spanish bride.

Across the bridge, in the widest part of Gracious Street, stood a most realistic-looking castle, but actually constructed, the chronicler is careful to explain, of timber covered with painted canvas. Its battlements were decorated with red and white roses, with gold fleur de lys, peacocks, greyhounds, white harts and other heraldic devices. Over the entrance hung a large portcullis 'and in every joint of the portcullis a red rose'. This was topped by the royal arms painted on a shield of mock stone, and 'on the highest of all the whole pageant, a red dreadful dragon, holding a staff of iron and on the staff a great crown of gold'. In Cornhill there was an astrological pageant, displaying the moon and other celestial bodies, with the angel Raphael waiting to remind the princess that marriage was ordained for love, with virtue and reverence and the procreation of children, and not for sensual lust and appetite. By the great conduit in Cheapside was a pageant of the sun, with a figure intended to symbolize Prince Arthur standing in a gilded chariot. By the standard in Cheapside, on a raised platform profusely embellished with red roses, greyhounds, lions and dragons, stood a great throne surrounded by burning tapers in gold candlesticks and 'innumerable angels singing full harmoniously'. Here was seated no less a person than God the Father, ready to exhort the princess to the love of God and of Holy Church in several stanzas of rather doubtful verse.

> 'Look ye', he declared, 'walk in my precepts and obey them well,
> And here I give you that same blessing that I
> Gave my well-beloved children of Israel;
> Blessed be the fruit of your belly.'

No one, least of all the Almighty's anonymous scriptwriter, could have guessed how bitterly ironical his words would turn out to be.

The Spaniards, of course, were accustomed to religious shows and processions, but they had never seen anything quite on this scale before and they rode wide-eyed behind the scarlet-robed Lord Mayor and aldermen through a fairy-tale city, with the trumpets braying and the Tower cannon booming in their ears. 'The princess', exclaimed the Licentiate Alcares, 'could not have been received with greater joy had she been the saviour of the world.'

The Londoners packing the streets and hanging out of every window along the route were regrettably inclined to laugh at the outlandish appearance of the foreigners, but for the princess herself there was nothing but praise. Catherine, in rich Spanish apparel, was riding a gorgeously trapped mule and wore 'a little hat fashioned like a cardinal's hat . . . with a lace of gold at this hat to stay it, her hair hanging down about her shoulders'. She must have made a charmingly exotic picture and young Thomas More, a law student at Lincoln's Inn, declared enthusiastically 'there is nothing wanting in her that the most beautiful girl should have'. The royal family, who were watching the show from a merchant's house in Cheapside, had every reason to be pleased, and for the King and Queen there was the added satisfaction of seeing ten-year-old Prince Henry carrying out his first important public engagement with perfect aplomb, as he rode through the crowded streets at his new sister's right hand.

The procession ended with a final pageant at the entrance to St Paul's Churchyard, and Catherine and her retinue were installed in the Bishop of London's palace which adjoined the west door of the cathedral. Next day, the eve of the wedding, there was a state reception for the Spanish dignitaries in the great hall of Baynard's Castle, the King sitting under a cloth of estate with his two sons on either side of him. In the afternoon the princess paid a ceremonial visit to the Queen and afterwards there was more dancing and merrymaking, so that it was quite late in the evening before she returned by torchlight to her lodging. 'Thus', remarks the chronicler, 'with honour and mirth this Saturday was expired and done.'

Prince Arthur arrived at St Paul's between nine and ten o'clock on the morning of Sunday, 14 November escorted by the Earls of Oxford and Shrewsbury, and shortly afterwards the bride emerged from the bishop's palace. She was met at the west door of the cathedral by the Archbishop of Canterbury, supported by eighteen other bishops and abbots mitred, and led down the six-hundred-foot length of the great church to the choir, Prince Henry giving her his right hand and Cecily of York bearing her train. Bride and groom were both dressed in white satin, Catherine's gown being made very wide 'with many pleats, much like unto men's clothing' and worn over a Spanish hooped farthingale, while a white silk veil bordered with pearls and precious stones covered her face.

After the marriage service conducted by the Archbishop, which lasted more than three hours, the newly-wedded pair went hand in hand towards the high altar, turning to the south and north so that 'the present multitude of people might see and behold their persons'. Trumpets, shawns and sackbuts sounded, and a great shout went up inside the cathedral, 'some crying King Henry, some in likewise crying Prince Arthur'. Outside, the bells crashed, the conduits ran with wine and the waiting crowds cheered themselves hoarse.

As soon as the long-drawn-out religious ceremonies were over, the wedding guests trooped across the churchyard to the bishop's palace, where a feast of 'the most delicate dainties and curious meats that might be purveyed and gotten within the whole realm of England' was laid out for them.

That day of pageantry, piety, emotion and over-eating ended with the customary ceremonious bedding of bride and groom, the prince being conducted by his lords and gentlemen (few of them entirely sober by this time) to the bridal chamber 'wherein the princess before his coming was reverently laid and disposed'. The marriage bed was blessed by the assembled bishops and at last the

Left: *Arthur, Prince of Wales, by an unknown artist.* Right: *Henry, Duke of York, second son of Henry VII and his eventual successor.*

young couple were left alone. A quarter of a century later, the details of that public bedding were to be as publicly re-hashed – even Arthur's boyish boast of the following morning was produced in evidence. He had called for a drink, remembered someone, saying he had been that night in Spain and found it thirsty work.

The celebrations lasted a full fortnight. On Monday, while the princess rested in her apartments, the Spanish visitors were entertained to dinner and supper by the King's mother and her husband, Lord Derby. On Tuesday, the King and all the quality went in state to hear mass at St Paul's and on Wednesday a number of new Knights of the Bath were created. On Thursday the Court moved to Westminster, where a tiltyard had been set up on the open space in front of Westminster Hall for a grand tournament in honour of the wedding – the champions vying with one another over the magnificence of their turn-out. On Friday, there was a state banquet inside the Hall with the new Princess of Wales seated on the King's right hand. There was more 'disguising': a castle set on wheels with ladies looking out of the windows and singing boys warbling on the turrets was drawn in by a team of prototype pantomime horses – four heraldic beasts painted gold and silver and each containing two men, 'one in the forepart and another in the hindpart'. This wonder was followed by a ship in full sail and

The betrothal of Prince Arthur and Catherine of Aragon; an early sixteenth-century Flemish tapestry.

finally by a third pageant 'in likeness of a great hill . . . in which were enclosed eight goodly knights with their banners spread and displayed, naming themselves the Knights of the Mount of Love'. When these set pieces had been exclaimed over and towed away, the musicians struck up for dancing. The younger members of the royal family took the floor and Prince Henry, energetically partnering his sister Margaret, 'perceiving himself to be accumbered by his clothes', threw off his gown and danced in his jacket, much to the amusement of his parents.

It was the end of November before the party began to break up. Catherine was to keep a permanent staff of about sixty Spanish attendants, but dignitaries such as the Count of Cabra, the Archbishops of Toledo and Santiago, and the Bishops of Malaga and Majorca had only come to see her safely married and now, surfeited with hospitality and laden with expensive presents, they were ready to leave for Southampton to face another sea crossing. When the moment of parting came, the little bride (she was not yet sixteen) shed some tears, and we have a glimpse of the King taking a rather woebegone princess into his library at Richmond and showing her 'many goodly pleasant books' in an attempt to cheer her up. The next few months were bound to be a difficult period of adjustment for the Spanish girl and, before the royal family returned to its normal routine, a decision had to be taken about her immediate future.

Arthur must go back to Ludlow where, as Prince of Wales, he represented his father on the Welsh Marches and where he was learning the business of government under the guidance of a small but carefully chosen band of advisers. The question which now arose was, should his wife go with him? Some people doubted whether, at barely fifteen, the prince was old enough or strong enough to undertake the duties of a husband. They also questioned the wisdom of exposing the newly arrived princess to the rigours of life on the north-west frontier, especially in the dead of winter. Surely it would be better to leave her at Court for a while, where the Queen could keep an eye on her and teach her something of English ways? This would certainly seem to have been the most humane and prudent course, but the King hesitated. Whether he was thinking about the expense of maintaining a separate establishment for his daughter-in-law, whether he was worried about possible difficulties with Spain if she was kept apart from her husband, or whether he simply felt that the two young people should be given a chance to get to know each other away from the distractions of the Court is nowhere recorded; but whatever considerations influenced his decision, when Arthur left for Shropshire in December, Catherine and her Spanish household went too.

They took the journey slowly, going by way of Abingdon, Oxford (where they spent Christmas, probably as guests of Magdalen College) and then north to Kenilworth. Here they turned westward, crossing the Severn at Bewdley and reaching the gloomy, medieval fortress of Ludlow Castle early in the New Year. We know very little of their life together but Arthur, who is said to have been 'very studious and learned beyond his years', would be kept busy working with his tutor, attending meetings of his council to listen while they debated points of local law and administration, and riding out on hunting expeditions when the weather was fine. Perhaps Catherine went with him sometimes, otherwise she would have had little to do but read or sit sewing with her ladies. There is nothing to suggest that she and Arthur ever succeeded in establishing any sort of close relationship. The prince was a quiet, shy boy, apparently content to stay in the background even at his own wedding, and the fact that they had no common language, apart from Latin and some schoolroom French, cannot have helped to break the ice. Catherine did not complain – she had been trained from babyhood to accept that her destiny would lie with strangers in a strange land – but it is hard to believe that she was happy.

There were some diversions, of course. The Welsh chieftains, led by that old friend of the family Rhys ap Thomas, came in to pay their respects and Rhys left his son Griffith to serve the Prince and Princess of Wales. Catherine made another friend at Ludlow – Margaret Plantagenet, now married to Sir Richard Pole (not to be confused with the de la Poles incidentally), chamberlain of Arthur's household. Margaret, tall, elegant and aristocratic, was the sister of the Earl of Warwick whose death had helped to make England safe for the Tudors, and for Catherine of Aragon. One might imagine that this would have created an impassable barrier between the two young women, but such situations were not uncommon in great families and the survivors learned to accept them with well-bred stoicism.

In January 1500 Dr de Puebla, the little Jewish lawyer who was King Ferdinand's resident ambassador at Henry's Court, had written triumphantly to his master that since Warwick's execution England had never been so tranquil or so obedient, and that not a drop of doubtful royal blood remained. De Puebla was being rather more optimistic than accurate. There was still quite enough doubtful, that is, Plantagenet, royal blood in circulation to cause Henry Tudor intermittent anxiety, and during the summer of 1501 disaffection centring round the remaining de la Pole brothers had been simmering under the surface of the wedding preparations. Some time in July or August, the eldest, Edmund, an arrogant and irresponsible young man who had nevertheless been treated with a good deal of forbearance by the King, fled to the Continent taking his next brother, Richard, with him. Richard sensibly adopted a career as a professional soldier and caused no further trouble to anyone, but Edmund, self-styled Duke of Suffolk and since 1499 the authentic White Rose, was taken up in a rather desultory way by the volatile Emperor Maximilian. Although Edmund de la Pole never looked like becoming a serious threat to the Tudor peace, Henry could not be quite comfortable in his mind while there was a Plantagenet on the loose in Europe.

Apart from this familiar vexation, in the spring of 1502 Henry was at peace with his neighbours and could congratulate himself on the fact that, after many months of patient negotiation, he had finally succeeded in signing a treaty of friendship with Scotland – soon to be sealed by another marriage, between his daughter Margaret and the Scottish king. So when tragedy struck early in April, it came out of a comparatively clear sky.

We are never likely to know exactly what Arthur died of. 'A consumption' say some authorities, but although the prince was almost certainly tubercular it wasn't that alone which killed him. Some accounts blame the sweating sickness and if they are right Fate could scarcely have played a crueller joke on the House of Tudor, for this disease – a violent malarial type of fever, often fatal within twenty-four hours – had first appeared in England in 1485, brought over by the Norman mercenaries who landed at Milford Haven with Henry and Jasper. Of course, Arthur may equally well have picked up some respiratory infection which an already consumptive adolescent had been unable to withstand. Whatever the cause, on 2 April the Rosebush of England, embodiment of all his father's hopes and dreams, was dead at the age of fifteen.

Richard Pole's courier found the Court at Greenwich in the early hours of the following Tuesday. The King's confessor undertook to break the news but it was the Queen who supported her husband through the first raging storm of his grief and shock, reminding him that his mother 'had never no more children but him only and that God had ever preserved him and brought him where he was'. They still had a fair prince and two fair princesses, and there might yet be more children. 'God is where he was and we are both young enough', said Elizabeth gallantly – she was thirty-six now and Henry forty-five.

Later, though, back in her own apartments, the Queen's brave front collapsed. 'Natural and motherly remembrance of that great loss smote her so sorrowful to the heart', says the chronicler, 'that those about her were fain to send for the King to comfort her; and then his Grace, of true gentle and faithful love, in good haste came and relieved her, and showed her how wise counsel she had given him before and he, for his part, would thank God for his sons, and would she should do in like wise'.

While the King and Queen clung together in their sorrow, struggling to come to terms with the will of a deity who could take their precious elder son on the very threshold of his manhood, and solemn dirges were sung in all the London churches, Arthur's body lay in his own room at Ludlow, the black-draped coffin surrounded by candles burning day and night. On St George's Day it was carried in procession to the parish church, with Griffith ap Rhys walking in front bearing the banner of the prince's arms and 'fourscore poor men in black mourning habits holding fourscore torches, besides all the torches of the town' bringing up the rear. Two days later the cortège set out for Worcester, the nearest cathedral, in the sort of weather which only an English April can produce – wild, wet and bitterly cold. The wind tore at the banners and trappings, pouring rain soaked the robes and hoods of the mourners and turned the road into a quagmire, so that at one stage oxen had to be used to draw the hearse. But the day of the funeral itself was mercifully fine and no detail of pomp or ceremony was omitted. The Earl of Surrey was chief mourner, supported by the Earls of Shrewsbury and Kent, and four bishops waited to conduct the service. 'He would have had a hard heart that wept not', remarked one eyewitness of the scene inside the cathedral and when the time came for the prince's household officers to break their staves and cast them into the open grave, everyone was in tears.

But in spite of disappointment and heartbreak, life and politics had to go on. Prince Henry, on whose health and well-being everything now depended, must be trained to take his brother's place, and the future of the widowed Princess of Wales must be settled. When the news of Arthur's death reached Spain, Ferdinand and Isabella's immediate reaction had been to ask for the return of their daughter. 'We cannot endure that a daughter whom we love should be so far away from us in her trouble', wrote Isabella. They also demanded that Henry should put the princess in possession of her widow's jointure – one-third of the revenues of Wales, Cornwall and Chester – and repay the first instalment of her dowry – 100,000 gold crowns. All this, though, was no more than the opening move in a fresh round of diplomatic bargaining intended to repair the broken link.

The House of Tudor was not alone in its recent misfortune. The Spanish king and queen had lost three heirs in quick succession – their only son, their eldest daughter, Isabella of Portugal, and Isabella's son, Dom Miguel. The kingdoms of

Aragon and Castile would now pass to their next daughter, Juana, wife of Philip von Hapsburg, Duke of Burgundy and son of the Emperor Maximilian. Juana's marriage, like Catherine's, had originally been a part of the general policy of containing France in a ring of pro-Spanish alliances, but by the early 1500s it had assumed a special significance; for it was Juana's son, Charles of Ghent, who would eventually inherit not only the rich Burgundian Netherlands and the Austrian domains of the Hapsburg family, but the crowns of Spain as well.

To see why the English alliance had become so important to the rulers of Spain, it is only necessary to look at the map. An unfriendly England or, worse, an unfriendly England allied with France, would be able to bar the Straits of Dover any time she pleased and thus effectively cut the future Spanish Empire in half. So when Hernan Duque, special envoy of the Catholic kings, arrived in London that summer, he brought with him full powers to negotiate a second marriage for Catherine – a marriage with her brother-in-law, 'the Prince of Wales who now is'.

The King of England received the proposal courteously, but was in no hurry to commit himself. Henry had no wish to break with Spain, whose friendship could only work to his advantage – especially bearing in mind that the Netherlands were far and away England's most valuable trading partners; but he was in a much stronger bargaining position now than he had been ten years ago. He had not forgotten the way Ferdinand had made him wait on Spanish pleasure during their previous dealings, making it humiliatingly clear that Spain was conferring a favour on his house. Now Ferdinand was the suitor and Henry would enjoy playing hard to get.

No one, it seems, thought of asking for Catherine's views on the subject, but there was one point on which she, or a senior member of her household, would have to be consulted. The princess had been ill, probably with the same infection that had killed Arthur, and it was several weeks before she was fit enough to leave Ludlow and travel slowly south in a black-curtained litter; but as soon as she reached London and had been installed at Durham House in the Strand to complete her period of strict mourning, Dr de Puebla began to make some discreet enquiries on a rather delicate matter. To put no finer point on it, he needed to know whether or not the Princess of Wales was still a virgin.

Of course, the mere fact that she had been through a church ceremony with Prince Arthur had created a canonical obstacle to her projected union with Prince Arthur's brother. If that first marriage had been consummated, then, under canon law, she and Prince Henry would be related in the first degree of affinity, a rather more serious impediment. In either case the Pope could issue the appropriate dispensation – it was simply a question of being sure of one's facts before approaching the Vatican.

De Puebla, therefore, had a quiet word with Don Alessandro Geraldini, Catherine's chaplain and confessor. Don Alessandro, possibly with the idea of being helpful, was quite definite. Certainly the marriage had been consummated, he declared, there might even be issue. Well, of course, if Catherine was by any chance pregnant, if she were to bear a posthumous child and that child were to be a boy, then the whole situation changed. But while de Puebla was digesting the implications of this interesting information, he heard a very different story from

Doña Elvira Manuel. Doña Elvira was furious. How dared the chaplain and the ambassador gossip about the princess behind her back? The marriage had *not* been consummated. Doña Elvira and all the matrons of their lady's household were prepared to swear a solemn oath that, of their personal knowledge, the princess was still *virgo intacta* – an assertion which could, if necessary, be easily verified. And having reduced de Puebla to an apologetic jelly, the duenna swept off to write her version to Queen Isabella. De Puebla believed her, and so did the Queen. 'It is already known for a certainty that the said Princess of Wales, our daughter, *remains as she was here*', she wrote to Hernan Duque in July 1502.

All the same, after a full discussion between the King, his council and the Spanish envoys, it was decided – presumably on the principle that it was better to be safe than sorry – to proceed on the assumption that the marriage had 'perhaps' been consummated, and the Pope was asked to dispense accordingly.

Some months before matters reached this advanced stage, the English royal family suffered its second bereavement within a year. By the late summer of 1502 Elizabeth of York had begun her eighth pregnancy and on 2 February 1503, while the Court was paying a visit to the City, she went into premature labour at the Tower of London. (The Queen had intended to be delivered at the comfortable, modern palace of Richmond and it was normal practice for a royal mother-to-be to retire from public gaze at least a month before the expected date of her confinement.) The baby, born 'upon Candlemas Day, in the night following the day', was a girl, christened Katherine; but Elizabeth, exhausted by successive childbearing, died a week later, on or about her thirty-eighth birthday, and the infant princess 'tarried but a small season after her mother'.

There was general and sincere mourning for the Queen who had always been popular. 'She was a woman of such a character', says Polydore Vergil, 'that it would be hard to judge whether she displayed more of majesty and dignity in her life than wisdom and moderation.' Everyone who knew her seems to agree that she was beautiful, noble, gentle and wise – a loving wife and mother, a dutiful daughter and a generous and affectionate sister. After allowing for the usual excesses of post mortem panegyric, a picture emerges of a placid, sweet-tempered, warm-hearted woman, conventionally pious and naturally indolent, content to let others take the lead. Some foreign observers hinted that the Queen was deliberately kept in the background by her mother-in-law and resented the older woman's dominating influence. Very possibly Elizabeth found the constant, busy presence of Margaret Beaufort something of a trial but she seems to have been willing enough to let 'my lady the King's mother' take over such tedious chores as drawing up rules of court etiquette and keeping an eye on the servants. As for her relationship with her husband, we know little enough about the private life of the first Tudor King and his consort but there is really no evidence to support the contention, first put forward by Francis Bacon, that Henry treated her with cold indifference. On the contrary, such evidence as does exist indicates that theirs was a good marriage, based on mutual tenderness and respect.

Elizabeth was given an elaborate and expensive funeral. On 22 February the coffin, resting on an open chariot draped with black velvet and followed by the officers of the household and representatives of the peerage, the judiciary and the church, was drawn by six horses through streets lined with torch-bearers to Westminster. Next day the Queen was buried in the Abbey, her sister Katherine Courtenay officiating as chief mourner. The King, according to custom, was not present. He had 'departed to a solitary place to pass his sorrow, and would no man should resort to him but those whom he had appointed.'

The fact that Henry began almost immediately to think of re-marriage need in no way detract from the sincerity of his grief. He was intensely conscious that the future of the dynasty, of everything he had worked and struggled for, everything he had built up over the past twenty years hung on the life of an eleven-year-old boy. Personal feelings set aside, it was the King's clear duty to his house and to his people to take another wife and beget more sons while there was still time.

Henry's first choice, which so horrified his nineteenth-century biographers, fell on his daughter-in-law Catherine of Aragon. By contemporary standards, though, there was nothing particularly shocking about this idea and, from Henry's point of view, it had a good deal to recommend it. Catherine was seventeen now, fully old enough for childbearing; she was ready at hand and no protracted negotiations would be necessary. It is true that her parents rejected the proposal indignantly, but they are more likely to have been motivated by political than by moral considerations. The Spanish monarchs were interested in providing for the next generation. They had no intention of wasting a young and nubile princess on a man old enough to be her grandfather. Henry, perhaps fortunately for his reputation, did not press the point and when Ferdinand offered his niece, the widowed Queen of Naples, as a more suitable candidate for the position of Queen of England, the King at once despatched an embassy with instructions to inspect the lady and report in detail on her physical and financial potentialities. Among a long list of items, the envoys were to notice whether or not she painted her face, 'to mark her breasts and paps, whether they be big or small', and, if possible, get close enough to smell her breath. There were a number of hidden hazards attached to long-distance courtship and Henry, always a prudent man, was guarding against as many as he could think of.

Meanwhile, the terms of the marriage contract between Catherine and young Henry were being finalized. Their betrothal was solemnized at the Bishop of Salisbury's house in Fleet Street on 25 June 1503, three days before the prince's twelfth birthday, and it was agreed that the wedding day should be set as soon as he had completed his fourteenth year – conditional on the necessary dispensation being forthcoming from Rome and on Spain being able to prove that the second half of the bride's dowry was in London ready for payment.

Marriage was in the air that summer. Two days after seeing his son betrothed, the King set out from Richmond to escort his eldest daughter, thirteen-year-old Margaret, on the first stage of her journey to the Scottish Border. As father and daughter travelled north through those long-ago June days they naturally had no conception of the far-reaching consequences which were to flow from the marriage of Margaret Tudor and James IV of Scotland; nor could they have foreseen that exactly one hundred years later Margaret's great-grandson would be making his journey south to be crowned at Westminster. It is true that when the Scottish marriage project was first being discussed at the council table, some councillors had put the case that 'if God should take the King's two sons without issue, then the kingdom of England would fall to the King of Scotland, which might prejudice the monarchy of England'; but Henry had replied that if such a thing were to happen, 'Scotland would be but an accession to England, and not England to Scotland, for the greater would draw the less.' This prescient piece of political wisdom 'passed as an oracle', at least according to Francis Bacon, and seems to have silenced any further criticism. In any case, the solid advantages of an alliance which would break the long-standing bond between England's ancestral enemies, Scotland and France, and secure her vulnerable land frontier, as well as put an end to the costly and destructive nuisance of organized Border raiding, obviously outweighed future imponderables and must be welcomed by all sensible men. The King, long-sighted though he was, could scarcely have envisaged the political complications or the personal tragedies which this union of 'the thistle and the rose' would inflict on his immediate descendants.

Henry accompanied the bridal party as far as his mother's house at Collyweston, which lay just south of Stamford, conveniently close to the Great North Road. Here the family goodbyes were said and young Margaret was handed over to the charge of the Earl and Countess of Surrey who would be responsible for delivering her safely to her husband. The King was sending his daughter off in style (apart from anything else, this was an excellent opportunity to show the Tudor flag in the seldom visited North Country) and as well as the Surreys and their train, 'there was appointed many great lords, nobles, knights, ladies, squires, gentlewomen and others for to convey her from place to place'. In addition to the regular escort, 'the nobles of the country, governors of towns, other officers of the lordships, mayors, sheriffs, aldermen, burgesses, and citizens of the towns through which she should pass' came out to greet the princess and 'make her all honour and reverence'. It was only to be expected, of course, that the county magnates, royal officers and civic dignitaries would be meticulous in paying their respects, but everywhere along the route the ordinary people left their harvesting to crowd the roadside to see the noble company, bringing 'great vessels full of drink' which they pressed on the thirsty travellers in a spontaneous gesture of hospitality. In every town and village the church bells pealed a welcome as soon as the cavalcade, in its cloud of summer dust, was sighted on the road; the royal trumpeters would answer with a fanfare, while 'Johannes and his company, minstrels of musick' struck up a tune on their instruments.

The English crossed the Border at Berwick on 1 August and were met by the Scots at Lamberton. King James, now a mature and experienced man in his late twenties, was known to be keeping a mistress – all the same, he was noticeably kind and attentive to his little bride, and taking every opportunity to kiss her and show her special courtesies in public.

The wedding took place at Edinburgh on 8 August, but although Margaret played her part gracefully enough in the various ceremonials and festivities, she was not happy. A plump, round-faced child, her somewhat stolid exterior concealed a passionate, headstrong nature, with a 'great twang' of the Tudor, or rather of the Plantagenet temper, and a sharp eye for a grievance. She felt that King James was taking altogether too much notice of the Earl of Surrey – 'he cannot forbear the company of him no time of the day' – also that Surrey was ganging up with the Scots against her, and she wrote querulously and rather incoherently to her father: 'He [Surrey] and the Bishop of Murray order everything as nigh as they can to the King's pleasure. I pray God it may be for my poor heart's ease in time to come . . . God send me comfort to His pleasure and that I and mine that be left here with me be well entreated such ways as they have taken.' The letter ended, rather pathetically, with a wish that 'I would I were with your Grace now, and many times more.'

Henry was probably not unsympathetic over his daughter's difficulties in finding her feet and adjusting to her new surroundings, but Margaret was on her own now – a Queen and a married woman – she would have to conquer her homesickness as best she could. In any case, the King was occupied that autumn getting to know his son and heir. There had, of course, been no question of sending this Prince of Wales away to Ludlow or anywhere else, he was far too precious, and Hernan Duque reported to Queen Isabella in January 1504 that the prince was now often in the King's company. Duque, after commenting approvingly on the affectionate relationship which existed between father and son, remarked that in his opinion the prince could have no better school than the society of such a wise and careful governor. Isabella, although no doubt pleased to hear about the satisfactory progress of her daughter's fiancé's education, was even more gratified by the information that he was growing into a big, strong youth and giving every promise that he would reach maturity.

Isabella did not live to see that maturity (perhaps it was just as well). She died in the following November and at once the European scene changed. Juana, Duchess of Burgundy and Archduchess of Austria, succeeded her mother as Queen of Castile and it began to look very much as if the unity of the Spanish peninsula – which had been founded on the union between Isabella and Ferdinand – might now collapse. Isabella had left instructions in her will that Ferdinand should continue to govern Castile in Juana's name, but not unnaturally Juana's husband had his own ideas on that subject. If Philip von Hapsburg could find a viable way of removing Castile from the King of Aragon's grasp, he would certainly use it. Meanwhile, the King of England, who disliked and distrusted Ferdinand, was thinking seriously of strengthening his ties with the Hapsburg family.

Henry wanted a personal meeting with Philip but did not achieve his objective until the beginning of 1506, and then only by a stroke of luck. On 7 January a fleet carrying Philip (now given the courtesy title of King of Castile), the Queen his wife, and a large retinue of Dutch and Flemish nobility sailed from Zeeland for Spain – though whether it went in peace or war nobody seemed very certain. As things turned out, it very nearly did not go at all. Gales in the Channel – the same 'tempest of wind' which in London blew down trees and tiles and the great weather-vane on St Paul's Cathedral – scattered the ships and forced them to seek refuge in ports all along the south coast from Rye to Falmouth. Philip's own vessel, battered, leaking and with one of its masts snapped off, staggered into Melcombe near Weymouth.

As soon as the news reached London, the King sent Sir Thomas Brandon to escort these unexpected but welcome visitors to Windsor and Philip found himself enveloped in a bear hug of Tudor hospitality. An English eyewitness of the splendid show, laid on at not much more than a week's notice, wrote complacently: 'I suppose few or none that were there ever saw castle or other lodgings in all things so well and richly appointed, and the great continual fair open household, so many noblemen so well appointed, and with so short warning as I think hath not been seen.'

If Philip chafed at the delay, he gave no sign of it. A large, fair, good-natured, rather slow-witted young man, he seems to have thoroughly enjoyed the entertainment provided for him – the hunting and hawking, the unlimited food and drink, the pageantry and display were all just what he liked. The other members of the royal family had also been summoned to Windsor, and on a non-hunting day Philip was invited 'for pastime' to watch the ladies dancing. His sister-in-law, Catherine of Aragon, showed off some of her Spanish dances, but Philip resisted her attempts to persuade him to take the floor himself. 'I am a mariner', he protested jovially, 'and yet ye would cause me to dance!' Catherine was followed by my lady Mary, the King's younger daughter, nearly eleven now and the beauty of the family. Mary performed her party pieces with great self-possession, dancing and then playing on the lute and virginals, 'and she was of all folks there greatly praised that of her youth in everything she behaved herself so very well.'

There was, of course, a purpose underlying all this jollity. Henry meant to take full advantage of a literally heaven-sent opportunity and the gay, relatively informal house-party atmosphere he had been at pains to create provided a useful screen behind which he and Philip could retire to talk business. There was plenty to talk about as the two Kings dined privately together in Henry's secret chamber or sat apart 'communing' while the rest of the company played cards or danced and made music. Henry wanted a new commercial treaty with the Netherlands, giving England most favoured nation treatment. He wanted a general alliance with the Hapsburgs. But most of all he wanted Edmund de la Pole, still at large in Flanders under the Duke of Burgundy's protection. The King had no illusions as to what might follow if he were to die before his heir was of full age – already reports of some disturbing gossip about 'the world that should be after him if his grace happened to depart' had reached his ears. The names of several possible successors had been mentioned, among them the Duke of Buckingham and Edmund de la Pole, but no one, ominously enough, had spoken of 'my lord prince'.

Philip, on his side, wanted English support, both moral and financial, in establishing his claims to Castile, and on 9 February 1506, he and Henry put their signatures to the Treaty of Windsor. Before the end of the month the Venetian, Vincenzo Quirini, who had sailed with the fleet from Zeeland and was now marooned at Falmouth – 'a very wild place which no human being ever visits' as he mournfully remarked – had nevertheless heard that 'the Kings of England and Castile have concluded and proclaimed a new and very close alliance, which was ratified and sworn at the altar'. On 16 March Edmund de la Pole was brought under escort to Calais and handed over to Henry's representatives. A fortnight later the White Rose had been safely deposited in the Tower.

Marriage, the usual cement for binding political treaties, was also discussed during those weeks at Windsor. In this case, three marriages – Henry's own to Philip's sister Margaret (the Queen of Naples had been discarded, not because she had bad breath but because it turned out she had no money), little Mary Tudor to Philip's son Charles, and ('very secretly' this one) the Prince of Wales to Philip's daughter Eleanor. When the King and Queen of Castile finally resumed their interrupted journey, matters seemed in a fair way to being settled and the result, so Henry sincerely hoped, would be the discomfiture of the King of Aragon.

In fact, the person who suffered most from the realignment of European power blocs was Ferdinand's unhappy daughter. When the contract for her second marriage was signed in the summer of 1503, Catherine had been required to renounce all claim to her dower rights as Arthur's widow – a renunciation which left her financially dependent on her father-in-law and very much at his mercy. At first Henry was not ungenerous, making the princess an allowance of a hundred pounds a month – enough, just, to support the establishment at Durham House. But later, as relations between England and Spain deteriorated and Ferdinand showed no sign of fulfilling his obligations, Henry had a means of retaliation ready to hand. Catherine's allowance was cut off and Durham House closed. Robbed of even the illusion of independence, forced to live on the fringes of the Court in whatever accommodation might be assigned to her, cold-shouldered by the English, her servants unpaid and mutinous, heavily in debt – though not, she assured her father pathetically, for extravagant things – the Spanish princess learned the hard way just what it could mean to be a pawn in the political chess game. Even such rare interludes as the visit to Windsor brought their own problems and Catherine had to sell some bracelets to pay for a new dress.

She got no help from Spain. God alone, wrote Ferdinand, knew the sadness of his heart whenever he thought of her miserable life, but he did nothing about paying over the rest of her dowry. The King of Aragon was, in fact, having something of a struggle to keep his own head above water and he chose to blame his daughter's predicament on the evil machinations of the King of Castile – although Philip had died in somewhat suspicious circumstances soon after arriving in Spain. Ferdinand, a talented and experienced practitioner of the art of survival, sent a fluent stream of regrets, excuses and promises to England, but meanwhile the Prince of Wales's fourteenth birthday had come and gone and his fiancée remained in limbo – lonely, humiliated and, so it seemed, betrayed.

It is hard not to blame Henry VII for the undoubted meanness with which he treated Catherine and this picture of a cold-hearted skinflint is the one that has come down to us. Like all such traditions, there is a grain of truth in it, but it is by no means the whole picture. The King was certainly very interested in money and skilful in amassing it, but he also knew how to spend it – witness the glorious chapel in Westminster Abbey which bears his name. Nor was his court the grim and joyless place it is sometimes painted. It was well regulated – Margaret Beaufort saw to that – and drunkenness, wasteful extravagance and anything which might be classed as 'goings on' were certainly discouraged; but there is plenty of evidence that the King's household was cheerful, comfortable and

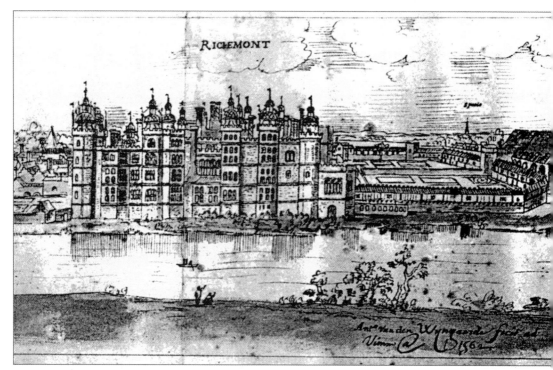

Richmond Palace; a sketch by Anthony van Wyngaerde. Beside the magnificent palace where Henry died in 1509 are the ruins of the old palace of Sheen burned down at Christmas 1498.

always suitably magnificent with, at least until 1503, a happy family life at its core. When the ancient royal manor of Sheen was destroyed by fire, a handsome new palace, built of brick and stone in the latest architectural style and surrounded by gardens and pleasure grounds, rose on the site, re-christened Richmond by Henry in memory of his own and his father's earldom. Improvements were also put in hand at Baynard's Castle and Greenwich.

The popular image of a killjoy King, spending every spare moment poring over his account books, is largely the creation of Francis Bacon, whose classic biography of Henry was published in the 1620s. 'For his pleasures', wrote Bacon, 'there is no news of them' but there is, in fact, quite a lot of news to be found in the Privy Purse accounts – enough at any rate to show that the King took his pleasures from a wide range of leisure activities: from hunting and hawking, tennis, archery, cards and dice; that he was fond of music, rewards to singers and musicians occur frequently; that, considering his many other preoccupations, he played a perfectly normal part in the busy social life of the Court. The account books also show that he was ready to be amused in a variety of ways – there are payments to 'a Welsh rhymer', to 'the blind poet', to 'a little maiden that danceth', to 'the children of the King's Chapel for singing of *Gloria in excelsis*', to

Henry VII in later life; a portrait by an unknown artist.

'a piper on the bagpipe', to 'a Spaniard that played the fool' and that is only a small, random selection. There is less evidence of interest in cultural matters. Henry himself was no intellectual and too conventionally-minded to feel much sympathy with the rising tide of intellectual excitement beginning to surge through the universities; but he respected learning in principle, saw to it that his children received the best possible education and encouraged his mother in her zeal for founding colleges. He was a pious man, neglecting none of his religious duties and giving special patronage to the Franciscan order of Observant Friars, but always a moderate man, he had none of his mother's religious fervour.

The last years of the King's life were marked by a noticeable deterioration in his health and by increasing loneliness. As early as 1501 he was complaining to his mother of failing eyesight – it sounds like cataract – and apologizing for the fact that it had taken him three days to write her a letter in his own hand. Probably he never really recovered from the shock of losing his elder son and his wife within a year of one another. He was seriously ill soon afterwards and by 1504 or 1505 it was being whispered that 'the King's grace is but a weak and sickly man, not likely to be a long-lived man'. By this time, too, there were many gaps in his small circle of intimate friends. Jasper Tudor had died back in 1495. John Morton had gone and so had Reginald Bray, two of his closest and most trusted confidants. It was a long time now since the glorious adventure of Bosworth and there were very few people left who remembered the fair-headed young Welshman who had landed at Milford Haven all those years ago.

None of the King's plans for a second marriage ever materialized. Margaret of Austria, a strong-minded lady already twice a widow, had declined the honour and his third choice, despite a most pertinacious pursuit, also proved to be beyond his reach. Henry Tudor's abortive courtship of the widowed Queen of Castile is the one bizarre episode in an otherwise unexceptional private life – not just because, as Catherine of Aragon's sister, she was closely related to him by marriage, but because she was, at least according to her own family, hopelessly insane.

Henry had met Juana briefly in 1506 (she had spent less than a week at Windsor) but in view of what followed it is tempting to believe that during those few days the sober, prudent King had fallen in love with another's man's wife. After Philip's death Juana, a Queen in her own right, naturally became a great matrimonial prize but this alone scarcely accounts for Henry's uncharacteristic, almost obsessive eagerness. He paid no attention to Ferdinand's hints and evasions, even stories that Juana had refused to allow Philip to be buried and was carrying his coffin about with her failed to discourage him. He continued to press his suit by every diplomatic means open to him, using every persuasion he could think of. Dr de Puebla was instructed to tell the King of Aragon that in different surroundings and under the care of an affectionate husband, the Queen of Castile might recover her wits; even Catherine was pushed into writing to her sister to commend the match. But all Henry could get out of Ferdinand was a vague promise that if Juana married anyone it should certainly be the King of England. As the King of England's disappointment and frustration increased, his temper got worse and Catherine, as his hostage, got the full benefit of it.

There is a certain amount of mystery attached to the question of whether the tragic Juana really was insane, or whether Ferdinand was deliberately exaggerating her undoubted mental instability for reasons of his own. Henry told a Spanish envoy in 1508 that when he had seen the Queen himself two years previously, she had spoken and acted rationally and with great dignity and grace. He had thought her sane then and he thought her sane now. He was receiving reports from Spain which said she was perfectly normal but that Ferdinand was keeping her shut up and spreading false rumours about her. If Henry believed these reports, and his intelligence service was usually reliable, then it would explain a good deal of his loathing of Ferdinand. It might also explain why the Prince of Wales, now a strapping young man taller than his father, was still unmarried – a fact which, considering the acute shortage of male Tudors, was worrying several members of the Council. But in spite of the obvious dangers inherent in such a delay, it seems that the King was using his son's marriage as bait, stubbornly hoping to catch his own fish on the hook.

Matters were still at this impasse when Henry died 'of a consuming sickness' on 21 April 1509. He was fifty-two years old and had ruled England for twenty-three years and eight months. Of his public abilities as King and statesman there can be little question and few people have disputed Bacon's judgement that he was one of the best sort of wonders – 'a wonder for wise men'. 'His spirit', wrote Polydore Vergil, 'was distinguished, wise and prudent; his mind was brave and resolute and never, even at moments of the greatest danger, deserted him.' John Fisher, Bishop of Rochester, making the King's funeral oration, declared that: 'His politic wisdom in governance was singular, his wit always quick and ready, his reason pithy and substantial, his memory fresh and holding, his experience notable, his counsels fortunate and taken by wise deliberation.' It is also worth remembering that Henry was a humane man. For a king with his problems the number of political prisoners executed during the reign was remarkably small.

As for the accusations of avarice and rapacity levelled against him both by his contemporaries and by succeeding generations, it is perfectly true that Henry had evolved some extremely efficient methods of soaking the rich. Nobody enjoys being parted from his money. Henry's victims, most of whom came from an articulate, influential section of the community, complained loudly and bitterly, and no doubt some injustices were done. But for the King, whose one overriding aim had always been to increase the authority of the Crown while strengthening his family's hold on it, money equalled power and power equalled security. As he grew older and more secure, paradoxically the urge to salt away just a little more and then a little more of the substance of power seems to have grown, until at the last it was threatening to overwhelm him and, as Polydore Vergil put it, to distort 'those qualities of trustfulness, justice and integrity by which the State must be governed'.

To his mother, who loved him, Henry was 'my own sweet and most dear king and all my worldly joy' – 'my good and gracious prince, king and only beloved son'. His subjects admired, feared and respected him, but there is little to suggest that they ever loved him. His was not an out-going personality. He never courted popularity and does not appear to have either wanted or expected it. The most he asked of the English people was that they should remain loyal and passive while he got on with the business of ruling them. And he ruled them well, leaving the country prosperous and at peace, the monarchy stronger and richer than it had been for generations. More than that, by his patient, unspectacular hard work, his unremitting attention to detail, the first Henry Tudor laid the foundations which alone made possible the achievements of his son and his grand-daughter.

CHAPTER 4

The Renaissance Prince

The Rose both white and rede
In one Rose now doth grow;
Thus thorow every stede
Thereof the fame doth blow;
Grace the sede did sow:
England now gather flowers,
Exclude now all dolours.

The new King of England was seventeen years old and the whole country promptly went wild with delight over 'our natural, young, lusty and courageous prince and sovereign lord, King Harry the Eighth'. Foreign diplomats sat down to write glowing reports of his magnificence and liberality, while John Skelton, the Poet Laureate, who had been the prince's first tutor – 'the honour of England I learned to spell' – hurried into enthusiastic verse:

Noble Henry the eight
　　Thy loving sovereine lorde,
Of Kingis line moost streight,
　　His titille dothe recorde:
　　In whome dothe wele acorde
Alexis yonge of age,
Adrastus wise and sage.

Adonis of fresh colour,
　　Of youthe the godely flower,
Our prince of high honour,
　　Our paves [shield], our succour,
　　Our king, our emperour,
Our Priamus of Troy,
Our welth, our worldly joy.

Noble 'Henry the eight' certainly seemed to have every advantage. Thanks to his father's statesmanship and careful housekeeping, he had succeeded unopposed to a secure and solvent throne – and that was something which had not happened to an English king for a long time. The second Henry Tudor was also of 'truly royal stock', embodying as he did the celebrated union of the red and white roses. But there was nothing of the pale, ascetic Lancastrian about Henry VIII. In him the Yorkist genes predominated and as a physical type he strongly resembled his maternal grandfather, Edward IV, who had been 'very tall of personage, exceeding in stature almost of all others . . . of visage lovely, of body mighty, strong and clean-made. Howbeit in his latter days, with over-liberal diet, somewhat corpulent and burly . . .'

Looking at portraits of the young Henry it is not easy to equate them with modern standards of male beauty, but his contemporaries were unanimous in their opinion that Nature could not have done more for the King. 'His Majesty', wrote the Venetian Piero Pasqualigo, 'is the handsomest potentate I ever set eyes on; above the usual height, with an extremely fine calf to his leg; his complexion fair and bright, with auburn hair combed straight and short in the French fashion, and a round face so very beautiful that it would become a pretty woman, his throat being rather long and thick.' Ten years after his accession, Henry was still being described as 'much handsomer than any other sovereign in Christendom . . . very fair and his whole frame admirably proportioned'.

This splendid red-headed young giant, with his round baby face and glowing pink and white skin had inherited more than good looks from his Yorkist grandfather. Edward IV had been a very popular king with the knack of making himself agreeable in all sorts of company. According to Polydore Vergil, he 'would use himself more familiarly among private persons than the honour of his majesty required' but Edward had known instinctively that popularity is often more valuable to a king – especially an English king – than majesty and his Tudor grandson knew it too, just as he knew how easily and cheaply it could be acquired. Henry VIII possessed the precious gift of personal magnetism which Henry VII had lacked and his charm, when he chose to exert it, was irresistible. Thomas More, an acute observer of human nature, put his finger on the secret when he wrote: 'The King has a way of making every man feel that he is enjoying his special favour, just as the London wives pray before the image of Our Lady by the Tower till each of them believes it is smiling upon *her*.'

The new King had also inherited the abundant energy of his Plantagenet forbears and he made tireless use of his superb athlete's body. He was a capital horseman, reported the Venetians, passionately addicted to hunting, who wore out eight or ten horses in a single day. He 'jousted marvellously', was a keen tennis player and could draw the bow with greater strength than any man in England. He loved hawking, was a good dancer and a crack shot who, at archery practice, surpassed the archers of his guard. In all the popular forms of mock combat and trials of strength – in wrestling and tilting, running at the ring and casting of the bar, in throwing a twelve foot spear and wielding a heavy, two-handed sword – the King soon proved himself more than a match for his competitors. He was, in fact, a first-rate, all-round sportsman and nothing could have been better calculated to endear him to a nation which idolized physical courage and physical prowess; which cared little for politics but a great deal for sport.

At the same time, there was more to Henry than a well co-ordinated hunk of

The Renaissance Prince: Henry VIII by Joos van Cleeve.

brawn and muscle. He had a good brain and had been given a good education. He liked to display his own learning and enjoyed the company of scholars, so that the intellectuals were as excited as everyone else over the appearance of 'this new and auspicious star', this lover of justice and goodness. Lord Mountjoy in particular could hardly contain himself. He wrote to his protégé in Rotterdam in May 1509:

> Oh my Erasmus, if you could see how all the world here is rejoicing in the possession of so great a Prince, how his life is all their desire, you could not contain your tears for joy . . . Our King does not desire gold or gems or precious metals, but virtue, glory, immortality. I will give you an example. The other day he wished he was more learned. I said: 'That is not what we expect of your Grace, but that you will foster and encourage learned men.' 'Yes, surely', said he, 'for indeed without them we should scarcely exist at all.'

No more splendid saying, thought Mountjoy, could have fallen from the lips of a prince.

There really seemed no end to the gifts and graces of this marvellous youth and it is hardly surprising that a great wave of optimism should have swept the country. In the spring of 1509 many people genuinely believed that a new era, 'called then the golden world', was dawning and that under the beneficent rule of an apparently ideal Christian monarch the bad old days of faction, suspicion and heavy taxes would be gone for ever.

Almost the first act of the ideal Christian monarch was to get married, and after all it was the despised and neglected Spanish princess who carried off the prize. The reasons behind this startling *volte-face* remain a little obscure. The bridegroom's own explanation, given in a letter to Margaret of Austria, was that his father, as he lay on his death-bed, had expressly commanded him to fulfil his obligations to the Lady Catherine and as a dutiful son he had no choice but to obey. Another account of the old King's last hours maintains that he expressly assured his son he was free to marry whom he chose and Don Gutierre Gomez de Fuensalida, the Spanish envoy who had been sent to England on a fence-mending mission, attributed the dramatic transformation of Catherine's affairs entirely to the direct, personal intervention of the new King, who imperiously swept aside all the pettifogging obstacles which had been holding up the marriage for so long and ordered Fuensalida to complete the financial arrangements as quickly as possible – something that much-tried individual had been trying his best to do for the past year.

Henry had seen very little of his fiancée for some time, so it is not likely that any tender feelings were involved. It looks very much as if he was simply impatient to prove his manhood by taking a wife, and the quickest and easiest way to achieve that was to marry the girl he was already engaged to, who was on the spot and patiently waiting his pleasure. Fortunately, King Ferdinand was now in a position to produce the second half of Catherine's dowry and Catherine, who had been at her wits' end to find the wherewithal to clothe herself and feed her servants, was caught up almost overnight in a whirl of wedding preparations, with nothing more serious to worry about than ordering a new trousseau.

As the King had set his heart on having his Queen crowned beside him, there was no time to be lost. On 10 May Henry VII was buried with all due ceremony in Westminster Abbey, to dwell 'more richly dead than he did alive', and as soon as the funeral was over Henry VIII bore his bride off to Greenwich. They were married very quietly in the church of the Observant Friars by the palace wall and although (at least so it was said later) the Archbishop of Canterbury had his doubts about the legality of this marriage of brother and sister-in-law, any scruples he may have felt were not strong enough to prevent him from performing the ceremony.

The coronation had been fixed for 24 June, four days before the King's eighteenth birthday. London was filling up with people who had come to town to see their monarch 'in the full bloom of his youth and high birth' and the City, which had not been *en fête* since Prince Arthur's wedding eight years before, was busy sweeping and sanding the streets and hanging out streamers and banners of tapestry and cloth of gold; while tailors, embroiderers and goldsmiths worked round the clock to fill orders for furred robes, new liveries, coats of arms and elaborate horse trappings.

On 23 June, the King made his ritual journey from the Tower to Westminster – a resplendent figure in crimson and gold, flashing with diamonds, rubies and emeralds and with a great golden baldric slung round his neck. As for his retinue, Edward Hall, that indefatigable chronicler of Tudor pageantry, declares 'there was no lack or scarcity of cloth of tissue, cloth of gold, cloth of silver, broderie or of goldsmiths' works: but in more plenty and abundance than hath been seen or read of at any time before'. The Queen's procession followed, with Catherine sitting in a litter draped with white cloth of gold and carried between two white palfreys trapped with the same material. She wore embroidered white satin and had a coronet 'set with many rich orient stones' on her head. Her marvellous russet-coloured hair hung loose down her back and Hall specially noticed that it was 'of a very great length, beautiful and goodly to behold'.

The next day Henry and his Queen were anointed and crowned by Archbishop Warham 'according to the sacred observance and ancient custom', and afterwards all the quality crowded into Westminster Hall for a banquet 'greater than any Caesar had known'. A grand tournament had been organized 'for the more honour and ennobling of this triumphant Coronation' and the next few days were given over to jousting, feasting and dancing.

The celebrations were brought to a temporary halt by the sudden death of the King's grandmother. Margaret Beaufort had been staying in the Abbot's house at Westminster for the coronation and she died there on 29 June at the age of sixty-six. The death of the foundress of the royal Tudor family broke another link with the past which everyone was now so busy forgetting and although she was given a suitably grand funeral and buried, according to her wish, beside her son and daughter-in-law in the Henry VII Chapel, the new King did not allow her passing to interfere with his pleasures any longer than was decently necessary.

Margaret, Countess of Richmond and Derby, is remembered for her piety, for her generosity in almsgiving, for her patronage of learning and as the founder of St John's College, Cambridge. It is possible, though, that her grandson's memories of this formidably virtuous *grande dame* were not particularly cheerful ones. Lady Margaret had always played an active part in the upbringing and education of her grandchildren and she would certainly have been associated in the King's mind with the last few years of his father's reign when, at least according to Fuensalida, the teenage Henry had been guarded as strictly as a young girl. He spent most of his time studying in a room leading off his father's chamber; he was only allowed out to exercise through a private door into the park and was surrounded by attendants chosen by his father. No outsider, wrote the ambassador, could approach or speak to him and he scarcely opened his mouth in public.

Fuensalida may well have been exaggerating the case but it is certainly true that the old King never permitted the Prince of Wales to take even the most minor independent share in government and made sure that, as he began to grow up, he stayed well out of the limelight. Whether this was simply because Henry VII considered his only surviving son too precious an asset to be let out of his sight, whether he doubted the boy's readiness to cope with independence or whether he was increasingly afraid of being outshone by his handsome, athletic heir we have no means of knowing. The fact remains that the future Henry VIII was kept a schoolboy under the constant surveillance of either his father or his grandmother until the moment of his accession. The prince seems to have borne this stultifying regime with exemplary patience, but it is hardly surprising that the moment he was free he should have thrown off all restraint – stating his intentions with engaging frankness.

> Pastance with good company
> I love and shall until I die
> Grudge who will, but none deny,
> So God be pleased this life will I
>> For my pastance,
>> Hunt, sing, and dance,
>> My heart is set;
>> All goodly sport
>> To my comfort
>> Who shall me let?

Who indeed? Here was a young man with the world at his feet, his father's money to spend and a good deal of boredom to make up for. He meant to enjoy himself and enjoy himself he did. For the rest of that first carefree summer the Court settled into a round of 'continual festival', with revels, tilts and tourneys, pageants, banquets and 'disguisings' following one another in an endless, glittering and expensive stream, and with the King always in the thick of the fun.

Henry had an insatiable passion for dressing up, and for charades. On one occasion, he and a bunch of cronies burst unannounced into the Queen's chamber 'all appareled in short coats of Kentish Kendal, with hoods on their heads and hosen of the same, every one of them [with] his bow and arrows and a sword and buckler, like outlaws or Robin Hood's men'. The Queen and her ladies, though

Henry jousting before Catherine of Aragon at the tournament held on 12 February 1512 to celebrate the birth of their son. An illustration from the Great Tournament Roll of Westminster.

'abashed' by this invasion, knew what was expected of them and danced politely with the strangers. Another time the King suddenly vanished in the middle of a banquet, to reappear 'appareled after Turkey fashion' in a gold turban and hung round with scimitars. His companions were dressed up as Russians and the torch-bearers had their faces blacked 'like Moriscos'.

The Queen's part in these merry pranks was to provide an admiring audience and she never failed to play up – to be suitably astonished and appreciative of the joke when Robin Hood, or the Saracen, or the mysterious Muscovite revealed himself as her husband. The King was delighted with her and, after less than two months of marriage, wrote to his father-in-law in elegant Latin, assuring him of 'that entire love which we bear to the most serene Queen, our consort'. When, on 1 November 1509 he was able to tell Ferdinand that 'the Queen, our dearest consort, with the favour of heaven, hath conceived in her womb a living child and is right heavy therewith', the young couple's happiness seemed complete.

Catherine was twenty-three now – a very different being from the shy, homesick child who had landed at Plymouth in 1501. During the seven lean years of her widowhood she had learnt some hard but useful lessons in patience, discretion, self-reliance and self-control and she had matured into a responsible, serious-minded and capable young woman. In the early years of their marriage Henry was not only devoted to her, he relied heavily on her judgement and experience, he respected her opinions and listened to her advice. It seemed an ideal match. Husband and wife shared many interests, both loved music and dancing, both had intellectual tastes, both were deeply religious. In addition, Catherine's good breeding and perfect natural dignity made an excellent foil for Henry's exuberance and her gently restraining influence saved the Court from any taint of vulgarity – attracting members of the older aristocratic families (some of whom became her special friends) who might otherwise have been repelled by the rollicking young men who flocked round the King.

But admirable creature though the Queen might be – and no one denied her many good qualities – her real business was to bear children, the sooner the better. No thinking man could forget that all the splendour and prosperity and high hopes of the new reign rested on the fragile foundation of one life. If the King were to have an accident in the tiltyard or the hunting field; if he were to fall victim to the sweating sickness, which notoriously attacked the upper classes; then the whole Tudor achievement would collapse overnight and the country revert into an anarchy far worse than any it had known under the faction fights of the rival Roses.

In May 1510 Catherine was delivered of her first child. It was a girl, born dead. Within a matter almost of days she was pregnant again and at Richmond Palace on 1 January 1511 she gave birth to a boy, alive and apparently healthy. Everyone breathed a sigh of relief. The Tower cannon fired a royal salute. Bells pealed and bonfires blazed in the streets of London. There were processions and Te Deums in the City churches and the authorities provided a ration of free wine for drinking the baby's health, while the baby's father dashed off impulsively to offer up his gratitude at the shrine of Our Lady of Walsingham.

As soon as the Queen was up and about again, the Court moved to Westminster where there was to be an extra special tournament to celebrate the birth of the Prince of Wales. The proceedings opened with a pageant of quite spectacular ingenuity. A whole 'mock forest' complete with rocks, hills and dales, its trees and flowers cunningly constructed of green velvet and damask and coloured silks, with a castle made of gold in the middle and concealing four armed and mounted knights was drawn in says Hall, 'as it were by strength of two great beasts: a lion and an antelope. The lion flourished all over with damask gold. The antelope was wrought all over with silver of damask, his beames and horns and tusks of gold.'

The King, not unlike some gorgeous heraldic beast himself in his gilded armour, entered the lists as Sir Loyal Heart. The royal pavilion of cloth of gold and purple velvet was lavishly decorated with the initials H and K embroidered in fine gold and, as a further compliment to the Queen, her badge, the pomegranate, was featured prominently among the display of Tudor roses.

The following night a great banquet was held in the White Hall during which Henry performed his famous vanishing act – reappearing with five companions and a chosen band of ladies in another pageant, this time 'a garden of pleasure'. The ladies were in Tudor white and green, Sir Loyal Heart and his friends in slashed purple satin heavily encrusted with ornaments of solid gold. But when the King began to distribute these as souvenirs to certain favoured guests, the common people, watching the fun from a distance, broke in to demand their share. They snatched the gold lace and spangles off the pageant, despite the efforts of the Lord Steward and his officers to stop them, and stripped the King and his companions to their doublets and hose. Eventually the guard had to be called to put the intruders out, but there was no ill-feeling. Nothing could spoil such a happy occasion and by the time the Court sat down to supper 'all these hurts were turned to laughing and game'.

The triumph at Westminster ended with 'mirth and gladness', but the gladness was pitifully short. On 22 February little Henry of Richmond was dead. He had lived just seven weeks. It was a dreadful blow, to the King and Queen and to the whole nation, but especially to the Queen. In the words of Hall's *Chronicle*, Catherine, 'like a natural woman, made much lamentation. Howbeit, by the King's persuasion, she was comforted but not shortly.' Henry's own grief had been genuine and violent, while it lasted, but it was not in his nature to be despondent for long. There would, after all, be plenty of time to beget more sons. The cloud on the horizon was as yet no bigger than a man's hand and the King quickly forgot his first serious disappointment in the thrill of preparing for his first war.

Henry VII had been a pre-eminently civilian monarch. His foreign policy had been concerned with drawing up commercial treaties and trade agreements, with forming useful and profitable alliances with other royal houses, and with keeping out of other people's wars. No one expected his son to continue along these sensible but unexciting lines. A king was still, in practice as well as theory, the war leader of his people and a fine upstanding young king like the second Henry Tudor would have to prove himself in battle as a matter of honour.

The second Henry Tudor was only too anxious for a chance to prove his mettle, but when he came to the throne he had found himself boringly at peace with all his neighbours – even with France who remained the ancestral enemy to every right-thinking Englishman. This was a state of affairs which the new King meant to change as soon as he could. Young Henry's head was stuffed with romantic dreams of the glorious past, dreams of Crécy and Agincourt and of reconquering England's lost empire. He saw himself as another Henry V and in the first summer of his reign, to the acute embarrassment of his Council, had hurled defiance at a surprised French ambassador in a scene which had only needed a tun of tennis balls to be complete.

But, to the King's irritation, France would not play. Louis XII was a middle-aged man intent on consolidating his recent territorial gains in Northern Italy. He was not in the least interested in the noisy challenges of a beardless boy or in becoming involved in a pointless war with England, and Henry was sulkily obliged to contain his impatience. Even he needed a *casus belli*, however slight. He also needed allies. Not even he was rash enough to take on an adversary twice his size singlehanded.

As it turned out, he did not have to wait very long for either of these two necessary adjuncts of military adventure. The Pope, becoming alarmed by the strength of the French armies on his doorstep, provided the first. The King of Aragon provided the second. Ferdinand had noted his son-in-law's bellicosity and Francophobia with quiet satisfaction and was only waiting for a favourable opportunity to use them for his own advantage. By the summer of 1511 this opportunity seemed to be at hand. Franco-Papal relations had deteriorated sharply and in October a Holy League directed against the 'schismatic' King of France was signed in Rome. Henry could now go to war well buttressed by allies and when Ferdinand suggested they should make a start by mounting a joint invasion of Gascony from the south, he fell in eagerly and quite unsuspectingly with his father-in-law's plans, though, oddly enough, he did not accompany the army which sailed from Southampton in April 1512.

From the Spanish point of view, the summer's campaign went off very nicely indeed. While the presence of some ten thousand English archers kept the French pinned down in Bayonne, Ferdinand was able to annexe the small neutral kingdom of Navarre on his north-western frontier. He showed no visible sign of being prepared to cross the frontier and the English expeditionary force received neither the co-operation nor the supplies they had been expecting. Marooned in the neighbourhood of San Sebastian with no fighting to do, the climate, the food and the harsh local wine played predictable havoc with their tempers and their stomachs. By the end of August the men were openly mutinous. By September the army was on its way home, leaving two thousand dead from fever and dysentery and having achieved precisely nothing. Ferdinand, keeping a perfectly straight face, accused his ally of deserting him – and just as the main operation had been about to begin! Other people passed unkind remarks on the subject of the sad decay of English military virtues, and Henry smarted under a devastating public humiliation. Next year, though, it would be different. Next year he would take the field himself and then these insufferable foreigners would see what an English army could do.

That winter was spent in hectic preparation for the forthcoming campaign and in working out a new strategy. Henry had now acquired another ally in the person of the Emperor Maximilian who, after a good deal of dickering about, had finally declared himself ready to join the anti-French league in return, naturally, for a handsome subsidy; and it was agreed that while Ferdinand, also subsidized to the tune of a hundred thousand English crowns, crossed the Pyrenees to conquer the duchy of Guienne for his daughter's husband, Henry and Max would make a joint assault on King Louis from the north. It was not until April 1513 that it became clear that the King of Aragon had once again defaulted on his obligations by arranging a year's truce with the enemy. This was treachery of the most blatant kind, but according to Ferdinand it had all been due to a most unfortunate misunderstanding – entirely the fault of his fool of an ambassador in London. Next year he would be only too pleased to help but just at the moment he was not at all well, in fact he had been practically at death's door and his confessor had urged him to make peace with his enemies for the sake of his soul.

Henry was understandably disappointed and aggrieved but Catherine, always loyal to her father and to Spain, was at hand to help smooth over any unpleasantness. In any case, the King was determined to go ahead with his own plans for a landing in Northern France. The Emperor, at least, was still loyal, though, as he mournfully explained, his financial difficulties were such that he would not, after all, be in a position to provide the troop contingents he had

Henry dining in his Privy Chamber; a sketch by Holbein.

promised. However, the King of England could have all the German and Burgundian mercenaries he cared to pay for, while Max himself would consider it an honour to fight under Henry's banner and would charge only a mere trifle, say a hundred crowns a day, just to cover his expenses.

By late spring everything was ready, but before Henry could feel free to leave the country there was a piece of unfinished business to be dealt with and on 4 May Edmund de la Pole was brought out of the Tower to his execution. When Philip of Burgundy had surrendered the White Rose seven years before, Henry VII had guaranteed the prisoner's life and had honoured his promise. His son was not so squeamish and information that Richard, the only remaining de la Pole still unaccounted for, was serving with the French army had sealed Edmund's fate.

There was another danger threatening the King's absence, and one a good deal more serious than the unhappy White Rose. Relations with Scotland had become increasingly strained during recent months and it seemed only too probable that, in spite of the treaty between the two countries, in spite of the fact that he was married to the King of England's sister, James IV would follow traditional practice by leading his army across the Border as soon as the English were otherwise engaged. Henry left the seventy-year-old Earl of Surrey with orders to guard the North, but otherwise he paid little attention to the rumbling noises coming out of Scotland. Nothing was going to deflect him now from his long looked-forward-to adventure and the fulfilment of his burning ambition to emulate and, if possible, exceed the rugged deeds of his ancestors.

The King set out from Greenwich on 15 June accompanied by the Queen, who was pregnant again, and a personal entourage which included a duke, two bishops and a score of noblemen, as well as minstrels, heralds, trumpeters, choristers, clerks and six hundred archers of the guard in new green and white liveries. The royal baggage-train contained suits of armour for every occasion, an enormous carved bed and enough gold-embroidered tents to accommodate the population of a small town. Henry never did anything by halves. The unwieldy, gorgeously dressed cavalcade made its way by easy stages to Dover, where the King created his wife Governor of the Realm and Captain General of the home forces before setting sail for Calais to join the main body of the army. Such a sight had not been seen since the days of the Hundred Years' War and the bosoms of those gentlemen of England with enough sense to stay at home swelled with vicarious pride.

Henry had a perfectly splendid time in France and duly astonished everyone by his courage and endurance in the face of the enemy. It is true that the enemy proved disappointingly elusive and it was bad luck that the King should have missed the best bit of action – a scrambling cavalry skirmish near Guinegate, later dignified as The Battle of the Spurs – but on the whole it was a very nice little war. Henry, firing a cannon with his own hands, dubbing knights on the field of battle and riding round the camp at night in full armour, enjoyed himself so much that he quite failed to notice that the two fortified frontier towns of Thérouanne and Tournai which, on Maximilian's advice, the allied army besieged and captured, were of strategic value only to Maximilian – forming as they did two awkward salients jutting into Hapsburg territory. But the Emperor was gratifyingly deferential towards his young commander and the King spent a charming month in Lille being royally entertained by the Hapsburg family.

While Henry was playing soldiers in Picardy, events in England were taking their expected course. King James had discovered that his country's ancient friendship with France carried more weight than any treaty with England and Catherine, left in charge with only a skeleton staff of councillors to help her, was soon 'horribly busy' organizing the defence of the northern counties and sewing badges and standards for the hastily mobilized home guard. She still found time, though, to worry about her husband, to send him supplies of clean shirts, to beg him not to 'adventure himself' too rashly, and to be sure and remember to change his clothes if he got wet or overheated. Henry, of course, was far too busy to write letters but Catherine received regular bulletins from his Almoner, Master Thomas Wolsey, and assured him in return that the King need not worry about the Scots. She and his subjects would deal with them gladly and 'take it for a pastime'.

By the end of August a formidable Scottish army had crossed the Tweed and on the afternoon of Friday 9 September came face to face with the Earl of Surrey's forces in the wild Border country at Flodden, a few miles south-east of Coldstream. The result, after some three hours of bloody fighting, was a shattering defeat for the Scots. James himself was killed 'within a spear's length' of the English commander and with him died nearly a third of his army and the flower of the Scottish aristocracy.

In real terms, of course, the victory at Flodden, which crippled Scotland for a generation, was worth more than a dozen French towns – a fact which did not escape experienced observers of the political scene – but Catherine was careful not to crow. Writing to Henry on 16 September and sending him a piece of the Scottish King's coat, she tactfully attributed 'the great victory that our Lord hath sent your subjects in your absence' entirely to the Lord, and, since Henry always took the deity's personal interest in his affairs very much for granted, he had no hesitation in accepting the credit.

The Queen was still busy dealing with the aftermath of victory. There was, for example, the embarrassing problem of what to do with James's body. He had died under a papal interdict and so could not be buried in consecrated ground. Catherine had the corpse embalmed and stored at the Carthusian monastery at Sheen pending further instructions. Then there was the widowed Queen of Scotland to be considered. This, too, was not without its awkwardness. How to condole with your sister-in-law when her husband has just been killed by the army under your command is not a situation normally covered in books of etiquette – not even sixteenth-century books of etiquette. But Margaret Tudor, who was understandably distracted with anxiety about her own future and that of her small son, now James V, had to be hastily soothed with assurances that she could continue to count on her brother's protection and support.

The campaigning season in France was coming to an end and on 20 October Henry, suddenly impatient to be home, slipped away from Tournai with a light escort. Three days later he was taking the Queen by surprise at Richmond, and husband and wife were reunited in 'such a loving meeting that every creature rejoiced'. The King was in high spirits and full of plans for next year's conquests. Before leaving Lille he had signed another treaty with Spain and the Hapsburgs binding the allies to make a three-pronged invasion of France in the summer of 1514, and had also settled that his sister Mary should marry Max's grandson, Charles of Castile, by the fifteenth of May. The only shadow lying across that triumphant autumn was the ending of the Queen's third pregnancy in a miscarriage.

The year 1514 marked an important stage in the development of young Henry Tudor. At any rate it marked his emergence from a fantasy world of knights in shining armour re-fighting the Hundred Years' War and brought him face to face with the realities of international diplomacy. The King owed this somewhat overdue awakening to Ferdinand of Aragon who had spent the winter quietly preparing to sell his son-in-law down the river for the third time. The plan, beneath its elaborate camouflage of verbiage, was simple enough. The King of France, having been suitably softened up by the Treaty of Lille and by the implacable hostility and growing military might of England, was offered a bargain: if he would relinquish his claims to Milan and Genoa, then Ferdinand and Max would be delighted to live like brothers with him for the rest of their days and would, naturally, come to his aid in the event of an English invasion!

But dealing with the guileless Henry seems to have made Ferdinand over-confident and he failed to take account of the fact that the King of France was also a poker player. Louis had no intention of submitting to a Spanish protection racket. On the other hand, he was perfectly prepared to pay any reasonable price for English neutrality. Accordingly he adopted the classic technique of stringing the King of Aragon along until that enterprising individual had been drawn into exposing his hand for all to see. Louis, of course, was hoping to catch England on the rebound and his expectations proved fully justified. Henry might still be inexperienced, but he was nobody's fool. By the spring of 1514 his opinion of Ferdinand was much the same as his father's had been, if not more so, and his one idea was to strike back.

This was the moment Louis had been waiting for and he went smoothly into action, using as intermediary the Duke of Longueville, who had been taken prisoner at the Battle of the Spurs and was now most conveniently residing at the English Court. In his present mood Henry was reluctant to trust anybody, but when the French offered peace on very gentlemanly terms, he was ready to listen. When Louis himself offered marriage to the Princess Mary, it opened up a prospect of so exquisite a revenge on his former allies that it was scarcely to be resisted.

This abrupt reversal of English foreign policy was made easier by the fact that Louis had now made his peace with Rome and that there was now a new and pacifically inclined Pope, anxious to see the Christian princes compose their differences. In any case, Henry's conscience was clear. He alone of the members of the Holy League had kept his word. 'I do not see any faith in the world save in me only', he told the Venetian ambassador, 'and therefore God Almighty, who knows this, prospers my affairs.'

There was quite a flurry of diplomatic activity between London and Paris during July and August as the peace treaty and the marriage contract were signed. The King and Thomas Wolsey, now rapidly becoming the King's right-hand man, could congratulate themselves on a very satisfactory outcome. Mary Tudor was less enthusiastic. Not that she had any reason to regret Charles of Castile, an unappealing pasty-faced boy of fourteen; but Louis, a widower in his fifties and unkindly described by some as 'old, feeble and pocky', could scarcely be said to offer a much more alluring prospect to a high-spirited nineteen-year-old who was generally conceded to be an exceptionally beautiful girl.

In the five years since her father's death Mary had experienced a degree of fun and freedom most unusual for an unmarried princess. But the King was very fond of his young sister. He liked her company and saw no reason why she should not enjoy herself. Mary shared his passion for parties and dancing and dressing-up and played a vigorous part in the hectic social life of the Court. The dangers inherent in this situation were obvious enough – it was not for nothing that princesses were normally shipped off to their husbands the moment they reached puberty. Mary was a warm-blooded young woman surrounded by all the best-looking young men in the kingdom – inevitably she had formed an attachment of her own, the object of her affections being Henry's closest friend, Charles Brandon, newly created Duke of Suffolk.

Charles Brandon owed his start in life to the fact that his father had been Henry VII's standard-bearer, killed at Bosworth by King Richard himself. The orphan obviously had a strong claim on the Tudor family and he had been brought into the royal household when he was about seven years old to be a companion to Prince Arthur. After Arthur's marriage he held various minor posts at Court, but it was pretty certainly his sporting prowess that had earned him admission to the charmed circle of intimates surrounding the new King. Charles was a tall, good-looking young man, like Henry a fine all-round athlete, tireless in the hunting field and a skilful and courageous performer in the jousts. A cheerful, good-natured extrovert, without very much in the way of intellectual equipment, he stood in no danger of out-shining his master, whom he followed about like a large, faithful dog. Henry found him excellent company, lavished favours on him and treated him as an honorary member of the family. Mary would, of course, have known him since childhood and, by the summer of 1514, what had most probably begun as a young girl's hero worship for one of her brother's lordly friends was ripening into something deeper.

There was no scandal – not a whisper of gossip linking the princess's name with the Duke of Suffolk reached the outside world – but inside the family circle the affair seems to have been an open secret. Indeed, Mary herself had confided in her brother, telling him frankly that she loved Charles Brandon and was only prepared to marry the 'aged and sickly' King of France on condition that, as soon as she was free again, Henry would allow her to make her choice as her own heart and mind should be best pleased. 'And upon that your good comfort and faithful promise', she wrote later, 'I assented to the said marriage; else I would never have granted to, as at the same time I showed unto you more at large.'

Whether this compromise was Mary's own idea, or whether it had been hammered out in a family conference we have no means of knowing. Nor do we know how seriously Henry took it. But he was particularly anxious that nothing should interfere with the smooth running of the new alliance. Mary was no longer a child and it would make things very awkward with the French if she turned difficult now. In the circumstances, he was ready to promise anything she wanted – anything to avoid tears and scenes and keep her happy until she was safely across the Channel.

The proxy marriage was celebrated at Greenwich on 13 August in the presence of the King and Queen and all the dignitaries of the Court. The Archbishop of Canterbury officiated and the Duke of Longueville acted as Louis' proxy. As soon as the solemn vows had been exchanged per verba de praesenti and the ring had been placed on the fourth finger of her right hand, Mary retired to put on an elaborate 'nightgown'. She and Longueville then lay down side by side and he touched her with his naked leg. After this rather curious piece of play-acting – intended to symbolize intercourse – the Archbishop pronounced the marriage consummated and Mary went off to change again, into a gown of chequered

Drawing of Henry's sister Mary as a young girl.

purple satin and cloth of gold worn over a grey satin petticoat. There was the usual great banquet with the usual display of expensive 'subtleties' and afterwards the floor was cleared for dancing. According to the Venetian ambassador, who was present by special invitation, 'the musical accompaniment was provided by a flute, a harp, a violetta and a certain small fife which produced a very harmonious effect'. The King and several other English lords danced in their doublets, and everyone was so gay and the music was so catchy that the ambassador felt distinctly tempted to throw off his own gown and join in. Prudently, though, he remembered his age and his dignity and abstained.

Wedding presents and letters of congratulations were now flowing in from all over Europe – Louis sent his bride a magnificent diamond and pearl known as 'The Mirror of Naples', valued by the London jewellers at sixty thousand crowns – and Mary was kept so busy during her last few weeks at home, receiving deputations, attending receptions and entertainments given in her honour, having fittings for her trousseau and undergoing a crash course in French that she had very little time for repining. At any rate, she was presenting a resolutely cheerful face to the world and one Italian observer remarked cattily that the princess did not appear to mind that the King of France was a gouty old man and she 'a young and beautiful damsel', so great was her satisfaction at becoming Queen of France.

Everything was French that year. There was even talk that the King was thinking of divorcing his Spanish wife, who could not give him an heir, and marrying a French princess. But by the late summer of 1514 Catherine was once more visibly pregnant. New linen and curtains were being ordered for her lying-in and Henry, joyfully trumpeting the news abroad, had invited King Louis to stand godfather to the new arrival – none of which sounds as if he was contemplating divorce.

From across the Channel came reports of Louis' eager impatience to see his bride. In spite of his age and his gout, he was said to 'yearn hourly for her presence' and according to the Earl of Worcester, who had gone over to France to act as Mary's proxy at the betrothal ceremonies, he had 'a marvellous mind to content and please the Queen'. It seemed the French king had shown Worcester 'the goodliest and richest sight of jewels' he had ever seen, telling him they were all for the Queen but that she should not have them all at once, 'for he would have at many and divers times kisses and thanks for them'. Worcester, much impressed by this lover-like attitude, told Thomas Wolsey he had no doubt that, by the grace of God, Mary would have a good life with her husband.

By mid-September everything was ready for her journey. There was a final outburst of entertaining and Mary herself gave a farewell reception to which all the foreign merchants in London were invited. Wearing a French gown of woven gold with the Mirror of Naples flashing on her bosom, the new Queen of France was very affable and gracious to her guests, giving her hand to everyone. She was obviously in her best looks, one witness going so far as to describe her as 'a nymph from heaven', but even allowing for a certain amount of over-enthusiasm there is no doubt that Mary Tudor was quite outstanding. Of slightly above average height, slender and graceful, she had a clear glowing complexion and a glorious mane of red-gold hair. Equally important, she had all the infectious gaiety and outgoing charm of manner which made her brother so attractive.

Mary left London on 19 September, accompanied by the King and Queen and an escort which, according to the Venetian merchant Lorenzo Pasqualigo, included 'four of the chief lords of England, besides four hundred knights and barons and two hundred gentlemen and other squires.' For the second year running the people of Kent were able to enjoy the spectacle of the royal family – the King riding with his sister, the Queen, because of her interesting condition, travelling by litter – pass through on their way to Dover. The Court on the move was always an impressive sight and seldom more so than on this occasion when, as Pasqualigo told his brother, 'the lords and knights were all accompanied by their wives and there were so many gowns of woven gold and with gold grounds, housings for the horses of the same material, and chains and jewels that they are worth a vast amount of treasure.'

The cavalcade reached the coast before the end of the month, but the September equinox was not the best time of year to choose for a Channel crossing. The weather was appalling and Henry rapidly got bored with waiting for it to improve. Dover in a howling gale and pouring rain offered few attractions and he was never a man to put other people's comfort before his own. So, when the wind dropped temporarily on the evening of 1 October, it was decided that the fleet should sail on the early tide, in spite of a forecast of more storms to come. Mary was woken in the small hours next morning and Henry went with her to the quayside. As they said their goodbyes in the chill grey damp of that dismal morning, Mary, in tears by this time, clung to her brother and rather desperately extracted from him a renewal of his promises about the future. He kissed her and committed her to God, the fortune of the sea (which, considering the look of the sea at that moment, can scarcely have been very cheering) and to the governance of her husband. Mary and her noble company then went on board while the King rode back to Dover Castle and a good breakfast.

The sea fully lived up to its unappetizing appearance. Of the fourteen ships conveying the Queen of France, her wardrobe and her retinue to Boulogne, only four arrived on schedule – the rest fetching up at various points along the coast from Calais to Flanders. The bride's own vessel made Boulogne but ran ingloriously aground just inside the harbour. Mary had to be transferred to an open boat and, soaked to the skin and prostrate with seasickness, was finally carried ashore through the waist-high surf by one of her gentlemen.

It was not a very auspicious start, but with the resilience of youth and health she recovered quickly and was soon winning golden opinions from the French, who were greatly struck with their new Queen's beauty, pretty manners and elegant, expensive clothes. For the journey from Montreuil to Abbeville she wore cloth of gold on crimson with tight English sleeves and a shaggy hat of crimson silk cocked over one eye. Her first meeting with Louis took place by carefully pre-arranged 'accident' on the outskirts of the town, and the King threw his arms round her neck and 'kissed her as kindly as if he had been five-and-twenty'. In Abbeville itself a royal welcome had been prepared and here on 9 October, amidst much lavish display by both nations, Mary was finally married to the King of France in person.

Not surprisingly such an oddly assorted couple were made the butt of unkind jokes in certain quarters – in Spain it was being freely predicted that his young wife would soon be the death of a bridegroom in his dotage who constantly licked his lips and gulped his spittle! However, to the outward eye, Louis appeared very jovial and in love. He had temporarily quite thrown off his invalidish habits and boasted that on his wedding night he had 'crossed the river' three times and would have done more had he chosen.

Apart from a brief unpleasantness over the dismissal of some of Mary's English attendants, Louis proved an indulgent and a generous husband and the newly-weds had established quite a cosy relationship by the time Charles Brandon paid a visit to France in November. The Duke of Suffolk had come over accompanied by the Marquis of Dorset and a number of other gentlemen, ostensibly to take part in a tournament forming part of the celebration for Mary's forthcoming coronation, but he also had certain confidential matters to discuss with the French government. Suffolk visited the King and Queen at Beauvais, where he found Louis lying on a couch with Mary sitting beside him, and was able to report to Henry 'that never Queen behaved herself more wisely and honourably, and so say all the noblemen of France'. Charles Brandon was clearly impressed by Mary's dignity and restraint which, he told Henry, 'rejoiced me not a little', adding significantly, 'your Grace knows why'. It sounds as though he had been afraid

In 1513 Mary Tudor married the aged Louis XII of France; an illustration by Pierre Gringoire, an eyewitness at the wedding ceremony. Louis died less than three months later.

Mary might embarrass him in public – this was their first meeting since her marriage. He need not have worried. The Queen of France knew what was due to her position and whatever her inner feelings on seeing Suffolk again, her self-possession was faultless.

It had been an eventful and generally satisfactory year for the Tudor family, but it was to end with an all too familiar disappointment. Queen Catherine was brought to bed at the beginning of December, but the baby, another boy, was either stillborn or lived for only a few days.

CHAPTER 5
Tudor Sisters

'Twas kenned that a woman *was Scotland's mail;*
A wean *wore Scotland's crown!*

'Sir, I beseech your grace that you will keep all the
promises that you promised me when I took my leave
of you by the water side . . .'

While Mary Tudor was occupying the centre of the stage in London and Paris, being petted and fêted as the beautiful young Queen of France, her elder sister was grappling with the realities of life and politics in Scotland after Flodden.

During the months immediately following the battle, Margaret Tudor, a pregnant widow of twenty-three, had been faced with the formidable task of trying to reassemble the shattered fragments of the English alliance, while holding at bay those Scottish warlords whose natural gut reaction was to pursue the blood feud straight across the Border and, at the same time, of taking what precautions she could to ensure the physical safety of herself, her unborn child and the eighteen-month-old James V.

Fortunately for all concerned, the Scots were too seriously weakened by defeat (in some families no males had survived the slaughter at Flodden) to be able to renew the war at once. Surrey's army had been disbanded but Lord Dacre, Warden of the Eastern Marches, was keeping up a suitably intimidating show of force along the Border while Margaret, acting with courage and resolution, had contrived to establish a precarious ascendancy over her sullen and largely hostile Council. Her authority as regent had been officially recognized but that, of course, did not for a moment restrain those Scots lords determined to put an end to Tudor domination of their country from plotting behind her back. They turned, as always, to France, and during the autumn of 1513 made contact with John Stuart, Duke of Albany, cousin and heir to the little king, inviting him to return to Scotland to 'share' the regency with the Queen who, as they pointed out hopefully, might well die in childbed.

John Stuart had lived all his life in France. (His father had been exiled for plotting against James III.) Himself half-French, wealthy, respected and happily married to a French wife, he was understandably reluctant to leave his comfortable home for the bloodstained jungle of Scottish politics. He therefore sent an evasive reply to his would-be hosts, obviously hoping they would not press the matter. But when Margaret got wind of this threatened renewal of the French connection, she was furious. Henry warned her on no account to agree to Albany's coming – not that she needed warning. She could see, quite as clearly as her brother, the dangers and complications which would follow, and anyway she had no intention of sharing her rule with anyone if she could help it. On the other hand, the Scottish Council was making it plain that unless she consented to receive the Duke, they would not come to the negotiating table with England. This not very dignified squabble dragged on until Margaret was forced to compromise. She undertook to welcome Albany at some future, unspecified date and in return the Scots sulkily agreed to observe a year's truce.

Matters had reached this stage when the Queen retired to Stirling Castle to wait for the birth of her child. The baby, a boy christened Alexander, arrived on 12 April 1514 and with this ordeal safely behind her – Margaret had a history of difficult confinements and had already lost four babies out of five – she felt better able to cope. Her circumstances had improved in other ways, too. The new Anglo-French understanding was taking much of the immediate pressure off her and, although the situation in Scotland remained potentially explosive, the long-term prospects of a peaceful and permanent settlement did now seem a good deal brighter. Henry was offering to adopt his nephews and was also dropping broad hints that if he had no children of his own, he would be prepared to acknowledge James as his heir – the very contingency once envisaged by Henry VII and his Council.

The best hope of reaching such a settlement obviously depended on the continued and successful regency of Margaret Tudor, so it was particularly unfortunate that it should have been Margaret herself who ruined everything by a single impulsive act. She had known little personal happiness as Queen of Scotland but now, for the first time in her life, she was in love and at the beginning of August 1514 – without observing even the formality of informing her Council or her brother – Margaret was married to nineteen-year-old Archibald Douglas, Earl of Angus, in a private ceremony at the church at Kinnoul.

She could scarcely have made a more unsuitable choice. Angus, whose father had been killed at Flodden, was head of the powerful Douglas clan and by singling him out as her husband, the Queen had destroyed at a stroke the delicate system of checks and balances, the whole intricate web of family feuds, jealousies and loyalties which made up the fabric of Scottish political life and which alone kept the rival chieftains from one another's throats. They might grudgingly acknowledge a foreign ruler; they would not for a moment stand for one of their number being preferred above the rest – especially a young, untried man who commanded no respect among his fellows either as a warrior or a leader. Angus, in fact, had little enough to recommend him beyond a handsome face and an ingratiating way with the ladies, and he soon proved to be both weak and arrogant – a fatal combination.

The announcement of the marriage led, predictably, to a renewed clamour for the return of Albany. The Council, quite beside themselves with annoyance over the underhand behaviour of the Douglas family, lost no time in informing the

Queen that by marrying without their consent she had automatically forfeited the regency and the custody of her sons. Margaret retorted by pointing out, with perfect truth, that there was nothing in James IV's will to stop her marrying anybody she chose and she proceeded defiantly to create the Earl of Angus co-regent. The Council retaliated by cutting off her income and forcing her to surrender the Great Seal. By September their attitude had become so threatening that the Queen felt it prudent to take sanctuary with her children in Stirling Castle, which had been garrisoned by Douglas men-at-arms.

From Stirling, expecting at any moment to be besieged by her enemies, she appealed to her brother for help. 'All the hope that my party adversary hath', she wrote, 'is in the Duke of Albany's coming, which I beseech you to let in any wise; for if he happen to come before your army, I doubt that some of my party will incline to him for dread. I shall keep this castle with my children till I hear from you.' Quite apart from her natural maternal feelings, Margaret knew that possession of the children was her trump card and she went on, 'the King, my son, and his brother, prospers well and are right lifelike children, thanked be Almighty God'. She warned Henry to disregard any letters he might receive signed only 'Margaret R', as these would either be forgeries or written under duress, and she ended: 'Brother, all the welfare of me and my children lies in your hands, which I pray Jesus to help and keep eternally to his pleasure. Your loving sister, Margaret R.'

Meanwhile, Margaret's 'party adversary', headed by the Earl of Arran, was urgently negotiating with Albany. The Duke, no less reluctant now to assume the regency than he had been the year before, had laid down a number of conditions for his return which made it clear that although he would naturally favour the Franco-Scottish alliance, neither he nor the King of France intended to offer the King of England any unnecessary provocation – indeed, one of his conditions was a stipulation that the Scottish lords must be prepared to behave in a civilized fashion towards Queen Margaret and her husband.

These terms were still under discussion when King Louis died at the beginning of January 1515 – an event which intimately affected the lives of both the Tudor sisters, for much would depend on the attitude adopted by the new French king. François, Count of Angoulême, a vigorous, athletic twenty-one-year-old, might be expected to be less pacifically inclined than his ailing predecessor and certainly his head was full of dreams of conquest, just as young Henry Tudor's had been. But François' dreams were of Italian conquest, of leading a triumphant army across the Alps, and it was no part of his plan to risk a war on two fronts. At the same time, he could scarcely ignore the claims of his country's ancient ally – especially when Scotland was being so obliging as to offer him a foothold on the British mainland! The knowledge that a French presence established north of the Border would alarm and annoy the King of England caused François no particular dismay. Henry Tudor was about to discover that he now had a serious competitor for the role of young lion among the European monarchs.

So, in the middle of May, despite a fusillade of diplomatic protests from London and a lurking English fleet in the North Sea, the Duke of Albany, attended by an impressive retinue, landed at Dumbarton to assume the Scottish regency. Margaret's first meeting with the interloper took place in Edinburgh and seems to have come as quite a pleasant surprise. Instead of the ogre she had apparently been expecting, she found an agreeable middle-aged Frenchman whose courtly manners and conciliatory approach might have been designed to soothe the fears of the most nervous lady. Albany, in short, was a gentleman and that was a good deal more than could be said for most of the Scottish nobility.

Left to themselves, the rival regents could probably have arrived at a mutually satisfactory power-sharing arrangement but there was never any chance of that. As soon as rumours that the Queen and the Duke were showing signs of becoming too friendly reached Lord Dacre in the Marches he hastened to warn Margaret to beware of French machinations, adding helpfully that she and her children were in great danger from Albany who was planning to murder his little cousins and seize the throne for himself. This was a libel, but the Duke, an honest well-meaning man and no fool, was hopelessly handicapped by the fact that he knew nothing about Scotland and could not even speak the language. Surrounded by a ring of greedy, suspicious magnates, whose one idea was to wring the maximum personal advantage from the situation and who would not hesitate to change sides any time it suited them, his freedom of action was severely limited. He was obliged to move against the Douglases if he wanted to preserve even a semblance of unity and this, of course, put an end to all hope of reaching an understanding with the Queen.

The unhappy Margaret was now pregnant again. She saw her only assured allies under attack and she was desperately short of money – Albany's promise that her dower rents would be restored had not been kept. It was becoming increasingly difficult to communicate with her brother and Henry, who was waiting on events, sent her nothing but vaguely worded messages that he was labouring for her more than she was aware of, which was not much comfort in the circumstances. Albany seemed to have gone over to the enemy and by July, Margaret, in fear for herself and her children and terrified for her husband, had once again sought refuge at Stirling. This time, though, there could be no evasion of the issue.

Albany and the Council had now decided on new arrangements for the custody of the little king and his brother. The Duke took his responsibilities towards the children very seriously and he knew that as long as they remained with the Douglases they would be in constant danger of kidnapping, or worse, by one or other of the rival factions. James, who stood so close to his uncle's throne, was a particularly hot property and rumours – not without foundation – were widespread that his mother was planning to escape with him to England. Albany, still trying hard to be fair to everyone, got the lords to agree that Margaret should be allowed to choose four guardians from a short-list of eight and given reasonable access to her sons; but she must be made to surrender them.

A deputation was sent off to Stirling to break this news to the Queen, but Margaret had enough warning of its approach to stage a scene which would, she hoped, advertise her cruel predicament to the world and gain her a little more time. She stood just inside the castle gates, holding three-year-old James by the hand, with Angus at her side and the nurse carrying Alexander, now fifteen months, standing behind her. As soon as the lords were within earshot, she called out to them to stand and show the cause of their coming. According to an eyewitness report:

> They showed they came from the Duke and governor, and that it was decreed by the parliament that they should come to ask deliverance of the king and his brother. And then she caused the portcullis to be letten down and made answer, saying that the castle was her own feoffment, given to her by the king her late husband . . . and that her said late husband had made her protectrix and given her authority to have the keeping and government of her said children, wherefore she could in no wise deliver them to any person. Natheless, she desired respite of six days to give her further answer.

Margaret got her six days respite, during which time Angus slipped unobtrusively away to try and raise his followers, but her 'further answer' to the Council was not acceptable. Angus, returning to Stirling with a force of sixty horsemen, found the castle surrounded by five hundred of Albany's soldiers and any rescue attempt clearly impracticable, but in the best tradition of romantic adventure stories he contrived to get through the besiegers' lines and enter the fortress by an underground passage. Husband and wife met for a hasty conference about future tactics and the Earl left the way he had come.

Meanwhile, Albany himself was advancing on Stirling at the head of an army 7,000 strong and Margaret knew that further resistance would be pointless. Heavily pregnant, and alone except for her ladies and the two little boys, she came out into the courtyard to surrender. In another well managed scene, she put the massive keys of Stirling into James' hands, telling the child to give them up to the Duke. Albany then knelt before his uncomprehending sovereign and swore allegiance. He told the Queen she could stay with the children but must accept their change of guardianship. He also assured her that she could rely on his protection and goodwill but when Margaret tried to plead her husband's cause, answered sternly that he could have no dealings with a traitor.

A few days later, in spite of the promise she had been given, Margaret was told she must leave her sons and go back to Edinburgh. She obeyed. She had no choice. In any case, her plan now was to lull suspicion by apparent compliance. She remained in Edinburgh for about a month, outwardly content and on friendly terms with Albany, but her letters to England were signed only 'Margaret R'. Albany was innocently unaware that other letters were leaving Edinburgh and going by secret channels to Lord Dacre, hovering on the Border.

At the beginning of September Margaret applied for permission to retire to Linlithgow to wait for the birth of her child. Permission was granted and the Queen departed to 'take her chamber'. She stayed at Linlithgow for precisely forty-eight hours and at midnight on 13 September set out on the first stage of her escape to England, escorted by Angus, his brother George and the Earl of Hume. A cautious reconnaissance of Stirling had shown that all ideas of carrying off the King and his brother would have to be abandoned and Margaret, forced to

Above left: *Margaret Tudor, c. 1520; an unauthenticated portrait attributed to Jean Perréal.* Above right: *James IV of Scotland was killed by his brother-in-law's forces at Flodden in 1513. His widow, Margaret Tudor, became Regent of Scotland for her infant son.* Right: *Margaret Tudor's second husband, Archibald Douglas, Earl of Angus; a contemporary engraving.*

choose between her husband and her children, unhesitatingly chose her husband. She believed that the children would be safe with Albany, while Angus indubitably would not. Angus might not have been able to do much to help her, but at least he had stood by her. She felt largely responsible for his present plight and she was still in love with him.

Having reached the Border, Margaret rested for a few days at Coldstream and then moved to Lord Dacre's house at Morpeth. At any rate that was the intention, but at Harbottle in Northumberland her pains began and there, on 7 October, she gave birth to a daughter. The infant Margaret Douglas seemed healthy and was christened next day 'with such convenient provisions as could or might be had in this barren and wild country'; but her mother, who had suffered a long and difficult labour, was desperately ill.

While Margaret lay helpless at Harbottle, an international storm of accusation and counter-accusation raged over her head. Henry was now noisily publishing his sister's wrongs to the world and Albany found himself being pilloried as a tyrant and a brute who had torn a mother from her little ones, forced a pregnant lady to flee for her life, insulted and abused an anointed Queen, stolen her jewellery and forged her handwriting.

As for the Duke, he was aghast at the turn events had taken. He had never questioned the sincerity of Margaret's submission, nor had it ever crossed his mind that a woman within weeks of being confined could be contemplating such an escapade – but then nothing in his experience had prepared him for the strong-minded ladies of the Tudor family. His attempts to defend himself and his pathetic pleas to Margaret to be reasonable and come home like a good Scotswoman were disregarded. When the French ambassador tried to put matters in perspective by declaring that the Queen had never been in the slightest danger of her life and had simply run away in a temper when she found she could not have her own way, he was ignored.

The weeks passed and Margaret remained at Harbottle Castle, suffering acutely from 'the great and intolerable ache that is in her right leg, nigh to her body'. This sounds like a severe attack of phlebitis, and was so painful that the invalid could not bear to sit up while her bed was made and screamed aloud whenever she had to be turned or moved. Lord Dacre was being driven distracted. Although he had repeatedly urged Margaret to seek his protection, he had not reckoned on having to provide for a royal lying-in. His life was not made any easier by the fact that the pain in her leg and reaction after so many months of nervous strain had combined to make the Queen exceedingly querulous. She was demanding comforts and medical attention unobtainable in the primitive Border country, refusing to see the local doctors, and complaining long and bitterly about the miseries of her situation.

At the end of November Dacre managed to transfer his exacting charge to the rather more civilized surroundings of Morpeth Castle, where he did his best to maintain her in the style to which she was accustomed – hanging new tapestries on the walls and displaying as much gold and silver plate as he could lay his hands on. By this time, too, couriers had begun to arrive with affectionate letters from Henry promising his sister and her husband a warm welcome at Court as soon as she was fit enough to travel and, even more important, bringing her a supply of new clothes. Margaret was carried in a chair to see 'all the stuff' which had come from London – gowns of cloth of gold and cloth of tissue, gowns of silk and furred velvet – spread out in the great chamber of Morpeth Castle. Much to Lord Dacre's relief, the sight cheered her up considerably and she invited the whole household to come and admire this reassuring evidence of her formidable brother's regard. 'You may see', she exclaimed triumphantly, 'that the king my brother hath not forgotten me, and that he would not I should die for lack of clothes.'

Her mind at this time seemed to be almost morbidly obsessed with clothes. In spite of the fact that she was still in no condition to wear anything but a nightdress, she was writing 'in all haste' to Edinburgh to order more silks, a purple velvet gown lined with cloth of gold, one of crimson velvet furred with ermine, 'and three gowns more and three kirtles of satin'. She had Henry's presents brought to her room two or three times a day so that she could gloat over them as she lay in bed; 'and this five or six days', wrote Christopher Garnish, Dacre's second-in-command, with a certain amount of awe, 'her grace hath had none other mind but ever to see her apparel'.

But although Margaret was able to derive some comfort from the splendours of her wardrobe, there was precious little comfort to be found anywhere else. Still very weak and in considerable pain, and with her whole political future in grave doubt, she was now beginning to have cause for concern about her husband. Angus visited her and the baby dutifully enough, but rumours that he was seeing a good deal of the beautiful Lady Jane Stuart of Traquair (to whom he had once been betrothed) soon filtered through to Morpeth Castle. There were rumours, too, that Angus was thinking of making his peace with Albany and the lords.

Margaret's year of trial ended in tragedy, with the death of little Prince Alexander after a short illness. Alexander was his mother's favourite. 'It hath pleased her to show unto me how goodly a child her younger son is' Christopher Garnish reported; 'and her grace praiseth him more than she doth the king her eldest son.' Both Garnish and Dacre were understandably nervous of the effect the news would have on their sovereign lord's 'dearest sister' and made up their minds to keep it from her as long as possible. In the end, of course, she had to be told and promptly collapsed with grief and shock. Dacre did not 'suspect any danger or peril of life', but his responsibilities weighed heavily on him and he wrote begging Henry to send a physician from London.

It would probably be fair to say that by this time Henry was becoming more than a little tired of both his sisters, whose affairs had demanded so much of his valuable attention during the past year. Margaret had at least been trying to look after his interests in Scotland, but Mary had come dangerously close to incurring his severe displeasure.

Mary's marriage to King Louis had lasted eighty-two days – an even shorter period than either she or Henry had envisaged – and some people did not hesitate to say that she had danced the old man into his grave with no thought for anything but her own pleasure. In fact, Mary, who was a kind-hearted girl, spent a lot of her time sitting at her husband's bedside, helping to keep him amused by singing to him and playing on her lute. The King, surprised and grateful, showed his appreciation by unfailing indulgence. 'The Queen', he wrote to Henry shortly before his death, 'has so conducted herself towards me, and continues so to do daily, that I know not how I can sufficiently praise and express my delight in her. More and more I love, honour and hold her dear.'

When Louis' worn-out body finally gave up its tenuous hold on life on New

Year's Eve 1514, Mary's position changed abruptly. No longer an old man's darling, cushioned in luxury and protected from every wind that blew, she had now become a childless dowager, alone in a foreign country and heavily dependent on the goodwill of the reigning monarch. That this could easily turn into an extremely uncomfortable position Mary knew from her sister-in-law's experience, but not even Catherine of Aragon had had to endure the forty days of strict seclusion imposed by French custom on a newly widowed Queen. This period of mourning or, more accurately, quarantine, was a purely practical measure designed to ensure that if a newly widowed Queen proved to be pregnant, there should be no doubt as to the paternity of her child. In Mary's case this was especially important. If by any chance she were carrying Louis' son, then François might stay plain M. d'Angoulême for the rest of his life.

Mary's assurances that, to the best of her knowledge, she was not pregnant were not attended to and she was bundled off to the Palace of Cluny to spend six weeks behind drawn curtains in a stuffy, black-draped mourning chamber. It was not an exhilarating prospect for an active, healthy young woman. Added to this, Mary was rather scared of François and even more so of his formidable mother, Louise of Savoy, and immured at Cluny she felt very much in their power. She had been separated from her English ladies and surrounded by a posse of hostile Frenchwomen, handpicked by François' sister Marguerite. She was suffering acutely from boredom, loneliness and toothache. But all these discomforts were as nothing beside her consuming anxiety that Henry or François might be bargaining her away to the highest bidder while she was cut off from the outside world and helpless to do anything to stop them.

Mary had received a letter from Thomas Wolsey, now Archbishop of York and Henry's most influential councillor, written during Louis' last illness, promising that her brother would not abandon her but warning her to do nothing without his advice. Above all, she must be careful to say nothing 'whereby any person . . . may have you at any advantage' and, of course, if any offers of marriage were made to her, she must refuse. 'And thus doing', went on Wolsey a shade patronizingly, 'ye shall not fail to have the King fast and loving to you, to attain your desire and come home again into England with as much honour as Queen ever had'.

This was all very well, but Mary knew she was now once again a first-rate matrimonial prize – and she knew her brother. Terror that he would break his word is apparent in every line of a somewhat incoherent letter written from Cluny early in January 1515, begging Henry to send for her as soon as possible, 'for as now I am all out of comfort, saving that all my trust is in your grace and so shall be during my life . . . Sir, I beseech your grace that you will keep all the promises that you promised me when I took my leave of you by the waterside. Sir, your grace knoweth well that I did marry for your pleasure at this time and now I trust that you will suffer me to marry as me liketh for to do . . . wherefore I beseech your grace for to be a good lord and brother to me.'

Exactly what Henry's long-term intentions were about his younger sister's future remain a trifle unclear. In the short term there is no doubt that he wanted her back in England. Neither he nor Wolsey trusted François and they were both afraid that he might use his present advantage to marry off his widowed *belle-mère* to some satellite of his own. Nevertheless, if the King did *not* intend to honour those promises made 'by the waterside', it was a serious mistake in tactics to appoint the Duke of Suffolk as head of the mission charged, among other things, with the task of winding up Mary's affairs in France and bringing her safely home. But Henry trusted his friend. Indeed he had no reason not to trust him. Like Thomas Wolsey, Charles Brandon was his own creation, dependent on royal favour and royal bounty for his very existence. The King did, however, take the precaution of asking Suffolk for a solemn promise that he would keep his relations with Mary on a strictly formal basis while they were abroad. Henry might trust his friend but he did not altogether trust his sister.

This promise was given at Eltham Palace shortly before the Duke left England. It was given quite freely and there is no reason to suppose that he did not fully intend to keep it – Charles Brandon was emphatically not a man to consider the world well lost for love. There may well have been a tacit understanding that if he succeeded in extricating the Queen Dowager on satisfactory financial terms, then the King might be prepared to consider giving them his blessing – certainly rumours of their coming marriage were already circulating – but the putative bridegroom was probably less concerned with thoughts of dalliance than with nervousness over the complex diplomatic chore which lay ahead, by far the most important yet entrusted to him. Suffolk, who was very much more at home in the tiltyard than in the conference chamber, could foresee hours of hard and difficult bargaining over Mary's plate and jewels and her dower rights. He did not foresee the other and infinitely more alarming complications lying in wait for him.

Henry and Wolsey had been right in their belief that François would attempt to persuade Mary into another marriage and he had already suggested two possible candidates, both of them his kinsmen. There were whispers, too, that he was making other suggestions to the widow 'in divers matters not according to her honour', and Mary herself later dropped hints that she had been persecuted by his attentions. Certainly François paid frequent visits to Cluny and may well have amused himself with a little amorous by-play – at twenty-one he was already an experienced and cynical womanizer. All the same, accusations that he was trying to blackmail Mary into becoming his mistress are based on conjecture rather than evidence. He naturally took a close interest in her future, but it was a political interest not a personal one.

The Anglo-French alliance was already showing distinct signs of strain and François was understandably anxious to frustrate any plans Henry might be nursing to use the Queen of France to secure a new anti-French alignment with the Spanish Hapsburg bloc. He told Mary he had definite information that her brother intended to revive her betrothal to Charles of Castile, and warned her that if she was foolish enough to insist on going back to England she would find herself being shipped off to Flanders to be married to the prince there. As this was exactly what Mary was most afraid of, such insinuations did nothing to soothe her already overwrought nerves. Embarrassed and affronted by François' gallantries (in spite of her three months in France she seems to have been still almost schoolgirlishly innocent) but not daring to offend him, exhausted by his nagging persistence that she should accept a husband of his choosing, profoundly suspicious of Henry's good faith and with no one she could trust to advise her, she 'wot not what for to do' and was steadily being driven into a course of action which might easily have ruined her.

On the eve of Suffolk's arrival, François decided it was time to stop playing games. Since Mary stubbornly rejected all his proposals for her future, he wanted to know if this meant that her affections were already engaged. Had she, in fact, ever made a promise of marriage to anyone? If she would only be frank with him, he would do his best to help her. This was just the sort of eventuality Wolsey had tried to warn her against, but by now Mary was past caring. Forgetting all caution, she proceeded to disclose 'the secret of her heart' and her fixed intention to marry Charles Brandon or no one. To her surprise and relief François proved wonderfully sympathetic. He quite understood how she felt and, of course, now that he knew the circumstances, he would not dream of teasing her any further. More than that, he promised on his faith as a true prince, that he would do everything in his power to promote the match. As well he might. Married to her English duke, Mary would present no danger to France and her confession had also given him a valuable bargaining counter in the forthcoming negotiations with her unsuspecting sweetheart.

Suffolk and his colleagues, Sir Richard Wingfield and Dr Nicholas West, arrived on 27 January and had their first audience with François at Senlis on the following Thursday. After the formal public exchange of compliments, Suffolk was summoned to a private interview with the King who wasted no time in coming to the point. He had been informed, he said, that the Duke had come to France to marry the Queen, his master's sister. Much disconcerted, Suffolk broke into vehement denials that he was contemplating any such breach of etiquette. But, with a sly smile on his big foxy face, François went on to reveal the full extent of Mary's indiscretion, even down to a certain 'ware word' – that is, some secret term of endearment used between the lovers – which Suffolk knew 'no man alive but she' could have betrayed.

Having thus neatly pulled the rug from under him and reduced him to a state of floundering dismay, François was ready to reassure his victim. He had promised Mary that he would help her to attain her heart's desire and Suffolk, too, would find him a kind and loving friend. 'I give you in your hand my faith and troth, by the word of a king', he declared impressively, 'that I shall never fail her or you but to help and advance this matter betwixt her and you with as good will as I would for mine own self.'

There was really no more to be said, and Suffolk emerged from this unnerving encounter uncertain whether to be more relieved or alarmed. He took the precaution of sending his own version of what had passed off to Wolsey post haste, but the acquisition of so influential a champion as the King of France could surely be counted as a favourable omen. It was not until some ten days later, when he saw Mary in private for the first time, that the real nature of his predicament was brought home to him.

The moment they were alone together the distracted widow unloosed all the pent up emotional strain of the past few weeks. The more she had thought about it, the more convinced Mary had become that François was right and that Suffolk's mission was nothing less than a trap to entice her back to England to be forced into another political alliance, and she would rather be torn in pieces she cried. Either that, or Suffolk's enemies on the Council would find some way of preventing their marriage. Nothing her harassed lover could say would pacify her, and in floods of tears – according to the Duke, he had never seen a woman so weep – she presented him with an ultimatum: either he married her now, at once, while they had the chance, or he 'might never look to have the same proffer again'. With his promise to Henry weighing heavily on his conscience, Suffolk tried to hedge but his expostulations were impatiently swept aside. Mary reminded him that she had her brother's promise that this time she could marry as she pleased; François was ready to help them; such an opportunity might never come again.

All this put Charles Brandon in a quite appalling quandary. His whole career had been founded on his total commitment to the Tudor family and now he was caught between the upper and nether millstones of Tudor passion and Tudor absolutism. The Duke was genuinely devoted to Henry and stood in very healthy awe of him but, on the other hand, it is not easy for a man to stand like a stone while the loveliest and most desirable princess in Europe is literally begging and praying him to marry her.

Personal feelings apart, Mary was too rich a prize to be surrendered lightly. Although it was not tactful to mention it, the fact that the King still had no living child could not be ignored. It was by no means impossible that his younger sister might found a new royal line and dreams of fathering a future king of England must at least have crossed Suffolk's mind. The temptation and Mary's tears were too much for him. He hesitated, wavered and was lost, and some time in February 1515 the Queen Dowager of France married Charles Brandon in the chapel at Cluny with a handful of her personal attendants as witnesses.

François had kept his promise to write to Henry in favour of the match (though he does not seem to have known it had already taken place) and was now beginning to raise the question of the restitution of Tournai. The town was still occupied by an English garrison and was, as François pointed out, only an expensive liability to Henry. He was ready to pay handsomely for its return and wanted Suffolk's help in arranging the deal. There was also the highly complicated business of Mary's finances. Her jointure, together with the plate and jewels she had brought from England, were secured to her; but a dispute was blowing up over the jewels showered on her by King Louis and the gold plate and furniture she had used as Queen of France. Both Henry and Mary contended that these should be regarded as her personal property, but François said it was unreasonable for her to expect to keep them after she had left the country.

In a letter to Suffolk, Thomas Wolsey had already made it clear that this was a matter of fundamental importance. He wrote:

Inasmuch as the King's grace hath great mind to the French King's plate of gold and jewels, I require and advise you substantially to handle that matter and to stick thereunto. For I assure you that the hope the King hath to obtain the said plate and jewels is the thing that most certainly stayeth his grace to assent that you should marry his sister. The lack whereof I fear me might make him cold and remiss and cause some alteration.

In the circumstances this was not reassuring. By the beginning of March rumours of the Cluny wedding were going round Paris and Mary thought she might be pregnant. Confession could no longer be postponed and on the fifth Charles Brandon sat down to write a difficult letter to Wolsey.

My lord of York, I commend me unto you. I know well that you have been the chief man that has been my friend, and therefore I will hide nothing from you, trusting you will help me now as you have always done. My lord, so it was that when I came to Paris I heard many things which put me in great fear, and so did the Queen both; and the Queen would never let me be in rest till I had granted her to be married; and so to be plain with you, I have married her heartily and have lain with her, insomuch as I fear me lest she be with child.

My lord, I am not in a little sorrow lest the King should know of it and be displeased with me; for I assure you I had rather have died than he should be miscontent. And therefore, my own good lord, since you have brought me hither, let me not be undone now, the which I fear me I shall be without your especial help . . . Beseeching you that I may have answer from you as shortly as it may be possible, for I assure you I have as heavy a heart as any man living and shall have till I may hear good tidings from you . . .

There followed a fortnight's painful suspense. Mary and Suffolk both knew that their 'privy marriage' could be set aside as invalid and both feared the Duke's enemies at home, who were already jealous of his spectacular rise in rank and riches, and who would certainly not consider him a fit match for the King's sister. There was also a strong conservative faction on the Council that disapproved of Wolsey's pro-French policy and favoured a renewal of the old ties with Spain and Flanders – a renewal in which Mary might have played such a useful part.

The newly-weds, who had begun rather late in the day to count the possible cost of their defiance, knew that everything would depend on how Henry took the news and waited with mounting anxiety for Wolsey's reply. 'My lord, with sorrowful heart I write unto you', it began ominously and went on to inform the Duke that the King's first reaction had been one of disbelief that his friend, the man in all the world he had loved and trusted best, could have so wantonly betrayed his confidence. Wolsey had had to show him Suffolk's letter before he would give it credence and now he was bitterly hurt and angry, 'for he doth well understand that he is deceived of the assured trust he thought to have found in you . . . Cursed be the blind affection and counsel that hath brought you hereunto', the Archbishop of York went on grimly, 'fearing that such sudden and unadvised dealing shall have sudden repentance.' Let Charles Brandon make no mistake, by his acts and doings he had put himself 'in the greatest danger that ever man was in'.

Wolsey could see only one possible way out of 'this great perplexity' and he was by no means certain whether it would answer. First, Suffolk and Mary must beg Henry's forgiveness, that went without saying. More important, they must bind themselves to repay the whole of Mary's marriage portion in annual instalments of £4,000, leaving her only £6,000 a year to live on. They must also give back all the plate and jewels she had taken to France, which were considered part of her dowry, and surrender the plate and jewellery King Louis had given her. 'This is the way to make your peace', wrote Wolsey; 'whereat if ye deeply consider what danger ye be in and shall be in, having the King's displeasure, I doubt not both the Queen and you will not stick.'

The effect of this letter was devastating. Shivering in their shoes, the culprits hastened to take Wolsey's advice. They were ready to strip themselves of every penny they possessed if it would appease the King, and now Suffolk cast himself at Henry's feet.

Most dread sovereign lord, with the most sorrowful heart I, your most poor subject, beseech forgiveness of mine offences and for this marriage in which I have done greatly amiss. Sir, for the passion of God, let it not be in your heart against me, and rather than you should hold me in mistrust, strike off my head and let me not live . . . If ever I thought or did anything, saving the love and marriage of the Queen, that should be to your displeasure, I pray God let me die as shameful a death as ever did man. But truly there was never master had a truer servant than your grace has had in me and ever shall have, whatsoever you or any man else shall think of me.

In her own letter, Mary tried hard to shield her husband and take the blame on herself. 'I will not in any wise deny that I have offended your highness', she wrote, 'for the which I do put myself most humbly in your clemency and mercy.' All the same, she assured her brother, she had not acted from 'sensual appetite' or because she had no regard for his displeasure. It was just that she had been in such terrible 'consternation, fear and doubt' that his Council would somehow manage to prevent her marriage – the one thing she wanted most in all the world. 'Whereupon, sir, I put my lord of Suffolk in choice whether he would accomplish the marriage within four days, or else that he should never have enjoyed me; whereby I know well that I constrained him to break such promises as he made your grace . . .'

Knowing her brother as she did, Mary had already taken steps to provide him with a tangible token of her repentance, sacrificing the most sumptuous of all Louis' gifts – the Mirror of Naples itself. But since this particular bauble unquestionably formed part of the French crown jewels, the King of France was justifiably irritated when he discovered its loss, and acrimonious (and perfectly fruitless) demands for its return played a considerable part in delaying and generally snarling up the final settlement of Mary's financial affairs. In the end, after a good deal of haggling, the English got rather better terms than might have been expected in the circumstances. As well as her widow's jointure, Mary received 200,000 gold crowns 'in contentation of her dower' and François agreed to let her keep a proportion of Louis' plate and jewels, on the clear understanding that this was to be recognized as his own generosity and not her right. With this they had to be content for, as Suffolk pointed out, they could not compel him to give so much 'without he list'.

It was April before the negotiations were completed and both Mary and Suffolk were longing to go home, but so far all their pleas for forgiveness had been ignored. They set out on their journey to the coast on 16 April and Charles Brandon addressed one more appeal to Henry from Montreuil. He had been told that his rivals on the Council were working on the King to have him put to death or at least thrown into prison. 'But, sir, your grace is he that is my sovereign lord and master who has brought me up out of nothing and to you, with most humble heart, I yield myself to do with my poor body your most gracious pleasure, not fearing the malice of others; for I know your grace to be of such nature that it cannot lie in their powers to cause you to destroy me . . .'

The couple reached Calais still without any word from England and Mary wrote this time, to inform her brother that she had put herself within his jurisdiction. She reminded him yet again of his famous waterside promise, begging him, 'for the great and tender love' which had always been between them, to let bygones be bygones and to certify her 'by your most loving letters of the same'. In the meantime, she and her husband would stay where they were. Mary was reasonably confident that Henry would come round, but she was not taking any unnecessary risks.

In fact, permission to cross the Channel and with it some hint of a break in the clouds was not long delayed, and the Suffolks sailed for Dover at the beginning of May. Their arrival was unmarked by any special ceremony and their first meeting with Henry took place in private at the manor of Barking on the eastern outskirts of London, but these were the only overt signs that they were still in disgrace. Although the reunion may have had its awkward moments, it was apparently quite cordial, the King, according to one contemporary observer, rejoicing greatly in his sister's honourable return.

All the accounts of his dire displeasure had, of course, been filtered through Wolsey in his role as intermediary and it is quite possible that they were somewhat exaggerated. Wolsey and Charles Brandon were natural allies in the running feud with the reactionary Duke of Norfolk and it would have suited the devious Archbishop to impress his friend with a proper sense of indebtedness. No doubt Henry had been both hurt and angry, but it is clear throughout that it was the breach of faith more than the actual marriage which had enraged him. It is equally clear that he had never intended to proceed to extremes against his old playmate and his favourite sister. He was genuinely fond of them both – though not fond enough to let them off paying reparations. Mary surrendered all the plate and jewels salvaged from France, which were later valued at just over sixteen hundred pounds, and as well as repaying her dowry she signed a deed undertaking to repay in annual instalments the £24,000 which had been laid out on her trousseau and the other expenses of her first marriage. It was a formidable sum and the debt was to hang round the Suffolks' necks for years, but by the standards of the time and considering the enormity of their offence, they had escaped pretty lightly. The Duke was allowed to keep all his offices and estates, and he and Mary were soon fully restored to the life-giving sunshine of royal favour.

They were publicly married at Greenwich on 13 May and Suffolk duly distinguished himself in a tournament held in honour of the wedding. But although the full Court was present and there was all the customary feasting and dancing, it was kept very much a family affair with none of the civic celebrations usual on such occasions. According to the Venetian ambassador, this was because 'the kingdom did not approve of the marriage' and the ambassador himself, who could not understand how the Duke had managed to keep his head on his shoulders, hesitated to offer congratulations until he was sure they would be acceptable.

It is true that there was a body of opinion which considered Mary had been thrown away on Suffolk but 'the wisest sort' were content, pointing out that another foreign marriage would have meant another expensive outfit and wedding journey, while as things were the Queen-Duchess was bringing money into the country. The Duke's easy-going amiability, good looks and athletic prowess made him a popular figure and few people, apart from his political rivals, seriously grudged him his good fortune. Few people, after all, could resist a romance, especially one with a happy ending – a rare enough event in royal circles. No one denied that it was an unequal match, but the general feeling on this aspect of Mary Tudor's love story was neatly summed up in the quatrain (said to have been composed by the bridegroom himself) which appeared beneath the double portrait of the happy pair painted about the time of their marriage:

> Cloth of gold, do not despise,
> Though thou be match'd with cloth of frieze.
> Cloth of frieze, be not too bold,
> Though thou be match'd with cloth of gold.

After the wedding the King went off on a summer progress to the West Country and the Suffolks retired to their East Anglian estates – partly to rest and recuperate after all the excitement of the past six months and partly as an economy measure. The Duke's visit to France had cost him a lot of money and in present circumstances he could scarcely apply to his brother-in-law for financial assistance. By the autumn, though, they were back at Court and attended a great banquet held at York House to celebrate the arrival from Rome of Thomas Wolsey's cardinal's hat. They were also much in evidence at the launching of a new warship, christened the *Virgin Mary* but more often called the *Princess Mary*. Mary herself was guest of honour at a dinner given on board at which the King presided, dressed in a sailor suit of cloth of gold, with an enormous boatswain's whistle hung round his neck on a gold chain which he blew as loudly as a trumpet on the least provocation. Everyone was in the highest spirits. Henry was never happier than when he was with the navy and the French Queen, as she continued to be known, having got everything she had ever wanted, was radiant.

The Suffolks expected their first child in the spring – Mary's supposed

In 1515 Mary Tudor married Charles Brandon, Duke of Suffolk; the wedding portrait of the Duke and Duchess of Suffolk.

pregnancy in Paris the previous March had turned out to be a false alarm – and Queen Catherine, too, was pregnant again. After so many disappointments, no one felt very optimistic of the outcome but hopes of a Prince of Wales could not be wholly discounted. In fact, on this occasion the Queen went her full time and at Greenwich, on 18 February 1516, she gave birth to a living child. True, the baby was a girl but at least it was healthy and gave every promise of survival. The new princess was christened with 'great solemnity' at the Friars' Church and given the name of Mary as a compliment to her aunt. Henry was apparently delighted with his daughter – his fondness for babies and small children was one of his more attractive traits – and when the Venetian ambassador ventured to commiserate with him over the baby's sex, he replied philosophically: 'The Queen and I are both young. If it was a daughter this time, by the grace of God the sons will follow.' Catherine was thirty-one now and Henry twenty-five.

Mary Brandon was to be more fortunate than her sister-in-law. Her baby, a healthy boy, made his appearance on Tuesday 11 March between ten and twelve o'clock at night and the same thought must have crossed the minds of everyone present in the birth chamber – the King's sister had succeeded where the King's wife had failed. Certainly the Brandon baby, named after his Uncle Henry, was given a princely christening. The ceremony took place at Suffolk's town house in Southwark with the King and Cardinal Wolsey as godfathers and Katherine Courtenay, once Katherine Plantagenet, as godmother.

It was a good year for babies and for family occasions. To Lord Dacre's unspeakable relief, Queen Margaret had at last recovered enough strength to leave her bed at Morpeth Castle. She reached London at the beginning of May, with her six-month-old daughter but without her husband – Angus had gone back to Scotland. Henry met his elder sister at Tottenham and escorted her in procession through the city to Baynard's Castle. Later he installed her at Scotland Yard, just below Charing Cross, the traditional lodgings of Scottish kings, and a lavish series of entertainments was planned in her honour.

The Suffolks were still in town, for although the Duke could ill afford the expense of a London season, he could not very well deny his wife the chance of a reunion with the sister she had not seen for thirteen years and they stayed on for a few weeks after Margaret's arrival. The Queen of Scotland and the Duchess of Suffolk enjoyed some cosy hours together, reminiscing, swapping experiences and comparing and showing off their babies. But for the elder sister the contrast can only have been painful. Margaret, already regretting her impulsive second marriage and prematurely aged by illness, worry and disappointment, knew that sooner or later she would have to go back to the Scotland she hated to fight for her son's future among the insolent, uncouth chieftains she hated still more; while Mary, the spoilt baby of the family, her beauty undimmed, was securely established in her own homeland and happily married to the man she loved – no one would ever take Mary's babies away from her.

The sisters had met with spontaneous pleasure and affection, but their ways had long since parted and they had little in common now apart from some childhood memories. A far deeper bond of friendship and shared experience existed between Mary and her sister-in-law. When, the following spring, Queen

Catherine made a pilgrimage to the shrine of Our Lady of Walsingham to pray for a son, Mary went with her and afterwards the Suffolks entertained her 'with such poor cheer as we could make her grace'.

Mary gave birth to her second child that year – a daughter christened Frances, probably as a gesture to the King of France – and two years later another daughter, Eleanor, was born. But all Catherine's prayers went unanswered. She miscarried again in the autumn of 1517 and in November 1518 she was delivered of another stillborn child. It was her last pregnancy.

CHAPTER 6
The King's Secret Matter

. . . when we remember our mortality and that we must die, then we think that all our doings in our lifetime are clearly defaced and worthy of no memory if we leave you in trouble at the time of our death.

In the spring of 1519 Henry VIII and Catherine of Aragon celebrated their tenth wedding anniversary and the six years difference in their ages was now cruelly apparent. Constant childbearing had spread and thickened Catherine's once slender waist and her lovely russet hair, so much admired by Edward Hall, had darkened to an indeterminate muddy brown. She had become a rather dumpy little woman, unshakeably dignified, formidably pious and increasingly preoccupied with the task of bringing up her precious daughter.

As for Henry, his youthful love affair with his wife had long grown cold. Some people dated the beginning of his withdrawal from 1514, the year of Ferdinand's third betrayal – and the year when rumours of divorce were circulating. Rumours were also circulating that the King of England had vented some of his rage against the King of Spain on his Spanish wife, but there is little hard evidence to support the gossipmongers and Catherine herself made it plain that she disapproved of her father's behaviour.

If Henry was already beginning to turn away from her, the reason is more likely to be found in the rise of Thomas Wolsey. In this burly son of an Ipswich grazier, with his brilliant brain, his unlimited capacity for sheer hard work and his total commitment to his master's interests, the King had found a councillor after his own heart and it was Wolsey's opinion which counted now, Wolsey whose advice was sought on all matters foreign and domestic, Wolsey who enjoyed the King's confidence. The Queen never liked or trusted the Cardinal Archbishop of York, but she never betrayed any personal resentment or jealousy of his steadily increasing influence over her husband.

Catherine showed no sign of jealousy either when, early in 1514, the King took one of her young maids of honour as his mistress. Not that there was anything remarkable in the King taking a mistress – indeed, by the standards of his day, Henry had been an unusually faithful husband. There may well have been some casual, temporary liaisons during the first five years of their marriage but it was not until the advent of Bessie Blount that the Queen had any acknowledged rival in her husband's bed.

We know very little about Bessie Blount. Catherine had first known the family, which came from Shropshire, in her Ludlow days. Bessie's father, John Blount of

Catherine of Aragon in middle age; a portrait by an unknown artist.

Kinlet, was related to her Chamberlain, William Blount, Lord Mountjoy, and it was possibly due to him that Bessie got a place at Court. She was very young, certainly no more than fifteen, when she first caught the King's eye and we are told that she was beautiful – 'a fair damosel' according to Hall's *Chronicle*, who 'in singing, dancing and in all goodly pastimes exceeded all other'. Lord Herbert of Cherbury, writing in the early seventeenth century, remarks (with a delightfully appropriate but unintentional pun) that Elizabeth Blount 'was thought for her rare ornaments of nature and education to be the beauty and mistress-piece of her time.' But the only really significant fact about Bessie Blount is that, in 1519, she bore the King 'a goodly man child of beauty like to the father and mother'.

The King acknowledged the infant with pride and pleasure and had him christened Henry, with Cardinal Wolsey once more a godfather. But Bessie Blount did not return to Court. 'The mother of the King's son', as she was now officially styled, had retired on her laurels and a year or so later she reappears in the record comfortably established as the wife of Gilbert Tailbois, a gentleman of substance with estates in Lincolnshire. Her place in the royal bed was taken, for a time at least, by Mary Boleyn, an experienced young woman of rather doubtful reputation who had gone to France with Mary Tudor in 1514.

The year 1525 is usually pin-pointed as the time when Henry first became seriously worried about the succession. On 18 June an investiture was held at Bridewell Palace and amongst those honoured were the King's nephew, Henry Brandon, now nine years old, who became Earl of Lincoln; the King's first cousin, Henry Courtenay, son of his aunt Katherine Plantagenet, who was raised to be Marquis of Exeter; and Sir Thomas Boleyn, created Viscount Rochford in recognition, it was supposed, of his daughter's services. But by far the most significant of the titles handed out that Sunday morning were those bestowed on the King's illegitimate son, Henry Fitzroy.

The six-year-old child had been brought over from Durham House in the Strand at about nine o'clock and taken to a private robing room to be dressed in the robes 'that pertained to the state of an Earl'. He was escorted into the richly decorated Presence Chamber by the Earls of Oxford and Arundel and solemnly created Earl of Nottingham, his patent being read aloud by Master Thomas More. Then the trumpeters blew a fanfare and the new Earl 'departed out of the King's presence in like manner and form as he was brought into it'.

A few minutes later he was brought back again, this time 'apparelled in the robes pertaining to the state of a Duke', supported by the Dukes of Norfolk and Suffolk and escorted by Garter King of Arms, the Marquis of Dorset and three earls who bore between them all the trappings of the ducal honour. The little boy stood stiff and uncomprehending as his father invested him with the mantle, the sword, the cap of estate and ducal coronet, before putting the gold rod into his hands. And thus, says a contemporary description of the event, 'was he created Duke of Richmond and Somerset, and at the conclusion of the ceremonies he stood aside in the King's presence above all the other peers of the realm'. A week later the Duke of Richmond was installed as a Knight of the Garter, and in July Letters Patent were issued creating him Lord High Admiral of England and Warden General of all the Marches towards Scotland.

Not surprisingly the sudden elevation of Henry Fitzroy caused a flurry of interest, especially among the diplomatic corps. There was talk of a royal marriage for the new Duke; there was talk of a kingdom to be created for him in Ireland and it was freely speculated that this healthy, handsome child, who had already been granted quasi-royal status, might yet 'be easily by the King's means exalted to higher things'.

Whatever the King's future plans, he contented himself in 1525 with granting his son an income of £4,000 a year and setting up a princely establishment for him at Sheriff Hutton in Yorkshire. The Warden General of the Scottish Marches set off to take up residence in his new domains in August, after bidding a formal farewell to the King at Hampton Court, Cardinal Wolsey's splendid riverside mansion. The Cardinal had presented his godson with a horse litter 'garnished with cloth of silver', but the Duke soon got bored with travelling in it and demanded successfully to be allowed to ride his pony instead. The journey north, which occupied more than a month, took on very much the character of a royal progress and in the privacy of the little Court at Sheriff Hutton my lord of Richmond was usually addressed in royal style; but, as nothing was said officially about exalting him to higher things, international interest in the King of England's bastard gradually faded.

The affair had, however, caused a certain amount of unpleasantness within the

Henry Fitzroy, Duke of Richmond, Henry's illegitimate son by Bessie Blount.

family circle. The honours and attentions showered on Bessie Blount's son had been too much for Queen Catherine's self-control, and she had protested angrily at what looked like a deliberate insult to herself and her daughter. Catherine's protests, though, did her no good and for the first time her husband turned on her, dismissing three of her Spanish ladies-in-waiting who were said to have encouraged her to criticize his actions. This, remarked a Venetian correspondent, was a strong measure, 'but the Queen was obliged to submit and to have patience'.

Catherine was obliged to submit, too, when Henry decided that the time had come for Princess Mary, now nine years old, to go to Ludlow to take up her duties as Princess of Wales. It was hard for the Queen, especially with her own gloomy memories of Ludlow, to face separation from her child, but she could take comfort from the fact that at least Mary was being treated with the consideration due to her father's heiress. Ludlow Castle was repaired and re-decorated for her, and her household would be under the control of her mother's old friend, Margaret Pole Countess of Salisbury.

All the same, it was a sad autumn for Catherine. Her health was poor and she had long since had to give up all hope of bearing a living son. She was estranged from her husband, separated from her daughter and missing the little girl badly. Internationally, too, the outlook was bleak, for relations with Spain were once more severely strained. Looking back over her life in September 1525 the Queen of England could see only a depressing catalogue of failure – repeated failure to give the King a male heir, failure to keep the Anglo-Spanish alliance in being, the failure, in short, of the whole purpose of her marriage.

But Henry came back to her. He no longer discussed his affairs with her and almost certainly he no longer slept with her, but there remained a bond of affection and respect, of shared experience and shared interests between them. They made up their quarrel and read Erasmus' latest book together. The King resumed his habit of receiving visitors in his wife's apartments and they kept Christmas together at Eltham, though with rather less indiscriminate hospitality than usual because of an outbreak of plague in London. Everything seemed to have settled back to normal and no one, least of all the Queen, could have guessed that this period of calm was the lull before the storm – the hurricane which was about to tear her world apart and destroy it for ever.

We do not know exactly when Henry was first seriously attracted by the sister of his discarded mistress Mary Boleyn. If we did, we should know a great deal more about the real origins of the King's Great Matter. The fortunes of the Boleyn family, tenant farmers from Sall in Norfolk, had been founded in the fifteenth century by Geoffrey, a younger son who had come up to London in classic Dick Whittington style and risen to be Lord Mayor. His son, William, had climbed further up the social ladder by marrying into the noble Anglo-Irish family of Butler and William's second son, Thomas, came to Court to make a career in the King's service – one of the new men attracted by the new dynasty. Thomas had also acquired an aristocratic wife, Elizabeth Howard, daughter of the second Duke of Norfolk, and there were three surviving children of the marriage – George, Mary and Anne.

Thomas Boleyn, Earl of Wiltshire and of Ormonde, father of Mary and Anne Boleyn; a sketch by Holbein.

In later years, when Anne Boleyn had become the most notorious woman in Europe, her lightest word, her every look and gesture were eagerly observed and reported on, but very little is known about her early life and there has long been controversy over her date of birth. William Camden, the Elizabethan antiquarian who was a friend of William Cecil and other near contemporaries with access to first-hand information, gives it categorically as 1507; but recent research, based on a new reading of an undated (an wildly misspelt) letter written by Anne to her father, has revived the case for an earlier date, around 1501, by placing her in the Netherlands at the court of Margaret of Austria in the spring of 1513. If this is correct, then it makes Anne well into her mid-twenties before she first caught the King's eye and in her early thirties before her daughter was born – unusually late for a first pregnancy.

Certainly one of the Boleyn girls, identified only as Mademoiselle Bullan, did go over to the Netherlands for a time, but this may have been Mary, the elder sister. Certainly it was Mary who went to France with Mary Tudor. Anne was probably born at Blickling in Norfolk, although tradition always associates her with Hever Castle, the Boleyns' Kentish property, and we know that she, too, spent some part of her girlhood in France. Either she joined her sister in 1514 or else, as has been suggested, it was not until 1519, when her father was appointed ambassador, that she crossed the Channel to be 'finished' in the household of Queen Claude, François' good dull wife, who maintained a school for young ladies at her court.

Whatever the true sequence of these events, Anne was unquestionably back in England by the end of 1521, when Anglo-French diplomatic relations were broken off and all English nationals called home. Her father had used his growing influence to get her accepted as one of Queen Catherine's maids of honour and she was present at the New Year Revels, wearing a dress of yellow satin and a caul of Venice gold. Thomas Boleyn was planning a match for his younger daughter with James Butler, one of her Irish kinsmen – a project which, for reasons connected with the political situation in Ireland, had the active support of the King and Cardinal Wolsey. But the negotiations made slow progress and Anne began to look round for a husband on her own account. Her choice fell on Henry Percy, son and heir of the Earl of Northumberland. This rather slow-witted youth was attached to Wolsey's entourage and 'when it chanced the Lord Cardinal at any time to repair to the court, the Lord Percy would then resort for his pastime unto the Queen's chamber and there would fall in dalliance among the Queen's maidens, being at the last more conversant with Mistress Anne Boleyn than with any other.'

The young people soon reached an understanding but as soon as rumours of a secret engagement reached Cardinal Wolsey, he took prompt and ruthless action to end it. He rated the unfortunate Percy in front of the servants of his chamber for so far forgetting himself and his position as to become entangled 'with a foolish girl yonder in the court', and ordered him 'not once to resort to her company' again on pain of his father's and the King's severe displeasure.

George Cavendish, Wolsey's gentleman usher, recording this episode in his biography of the Cardinal, believed that the King had ordered Wolsey to intervene because he had already conceived a secret passion for Anne. In view of later events, this must have seemed a reasonable assumption to Cavendish, writing with the benefit of hindsight, but there is, in fact, no evidence whatever that Henry had any amorous feelings for Anne Boleyn as early as 1522 – a time when he was probably still sleeping with her elder sister. A less romantic but far more likely explanation is that the Cardinal had simply acted to prevent a young nobleman entrusted to his care from being trapped into matrimony by a scheming young woman of no particular family. As for Anne, she showed her furious disappointment so openly that she was sent home in disgrace and, as far as we know, did not return to Court until the end of 1525 or the early part of 1526.

By this time the Butler marriage had finally fallen through and Anne was still unbetrothed. There were apparently no other suitors under consideration and she had begun to amuse herself by flirting with Sir Thomas Wyatt, the witty, sophisticated courtier, diplomat and poet who was a neighbour of the Boleyns down in Kent. Wyatt, like the King, was a married man and it seems possible that it was his obvious interest which first roused Henry to take notice of Anne. There was some by-play between the two men over a trinket belonging to Anne and flourished by Wyatt during a game of bowls with Henry. Henry, in turn, produced a ring that he declared had been given to him and the episode, which had begun half in joke, ended with the King striding off 'showing some discontentment in his countenance'.

'Who list her hunt', wrote Thomas Wyatt in a sonnet that may or may not refer to Anne Boleyn, but which could hardly be more apt,

> Who list her hunt, I put him out of doubt,
> As well as I may spend his time in vain:
> And, graven with Diamonds, in letters plain
> There is written her fair neck round about:
> *Noli me tangere*, for Caesar's I am;
> And wild for to hold, though I seem tame.

Whether or not Wyatt had spent his time entirely in vain (it was whispered later that Anne had not always been so hard to get), he was wise enough to abandon the chase as soon as Caesar set foot in the stirrup and by some time in the summer of 1526 the field had been cleared for the most remarkable courtship in English history.

No other woman in English history has ever aroused so much and such violent controversy as Anne Boleyn. In her own lifetime she was 'the other woman', the home-wrecker, the wicked stepmother; she was the concubine, *la grande putain*, the goggle-eyed whore, 'that naughty pake Nan Bullen'. Succeeding generations have seen her as a wronged and virtuous Protestant heroine, as a helpless victim of circumstances, as a commonplace little gold-digger. It is virtually impossible now to find the real woman beneath all the passion and the politics, the prejudice and the special pleading, and often the seeker feels, like Wyatt, that he is trying to catch the wind in a net. She can only be glimpsed occasionally – defiant, tricky, 'wild for to hold' though she seems lame – and always there is that faint but unmistakable whiff of the feral, the untameable, wherever she has been.

Anne Boleyn; a drawing by Holbein.

She was not conventionally beautiful, especially not by the standards of an age which admired blue-eyed, fair-skinned blondes. Anne's dark brunette colouring earned her another of her nicknames, 'the night crow'. She had thick, glossy black hair and fine dark eyes, which seem by all accounts to have been her best feature, but she was inclined to be flat-chested and her complexion is variously described as 'sallow' or 'swarthy', which sounds as if she had the rather greasy, coarse-textured skin which often goes with black hair and eyes. There were other blemishes, too. She is said to have had a projecting tooth, a rudimentary sixth finger on her right hand and a large mole or strawberry mark on her neck. But Anne was always clever at making the best of herself. She dressed well and soon became a leader of fashion, being described as 'the model and mirror of those at Court'. She sang, played the lute and was a graceful dancer. But, apart from the extra polish of her French education, she does not appear to have had any special accomplishments to mark her out from her contemporaries. She is said to have had a ready wit, but no examples of it have survived. She certainly had a venomous temper and a sharp tongue which made her many unnecessary enemies. It is not easy to define the secret of her undoubted fascination, but probably it lay partly in her general air of elegance and vivacity, and partly in that special quality of sexual magnetism which eludes description, defies portraiture and has little or nothing to do with physical beauty.

It was not long, of course, before the whole Court knew that Mistress Anne Boleyn was the King's latest fancy, but no one as yet 'esteemed it other than an ordinary course of dalliance'; nor is there any reason to suppose that Henry himself was contemplating anything other than an ordinary course of dalliance – not, that is, until Anne made it clear that she had no intention of allowing him into her bed. This disobliging attitude may well have surprised the King, but from Anne's point of view it was reasonable enough. Her sister Mary had received no very startling reward for her services, having been married off to William Carey, one of the King's boon companions but otherwise of no special consequence. Even Bessie Blount, who had given the King a son, had achieved no more than a respectable marriage. Anne, intelligent, ambitious and, since the Percy *débâcle*, with something of a chip on her shoulder, wanted to do better than that.

In spite of his highly-coloured reputation, Henry was no lecher and held, with perfect sincerity, strong moral views on female chastity. He could understand and respect Anne's veto and, having satisfied himself that she was not to be enjoyed without marriage, he made up his mind to give her marriage. Just when this majestic decision was taken is yet another unanswered question. All we know for certain is that in May 1527 the King made the first moves in the divorce or, to be strictly accurate, the nullity suit which was to have such incalculable effects on the whole course of English life.

Henry based his case quite simply on the Old Testament text: 'If a man shall take his brother's wife, it is an unclean thing . . . they shall be childless.' Henry had married his brother's wife and they were childless, or as good as childless. This was obviously a sign of God's displeasure and the King began to feel qualms of conscience, soon to develop into an unalterable conviction, that his marriage was against God's law – that for the past eighteen years he and Catherine had been living together in incestuous adultery. Why else, after all, should the Almighty, who had always taken such a flattering interest in his affairs, deny him a male heir?

It is generally accepted by serious historians that Henry's desperate need for a son to succeed him was the spur which goaded him into seeking a divorce in the first place, the driving force which sustained him through the bitter legal battle that followed. Of course Henry wanted a son and his anxiety about the succession was to play an increasingly important part in the general conduct of his policy. (In the matter of the divorce, it provided an unexceptional excuse for some highly questionable proceedings.) But at the same time, it is worth remembering that in 1527 it was very nearly nine years since Catherine's last pregnancy, six or seven years at least since Henry had known she would never have another child – a lapse of time which does not exactly promote an impression of desperation.

It is difficult, therefore, not to wonder whether, if Henry had never become infatuated with Anne Boleyn, we should ever have heard about that famous scruple which 'pricked' his conscience. His own subjects certainly wondered. 'The common people', wrote Edward Hall, 'being ignorant of the truth and in especial women and others that favoured the Queen talked largely and said that the King would for his own pleasure have another wife.' This sort of talk became so widespread that the King found it necessary to explain his position in a public statement made to the Lord Mayor and aldermen of London and various other notables at Bridewell Palace. Henry began by reminding his audience that throughout almost twenty years of his reign they had enjoyed a period of peace and prosperity, that he had protected them from 'outward enemies' and had never undertaken a foreign war without achieving victory and honour. 'But', he went on, 'when we remember our mortality and that we must die, then we think that all our doings in our lifetime are clearly defaced and worthy of no memory if we leave you in trouble at the time of our death. For if our true heir be not known at the time of our death, see what mischief and trouble shall succeed to you and your children.' It was perfectly true that it had pleased God to send him a fair daughter, but learned men were now telling him that Mary, begotten on his brother's wife, was not his lawful daughter, that he was not lawfully married, but living 'abominably and detestably in open adultery'. This fearful possibility daily and hourly troubled his conscience and oppressed his spirits. It was, on his word as a prince, the only reason why he had sought counsel from experts, so that the matter could be decided. He intended no disparagement of the Queen, a most excellent and virtuous woman. Henry would be grieved if he had to part from 'so good a lady', his loving companion for nearly twenty years, but he could not risk God's continued displeasure or the danger of having no true heir of his body to inherit the realm.

It was a good speech, moving, dignified and manly. It had the additional merit of being absolutely sincere: Henry had long since convinced himself of the purity of his motives. It did not, of course, contain any mention of Anne Boleyn but by the time it was delivered, November 1528, no one who had seen them together could any longer be in the slightest doubt about his feelings for her. The one thing which emerges with total clarity from the confusion surrounding the genesis of the King's Great Matter is that the King, for the first and perhaps only time in his life, was deeply, genuinely in love. The little bundle of letters (undated but ascribed to the summer of 1527) written to Anne while she was staying down at Hever, show that Henry had forgotten he was a mature, almost a middle-aged man with a faithful wife and an eleven-year-old daughter. In the words of George Cavendish, he had become 'so amorously affectionate' that 'high discretion was banished for the time'. Honest Master Cavendish, watching the progress of events from his place in Wolsey's shadow, was moved to moral reflection on the wilfulness of princes. 'And above all things', he lamented, 'there is no one thing that causeth them to be more wilful than carnal desire and voluptuous affection of foolish love.'

Henry does not seem to have anticipated any very serious difficulty in getting his divorce. The ending of a marriage with a decree of nullity was by no means unprecedented or even particularly unusual (provided, of course, that the litigants commanded the necessary influence and resources) and in normal circumstances the Pope would be unlikely to disoblige so distinguished and dutiful a son of the Church as the King of England. Unfortunately, in the summer of 1527, circumstances in Rome were far from normal. France and Spain were once more at one another's throats over their rival claims to Northern Italy and in

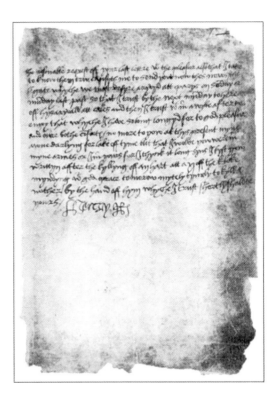

A letter from Henry to Anne Boleyn, September 1528, telling her of the imminent arrival of Cardinal Campeggio. Henry writes: 'I would you were in mine arms, or I in yours, for I think it long since I kissed you.'

consequence, the Holy Father was currently to all intents and purposes a prisoner of the Holy Roman Emperor. And the Holy Roman Emperor, Charles von Hapsburg, happened to be the Queen of England's nephew, the son of her sister Juana.

As soon as Catherine heard that the legality of her marriage and the legitimacy of her daughter were being called in question (and she had heard sooner than Henry meant her to), she had appealed to Charles, now the head of her house, begging him to prevent any hearing of the case in England and especially any hearing of it by Wolsey.

Charles V was, on paper at least, the most powerful monarch in Christendom. He also carried most of the problems of Christendom on his shoulders, but he had a strong sense of family honour. He assured his aunt that she could count on his devoted support and he despatched an experienced canon lawyer to Rome to watch her interests. Henry was also sending envoys to Rome to badger the Pope for a commission giving Wolsey full power to grant his divorce and the Holy Father, assailed on all sides, shed tears and tore his beard in anguish. But the tide of war was now turning in favour of France, the Imperial army retreated and the Pope finally agreed to send Cardinal Lorenzo Campeggio to England with authority to hear the case jointly with Wolsey and declare the King's marriage null, if the facts seemed to warrant it. Campeggio was also instructed to take no irrevocable action without reference to Rome, to delay taking any action for as long as possible and to do his best to effect a reconciliation between the parties.

The Cardinal reached London in October 1528. He found Henry growing restive and not in the least interested in reconciliation. He appeared so completely satisfied with the justice of his cause, that Campeggio reported 'an angel descending from heaven would be unable to persuade him otherwise'. Catherine proved equally unpersuadable. Henry was taking the prohibition in the Book of Leviticus as a clear statement of God's law, and questioning the power of any Pope to dispense it. Catherine's reply was devastatingly simple. Her marriage to Arthur had never been consummated. She had been *virgo intacta* when she married Henry. Therefore his arguments were irrelevant. She was, always had been and always would be the King's true and lawful wife, their daughter was his legitimate heiress. And during the nine years of life which remained to her, Catherine never budged from this stand. She was uninterested in bribes, unimpressed by threats, unmoved by an increasingly mean and spiteful campaign of persecution. If she blasphemed against the sacrament of marriage, she would be damning her immortal soul and consenting to the damnation of her husband's. Apart from this, if she agreed that she had been living in sin, 'the King's harlot', for the past twenty years, then she would be admitting that her whole life had been a useless waste of time; she would be denying her daughter's rights of inheritance; perhaps even more to the point, she would be opening the door for Anne Boleyn. Catherine has been accused by Henry's partisans of being bigoted, pig-headed and perverse but all her deepest instincts as a woman, wife and mother had been outraged and she reacted accordingly. With all the iron courage and stubborn pride of her race, she fought her lonely battle to the end.

By the summer of 1529 Campeggio had run out of delaying tactics and was obliged to convene the legatine court which was to investigate the King of England's marriage. The Queen promptly lodged a formal protest against its jurisdiction and appealed to the Pope to decide the case himself. But she did make one appearance before the Cardinal's court. Kneeling at her husband's feet in the great hall at Blackfriars, she begged him, for all the love that had been between them, to let her have justice and right and to take some pity on her. She reminded him that she had always been a true, humble and obedient wife, ever comformable to his will and pleasure. 'And when ye had me at the first', she went on, 'I take God to be my judge, I was a true maid without touch of man; and whether it be true or no, I put it to your conscience.' Henry looked straight ahead, stony-faced. Catherine finished her speech. Then she rose from her knees, curtsied and turned to go, leaning on the arm of her gentleman usher – the same Griffith ap Rhys who had ridden in to Ludlow with his father all those years ago to take service with the Princess of Wales. When Griffith ventured to point out that the court crier was summoning her to return, Catherine answered 'it makes no matter, for it is no indifferent court for me. Therefore I will not tarry.' 'And thus', says George Cavendish, an eyewitness of the scene, 'she departed out of that court without any further answer . . . nor would never appear in any court after.'

Catherine had been quite right when she said that she would never get a fair hearing in any English court. At Blackfriars only one person, John Fisher, Bishop

Cardinal Thomas Wolsey by
Jacques le Boucq.

of Rochester, once the spiritual director and close friend of Margaret Beaufort, had the courage to contradict Margaret's grandson. Much of the court's time was taken up in a pointless and distasteful wrangle about the Queen's virginity at the time of her second marriage, and with hearing witnesses who had been present at the public bedding of the Prince and Princess of Wales more than a quarter of a century before. These individuals obligingly dredged their memories for details which would convince Campeggio that there had been carnal copulation but, as Cavendish sensibly remarked, this was a matter on which no man could know the truth. Anyway, it all turned out to be a waste of time. There was another shift in the see-saw pattern of European politics and the Pope, yielding to Imperial pressure, transferred any further hearing of the case to the Roman courts.

This marked the beginning of the end for Thomas Wolsey – the first major casualty in the long, blood-stained battle for the divorce. Predictably he became the scapegoat for Henry's rage and disappointment, and by October the Emperor's new ambassador in London was reporting that the downfall of the Cardinal seemed complete. Messire Eustace Chapuys added that the King and his 'Lady' had come up from Greenwich to cast an appraising eye over the treasures of York House and had been surprised and pleased by what they found.

The King's domestic arrangements at this time were, to put it mildly, unusual.

Anne Boleyn now went with him everywhere and 'kept an estate more like a Queen than a simple maid'. She had her own apartments at Greenwich, Henry's favourite residence, and was receiving all the attention due to a royal bride-to-be. Meanwhile, in another part of the palace, Queen Catherine, ignoring the existence of her rival with well-bred indifference, continued to preside over the household, mending her husband's shirts and seeing to his comfort just as she had always done. Such a situation, while not without its comic side, inevitably led to friction and on one occasion, after a lot of talking and raised voices, Henry was seen to leave his wife's room in a hurry looking 'very disconcerted and downcast'. He got no sympathy from Anne who told him that Catherine would always get the better of him in argument. 'Some fine morning you will give in to her persuasions', cried Anne, 'and then you will cast me off.' And she went on to reproach her harassed sweetheart, reminding him that she had been waiting a long time – nearly three years now – and was sacrificing her youth, her chances of making an honourable marriage and having children, all apparently to no purpose.

That December, Thomas Boleyn, Viscount Rochford, was created Earl of Wiltshire and at a splendid banquet held to mark the occasion, his daughter took precedence even over the Duchesses of Suffolk and Norfolk, occupying the place of honour at the King's side – a place usually occupied by the Queen. 'After dinner', wrote Eustace Chapuys scornfully, 'there was dancing and carousing, so that it seemed as if nothing were wanting but the priest to give away the nuptial ring and pronounce the blessing.'

But appearances were deceptive and although the Pope was being pressed by both sides to come to a decision, he had still not even begun to hear the case. Henry was already threatening to break with Rome if judgement went against him. But as long as no judgement was given, the pious and conservative King might hesitate to take such a drastic step – or so at least the Holy Father seems to have reasoned. Then again, the problem might go away of its own accord. One of the disputants might die, or Henry might tire of Anne – most people, naturally enough, believed she was already his mistress. There was also just a faint hope that the disapproval of his subjects might force the King to go back to his wife.

Certainly popular disapproval of the divorce in general and of Anne in particular was strong among all classes of Englishmen and their wives, especially their wives – Anne was once nearly lynched by an angry mob of women. But no amount of disapproval, at home or abroad, could touch the King's passionate attachment for his Lady. Her will was law, reported one ambassador and Henry sometimes gave the impression of being rather frightened of her. Chapuys, who had quickly become Queen Catherine's devoted champion, described one interview with the King during which Henry took every opportunity to bring up the subject of the divorce, speaking of it 'with much eagerness'. The ambassador, though, had caught sight of Anne eavesdropping at a window overlooking the gallery where he and the King were talking and took a malicious pleasure in bringing forward his best arguments in favour of the Queen, so that Henry, 'fearing lest the Lady might overhear something that would offend her', steered him away into the middle of the room.

It was during the year 1530 that the King first began to see a way through his matrimonial difficulties. Really it was very simple. If the Pope would not give him a divorce, then he must manage without the Pope. If he assumed supreme religious power in his own realm, the clergy would become dependent on the King and would soon learn to do as they were told; the appearance of law could be preserved and the very considerable wealth of the church in England would be at the disposal of the Crown. This radical solution may have been suggested by Henry's new secretary, Thomas Cromwell – certainly his was the administrative genius which turned it into a practical possibility – but the idea itself somehow bears the stamp of Henry's ruthless single-mindedness in the pursuit of his own way.

The general momentum of events now quickened perceptibly. In July 1531 Henry finally separated from his wife. He had been away on a hunting trip, accompanied as usual by Anne, and sent a message back to Windsor ordering the Queen to leave the Court before his return. He never saw her again. In May 1532 the English church finally surrendered its ancient, jealously guarded immunity from lay authority. In August death removed the last obstacle in the King's path. William Warham, Archbishop of Canterbury, was old and sick and frightened, but he had always steadfastly refused to defy the Pope's ban on any re-opening of the 'Great Matter' in an English court. Now he was gone, and the King and Thomas Cromwell knew just the man to replace him. Thomas Cranmer, an obscure don from Jesus College, Cambridge and one-time chaplain to the Boleyn family, was a gentle, mild-mannered individual who could be trusted to obey orders.

In October 1532 Anne Boleyn, decked out in Queen Catherine's jewels, was to accompany the King on a state visit to France; but before the ambiguous couple crossed the Channel another event of considerable significance had taken place. With victory in sight, Anne had at last surrendered the citadel and had given Henry what he had been waiting for since 1526. In return, she was created Marquess of Pembroke in her own right, with an independent income of a thousand pounds a year. Further reward came the following January, when she and Henry were married under conditions of great secrecy in a turret room at Whitehall, 'very early before day' in the presence of only three witnesses. This furtive ceremony was performed by Dr Rowland, the King's chaplain, 'to whom the King told that now he had gotten of the Pope a licence to marry another wife'.

If Henry really told his chaplain that he had a licence from the Pope, it was a flat lie, but the reason for it soon became apparent. Towards the end of February 1533 Eustace Chapuys heard how Anne Boleyn had emerged from her private apartments into the gallery, where a crowd of people was milling about. Seeing a particular friend among the company – it may very likely have been Sir Thomas Wyatt – she cried out to him that for the past three days she had had an 'incredible fierce desire to eat apples'. The King had told her it was a sign she was with child but she said no, no, it couldn't be. And then, with one of her sudden, disconcerting shrieks of laughter, she turned and disappeared back into her rooms, leaving the onlookers staring at one another 'abashed and uneasy'.

In fact, Anne must have been nearly three months pregnant by this time and Henry would have to move fast if her child was to be born in wedlock. In March, Thomas Cranmer was consecrated Archbishop. In April, the last shreds of

Title page of The noble tryumphaunt coronacyon of quene Anne, *1533.*

reticence about the exact nature of Anne's position were cast aside. On Easter Saturday she went to Mass in royal state for the first time, 'loaded with diamonds and other precious stones and dressed in a gorgeous suit of gold tissue'. She was now being officially prayed for as Queen – this caused more than one congregation to walk out in protest – and the nobility, with the King's watchful eye fixed on them, were required to pay their respects to her. Chapuys reported that the whole thing seemed like a dream and even her own supporters did not know whether to laugh or cry.

On 10 May Thomas Cranmer set up his court at Dunstable to enquire into the King's 'great cause of matrimony' and by 28 May had pronounced Henry's first marriage null and void and his second good and lawful. Three days later, Anne, now visibly pregnant, rode in triumph through the City to her coronation, wearing a necklace of pearls as big as chick peas, her splendid mane of black hair hanging loose about her shoulders.

On 1 June, Queen Anne went in procession from Westminster Hall 'with all the monks of Westminster going in copes of gold, with thirteen abbots mitred and after them all the King's Chapel with four bishops and two archbishops, and all the lords in their Parliament robes'. The crown was carried before her by Charles Brandon, Duke of Suffolk and her two sceptres by two earls. She herself walked under a canopy of cloth of gold, wearing a kirtle of crimson velvet under a robe of purple velvet furred with ermine, a rich coronet with a caul of pearls on her head. 'And so was she brought to the Abbey of St Peter's at Westminster', wrote a contemporary chronicler, 'and there was she anointed and crowned by the Archbishop of Canterbury and the Archbishop of York.'

This was Anne's moment of glory – not since the days of Elizabeth of York had so much honour been paid to a Queen consort. She is said to have complained that she saw too many caps on heads and heard too few 'God save you's' as she passed through the streets, but that scarcely mattered. She was safely married and safely crowned. If her child was a boy and healthy, nothing would matter.

Preparations were now under way for the all-important confinement. Henry, reported Eustace Chapuys, apparently believing implicitly in the bulletins being fed to him by the court physicians and astrologers, was confident that his Lady would give him a male heir and had made up his mind to celebrate the event with a pageant and tournament. But, Chapuys also reported that there had been a definite coldness lately between the newly married pair. Anne, it seemed, had already been given some cause for jealousy, but when she complained the King had told her brutally that she must learn to shut her eyes and endure, as her betters had had to do. The ambassador added regretfully that he thought this was only a 'love quarrel' – all the same it was a red light, the first indication that the honeymoon was over.

Towards the end of August the Court moved from Windsor to Greenwich, where Henry himself had been born, and there at about three o'clock in the afternoon of Sunday 7 September Anne give birth to 'a fair daughter'. It was a bitter and grievous disappointment. Henry had turned the world upside down, made powerful enemies abroad and alienated some powerful people at home all for another useless girl. Not only had he failed to secure the succession (in fact, he had made matters rather worse by introducing a new element of doubt and confusion), but he had once more demonstrated to a sniggering Europe his unfortunate inability to get sons – especially embarrassing this for such a flamboyantly masculine figure as the King of England.

There was nothing to be done except put the best possible face on it. A Te Deum for Anne's safe delivery was sung in St Paul's Cathedral and on 10 September the newest member of the Tudor family, named after her Plantagenet grandmother, was christened with all due ceremony in the Friars' Church at Greenwich. Archbishop Cranmer stood godfather and when the baby had been brought to the font and baptized by the Bishop of London, Garter King of Arms prayed sonorously that God of his infinite goodness would send prosperous life and long to the high and mighty Princess of England, Elizabeth.

CHAPTER 7

England's Treasure

God save King Henry with all his power,
And Prince Edward, that goodly flower,
With all his lords of great honour –
Sing on, troll away, sing, troll on away
Heave and how, rumbelow, troll on away.

For Anne Boleyn the birth of Elizabeth brought the beginning of fear. In January of 1534 there was a rumour that she was pregnant again but either she miscarried at a very early stage or, more likely, the rumour was a false one. In March the Pope at long last pronounced judgement on the King's first marriage – judgement in Catherine's favour. Almost simultaneously Parliament at Westminster passed the Act of Succession recognizing the legality of Henry's second marriage and entailing the crown on Anne's children. It now became high treason to question the validity of the divorce by deed or writing and, to drive the point home, every member of Parliament, 'all the curates and priests in London and throughout England' and 'every man in the shires and towns where they dwelled' were required to swear a solemn oath 'to be true to Queen Anne and to believe and take her for lawful wife of the King and rightful Queen of England'. In one sense, of course, this set the final seal on Anne's victory, but it also underlined her obligation to fulfil her side of the bargain and provide the country with a Prince of Wales.

In April the King and Queen were at Eltham with their baby daughter, 'as goodly a child as hath been seen' gushed somebody, and my Lady Princess was noticed to be much in her father's favour, 'as goodly child should be, God save her'. Henry never could resist babies, but while he fondled and played with the six-month-old Elizabeth there were ominous signs that her mother no longer occupied a similarly favoured position. By mid-summer rumours that the Queen was pregnant were going round again, but again nothing came of it. By September Chapuys was writing that 'since the King began to entertain doubts as to his concubine's reported pregnancy, he has renewed and increased his love to another very handsome young lady of this court'. The young lady's name is not mentioned, but it is possible that Henry was already becoming attracted by pale, prim Jane Seymour.

Anne tried to get rid of the girl, and Chapuys heard that Henry had told his concubine to be satisfied with what he had done for her; that 'were he to begin again, he would certainly not do as much; that she ought to consider where she came from, and many other things of the same kind'. But although the Emperor's ambassador lovingly collected scraps of gossip like this, he still believed that no great importance should be attached to them, 'considering the King's fickleness and the astuteness of the Lady, who knows perfectly well how to deal with him'. Everyone was so conditioned by this time to the idea of Anne's power over the King, that at first it was difficult to grasp that her magic had begun to desert her. All the same, by the end of the year, it was clear to any discerning observer that Henry's grand passion had burnt itself out, leaving only cold, sour ashes behind. Anne's growing sense of insecurity drove her on into making scenes which bored and irritated him, and the elegant, lively dark-eyed girl was becoming a shrill, haggard virago, who could not always control her hysterical outbursts and made no attempt at all to control her bitter tongue.

But although his domestic problems were potentially worrying, the King had other things on his mind during the winter of 1534. In November the Act which declared the King officially and unconditionally Supreme Head of the Church in England came before Parliament, and as from the following February it would be high treason 'maliciously' to deny this startling addition to the royal style. Sir Thomas More, who had a gift for putting things in a nutshell, described the Act of Supremacy as 'a sword with two edges, for if a man answer one way it will destroy the soul, and if he answer another it will destroy the body'. Neither More nor John Fisher, Bishop of Rochester, shared the King's confidence in his special relationship with God; neither was prepared to recognize Henry Tudor as their supreme earthly authority on spiritual matters, and in the summer of 1535 both paid the penalty. As he stood on the scaffold, Thomas More once again summed up the situation in a single telling phrase. 'I die the King's good servant', he said, 'but God's first.'

Thomas More, a scholar renowned throughout the civilized world, and John Fisher, a prince of the Church, were by no means the only men in England who considered their souls more important than their bodies but they were by far the best known and the news of their deaths sent a shockwave of revulsion and dismay around Europe. But Henry had learnt his own strength now. Ironically enough, it was Thomas More who, not long before, had warned Thomas Cromwell 'if a lion knew his own strength, hard were it for any man to rule him'. In future no man, and no woman either, could rule Henry Tudor. The easy-going, malleable young King had gone forever.

Towards the end of the summer Henry went off on a progress through the south-western counties, during which he stayed three nights at Jane Seymour's family home at Wulfhall in Wiltshire. Just what his plans were (if indeed he had any at this stage) we do not know, but he was still sleeping with Anne for in November she was definitely pregnant again. Then, in the first week of January 1536, Catherine of Aragon died at Kimbolton Castle, the gloomy, semi-fortified manor house in the Midlands, where she had been living for the past two years in increasingly miserable seclusion. Henry made no pretence of mourning. 'Thank God we are now free from any suspicion of war', he exclaimed to the Emperor's ambassador and a shocked Chapuys reported that on the day after the news reached the Court, Henry appeared dressed in yellow from head to foot, carrying his bastard daughter (Elizabeth was nearly two-and-a-half now) about in his arms, making a great fuss of her and showing her off to all and sundry.

Anne, also wearing yellow, rejoiced with Henry – at least in public. But she was far too intelligent not to have reflected on the possible consequences of Catherine's death. The King was unlikely to complicate an already complicated situation any further by embarking on a third marriage while his first wife – still regarded, of course, by all orthodox Catholics as his only legal wife – remained alive. He had not dared to kill Catherine as he had killed More and Fisher, and as Chapuys had feared he might, but now that she had at last had the tact to die of natural causes he would find it a great deal easier to make a fresh start.

Catherine was buried at Peterborough on 29 January as Arthur's widow, Dowager Princess of Wales, the title she had so resolutely refused to accept in life, and on that very day 'Queen Anne was brought abed and delivered of a man child before her time, for she said that she had reckoned herself but fifteen weeks gone with child'. Henry had just had a bad fall in the tiltyard which, it was said, caused the Queen to take a fright and fall into travail. But according to gossip, it was not so much concern for her husband's welfare as jealous rage over his continuing attentions to Jane Seymour which had caused that fatal miscarriage – either that, or her own 'defective constitution'. Whatever the reason, it spelt disaster for Anne who, by a certain rough justice, was now experiencing something of what her predecessor had suffered. Henry showed her no sympathy. He scarcely bothered to speak to her and when the pre-Lenten festivities began, went off to 'disport himself' in London without her – an ominous contrast to the days when he could not bear to have her out of his sight for more than half-an-hour at a time. Chapuys heard that the King was telling certain close friends, in the strictest confidence, that he had been tricked into his second marriage by charms and witchcraft and therefore considered it to be null and void. God obviously shared this view and was manifesting his displeasure by denying him male children. By Easter it was obvious that the end would not be long in coming. Anne had failed and, like Thomas Wolsey before her, she must pay the price of failure.

Secretary of State Thomas Cromwell knew what was expected of him. A discreet whisper in a receptive royal ear that treason was brewing and it might be as well to set some enquiries on foot, and the thing was as good as done. The arrests began on 1 May. Mark Smeaton the lute-player, Henry Norris, Francis Weston and William Brereton of the Privy Chamber, and Anne's brother George were taken to the Tower. On the following day the Queen herself was brought up-river from Greenwich to share the imprisonment of the five men accused of having been her lovers.

Apart from her adultery with 'divers of the King's familiar servants' and incest, inciting her own natural brother to violate her by 'alluring him with her tongue in his mouth and his tongue in hers', Anne was charged with despising her marriage and entertaining malice against the King. She and her lovers were said to have conspired the King's death and Anne was also accused of promising to marry one of them after the King was dead and of affirming 'that she would never love the King in her heart'.

No shred of evidence was ever produced to substantiate any of these charges – unless a 'confession' extorted from the poor terrified musician Mark Smeaton counted as evidence. Anne had undoubtedly been indiscreet, perhaps recklessly so. When Henry began to seek his pleasures elsewhere, relegating her to the role of brood mare, she seems to have turned more and more to the company of the young professional gallants who thronged the Court, allowing, even encouraging them to flirt with her. She may have known she was playing with fire and have enjoyed doing it, but it is hard to believe that she would have deliberately burnt her fingers.

The government was making the most of the horrid scandal of the Queen's adultery and the stories of her 'abominable and detestable crimes' and her 'incontinent living' soon became so exaggerated that the more level-headed started to discount them. Henry, of course, believed them all – or said he did. He told the Bishop of Carlisle excitedly that he believed Anne had had to do with more than a hundred men. He had long been expecting something of this sort to happen and had written a tragedy on the subject which he carried about with him in his bosom! 'You never saw prince or man who made greater show of his horns or bore them more pleasantly', commented Eustace Chapuys. Certainly for a man who believed he had been cuckolded on such a grand scale Henry appeared to be in excellent spirits and the Court had seldom been gayer. Jane Seymour was now installed in a house on the river and being visited regularly by the King who would return to Greenwich late at night, his barge filled with minstrels and musicians playing and singing lustily. 'This state of affairs', wrote Chapuys, 'has been compared by many to the joy and pleasure a man feels in getting rid of a thin, old, vicious hack in the hope of having soon a fine horse to ride.' Although no one felt much sympathy for Anne personally (only gentle Archbishop Cranmer showed any real compassion), some people were not happy about the way the proceedings against her were being conducted. Many people felt that Henry's blatant courtship of another woman while his wife lay in prison awaiting trial for her life was not the sort of behaviour generally expected of a monarch and a gentleman.

Anne's trial took place on 15 May. It was, of course, a mere formality but the Queen faced her judges with courage and dignity and heard the sentence, pronounced by her uncle Norfolk, of burning or beheading at the King's pleasure without flinching. She was ready for death, she said, and only regretted that so many innocent men were to die for her sake. The other prisoners died two days later and Anne's execution was fixed for the eighteenth. But there was a last minute delay, caused by the King's determination to have his second marriage annulled. Thomas Cromwell had tried to prove a pre-contract between Anne and Henry Percy, but the now Earl of Northumberland denied this so furiously and so categorically that Cromwell had been obliged to fall back on Henry's own misconduct with Anne's elder sister. This was embarrassing because, since canon law made no distinction between a licit and an illicit relationship, the King's intercourse with Mary Boleyn made Anne as much his sister-in-law as ever Catherine of Aragon had been – an inconvenient fact which Henry had always been careful to ignore. However, this was no time to be fussy about details and on

18 May Thomas Cranmer obediently provided a decree of nullity. The fact that Anne was to die for adultery having never been a wife was brushed aside as another unimportant detail.

During the time since her arrest Anne's moods had fluctuated wildly between resignation, hope and hysteria. 'One hour she is determined to die and the next hour much contrary to that', reported William Kingston, Constable of the Tower. But now she was anxious to make an end. The stories of her impatience and her unseasonable high spirits are well known and William Kingston was greatly disconcerted by his prisoner's shrieks of merriment and the rather tasteless jokes she would keep making about the smallness of her neck. It was not at all what Kingston was used to. 'I have seen many men and also women executed', he wrote, 'and all they have been in great sorrow. But to my knowledge this lady had much joy and pleasure in death.'

Death came at eight o'clock on the morning of 19 May when Anne was brought out on to the little square of greensward where the carpenters had been hammering and shouting all the previous night as they put up the scaffold. The Queen had dressed carefully for her last public appearance, wearing a long robe of grey damask over a crimson underskirt, and looked, according to one eyewitness, 'as gay as if she was not going to die'. The executioner, specially imported from Calais at a cost of £23 6s 8d, drew his sword from its hiding place in a pile of straw and it was all over. Head and trunk were bundled into a makeshift coffin and buried that same afternoon in the chapel of St Peter-ad-Vincula hard by the execution ground. There were no mourners and it was left to Eustace Chapuys, Anne's bitterest enemy, to pay her a final tribute. 'No one ever showed more courage or greater readiness to meet death than she did', he commented in a despatch to the emperor dated 19 May, and went on to tell his master that he had been told by a reliable source that both before and after receiving the sacrament Anne had sworn, on the peril of her soul's damnation, that she had never been unfaithful to the King.

The King who had loved her and destroyed her wasted no time on mourning, not even on a decent interval of widowerhood. On 20 May he and Jane Seymour were betrothed in a private ceremony at Chelsea, and ten days later they were married in the chapel of York Place. Henry's third wife was a small, quiet, colourless blonde in her late twenties, undistinguished by looks or noble birth. She had served both her predecessors as maid of honour, but her loyalties were said to be with Queen Catherine. For this reason Chapuys welcomed the marriage, for he hoped and believed that the new Queen would befriend Catherine's daughter.

Mary Tudor had suffered cruelly as a result of her parents' divorce, enduring insult, humiliation, personal sorrow and physical fear which permanently ruined her health and spoilt her disposition. She had always ranged herself beside her mother on the domestic battlefront as, quite apart from her strong natural affections and deep religious convictions, she was bound to do – for if she admitted the justice of her father's case, she would be admitting her own illegitimacy and denying her rights of inheritance.

During the early years of the struggle Mary had been left more or less alone,

Jane Seymour; a portrait by Holbein.

living in one or other of the royal manor houses scattered about the Home Counties and still chaperoned by her friend and Lady Governess, Margaret Countess of Salisbury. She had not seen her mother since Catherine's expulsion from the Court in 1531, but she knew well enough what was happening to her and had been obliged to watch in helpless rage and misery while the wicked – especially Anne Boleyn – flourished and Catherine's predicament grew steadily worse. This was damaging enough for a sensitive adolescent but it was not until the birth of Elizabeth that Mary's troubles began in earnest.

Just as the King could not have two rival Queens in his realm without running the risk of looking ridiculous, he could not have two rival heiresses without running even more serious risks. Towards the end of September 1533, Mary's chamberlain, Lord Hussey, was instructed to inform the Princess of her father's pleasure 'concerning the diminishing of her high estate'. Mary, standing full on her seventeen-year-old dignity, froze the embarrassed chamberlain with a cold Tudor eye. She was 'much astonished' that Hussey should have the impertinence to declare such a thing without a written authority from the King. A few days later came an order from William Paulet, Comptroller of the Royal Household, that Mary was to leave her present home, Newhall in Essex, for Hertford Castle. Mary demanded to be shown Paulet's letter and there, for the first time in black and white, she saw herself baldly described as 'the Lady Mary, the King's daughter'. She tried sending a letter to her father, in the faint hope that a personal appeal might be able to move him, 'for I doubt not', she wrote with pathetic optimism, 'but you take me for your lawful daughter born in true matrimony. If I agreed to the contrary I should offend God; in all other things Your Highness shall find me an obedient daughter.'

Henry's response was to send a commission, headed by Dr Simpson, Dean of the King's Chapel, to visit Mary at Newhall. The King had been surprised and pained to hear that his daughter had so far forgotten her filial duty and allegiance as to 'arrogantly usurp the title of Princess' and pretend to be his heir presumptive. The commissioners proceeded solemnly to warn her of the folly and danger of her conduct and to point out that if she persisted, she would worthily deserve the King's 'high displeasure and punishment by law'. However, if she repented and conformed to his will, he might be graciously pleased 'of his fatherly pity' to forgive her and even to promote her welfare.

Mary may have been prepared for a rebuff, but to be accused of 'arrogantly usurping' a title she had held since birth and to be so accused by the one whose paternity had conferred that title on her was something monstrous enough to destroy her sense of identity for ever. But the former Princess of England had inherited stubborn characteristics from both her parents; she had her religious faith and her mother's indomitable example to support her; she would not conform and so the battle between father and daughter was joined.

Mary did not have long to wait for the first consequence of her defiance. Early in November Eustace Chapuys heard with horror that 'not content with having taken away from his own legitimate daughter the name and title of Princess', the King was threatening to make her go and live as maid of honour to his base-born daughter. Not was this an idle threat. A separate household had been set up for the baby Elizabeth at the old bishop's palace at Hatfield and about a week before Christmas 1533, the Duke of Norfolk descended on Mary at Hertford Castle and bundled her off at half-an-hour's notice to join the nursery establishment.

Mary had always known her father as a kindly, affectionate figure who used to carry her about in his arms showing her off proudly to foreign visitors and had once teased her at a solemn state function by pulling off her cap, so that her long reddish blonde hair had tumbled down over her shoulders. Now he seemed to have become a totally different person. Like her mother, Mary naturally ascribed this terrifying change to the malign influence of Anne Boleyn and at Hatfield she would be living in a house ruled by Anne's relations. But if Mary was afraid she never showed it. When Norfolk asked her whether she did not think she should pay her respects to the princess, she answered fiercely that she knew of no princess in England except herself. If, with splendid scorn, the King acknowledged Madame of Pembroke's daughter as his own, then Mary would call her sister, just as she called Henry Fitzroy brother, but no more. Well then, said Norfolk, had she any message for the King? None, came the immediate retort, 'except that the Princess of Wales, his daughter, asks for his blessing'. Norfolk told her roundly that he dared not deliver such a message. 'Then go away', cried Mary, 'and leave me alone.'

She was about to learn what it meant to be truly alone. Shut up at Hatfield,

Mary Tudor as a young girl; a drawing by Holbein.

given (so Chapuys heard) the worst room in the house and forced to eat all her meals in the crowded Great Hall Mary was also learning the bitter lessons taught by impotence, hatred and injustice. When Henry came to visit Elizabeth, she was kept out of sight. Chapuys believed this was Anne's doing, that she was afraid the King's resolution might weaken if he saw his elder daughter. Chapuys also heard that Anne had sent a message to her aunt, Lady Shelton, now Mary's 'governess', telling her to give the girl a box on the ears 'for the cursed bastard she is'.

If any news was reaching Mary from her mother, it cannot have made her life any easier to bear. At about the same time as she was taken to Hatfield, a deputation headed by the Duke of Suffolk had gone to Catherine, then at Buckden in Huntingdonshire, to make another attempt to bully her into accepting the title of Princess Dowager. But Catherine was not taking anything from Charles Brandon. She told him flatly that she still considered herself to be Henry's Queen and his legal wife, and that she would 'rather be hewn in pieces than depart from this assertion'. The Duke had orders to move her to Somersham, a house situated in the marshy wastes of the Fen country and a notoriously unhealthy spot. Catherine refused to go. It would, she declared, be tantamount to conniving at her own death. She locked herself in her bedroom and told Suffolk through a crack in the wall that if he wanted to take her, he would have to break down the door and bind her with ropes. This was too much for Charles Brandon, already a reluctant emissary, and nothing more was said about Somersham, but shortly afterwards the former Queen of England was transferred to Kimbolton. There, ignoring the existence of those household officers sworn to her as Princess Dowager, she confined herself to her own room, waited on by the handful of faithful Spaniards still with her, who cooked her food before her eyes for fear of poison.

While it is impossible to justify Henry's treatment of his discarded wife and elder daughter in any human terms, he did have some political excuse for his apparent ferocity. Catherine and Mary were both the objects of considerable popular sympathy and, as long as they continued to stand out against him, would make a natural rallying point for all those people who hated his new order. This applied especially to Mary, still regarded as the true heiress by the majority of Englishmen, and it was she who now had to bear the brunt of her father's ruthless intimidation.

Some time during the spring of 1534 the royal commissioners visited the Princess Elizabeth's household to exact the Oath of Succession from its inmates – that oath which, among other things, required the lieges to take the Lady Mary 'but as a bastard and thus to do without any scruple of conscience'. The Lady Mary, of course, refused to swear. Not that it mattered, Lady Shelton told her roughly. It did not matter whether she surrendered her title or not, she was still a bastard whatever she did. But, added the lady, if she were the King, she would kick Mary out of the house for her disobedience and then she said something else which brought a new and colder fear.

Mary at this time had no means of communicating with Chapuys, the only friend she seemed to have, but terror sharpened her wits. She asked to see 'a physician who formerly was her tutor and usual doctor' who happened to be staying in the house. A private interview was refused but somehow she had to find a way of using this man as a messenger. She was able to see him in public and told him she had been so long without speaking Latin that now she could hardly say two words correctly. The doctor, unwittingly picking up his cue, suggested she should try and Mary, knowing that no one else in the room would be able to understand, told him that the King had been heard to say, only the day before, that he would have her beheaded for disobeying the laws of the kingdom. 'Hearing which', wrote Chapuys, 'the physician was much astonished and knew not what to answer, except that the Princess's Latin was not very good and he could not understand it.' However, the small desperate subterfuge worked. The good doctor had understood enough of what his former pupil was trying to tell him and passed it on to Chapuys.

Lady Shelton's spite regardless, Mary's treatment actually improved a little during the summer. She was allowed more servants and, by their means, was able to reopen her secret correspondence with Chapuys. But she saw any improvement as a trap of some sort intended to take her off her guard and told Chapuys – she was eighteen-and-a-half now – that her only hope was to die. She did, in fact, become seriously ill soon afterwards. Thomas Cromwell had been hinting that a lot of problems would disappear if only God would decide to take the Lady Mary to himself; but it would, nevertheless, have been highly embarrassing for the government if she were to die in her present circumstances and one of the royal physicians was sent to visit her. Dr Buttes, a sensible, kindly man, suggested that the girl should be sent to be with her mother who, at least, could not be suspected of trying to poison her. Catherine got wind of this scheme and, grasping at a sudden straw of hope, wrote to Chapuys begging him to try and persuade the King 'to do such a charity as to send his daughter and mine where I am'. She would nurse Mary herself and the 'comfort and mirth' they would have together would be half her cure. But Henry refused to contemplate such a thing. Catherine and Mary were causing him enough trouble separated – let them once be together and all the effort he had been expending on trying to break Mary's will would be wasted. He also hinted that he suspected a security risk.

Although Catherine indignantly denied any knowledge of a plot, Chapuys had for some time been investigating the possibilities of getting Mary out of the country. He thought it should not be too difficult, provided the princess was somewhere fairly close to London and if an oared boat, independent of the tides and strong enough to fight off pursuit, was ready to take her to the mouth of the Thames, where one of the Emperor's ships would be waiting.

In April 1535 it looked as if an opportunity had come. Mary had been at Greenwich with Elizabeth but had then been suddenly moved to a house about twelve miles from the river. Chapuys reported that it would be comparatively easy for a party of well mounted men to snatch her while she was out walking (it would be better to make it look like kidnapping for Mary's own sake) and put her on board a ship below Gravesend. Mary herself was only too willing to co-operate, but the ambassador dared not act without authority. 'The matter is hazardous', he wrote conscientiously to the Emperor, 'and Your Majesty will take it into due consideration.' The Emperor would have liked to be able to rescue his cousin – he had been doing his best to persuade Henry to allow her to make a suitable marriage – but to abduct the daughter of a brother monarch smacked uncomfortably of brigandage. Charles was a cautious man. He considered too long and the opportunity was lost. There would be no great adventure for Mary – no wild ride across the Essex marshes to the sea. She fell ill again. The summer passed and her hopes of deliverance faded.

As autumn approached Chapuys could smell danger on the wind. He could get no access to Mary and all his persistent, nagging protests and enquiries met with the same stonewalling response. There was not the slightest need for anyone to feel anxious about the Lady Mary, Cromwell assured him blandly, since no one was more concerned for her welfare than her own father. But Henry had tasted blood that year and Anne, who feared and hated Mary, was still beside him. Chapuys believed that the concubine would not rest until she had engineered the death of the legitimate heiress. He and Catherine were both afraid that the King meant to put Mary to the test over the Oath of Succession when Parliament met again. Then Catherine died – and even when her illness was known to be mortal Henry would not allow her daughter to go to her. A few months later Anne, too, was gone. For Mary at least this altered everything. She waited a week and then wrote to Thomas Cromwell asking him to open the way for a reconciliation with her father – to obtain for her 'his Grace's blessing and favour'. She would have written sooner, she told Cromwell, only she knew that no one would dare to speak for her as long as 'that woman' lived.

Mary was still clinging to the belief that all her own and her mother's sufferings, all the sufferings which had fallen on other loyal and orthodox Catholics, were due to the evil influence of 'that woman'; that Henry remained at heart the same good-natured, conventionally pious man she remembered from her childhood, and now that he was no longer bewitched by the she-devil everything would somehow come right again. This was not a very realistic attitude but it was a very understandable one. Mary had not seen her father to speak to for five years and she had no conception of the quality of the change in him. Anne Boleyn had for so long been a convenient scapegoat that both Mary and Catherine had been able to shut their eyes to the truth. Neither had faced the fact that Anne had merely provided the catalyst; that the transformation of a loved and loving husband and father into a cold, unfeeling despot was due to characteristics inherent in his own nature. Catherine had been spared the bitter awakening. Mary was not.

At first all seemed to be well. Thomas Cromwell, a practical man of affairs, could see no sense in the continuing estrangement between the King and his elder daughter. To him, these destructive family quarrels were both a waste of time and an unnecessary political complication. So, as God was apparently not going to assist by removing Mary, Cromwell cast himself in the role of peacemaker. He got permission for Mary to write to the King which she did, 'in as humble and lowly manner as is possible for a child to use to her father', begging forgiveness for all her offences and 'beseeching your Highness to consider that I am but a woman and your child, who hath committed her soul only to God and her body to be ordered in this world as it shall stand with your pleasure.' She ended by congratulating Henry on his new marriage and assuring him that she was praying God to 'send your Grace shortly a prince'.

The only response to this painful effort was a letter from Cromwell, enclosing the draft of a formal apology which he advised her to copy. The draft was abject enough and Mary duly made two copies which she returned to Cromwell with a covering letter, telling him that she had now done 'the uttermost my conscience will suffer me'. But when Cromwell read his copy he found that Mary had added a fatal reservation – she was prepared to submit to her father 'next to Almighty God'. This was not good enough and Cromwell wrote again, more sharply this time, for Henry's temper was rising. The Secretary enclosed another draft, to be copied exactly.

Mary, tormented by neuralgia which gave her 'small rest day or night', knew now that she would be lucky to get away with a general submission, however abject, without being forced to take the dreaded Oath of Succession. She was no longer in a position to quibble over a form of words and she copied Cromwell's second draft without 'adding or minishing' – only one copy though, for she 'cannot endure to write another'. Still it was not enough, and a commission – headed by that bird of ill-omen, the Duke of Norfolk – came down to her at Hunsdon in Hertfordshire. They brought with them a document for her signature, a document which spelt out Henry's terms for unconditional surrender.

When Mary refused to sign, the behaviour of the commissioners effectually extinguished any lingering hopes of making peace with honour. She was such an unnatural daughter, cried one, that he doubted if she was even the King's bastard. Another added pleasantly that if she were his daughter, he would beat her to death and knock her head against a wall until it was as soft as a baked apple. They told her she had shown herself a traitor to the King and his laws and would be punished as such. Finally, they said she might have four days to think the matter over and ordered Lady Shelton to see that she made no contact with the outside world and not to leave her alone for a moment, either by day or night.

In spite of this, Mary did manage to make two last frantic appeals – one to Eustace Chapuys, the other to Thomas Cromwell. But the ambassador, for so long her faithful friend and ally, could only advise her to yield if she felt her life was really in danger. Trying to comfort her, he wrote that God looked more at the intentions than the deeds of men and she would be better able to serve him in the future if she gave way now. As for Thomas Cromwell, he was discovering the perils of getting trapped between two battling Tudors and was badly frightened. He told Chapuys that for several days he had considered himself a dead man, for when the commissioners reported their failure with his daughter the King had flown into a towering rage and had been heard to swear that not only Mary should suffer for her obstinacy but many others, including Cromwell.

In his reply to Mary's last cry for help, the Secretary made his feelings abundantly clear. 'To be plain with you, madam', he wrote, 'I think you the most obstinate and obdurate woman that ever was.' If Mary did not speedily abandon the 'sinister counsels' which had brought her to 'the point of utter undoing', Cromwell wanted nothing more to do with her ever again; she had shown herself such an unnatural and ungrateful daughter to her 'most dear and benign father' that she was not fit to live in a Christian congregation. All the same, he gave her one last chance, sending her 'a certain book of articles' which she was to sign and return with a declaration that she thought in heart as she had subscribed with hand.

When Cromwell's letter reached her, Mary knew that she was beaten. For very nearly three years she had fought gallantly to defend her principles and her good name. As long as her mother lived and, for that matter, as long as Anne Boleyn was alive, she had been armoured against all attack but now, utterly alone, ill, exhausted and despairing she gave in. At eleven o'clock on a Thursday night about the middle of June, she signed the 'book of articles' recognizing 'the King's highness to be supreme head on earth under Christ of the Church of England' and utterly refusing 'the Bishop of Rome's pretended authority, power and jurisdiction within this realm'. She also acknowledged that her mother's marriage had been 'by God's law and man's law incestuous and unlawful'.

Her reward came about three weeks later, when she was brought from Hunsdon 'secretly in the night' to Hackney for a private interview with the King. According to Chapuys it was impossible to exaggerate Henry's kind and affectionate behaviour on this occasion. 'There was nothing but conversing with the princess in private, and with such love and affection and such brilliant promises for the future that no father could have behaved better towards his daughter.'

Chapuys, of course, was enormously relieved that the crisis had been resolved and so, it is clear, was Henry. Whether or not he would really have treated his daughter as he had treated Thomas More and John Fisher we shall never know, but many people close to him had believed that he might – as the King intended they should. Most likely it had all been a war of nerves – pressure applied relentlessly until the victim finally cracked under it. It is easy to dismiss Henry as a monster for his brutal treatment of Mary, but it was becoming increasingly necessary to secure her capitulation. Serious unrest was brewing in the north, where opposition to the King's revolutionary politics was strongest and where a variety of social, economic and religious discontents presently erupted in the Pilgrimage of Grace. Mary represented the old, familiar ways and she had many friends and sympathizers among the older, more conservative nobility and gentry. Until she herself had renounced her birthright, there was a real enough danger that she might be used as a figurehead for rebellion at home and even invasion from abroad.

This, at least, is the explanation usually given and it is a perfectly viable one – as far as it goes; but it takes no account of the dark undercurrents of pride and passion, fear, hate and guilt flowing beneath the surface. Henry needed to break his daughter for political reasons but he needed to win the battle for other reasons, too. Catherine had defeated and escaped him – he could not endure that Mary should do the same. Nor could he endure any reminder of the past he put behind him, the guilt he had buried and purged. Now everything was all right again and Mary was once more his 'dear and well-beloved daughter'. And, astonishingly, she really was. Henry was genuinely fond and proud of all his children – so long, of course, as they showed no signs of having minds and wills of their own.

For Mary it was not so simple. She rode back to Hunsdon with a fine diamond ring, a present from Queen Jane, on her finger and a cheque for a thousand crowns from her father, together with an assurance that she need not worry about money in the future. But none of this could help her in the anguish of her remorse. Mary did not possess Henry's monumental capacity for self-deception and, although she begged Chapuys to ask the Pope to give her secret absolution for what she had done under duress, nothing would ever alter the fact that she had knowingly betrayed the two things which meant most in the world to her – her religious faith and her mother's memory. That betrayal, made by a frightened girl of twenty, was to haunt her for the rest of her life and help to make her, as she once bitterly described herself, 'the most unhappy lady in Christendom'.

Meanwhile, the King's younger daughter, the cause of so much of her sister's unhappiness, was being bastardized and disinherited in her turn. Parliament met in June and passed a second Act of Succession, ratifying the annulment of Henry's second marriage and officially declaring Elizabeth to be illegitimate. The succession was now to be vested in the offspring of Jane Seymour. Failing this, the King was given power to appoint an heir by will or letters patent. Such an unprecedented step shows just how acute the problem was becoming and, not surprisingly, there was renewed talk of naming the Duke of Richmond. As the Earl of Sussex remarked, if all the King's children were bastards, why not choose the boy and have done with it.

But if Henry was seriously considering the idea, he was frustrated, for Henry Fitzroy died on 22 July 1536 'having pined inwardly in his body long before he died' – a victim, almost certainly, of tuberculosis to which the young Tudor males were so fatally susceptible. Richmond seems by all accounts to have been an unusually attractive boy and a loss to the nation. He had been married in 1533 to Mary Howard, the Duke of Norfolk's daughter, and was a close friend of Norfolk's son, the Earl of Surrey, who later celebrated in verse an idyllic year the two young men spent together at Windsor Castle.

> The wild foreste, the clothed holts with greene;
> With reins availed, and swift-y-breathed horse
> With cry of hounds and merry blasts betwene
> Where we did chase the fearful hart of force,
> The voide walls, eke, that harborde us eche night;
> Wherewith, alas! revive within my breast
> The sweet accorde, such slepes as yet delight
> The pleasant dreams, the quiet bed of rest;
> The secret thoughtes, imparted with such trust;
> The wanton talke, the divers change of play;
> The friendship sworne, eche promise kept so just,
> Wherewith we past the winter nightes away.

Chapuys thought that Richmond's death would greatly improve Mary's chances of resuming her proper place as heiress presumptive, but no move was made to reinstate her. Actually, though, it hardly mattered that her official title remained no more than 'the Lady Mary the King's daughter'. Unless and until the King fathered a legitimate son, she would always be regarded as the King's heir by everyone who mattered. Not that the King had given up hope of fathering a legitimate son – far from it – and when, in March 1537, it was officially announced that the Queen was pregnant, the hopes of the whole country revived.

At two o'clock in the morning of Friday 12 October 1537, after a labour which lasted for three days and two nights, Jane Seymour gave birth to a healthy boy. By eight o'clock the news had reached London and solemn Te Deums were immediately sung in St Paul's and every parish church in the city. Bells pealed, two thousand rounds were fired from the Tower guns, bonfires blazed up dangerously among the crowded timbered houses and everyone shut up shop and surged out into the streets to celebrate. Impromptu banquets were organized as bands of musicians went about playing and singing loyal ballads in honour of the occasion, and everyone drank the prince's health in the free wine and beer which flowed in profusion from the conduits and from hogsheads provided by the civic authorities and by other prominent citizens. Even the foreign merchants of the

Steelyard joined in – burning torches and contributing a hogshead of wine and two barrels of beer for the poor.

All that day, throughout the night and well into the next day the capital rocked and clashed in a great crescendo of thanksgiving and relief that at last England had a Prince of Wales born in undisputably lawful wedlock. Messengers were despatched to 'all the estates and cities of the realm' spreading the glad tidings and the whole country went hysterical with joy. As Bishop Latimer wrote to Cromwell from his Worcester diocese: 'Here is no less rejoicing in these parts from the birth of our prince, whom we hungered for so long, than there was, I trow, at the birth of St John the Baptist . . . God give us grace to be thankful.'

The christening of England's Treasure, 'Prince Edward that goodly flower', took place in the chapel at Hampton Court three days after his birth and was, of course, suitably magnificent. The Dukes of Suffolk and Norfolk and Archbishop Cranmer were godfathers. The Lady Mary was godmother. The baby's other sister was also present, carrying the heavily jewelled and embroidered baptismal robe. This burden proved rather too much for the four-year-old Elizabeth, so she herself was carried in the procession by Queen Jane's elder brother.

During the past decade, while Henry's personal affairs had been occupying everybody's attention, the family scene had been changing and the biggest gap at Edward's christening was caused by the absence of Mary Tudor, Queen of France. Mary never seems to have regretted her tearful ultimatum to Charles Brandon, and that rash runaway marriage in the chapel at Cluny could be counted as a success. But in recent years, although the Duke remained in constant attendance on the King, the Duchess of Suffolk had preferred to spend most of her time down at Westhorpe, the family's principal residence in East Anglia. She was increasingly preoccupied with bringing up her family and her health had begun to fail. The exact nature of Mary's long wasting illness remains a mystery – its only recorded symptom was a pain in the side – it may have been cancer, it may have been tuberculosis. Whatever it was, it was usually given as the reason for her non-appearance at Court. Another and equally cogent reason may well have been the Queen-Duchess's natural reluctance to yield precedence to Mistress Anne Boleyn and revulsion at the way her once dear friend and sister-in-law was being treated.

Mary's last visit to London was in the spring of 1533, when she came up for the wedding of her elder daughter, Frances, now sixteen, to Henry Grey, Marquis of Dorset at Suffolk House and the betrothal of the younger, Eleanor, to Henry Clifford, the Earl of Cumberland's heir. Suffolk had to stay in town – he was very busy with preparations for Anne Boleyn's coronation – and Mary travelled back to Westhorpe alone with Eleanor. On Midsummer Day the loveliest princess in Europe was dead at the age of thirty-eight, and in March 1534 her son Henry, Earl of Lincoln, followed her to the grave. Remarkably little is known about this young man, who stood so close to the throne and who lived to the age of eighteen before succumbing, again most probably, to tuberculosis. But his death was regarded as a windfall for his cousin, the King of Scotland, since the pundits considered that Henry's younger nephew, being native born, might be preferred to the elder in the succession stakes.

Charles Brandon survived this double tragedy with reasonable equanimity. He had made Mary Tudor a faithful and affectionate husband, but he replaced her within a couple of months. To do him justice, financial necessity had something to do with this almost indecent haste. He was, as usual, heavily in debt – Frances' wedding had cost him over fifteen hundred pounds and there was Eleanor's still to come. The Duke of Suffolk needed a rich wife and he picked the candidate closest to hand, his ward Katherine Willoughby, daughter and heir of Lord William Willoughby and Maria de Salinas, one of Catherine of Aragon's Spanish ladies. The fact that Katherine Willoughby was about the same age as his own younger daughter – fourteen to his forty-eight – and was betrothed to his own son, did not apparently detract from her eligibility in the Duke's eyes, though it did give rise to some unkind gossip. In fact, the marriage proved a very happy one. Young Katherine was an intelligent, high-spirited girl (she later became notorious for her outspoken Protestantism) and quickly gave her husband two more sons. In the same month of the same year that Prince Edward was born there was another addition to the clan and to what was to become known as the Suffolk line, when Frances Grey, née Brandon, gave birth to a daughter, Jane, named perhaps in honour of the Queen.

But Jane Seymour was in no condition to appreciate the compliment. A few days after Edward's christening she became so ill that the last sacraments were administered. She rallied briefly, but by 24 October she was dead. According to Cromwell, her death was due to the negligence of her attendants, who had allowed her to catch cold and to eat unsuitable food. In fact, of course, she died of puerperal sepsis – the scourge of all women in childbed.

Jane was given a state funeral at Windsor Castle with the Princess Mary officiating as chief mourner. She was the first and, as it turned out, the only one of Henry's wives to be buried as Queen and perhaps this was fair – she was, after all, the only one who had fulfilled her side of the bargain to his satisfaction. The King 'retired to a solitary place to pass his sorrows' and his grief was probably sincere enough, while it lasted. But he was soon back at Hampton Court so that he could see his son every day and make sure that 'the realm's most precious jewel' was being properly cared for.

Edward spent the first few months of his life at Court under his father's eye, but with the approach of summer, always the most dangerous time of year for plague and other contagions, the nursery was moved out into the country. The most elaborate precautions against infection were laid down in a series of ordinances, written out in the King's own hand. No officers of the prince's privy chamber might go to London without permission and on their return must observe a period of quarantine, in case they had picked up anything nasty. If anyone in the household did fall ill, they were to be removed at once. Everything was to be kept scrupulously clean – all galleries, passages and courts were to be swept and scrubbed twice a day, everything the prince touched or used was to be carefully washed and handled only by his personal servants, no dirty utensils were to be left lying about and all dogs, except the ladies' pets, had to be confined to kennels.

Under these sensible hygienic rules, Edward grew and thrived. He was a large, fair, placid baby – a type much admired – and Eustace Chapuys described him as

PARVVLE PATRISSA, PATRIÆ VIRTVTIS ET HÆRES
ESTO, NIHIL MAIVS MAXIMVS ORBIS HABET.
GNATVM VIX POSSVNT COELVM ET NATVRA DEDISSE,
HVIVS QVEM PATRIS, VICTVS HONORET HONOS.
ÆQVATO TANTVM, TANTI TV FACTA PARENTIS,
VOTA HOMINVM, VIX QVO PROGREDIANTVR, HABENT
VINCITO, VICISTI, QVOT REGES PRISCVS ADORAT
ORBIS, NEC TE QVI VINCERE POSSIT, ERIT.

Above: *Edward, Prince of Wales, by Holbein.*
Left: *Mistress Jak, Prince Edward's nurse, drawn by Holbein.*

'one of the prettiest children that could be seen anywhere'. Details of his progress were minutely recorded: his first teeth appeared without difficulty; at a year old he was a little thinner, but shooting out in length and trying to walk; at eighteen months he threw a rather embarrassing tantrum in front of some queerly dressed foreign visitors, hiding his face in his nurse's shoulder and howling with rage; at nearly two the Lady Mistress of his household told Thomas Cromwell that his grace was in good health and merry. 'I would to God', she went on, 'the King's grace and your lordship had seen him yesternight, for his grace was marvellously pleasantly disposed. The musicians played and his grace danced and played so wantonly that he could not stand still, and was as full of pretty toys as ever I saw a child in my life.' To his father, of course, Edward was perfect and Henry lost no opportunity to hang over the cradle or display the prince to the people.

But as the prince cut his teeth and began to grow out of the cradle and the King continued to worry in case some disrespectful germs should dare to approach his darling, danger threatened, or seemed to threaten, from abroad. In December 1538 the Pope, encouraged by the Pilgrimage of Grace and other hopeful signs of unrest among the islanders, at last summoned up enough resolution to promulgate his long-delayed Bull of Excommunication against the defiant and irreligious King of England. This somewhat antique weapon which, in theory, deprived an offending monarch of his throne and put him and his subjects outside the Christian pale, had lost most of its teeth by the middle of the sixteenth century, but it still inspired a good deal of superstitious dread among the faithful. This, coupled with the fact that the Holy Roman Emperor and the King of France (on whom, in theory, would fall the duty of deposing the King of England) had temporarily buried the hatchet, gave rise to a short-lived but excitable invasion scare along the south coast. But neither Charles nor François, good papists though they declared themselves to be, had any real intention of moving against Henry and the chief result of the Pope's action was to give the King an excuse to complete the virtual annihilation of his remaining Plantagenet cousins.

The Holy Father had sent Reginald Pole, son of the Countess of Salisbury, on a mission to both France and the Emperor to rouse them against 'the most cruel and abominable tyrant' across the Channel. Pole was a high-minded if not very realistic individual, a Cardinal since 1536 and an exile for his religious principles. His errand was a dismal failure, but, as he might have foreseen, it spelt doom for his family at home. His elder brother Henry, Lord Montague, was promptly executed and his mother arrested. Royal vengeance also fell on the Courtenay family. The Marquis of Exeter with his wife and young son went to the Tower, the Marquis soon leaving it again for Tower Hill and the block. Two years later, Henry finally completed the work of safeguarding his son's inheritance by carrying out the death sentence on the old Countess of Salisbury herself. Margaret Pole, née Plantagenet, once long ago, the dearest friend of Queen Catherine of Aragon, a second mother to the Princess Mary Tudor and 'a lady of virtue and honour if there was ever one in England' was taken out on a May morning to be literally hacked to pieces by an apprentice executioner: an action which more than any other lent considerable point to Reginald Pole's book in which he had compared the King of England to the Emperor Nero.

CHAPTER 8

The Old Fox

He is an old fox, proud as the devil and accustomed to ruling.

It was the nervous international situation with England threatened with encirclement by the Catholic powers which propelled Henry into his fourth marriage. To guard against political isolation, the King needed friends among the emergent Protestant nations. So an alliance and a new Queen were sought from among the Lutheran states of Northern Europe and finally found in the small duchy of Cleves on the northern Rhine.

Anne of Cleves landed at Deal on 27 December 1539, having been delayed for a fortnight at Calais by bad weather and the King, suddenly boyishly impatient for a sight of his bride, dashed down to Rochester 'to nourish love'. It was quite like the old days, just Henry and a few companions riding incognito on a romantic errand. Unfortunately, though, it ended in an embarrassing fiasco. To begin with Anne, not so well versed as the English ladies in the King's little ways, failed to realize who he was and was understandably taken aback when this enormous, middle-aged man in a marbled cloak and hood burst unannounced into her room to enfold her in an ardent embrace. But even when the situation had been painstakingly explained to her, she displayed none of the delighted surprise proper to the occasion and would only edge nervously away from her alarming fiancé. It did not help, of course, that she could speak no English, or indeed any other language but her native German and Henry left as soon as he decently could, taking with him the present of expensive furs which he was not going to waste on such an undeserving object.

He complained bitterly all the way back to Greenwich that he had been monstrously deceived; that this dull, plain, lumpish girl was nothing like the paragon he had been led to expect; and that if he'd known what she was really like 'she should never have come into this realm'. 'Is there none other remedy but that I must needs, against my will, put my neck in the yoke?' he asked Thomas Cromwell. None immediately suggested itself. Anne was here now and Henry would have to go through with the wedding whether he liked it or not. The ceremony took place on Twelfth Night but although he slept beside his bride for a few nights, nothing – not even the inducement of begetting another son – could bring the King to consummate the marriage. Anne was as disappointing in bed as she was out of it and after feeling her breasts and belly Henry told Cromwell disconsolately that he had 'neither will nor courage to the rest'.

Left: *Anne of Cleves, by Holbein*. Right: *Thomas Cromwell, Henry's chief minister throughout the 1530s and the architect of his marriage to Anne of Cleves.*

Obviously some remedy would have to be found, especially as by Easter the whole Court knew that the King's fancy had been caught by one of the new Queen's maids of honour – plump, lively little Catherine Howard who, by a curious coincidence, was a cousin of Anne Boleyn. Fortunately divorce was easier nowadays and before the summer was half over the King and his legal advisers had discovered ample grounds for a nullity suit. It was all very civilized and amicable. Anne had accepted dismissal with a docility, an alacrity even, which quite surprised the King, and opted to remain in England on a pension of £500 a year, with two royal residences allocated to her use. She settled down apparently quite content with her position as Henry's 'adopted sister', and was to become a valued friend of the royal family – a sort of honorary maiden aunt.

Having got his freedom, Henry wasted no time. On 28 July 1540 he married Catherine Howard and that same day Thomas Cromwell was executed for high treason. Cromwell's fall, although still shrouded in a fair amount of confusion, closely parodied that of the King's other great minister, Cardinal Wolsey. Like Wolsey, Cromwell had served his master faithfully and well. Like Wolsey, he had no aristocratic family connections (he is generally believed to have been the son of a blacksmith) and therefore depended heavily on the King for protection from his enemies.

Henry did not want to be bothered with politics just then. He had temporarily forgotten his increasing age and girth and his bad legs and was enjoying an Indian summer of renewed youth and vigour in the entrancing company of his 'rose without a thorn'. The French ambassador remarked that 'the King is so amorous of Catherine Howard that he cannot treat her well enough and caresses her more than he did the others'. Henry showered jewels, expensive dresses and grants of land on his new pet and carried her off on an extended honeymoon which lasted into the autumn.

There were no problems about consummating this marriage; but while Anne of Cleves had been a timid, unawakened virgin, Catherine at nineteen was already sexually experienced – a significant fact which seems to have escaped Henry's notice. However, it did not long escape the notice of the Court that the Queen's behaviour could, at the least, be described as indiscreet. In the spring of 1541 the King set off on a progress northward – the first time he had ever visited this recalcitrant part of his dominions – taking with him his wife, his elder daughter and a personal retinue over a thousand strong. The weather was bad and the King of Scots, whom Henry had been hoping to meet at York, failed to turn up at the rendezvous – a deliberate snub which annoyed his uncle very much – but otherwise the trip could be counted as a success and the King arrived back at Hampton Court in October in a complacent frame of mind. He did not know that throughout the summer's journeyings and very likely before, the Queen had been slipping off up the backstairs to meet one of the gentlemen of his Privy Chamber, her 'little sweet fool' Thomas Culpepper.

This was not the only thing Henry did not know about his 'jewel of a wife' but those people who did know – people with special knowledge about her casual, scrambling girlhood in her grandmother's house down at Horsham where the Dowager Duchess of Norfolk had shut her eyes to goings on in the maids' dormitory after lights out – were beginning to wonder if it was altogether wise to keep this knowledge to themselves. Finally, John Lascelles, who had his own reasons for disliking the whole Howard tribe and whose sister Mary had been a member of the household at Horsham, laid certain information before the Council. He told how one Henry Manox, a music teacher, had been familiar with the secret parts of Catherine's body when she was only fourteen; how one Francis Dereham, now the Queen's secretary, had been made welcome in her 'naked bed' and had known her carnally many times before her marriage to the King.

Gossip was one thing, but detailed accusations like these could not be suppressed. Henry's first reaction was furious incredulity. This was all a plot to blacken the Queen's name and he ordered an immediate investigation. But when the whole, rather squalid little story had been dragged painfully into the light, the facts were undeniable. There could be no doubt whatever that Catherine had been promiscuous before her marriage and that her behaviour since had been at best criminally foolish. Actual adultery with Culpepper was never proved conclusively but the presumption of guilt was very strong and, in any case, Culpepper confessed both desire and intention which was quite enough.

This time Henry did not wear his horns so pleasantly. Catherine had wounded an ageing man where it really hurt and the French ambassador reported that the King 'has changed his love for the Queen into hatred, and taken such grief at being deceived that of late it was thought he had gone mad, for he called for a

Catherine Howard; an unauthenticated
portrait by an unknown artist.

sword to slay her he had loved so much.' Later, to the acute embarrassment of the
Council, rage gave way to tears of self-pity as the King bemoaned his 'ill-luck in
meeting with such ill-conditioned wives'. The wretched Catherine, too, was in a
sorry state and when Cranmer was sent to visit her to bring her to a proper sense
of her iniquity, he found her in such a 'franzy' of terror and remorse that the
kind-hearted Archbishop was moved rather to pity and to fear for her reason.

It was a miserable Christmas all round, made worse by anxiety about Edward,
who had been seriously ill with a malarial-type fever. But by early February 1542,
when that poor, silly little trollop Catherine Howard had been beheaded on
Tower Green and had gone to join her cousin Anne under the stones of St Peter-
ad-Vincula, Henry was slowly recovering his normal self-esteem. All the same, his
last two disastrous experiences had put him right off marriage for the time being
and he turned instead to more congenial pastimes, such as bullying the Scots and
planning further adventures in France.

Margaret Tudor had died the previous autumn at the age of fifty-two, but
although her death snapped another link with the past, it made little material
difference to the crisis situation building up in Scotland. Margaret's uncontrolled
temper and her unfortunate tendency to allow her private passions to influence
her public life had dissipated much of her political credibility and, in any case, she

and her brother had been on bad terms for some time. Henry had always disapproved strongly of his sister's determination to divorce her unsatisfactory second husband, the Earl of Angus, and Margaret never quite forgave Henry for taking Angus's side in their long, bitter and immensely complicated matrimonial dispute. The Earl eventually sought asylum in England, while his daughter and the King's niece, Lady Margaret Douglas, was brought up at the English Court.

But if Margaret Tudor had largely failed the cause of Anglo-Scottish friendship, her son's attitude was even more disappointing. As soon as he was in a position to manage his own affairs, young James had turned obstinately back to France, marrying first one and then another French wife. Equally irritatingly, he remained an orthodox Roman Catholic steadfastly refusing to follow the example of his schismatic and iconoclastic uncle – even when Henry generously offered him the benefit of his experience and sent him detailed instructions on 'how to create your own national church'. James's Romanism was an especially sensitive issue in view of his proximity to the English throne. If anything were to happen to Edward, who was still only five years old and had only just recovered from a dangerous illness, James would have a very strong claim to be considered Henry's heir – particularly bearing in mind the fact that Henry himself had disinherited both his daughters.

The King had expended a lot of time and trouble in wooing his nephew but now he was getting impatient. He wanted to secure his back door without further delay and by October 1542 he was ready to take direct action. The Duke of Norfolk led an army across the Border in a full scale raiding expedition which cut a swathe of wreckage and destruction but failed to intimidate the Scots. Instead, predictably, it stirred them to retaliate and on 21 November an army of ten thousand attacked a greatly inferior English force at Solway Moss, north of Carlisle. The outcome was a disaster even more horrifying than Flodden. The Scots were routed utterly and completely at a cost, so it was boasted, of only seven English casualties. This was disgrace as well as disaster and three weeks later Scotland's misfortunes were crowned by the death of her king. James V, always a melancholic and unstable character, had turned his face to the wall and now the Scottish throne passed to the week-old girl baby born to James's second wife, Mary of Guise, in the dismal aftermath of Solway Moss.

Fate had dealt Henry triumph in spades and presented him with a first-rate opportunity to solve the Scottish problem. Instead, by a mixture of arrogance, impatience, over-confidence and greed, the King not only wasted his chances but helped to sow the seeds of his little great-niece's tragedy. The obvious way to achieve a peaceful and (with any luck) permanent union between England and Scotland was by a marriage between the infant Mary Queen of Scots and Edward Prince of Wales; but this was a matter for delicate and tactful negotiations, needing sympathetic consideration of Scottish national pride – which was prickly enough at the best of times – and generous guarantees of Scottish liberties. The Scots could see as well as anyone that the logical result of the proposed alliance would be a swallowing whole of Scotland by England. 'If your lad were a lass and our lass were a lad, would you then be so earnest in this matter?' one Scotsman enquired of the English ambassador.

In these circumstances, Henry's bullying demands that Mary should be sent to England at once; that he should become, in effect, Scotland's regent; that Scotland should renounce her treaty of friendship with France and make no other foreign treaties without his consent; and that English garrisons should be admitted to Edinburgh, Stirling and Dumbarton had the immediate effect of raising every Scottish hackle and of dismaying and alienating even the pro-English lords. Such demands were, of course, not merely unacceptable, they were – short of total military conquest – unenforceable and Henry had to climb down. In the treaty finally signed at Greenwich on 1 July 1543 it was agreed that Mary should remain in Scotland until she reached marriageable age and the break with France was no longer insisted on. But the damage had been done and the French party in Scotland was rapidly regaining its ascendancy. There was no Duke of Albany to call home on this occasion, but Cardinal Beaton, the powerful and unscrupulous Catholic leader, was strongly pro-French in his sympathies and so, naturally enough, was the Queen Mother, an intelligent and tough-minded Frenchwoman.

Before the end of the year the Scottish Parliament had repudiated the Treaty of Greenwich and was busily refurbishing all the old ties with France. Henry was back where he had been before Solway Moss – in fact he was rather worse off – and a savage punitive expedition against Edinburgh and Leith in the spring of 1544 achieved nothing in the long-term except a further hardening of Scottish attitudes and a strengthening of Scottish determination to keep their baby Queen out of the clutches of her wicked great-uncle whatever the cost. As his old friend Charles Brandon told him, the King would get nothing out of Scotland now save by the sword.

While he had been making a considerable hash of his son's marriage prospects, Henry had done rather better for himself and on 12 July 1543, in a quiet ceremony at Hampton Court, he took his sixth and last wife. Lady Latymer of Snape Hall, born Katherine Parr, daughter of an old-established Northamptonshire family, proved in many ways his best and most successful choice. Already twice married and twice widowed, the new Queen at thirty-one was still a pretty woman. Even more important, she was a mature and sensible woman, experienced in the ways of husbands. As the anonymous author of the *Spanish Chronicle* put it, she was 'quieter than any of the young wives the King had had, and as she knew more of the world, she always got on pleasantly with the King and had no caprices.'

Katherine Parr had not sought the honour done to her – rather the reverse. Apart from the obvious perils involved in becoming Henry's wife, the King was no longer a very attractive proposition physically. He had aged quite noticeably since the Catherine Howard episode and at fifty-two he was grossly fat with suppurating, foul-smelling and acutely painful ulcers on both legs. His mind was still sharp enough but he was growing increasingly moody and suspicious. Often morose and unpredictably bad-tempered, he could be as dangerous as a wounded tiger and it is hardly surprising that Katherine should have quailed at the prospect before her – especially as she was already being courted by Henry's brother-in-law, the dashingly handsome Thomas Seymour. But Thomas

*Katherine Parr, a portrait
attributed to William Scrots.*

Seymour, like Thomas Wyatt before him, knew better than to enter into amatory competition with his sovereign lord and as soon as the King's interest became clear, he melted hastily into the background, leaving Katherine to accept the fact that it was plainly God's will that she should be Queen of England. In the circumstances, it is very much to her credit that she accepted it cheerfully and gave Henry loyal and sympathetic companionship during the last years of his life.

As well as being a good wife, Katherine Parr was also a good stepmother, taking a conscientious and constructive interest in the welfare of her husband's curiously assorted brood and trying to create some sort of home life for them. She was not, of course, a stranger to the royal family. Her mother had been one of Catherine of Aragon's ladies and she herself had spent some of her early years at Court. Now she renewed her childhood acquaintance with the Princess Mary – there was only four years' difference in their ages – and the two women became very friendly. Mary was still spending most of her time in the country, at Havering or Hunsdon or Beaulieu in Essex, a quiet, informal existence usually shared with either her little sister or her brother; but Katherine encouraged her to come to Court more often, wrote to her regularly, lent her money and sent down one of her own servants whom she knew would be welcome 'for the sake of his music'.

Following in the tradition of those pious and serious-minded royal ladies,

Margaret Beaufort and Catherine of Aragon, Katherine Parr took an informed and practical interest in educational matters and was a lively patron of the New Learning. She played an active part in the reorganization of the royal schoolroom which took place during the summer of 1544 and is generally credited with securing the appointment of the Cambridge humanist and Greek scholar, John Cheke, as principal tutor to Prince Edward who, at six-and-a-half, was just beginning his classical training in earnest. The Queen picked another Cambridge man, William Grindal, to tutor the Princess Elizabeth.

Anne Boleyn's daughter was ten years old now – a pale, sharp-featured, carrotty-haired girl who had not so far attracted much notice in the outside world. As the bastard of a notorious adulteress, she had little value on the international marriage market and at home she had always been over-shadowed by her brother and sister. Her father was apparently quite fond of her, when he remembered her existence, and she took her place as a member of the family on state occasions; but since her mother's disgrace, the up-bringing of the once 'high and mighty princess of England' had been left almost entirely in the hands of her governess. Katherine Parr was the first of Elizabeth's numerous stepmothers to take the trouble to get to know the child of Henry's 'great folly', who seemed doomed to the life of a poor relation or, at best, marriage to some useful supporter who would be prepared to overlook her unfortunate maternity in exchange for a toehold in the royal family. It may have been politic to gain the support and affection of Edward and Mary, but the Queen was acting out of disinterested kindness when she brought young Elizabeth to Court, gave her apartments next to her own at Greenwich, saw that something was done about her education and offered her friendship and guidance at a time when she was beginning to need them most.

In July 1544 Henry crossed the Channel for the last time to take part in his last foreign war, but before he left a third Act of Succession had reached the Statute Book. This Act confirmed the King's right to dispose of the crown by will, but made it clear that should Edward fail to leave an heir, and failing any children of Henry's latest marriage, the throne would pass first to Mary and then to Elizabeth, subject to conditions to be laid down by the King in his will. Neither Mary nor Elizabeth was legitimized by the new Act – the question of their legitimacy was simply ignored – and their constitutional position remained peculiar to say the least.

On 7 July Henry appointed his wife Regent in his absence abroad – an honour not accorded to a Queen consort since the days of Catherine of Aragon – and on the twelfth he set sail for Calais. The attack on France, undertaken in conjunction with the Emperor, was not a great success either politically or militarily, though Henry did achieve what was probably his main objective – the capture of Boulogne, the port used by the French to send military aid to Scotland – and he thoroughly enjoyed himself superintending the details of the siege, riding about the trenches happily occupied in 'foreseeing and caring for everything'.

The Council and the army commanders had done their best to dissuade the King from taking the field in person, believing not only that it would be the death of him but that he would be very much in the way. Nothing, though, was going to

'Henry VIII and his Family': Princess Mary, Prince Edward, Jane Seymour and Princess Elizabeth.

stop Henry from grasping this opportunity to go campaigning again and to re-create the triumphs of his glorious past. It was not the same, naturally. The sick old man who had to be hoisted painfully on to his horse, or carried round in a litter, bore little resemblance to the splendid young warrior of thirty years ago, but even so his two months' holiday in France did him a lot of good and he was noticeably better in health and spirits as a result.

It was, it could only be, a temporary improvement, and the following March he was very poorly again with one of the recurring fevers – caused most likely by a flare-up of his inflamed leg – which had been troubling him for the past three years. The King tried hard to conceal his growing infirmity from the public; he continued to hunt and to travel about the country round London, but those closest to him could see a steady deterioration and certain people were already looking towards the future. Already the jockeying for position during an

In fact Jane Seymour died soon after Edward's birth; this painting was probably executed in 1545.

inevitable royal minority had begun and by the summer of 1545 two distinct parties were forming. On the one side stood the conservatives – the old Duke of Norfolk, the right-wing bishops, Gardiner of Winchester and Bonner of London, and the Lord Chancellor Thomas Wriothesley. Opposing them were the progressives, led by the Prince of Wales's uncle, Edward Seymour Earl of Hertford, and John Dudley Lord Lisle, both able men who had been making a name for themselves in the royal service as diplomats and as military commanders. Behind these two were a number of other privy councillors and courtiers, up-and-coming families like the Parrs and the Herberts and, though he was careful not to draw too much attention to the fact, Archbishop Cranmer himself.

The developing conflict was basically about power and politics, but it was fought out over religious issues – logically enough when one remembers that in the sixteenth century politics and religion were, for all practical purposes, one and the same thing. Certainly Henry's religious policy had been dictated by political and, to some extent, personal necessity. A natural, dyed-in-the-wool conservative himself, it is highly improbable that the King would ever have considered breaking with Rome if the Pope had not been so disobliging as to refuse to give him his divorce. Having once considered it, the advantages in terms of increased revenue and enhanced royal power and status became splendidly apparent, but Henry remained a conservative at heart and while he lived the Church of England remained Catholic in the sense that all the basic tenets of the Catholic faith continued to be observed and were indeed enforceable by law.

It was not, of course, as simple as it sounded. The King may not have meant to start a revolution when he rejected the Pope and all his works but that, in effect, was what he had done. There was a long tradition of anti-clerical feeling and smouldering religious radicalism in England and Henry's personal quarrel with Rome had provided the spark which set a quantity of tinder-dry undergrowth alight. The subsequent conflagration proved, not surprisingly, difficult to control – especially when the Great Bible, based on Tyndale's and Coverdale's translation, was made available to the general public. The average concerned and educated layman was now, for the first time, in a position to study and interpret the word of God for himself and, in the 1530s and 1540s, this was the very stuff of revolution. It led naturally to the spread of revolutionary ideas; to the realization that it was possible for an individual to hold direct communion with God, that the ordinary layman (or woman) was no longer totally dependent on the priest to act as his intermediary, and the sense of excitement and emotional release this brought to many people cannot be emphasized too strongly.

Henry's attitude towards the force he had unloosed remained ambivalent. As long as it seemed politically expedient, he had encouraged or, at any rate, had not seriously discouraged a limited amount of progressive thinking. On the other hand, he had no intention of allowing the radicals to get above themselves, and from time to time they received a sharp reminder that the Supreme Head was watching them. The King's policy, generally speaking, was to hold a balance between the opposing factions and he would, with splendid impartiality, hang Catholics for treason and burn Protestants for heresy. But during the mid-1540s it seemed as if the progressive party was having things pretty much its own way. Certainly very few heresy prosecutions were brought during 1544 and 1545, and in London especially the law was being openly flouted. The conservatives thought they knew where to lay the blame for this distressing state of affairs.

Queen Katherine Parr was known to favour the new humanistic brand of piety which laid great stress on the importance of private devotion and played down the organized, sacramental aspects of religion. She had gathered round her a number of like-minded ladies and together they spent much of their time studying and discussing the Gospels and listening to discourses by such fashionably advanced clerics as Nicholas Ridley, Hugh Latimer and Nicholas Shaxton. Katherine's circle included the young Duchess of Suffolk, who made no secret of her poor opinion of the conservative bishops; Joan Denny, wife of one of Henry's favourite gentlemen; the Queen's sister, Anne Herbert, and her stepdaughter, Elizabeth

Tyrwhit; Lady Lisle, the Countess of Hertford and the Countess of Sussex. Between them these ladies commanded a considerable weight of influence and they were, in the estimation of men like Stephen Gardiner, rapidly turning the Court into a hotbed of the most pernicious heresy.

The climate began to show signs of change in the late summer of 1545. In August of that year the Duke of Suffolk died suddenly while the Court was on a progress. For Henry it was a grievous personal loss. Charles Brandon was one of his oldest friends and one of the very few who could still remember those golden summers long ago when life was spent in 'continual festival'. His death was also regarded as a loss for the friends of the Gospel, since the Duke had become closely associated with the progressive party in recent years. By Christmas it was clear that the King himself was getting worried about the increasing dissension between the rival factions, and in a speech delivered to Parliament on Christmas Eve, he reproved the nation via its elected representatives for speaking slanderously of priests and for having the temerity to follow its own 'fantastical opinions and vain expositions' in high matters of religious doctrine. Henry reminded his audience that licence to read Holy Scripture in their mother tongue had been granted them only to inform their consciences and so that they might instruct their children and families. It was emphatically not a licence for every Tom, Dick and Harry 'to make Scripture a railing and a taunting stock against priests and teachers'. The King was very sorry, he went on, 'to hear and know how unreverently that most precious jewel, the word of God, is disputed, rhymed, sung and jangled in every alehouse and tavern, contrary to the true meaning and doctrine of the same'.

Unfortunately, this royal scolding had little effect on that section of the population which had discovered the heady delights of theological and, by implication, political debate. 'Religious novelties' continued to proliferate and by the spring of 1546 the bishops were pressing urgently for an anti-heresy drive. This was in full swing by late March, but Gardiner, Wriothesley and other leading conservatives remained convinced that the key to the situation lay with the Queen; that the way to bring down the progressives was to attack them through their wives.

It was June before an opportunity presented itself. In the story as told by John Foxe, the Protestant propagandist, it was the Queen's habit to sit with her husband in the evenings and to entertain him with intellectual conversation which naturally turned to the absorbing topic of religion. This was all very well, up to a point. Henry always enjoyed good talk, he was fond of his wife and pleased that she should take an interest in serious matters. But on one occasion, about the middle of June, Katherine allowed her enthusiasm to run away with her and unwisely forgot the cardinal rule of debate with the King – that he must win any argument, especially theological argument, hands down. Henry's legs were particularly troublesome just then and his temper was consequently shorter than usual. He lost patience, changed the subject abruptly and, after the Queen had said goodnight turned to Stephen Gardiner, who happened to be present, grumbling that he did not know what the world was coming to and that it was a fine thing at his age to be taught by his wife.

This was just the opening Gardiner had been waiting for. He agreed warmly with his sovereign lord and went on to warn him of the danger of the opinions so 'stiffly maintained' by the Queen – opinions which not only disallowed and dissolved the politic government of princes, but also taught the people that all things ought to be in common. Beliefs of this kind, Gardiner pointed out, 'were indeed so odious and for the Prince's estate so perilous, that . . . the Council was bold to affirm that the greatest subject in this land, speaking those words that she did speak and defending likewise those arguments that she did defend, had with impartial justice by law deserved death.'

This was fighting talk and Henry was, or pretended to be, seriously disturbed. Was he nourishing yet another serpent in his bosom? Had such rank and wicked heresies really been finding sympathy under his own roof? Obviously something must be done, and the King immediately authorized an enquiry into the conduct and beliefs of the members of the Queen's household. If any evidence to support the Council's allegations came to light, then the Queen herself and anyone else involved were to be arrested pending further investigation. This was all Gardiner needed and he hurried off to set the wheels in motion, though – and he was not known as 'wily Winchester' for nothing – he carefully left the actual dirty work in the hands of Thomas Wriothesley.

In preparing their case against Katherine, the conspirators held what they hoped would be a trump card in the person of Anne Kyme, better known by her maiden name of Anne Askew. Anne, a truculent young woman from Lincolnshire, was a notorious heretic, already convicted and condemned. The interesting thing about her from Wriothesley's point of view was that she was known to have had close connections with the Court. If it could be proved that the Queen, or any of the Queen's ladies had been in touch with her since her arrest; if it could be shown that they had been encouraging and supporting her, then the Chancellor would have more than enough evidence to justify a dramatic series of further arrests. Anne was therefore transferred to the Tower and interrogated by Wriothesley and his henchman, the Solicitor General, Richard Rich. But apart from the fact that she admitted receiving some small sums of money, through her maid, from servants wearing the livery of Lady Denny and Lady Hertford, Anne told them nothing. Exasperated, Wriothesley ordered her to be put on the rack, but since it was illegal to resort to torture without a proper authorization from the Privy Council and, in any case, unheard of to apply it to a gentlewoman like Anne Askew, the Lieutenant of the Tower hastily dissociated himself from the proceedings. There followed a quite extraordinary scene, with the Lord Chancellor of England stripping off his gown and himself turning the handle of the rack. It did him no good. Anne either would not or could not (probably could not) provide him with any useful information. All he succeeded in doing – for naturally the story soon got about – was to turn her into a popular heroine.

Having failed with Anne Askew, the Queen's enemies were obliged to fall back on charges of a more general nature – such as possession of banned books which they felt pretty certain would be found in her apartments, or which could always be planted there. A list of charges had, in fact, been drawn up by early July and, according to Foxe, was shown to the King and signed by him. The Queen's arrest would now follow, but a few days before it was due to take place Henry told one of his physicians, Dr Wendy, all about the plan – at the same time swearing him to secrecy. Then, a copy of the 'articles' against the Queen was dropped by convenient 'accident' in the passage outside her rooms. It was, of course, quickly found and shown to Katherine who, for the first time, became aware of her danger. Terrified, she collapsed, falling 'incontinent into a great melancholy and agony'. Dr Wendy was sent to attend her and naturally passed on everything the King had told him. He advised his patient to get rid of any incriminating books without delay and to throw herself on her husband's mercy.

But Katherine Parr could think of a number of people, including her immediate predecessor, who had thrown themselves on Henry Tudor's mercy without result. She would have to do better than that if she was to save her life. Whatever happened she must contrive to see and speak to her husband before her enemies struck and on the evening of 13 July she made her way to the King's Privy Chamber, accompanied only by her sister, Anne, and her cousin Lady Lane. If she was afraid, she did not show it.

Henry greeted her with bland good humour, congratulated her on her recovery from her sudden indisposition – and then he pounced. He had been troubled about some knotty point of theology. Perhaps the Queen could resolve his doubts. This was Katherine's cue and she picked it up calmly. She was only a poor, ignorant woman. Why should the King require her judgement 'in such diffuse causes of religion' which were far beyond her understanding? Even if she were to venture an opinion, she would still refer 'in this, and in all other cases, to Your Majesty's wisdom, as my only anchor, supreme head and governor here on earth, next under God, to lean unto'.

'Not so, by St Mary!' came the menacing reply. 'You are become a doctor, Kate, to instruct us, as we take it, and not to be instructed or directed by us.'

'If Your Majesty take it so', answered the Queen, 'then hath Your Majesty very much mistaken me.' It was, of course, quite unsuitable – against the ordinance of nature, in fact – for any woman to presume to teach her husband. It was she who must be taught by him. As for herself, if she had ever appeared bold enough to attempt to argue with her lord and master, she had meant it for the best; hoping by intellectual discussion to amuse and distract him and take his mind off the pain in his legs. She admitted that she had also encouraged such discussion for her own sake, 'that I, hearing your Majesty's learned discourse, might myself profit thereby'.

Henry was immensely pleased and relieved. 'And is it even so, sweetheart?' he exclaimed. 'And tended your arguments to no worse end? Then perfect friends we are now again, as ever at any time heretofore.' The reconciliation was complete. The King embraced his wife and told her she had done him more good than if someone had given him a hundred thousand pounds. Never again would he misjudge her, and 'with great signs and tokens of marvellous joy and liking' he kept her at his side far into the night. Next day, Henry, still in the best of tempers – 'as pleasant as ever he was in all his life before' – summoned Katherine and her ladies to join him out in the summer sunshine in the palace gardens. This idyllic scene was presently interrupted by the arrival of the unsuspecting Thomas

Wriothesley, with forty yeomen of the guard at his back and a warrant for the Queen's arrest in his pocket. But instead of the triumph he had been anticipating, the Chancellor was greeted with a tirade of royal abuse and sent packing with his tail between his legs, 'the whole mould of all his device being utterly broken'. This, at any rate, is the traditional story as related with much glee and a wealth of circumstantial detail in John Foxe's *The Book of Martyrs*.

It has been suggested that Henry, increasingly melancholic and pathologically distrustful of everyone around him as he felt old age and physical infirmity creeping up on him, had allowed Stephen Gardiner to poison his mind against his faithful and devoted wife – even that his mind was becoming clouded by pain and disease, that he was becoming a pathetic, irresponsible old man, easily manipulated by whoever happened to be fortunate enough to catch his ear. At the same time, it is noticeable that anyone rash enough to assume that the ageing King could be manipulated ended up by regretting it and Henry's manoeuvres more closely resemble those of a seasoned political operator, up to every trick in the game, than a senile dotard. In view of later developments, it seems highly probable that he had seen through Gardiner from the beginning and had adopted the classic technique of appearing to go along with the conspirators until they had been drawn into exposing their hand. It is significant that the King made sure that his wife should receive some advance warning of her impending doom and also gave her an opportunity to defend herself – an opportunity not granted either to Anne Boleyn or to Catherine Howard.

The collapse of the plot against the Queen marked the end of the short-lived right-wing resurgence on the Council and by the autumn the conservative Catholic party had suffered a virtual death-blow in the disgrace of the Duke of Norfolk and the sudden removal of Bishop Gardiner from the list of executors of the King's will. The ruin of the influential Howard family seemed complete. Norfolk's arrogant soldier-poet son, the Earl of Surrey, was executed for the technical treason of quartering his arms with those of Edward the Confessor, and the old Duke himself escaped a similar fate by the skin of his teeth. As for that brilliant but tricky lawyer and diplomat Stephen Gardiner, Henry would give no reason for excluding him from the projected Council of Regency, except to say that 'he was a wilful man and not meet to be about his son'. He himself could control Gardiner and 'use him and rule him to all manner of purposes', but no one else would be able to.

The motives behind this sudden, savage assault on the conservatives remain somewhat obscure, but one thing is certain – that the driving force came directly from the King. Henry may have doubted whether either Norfolk or Gardiner, both old-fashioned Catholics at heart, were entirely sound on the question of Royal Supremacy. This was a point on which the King was always ultra-sensitive and may account for the fact that in the closing months of his life he personally ensured that in his son's reign the balance of power would be decisively tilted in favour of those who advocated a far more radical programme of reform than anything he had been prepared to countenance; but with men like Edward Seymour and John Dudley in the saddle there would be no danger of any return to papal domination.

As Christmas approached, it was becoming obvious that the King had begun to fail. He who had once been the handsomest prince in Christendom was now a swollen, rotting hulk, suffering such agony from his ulcerated legs that his physicians despaired of his recovery. The exact nature of Henry's illness remains a matter for speculation and suggestions have included malaria, gout, alcoholism, heart disease, osteomyelitis and, of course, syphilis. This hypothesis was first put forward in the late nineteenth century and was pounced on joyfully by all those who enjoy a bit of historical dirt. But, in fact, there is not a shred of contemporary evidence that the King had venereal disease, no hint that he ever underwent the recognized treatment for 'the great pox', and this was just the sort of interesting information which foreign ambassadors were paid to ferret out.

Modern medical opinion inclines to the view that Henry's 'sorre legge', which first began to trouble him as early as 1528, was caused by varicose ulcers, or that he may have been suffering from a chronic septic infection of the bone following an injury received in one of his mishaps in the tiltyard. He had a serious accident in 1536 (the same on which Anne Boleyn tried to blame her disastrous miscarriage) when he fell heavily from his horse while jousting and was unconscious for two hours. This had put an end to his jousting days and although he still rode and walked energetically, he was obliged to give up most of the violent physical exercise he loved. He had already begun to put on weight and from then on all his enormous muscular body turned steadily to fat. The strain this imposed on the heart, added to unwise diet, the terrifying ministrations of Tudor doctors, constant pain and recurring high fever would have been enough to kill most people, and probably only Henry VIII's will-power and his magnificent constitution kept him going during those last weeks.

Early in January the Imperial ambassador was reporting that the King could not live much longer, but the King was not dead yet. He was still obstinately alive and refusing to sign his will — making it perfectly clear that anybody foolish enough to trade on their expectations would suffer the same fate as Stephen Gardiner. As long as the will remained unsigned Henry could cling at least to the illusion of power — the absolute power over other people's lives which fed his insatiable egotism. As long as the future remained uncertain the atmosphere at Court was thick with tension and suspicion, as hopeful councillors eyed one another jealously and the old man propped on his pillows looked on with malevolent amusement.

In the end he left it too late. On 27 January, when it was obvious that death was very near, the Council, faced with the horrifying possibility of the King dying intestate, took matters into their own hands and ordered the will to be signed with the dry stamp — that is to say, an outline facsimile of the royal signature was embossed on the paper and inked in by a clerk. This, at any rate, is one version of the story. Another says that the final draft of the will had been stamped and handed over to the Earl of Hertford on 30 December; but it would have been entirely typical of Henry to have kept his anxious servants on tenterhooks and to have enjoyed doing so. Not had he yet come to terms with the fact of his dying and had dealt with this particular problem by ignoring it.

Since it was treasonable to prophesy the King's death, those at his bedside were understandably reluctant to draw his attention to its inexorable approach and it was not until the evening of the twenty-seventh that Sir Anthony Denny, chief gentleman of the Privy Chamber, plucked up courage to tell his master what case he was in – 'to man's judgement not like to live'. Henry received the news calmly. He felt confident that, in the circumstances, the Almighty, whom he had always regarded very much in the light of a working partner, would not hesitate to pardon all his sins, 'though they were greater than they be'. Denny asked if he would like to unburden his conscience to some learned man and Henry replied that if he wanted anyone it would be Cranmer, but he would 'take a little sleep' before deciding. Cranmer was fetched from Croydon but by the time he arrived the King was past speech and could only grasp his old friend by the hand. His little sleep was turning into the longest sleep of all, and at about two o'clock in the morning of 28 January 1547 Henry Tudor drifted quietly out into the dark. He was fifty-five years old and had ruled England for very nearly thirty-eight years.

A wide variety of adjectives can and have been applied to the second Tudor King – from patriotic, wise and courageous, to tyrannical, sadistic and paranoid. Somewhere between these two extremes lies a man of many talents, of intelligence and considerable native shrewdness, who had acquired a good deal of political acumen (though often at quite unnecessary expense); an intellectually lazy man, who quickly became bored with the dry business of government but who had an unerring eye for picking men and for using them; a man of enormous personal charm and outward warmth, capable of giving and inspiring affection but fundamentally cold-hearted, fundamentally ruthless. 'He is a wonderful man', a French ambassador once observed of the King of England, 'and has wonderful people around him, but he is an old fox.'

Henry's most outstanding characteristic, which coloured his every action, both public and private, throughout his reign, was his sublime, sometimes preposterous, egotism. 'Squire Harry', remarked Martin Luther, 'wishes to be God and to do as he pleases.' What inner fears and deep-seated insecurity lay hidden behind the dazzling, high-gloss façade which Henry presented to the world; what sense of inadequacy was concealed by that terrifying joviality, those outbursts of murderous rage, we can only guess. The great majority of his subjects, untroubled by Freudian speculation, saw only the façade – the princely courage, the huge bejewelled figure which seemed to embody the very essence of the kingly ideal – and were content. And after all, why not? Henry had given them strong government and internal peace and had offered a highly satisfying focus for their growing sense of national identity. In defying the monolithic power of the Roman Church, he had done something which no English king before him had dared to do and he had got clean away with it. If a number of harmless individuals had been hurt in the process and if he had wasted a unique opportunity to use the wealth of the Church to provide social benefits for the people – well, the people on the whole were not complaining. They may not always have approved of Henry's goings on, but he had been a king who *was* a king, a king to be proud of and to this day Bluff King Hal remains one of the very few English monarchs who is instantly recognizable to their descendants.

As for his private life, Henry VIII is naturally remembered as the King with six

Henry in the last years of his life.

wives – an unusual achievement for any man, but in Henry's case its importance can easily be exaggerated. For in spite of the highly-coloured sexual reputation which his matrimonial marathon has earned him, he was no Don Juan. On the contrary, he had an almost bourgeois respect for convention – his wives far out-numbered his mistresses – and in general he took a severely practical view of the married state. It was intended for the procreation of children and the Queens' primary function had always been to produce sons. Henry had, in fact, left instructions that he was to be buried at Windsor beside Jane Seymour, the only Queen who had fulfilled her primary function, and on 16 February, after a solemn funeral mass conducted by Stephen Gardiner, he was laid to rest between the stalls and the altar in St George's Chapel.

And so he was gone. He had hounded his blameless first wife into her grave and wrecked his elder daughter's life. He had killed his own great love. He had callously abandoned his most faithful servants naked to their enemies. And yet, in spite of it all, he was not a monster. The nation mourned him sincerely and within weeks of his death he was becoming a national symbol.

CHAPTER 9

A Boy of Wondrous Hope

Sing up, heart, sing up, heart, and sing no more down,
For joy of King Edward, that weareth the crown!

Henry VIII was the last of the adult Tudor males. When he died the only males with royal Tudor blood in their veins were Henry's own son, Edward, now nine years and three months old, and the infant Lord Darnley, son of his niece Margaret Douglas, who had married into a collateral branch of the Stuart family. Apart from these two children, the English royal house had become exclusively and depressingly female. There were Henry's two daughters, the Ladies Mary and Elizabeth; his other two nieces, Frances Grey, Marchioness of Dorset and Eleanor Clifford, Countess of Cumberland and their daughters – three Greys, Jane, Katherine and Mary, aged respectively nine, seven and two, and one Clifford, Margaret, now seven years old – while the main branch of the Stuart-Tudor line was solely represented by the young Queen of Scotland.

This preponderance of women and little girls was politically as well as dynastically unfortunate, for it meant that until Edward was old enough to take over – at least another six or seven years – control would pass out of Tudor hands. King Henry's will had provided for a council of sixteen executors, each 'with like and equal charge', to rule the country during his son's minority – an arrangement so patently unworkable that it had been set aside within a week of the old King's death. At a meeting of the executors held on 31 January it was agreed that 'some special man' would have to be preferred before the rest. The choice was an obvious one and the council obediently proceeded to confer on Edward Seymour, Earl of Hertford, 'the name and title of Protector of all the realms and dominions of the King's majesty that now is, and of the Governor of his most royal person'.

There were, of course, plenty of precedents for appointing the uncle of a child King as regent and guardian, and Edward Seymour had other qualifications. He was a man of proven ability, an experienced and successful soldier and diplomat, generally respected by his colleagues and trusted by the late King. But he was not of the blood royal. The son of a Wiltshire landowning family, he owed his earldom in part to his own exertions, but more to the fact that his sister had had the singular good luck to become Queen. His elevations to vice-regal status would inevitably give rise to jealousy and faction, and it remained to be seen whether he possessed the ruthlessness needed to fight off competition.

He had begun promisingly. Guided by his friend and ally, that shrewd political

Edward VI, a portrait by an
unknown artist.

tactician, Secretary of State William Paget, Seymour had left Whitehall in the early hours of 28 January, before the old King's body was cold. His destination was Hertford Castle, the current residence of the new King; his purpose to get custody of his nephew while Paget handled his interests in London. Largely thanks to Paget, the *coup* was so skilfully managed that by the time the council met on the thirty-first, they were simply rubber-stamping an already accomplished transference of power.

Seymour brought Edward as far as Enfield to join the Princess Elizabeth before breaking the news of their father's death. Brother and sister clung together in such floods of tears that the onlookers were deeply moved, but whether the children cried from grief, from shock or just in sympathy with each other, it is impossible to say. Henry, at least in his own estimation, had been a concerned and affectionate father – Edward certainly had been the apple of his eye. Yet it is not easy to believe that either Edward or Elizabeth felt genuine human sorrow at his loss. In spite of Katherine Parr's well meant efforts, neither had ever known any real family life; neither had ever been given the opportunity to form a genuine human relationship with their awesome parent. But they both knew that his death meant their sheet anchor had gone; that in spite of the kneeling courtiers, the elaborate deference and the fine words, they were now, at nine and thirteen, alone and all too vulnerable in a potentially very dangerous world.

The small, solemn, blond boy who rode through the mid-winter landscape on his way to take possession of his capital seemed a very different type from the bouncing, rumbustious extrovert his father had been at a similar age, and if anyone noticed an ominous resemblance to his uncle Arthur, no one commented on it. Physically Edward was an attractive child, with delicately modelled features, big grey eyes and the family's reddish gold hair, while mentally and intellectually he showed the greatest promise. An enthusiastic contemporary wrote:

> If you knew the towardness of that young Prince your heart would melt to hear him named . . . the beautifullest creature that liveth under the sun, the wittiest, the most amiable and the gentlest thing of all the world. Such a spirit of capacity, learning the things taught him by his schoolmasters, that it is a wonder to hear say. And finally he hath such a grace of deportment and gesture in gravity when he cometh into any presence, that it should seem he were already a father, and yet passeth he not the age of ten years.

Allowing for the fact that almost any child of average intelligence being put through the academic forcing process devised by Edward's tutors might seem a prodigy to the uninitiated, it is still fair to say that Edward was well above average intelligence. As for his gravity of deportment and gesture, the priggish, unchildlike behaviour which often makes the young King appear both pathetic and repulsive, this was simply the natural result of his training and background.

There was no sentimental cult of youth in the sixteenth century. Childhood was widely regarded as an unfortunate but unavoidable preliminary to useful adult life – a period of mental and physical infirmity which, for everyone's sake, should be got through as quickly as possible. Precocity or 'towardness' was therefore to be encouraged and cultivated. Edward was naturally a serious-minded boy. He had been brought up from infancy as the heir to the throne and there is no reason to suppose that at nine years old he did not fully understand and accept the duties and the responsibilities of his position. Childish behaviour in these circumstances would obviously have been quite unsuitable.

Edward arrived in London during the afternoon of 31 January and received an ecstatic welcome from the waiting crowds as he was escorted through the city to the fortress palace of the Tower, where his apartments had been 'richly hung and garnished with rich cloth of arras and cloths of estate as appertaineth unto such a royal King'. Next day came his formal introduction to 'the most part of the nobility of his realm, as well spiritual as temporal' who had gathered in the presence chamber to kiss his hand and to hear the official promulgation of Seymour's appointment as Protector and Governor of the King's person. The assembled lords declared that they would be ready at all times 'with all their might and power' to defend the realm and the King, and finally 'cried all together with a loud voice, "God save the noble King Edward!"'. In reply to this very proper demonstration of loyalty, the noble King Edward took off his cap and recited his piece. 'We heartily thank you, my lords all; and hereafter in all that you shall have to do with us for any suits or causes, you shall be heartily welcome to us.'

The coronation procession of Edward VI. The procession is seen leaving the Tower, moving along East Cheap and down the Strand to Charing Cross and Westminster.

These preliminaries being out of the way, the regime began to settle down and to make plans for the coronation which was to take place on 20 February, agreeing that, as a grudging concession to the King's youth, the antique ceremony should be shortened from the usual eleven or twelve hours to about seven. On 18 February there was a grand investiture, as the new rulers of England made their first experiments with the sweets of power. Edward Seymour, Earl of Hertford, was created Duke of Somerset to emphasize the grandeur of his position. John Dudley, Viscount Lisle, became Earl of Warwick, and the younger Seymour brother, Thomas, Baron Seymour of Sudeley.

On the nineteenth Edward made the recognition procession from the Tower to Westminster. Dressed all in white and silver with the tall, imposing figure of the Duke of Somerset at his side, the third Tudor King rode through gaily decorated, freshly gravelled streets, surrounded by all the pomp and panoply amassed by his ancestors, the cheers of the people breaking over him in warm, generous waves. The city had, as usual, put on a royal show, with allegorical pageants, singing boys and Latin orations at every corner; but, as far as Edward was concerned, the high spot of the afternoon was undoubtedly the acrobat who performed 'masteries' on a rope stretched above St Paul's Churchyard, and who delayed the King's majesty with all the train 'a good space of time'.

The coronation ceremony itself, performed by Edward's godfather Archbishop Cranmer, went without a hitch, though it was perhaps ironical that the first King of England to be crowned as Supreme Head of the Church, God's vice-regent and Christ's vicar within his own dominions should have been a child of nine. If anyone found anything faintly ludicrous in the idea, they were careful not to say so and in sermon after sermon preached in the weeks following the coronation

Edward was compared to Old Testament heroes such as David, Josiah and the young Solomon. The age of the spiritual father of the people was immaterial, his extreme youth a mere temporary inconvenience. What mattered was the fact that he was God's anointed, 'elected of God and only commanded by him', divinely ordained to guide the people into the paths of righteousness. Edward certainly believed this. Whatever inner misgivings he may have felt were not connected with God's purposes but with man's.

As soon as the excitement of the coronation and its attendant festivities were over, the King went back to his lessons and the other members of the royal family were able to start adjusting to their new situation. The Queen Dowager had been left with no further say in the upbringing of her stepson, but she had been generously provided for in her husband's will. Katherine Parr was now an extremely wealthy lady and, until the King married, she remained the first lady in the land, taking precedence even over the princesses. But the most important thing as far as Katherine was concerned, was that she was now for the first time in her life entirely independent and free to please herself. Soon after Henry's death she had moved to her dower house at Chelsea – a modern, red-brick building, convenient for London and pleasantly situated overlooking the Thames. Here she was joined by the Princess Elizabeth and also by young Jane Grey, thus continuing the time-honoured custom of turning a royal lady's household into a finishing school for girls. With the progressive party now in the ascendant Katherine could indulge her religious and intellectual proclivities without fear or concealment, and Chelsea Palace rapidly became a recognized centre of advanced godliness where the minds of two potentially very important wives and mothers were being moulded.

Unfortunately, this feminine mini-paradise was soon to be invaded by old Adam in the shape of Katherine's former sweetheart, Thomas Seymour. The Protector's younger brother was currently labouring under an acute sense of grievance. Not altogether surprisingly he thought poorly of an arrangement which allowed one of the King's uncles to enjoy all the fruits of this valuable relationship, while leaving the other out in the cold. Thomas regarded his barony and his new office of Lord Admiral, passed on to him by John Dudley, as mere consolation prizes and he had every intention of redressing the balance as soon as he was in a position to do so.

As an eligible bachelor in his late thirties, his obvious first step towards political advancement was a good marriage and, according to gossip, his first choice had been the thirteen-year-old Elizabeth. Warned off by his brother and the council, Thomas turned back to the Queen whose feelings for him, he was confident, had not changed. He was quite right in this assumption and Katherine made no attempt to conceal her delight at his renewed attentions. 'I would not have you to think that this mine honest good will toward you to proceed of any sudden motion of passion', she wrote to him from Chelsea. 'For as truly as God is God, my mind was fully bent the other time I was at liberty to marry you before any man I knew.' God, on that occasion, had withstood her will 'most vehemently' but now she was to have her reward for self-abnegation, and at thirty-four the pious, high-minded Queen was radiant as any teenager at the prospect of marrying the man she loved.

...ward Seymour, Duke of Somerset and brother of
...ne Seymour. On Henry's death he became Lord
...otector for his nephew, Edward. A miniature by
...icholas Hilliard.

The Lord Protector's brother, Thomas Seymour, who
married Henry VIII's widow, Katherine Parr.

Certainly Katherine deserved some happiness. The pity was that she had not
made a better choice. Thomas Seymour was physically a very attractive man with
plenty of surface charm. 'Fierce in courage, courtly in fashion; in personage
stately, in voice magnificent, but somewhat empty of matter' runs the well-
known, near contemporary assessment. He was also a vain, greedy, selfish man –
dangerous both to himself and to others.

The Queen Dowager and the Lord Admiral were married privately – so
privately in fact that no one knows exactly where or when the ceremony took
place, although it was probably no later than the beginning of May 1547.
Katherine had talked rather half-heartedly about delay and observing a decent
period of mourning but Thomas, who was anxious to avoid delay, had
experienced very little difficulty in cajoling her out of her scruples.

The next thing was to find a tactful way of breaking the news to the rest of the
family and Thomas wrote to the Princess Mary, asking if she would further his
suit with the Queen. He got severely snubbed for his pains. Mary was old-

fashioned enough to disapprove of hasty re-marriage, especially in this case 'considering whose wife her grace was of late'. But, of course, it was the King's opinion which really mattered. Thomas Seymour had few opportunities of seeing his nephew – this was one of his principal complaints – and he had already taken the precaution of suborning John Fowler, a gentleman of the Privy Chamber, to carry messages and generally act as go-between. He now instructed Fowler to broach the subject of his marriage to Edward in general terms and received the, for Edward, waggish response: 'Wot you what? I would he married my sister Mary to turn her opinions.' Thomas progressed to enquiring, again via Fowler, if Edward 'could be contented I should marry the Queen', and then Katherine herself took a hand. Some time towards the end of May she paid a visit to Court and discussed the whole question of her re-marriage with the King, explaining that no disrespect was intended to his father's memory. Reassured on this point, Edward raised no objections. He was genuinely fond of his stepmother and had nothing against his uncle Thomas – who was busily currying favour with surreptitious gifts of pocket money.

When news of his brother's matrimonial activities reached the ears of the Lord Protector he was, as Edward noted laconically in his Journal, 'much displeased'. But the thing was done now and, in any case, the Protector had weightier matters on his mind that summer. Towards the end of August he left for the North to pursue Henry VIII's policy of attempting to intimidate the Scots into surrendering their little Queen to the cousinly care of her English fiancé and accepting English suzerainty. Somerset succeeded in inflicting yet another devastating defeat on the Scots at the battle of Pinkie, but he did not persuade them to become Englishmen. On the contrary, his 'rough wooing' had the extremely predictable result of driving Scotland ever more firmly into the arms of France. The four-year-old Mary was hastily moved to the island sanctuary of Inchmahone, and the following spring she was spirited away to the Continent and betrothed to the Dauphin. King François had not long survived his old rival Henry Tudor, but the French throne was now occupied by his son, Henri II – a resolute individual who would know how to protect his future daughter-in-law. The King of England would have to look elsewhere for a bride and any chance of uniting the British kingdoms had gone for another generation.

Thomas Seymour should have commanded the fleet during the Scottish campaign, but the Lord Admiral preferred to delegate his duties and remained at home to develop certain projects of his own. He was now living openly as Katherine's husband – sometimes at Chelsea, sometimes at the Queen's manor of Hanworth and sometimes at his own town house, Seymour Place. Katherine was transparently happy in her new life and the Admiral, having achieved the first of his objectives, in high good humour. With the irruption of his loud-voiced, ebullient male presence the atmosphere of the Queen's household had become noticeably more relaxed and informal – in one direction at least unusually so, for Thomas Seymour soon began to amuse himself by teasing his wife's stepdaughter. He 'would come many mornings into the Lady Elizabeth's chamber, before she were ready, and sometimes before she did rise. And if she were up, he would bid her good-morrow, and ask how she did, and strike her upon the back or on the buttocks familiarly . . . and sometime go through to the maidens and play with them, and so go forth.' If Elizabeth was still in bed, 'he would put open the curtains, and bid her good-morrow, and make as though he would come at her. And she would go further into the bed, so that he could not come at her.'

Katherine saw no harm in this sort of romping – she sometimes accompanied the Admiral on his early morning forays and together 'they tickled my Lady Elizabeth in the bed, the Queen and my Lord Admiral'. But the princess's governess took a more realistic view of the situation. Mrs Katherine Ashley, a disapproving spectator of much giggling and shrieking and games of hide-and-seek round the bed-curtains, was devoted to her charge and she knew that the sight of a man – even one who might, at a pinch, be considered a member of the family – apparently welcome to invade her bedroom in his nightgown and slippers would inevitably set tongues wagging. After all, Elizabeth was fourteen that September and no longer a child. Mrs Ashley therefore attempted to remonstrate with the Admiral, telling him that his behaviour was complained of and that her lady would be 'evilly spoken of'. The Admiral, of course, swore by God's precious soul that he meant no harm, that the Lady Elizabeth was like a daughter to him and that he would know how to deal with slanderers. But Mrs Ashley, whose sharp nose for gossip had already picked up the rumour that if my lord could have had his own will he would have married the Lady Elizabeth before he married the Queen, was unconvinced and went to lay her problem before the Queen herself. Katherine 'made a small matter of it' – she was not in the mood to take anything very seriously that summer – but she did promise to chaperone her husband more closely in future.

Just what, if anything, Thomas Seymour expected to gain by his barely-concealed sexual pursuit of Elizabeth is hard to say. Most likely it had begun simply as his idea of a joke but no doubt it also gave him a gratifying sense of power to be on such terms with Henry VIII's daughter. He never attempted similar tactics with the other young girl living under his wife's roof – Lady Jane Grey was still too undeveloped physically to give any spice to slap-and-tickle and besides the Admiral had other plans for her.

Under the terms of his will, Henry VIII, using the powers conferred on him by the 1536 Act of Succession, had settled the crown, in default of heirs from his own children, on the descendants of his younger sister – arbitrarily excluding the senior Scottish line. Jane Grey's dynastic importance had therefore increased dramatically and Thomas Seymour wasted no time in cultivating the friendship of her father. He experienced no particular difficulty in persuading the Marquis of Dorset to put Jane's future in his hands in exchange for certain financial considerations and a promise that the Admiral would see her placed in marriage much to her father's comfort. When Dorset asked for details, John Harington, one of Seymour's most trusted agents who was conducting the negotiations, replied impressively 'I doubt not but you shall see he will marry her to the King', and on this understanding the bargain was struck.

No one, of course, thought it necessary to ask Jane's opinion and Jane herself would not have expected it. A formidably intelligent and 'toward' child, she took very little interest in anything but her lessons. Like her cousins Edward and

Elizabeth, she was already well grounded in the classics and was also studying Greek, French and Italian; but unlike her cousins she, alone of the royal family, was a true scholar, content to devote herself to the pursuit of knowledge for its own sake and not as a means to an end.

Jane was not getting the intensive academic training she so much enjoyed because her parents had any great respect for learning – Frances Dorset, a buxom, vigorous, hard-riding woman who bore a frightening resemblance to her late uncle Henry, and her ambitious but weak-minded husband were very much more interested in worldly advancement – but because, largely thanks to Katherine Parr, higher education for girls had become fashionable and therefore desirable. Jane did not get on with her parents (she once went so far as to tell that sympathetic educationist Roger Ascham that she thought herself in hell when in their company) and was unhappy at home. In the Queen's household she was petted and praised; her cleverness, accomplishments and piety were openly discussed and admired, her brilliant prospects whispered over – and at this time her future did look extremely promising. Katherine, whose influence was still considerable, had quickly become very fond of her, the Admiral was kind to her and in this congenial atmosphere she naturally began to blossom.

But although Jane Grey was a child of whom any family might justly have been proud, of the half dozen or so young people who represented the rising generation of the House of Tudor it was on Edward that attention naturally focused. Edward himself was beginning to find some of this attention a trifle burdensome – especially the attentions of his maternal relatives. The Duke of Somerset was proving a strict guardian and by the end of the first six months of his reign the young King had conceived a perfectly dispassionate dislike of his elder Seymour uncle, who kept him short of money, treated him like a child and was using the royal 'we' in his own correspondence. To do the Protector justice, there is no reason to suppose that his intentions towards his nephew were ever anything but honourable, but he was a cold, stiff man, 'dry, sour and opinionated' was the verdict of the Imperial ambassador, with very little idea of how to make himself agreeable to a child like Edward – incapable of striking the admittedly difficult balance between the deference due to the royal *persona*, the warmth of a close blood tie and the authority needed to guide and to guard this exceptional small boy.

Edward's uncle Thomas was, by contrast, jovial and open-handed. Edward did not hesitate to take advantage of the open-handedness and soon fell into the habit of despatching terse demands for cash by means of the useful John Fowler. But he was becoming irritated and a little frightened by the Admiral's persistent, half-bullying suggestions that he should do more to assert himself and his attempts to involve him in the Seymour family feuds. A particularly acrimonious dispute had arisen that autumn over some items of the Queen Dowager's jewellery which Katherine claimed were her own property, gifts from the late King. But the Protector insisted they belonged to the crown and refused to give them up. Matters were exacerbated by the attitude of the Duchess of Somerset, a vindictive shrew who furiously resented the fact that Katherine continued to take social precedence over her and made no secret of her feelings on the subject.

Edward's first Parliament was due to meet in November and the Admiral, inspired with a renewed sense of his various wrongs, stamped about shouting that, by God's precious soul, he would make this the blackest Parliament that ever was in England. When his cronies, alarmed by his violence, tried to calm him down, he roared defiantly that he could live better without the Protector than the Protector without him, and that if anyone went about to speak evil of the Queen he would take his fist to their ears, from the highest to the lowest.

Thomas Seymour had tried to inveigle Edward (now quite considerably in his debt financially) into signing a letter to be presented to the House of Lords, asking them to favour a suit which his uncle meant to bring before them. According to the Admiral, this was merely a petition to recover Katherine's jewels but more likely he was hoping to get the Lords' support for his plan to have the offices of Protector of the Realm and Governor of the King's person divided between his brother and himself. Edward was clearly suspicious. Beneath that impassive, childish exterior an alert Tudor brain was picking up danger signals and the King turned for advice to his principal tutor, Sir John Cheke, the one person he trusted completely. Cheke warned him very seriously against signing anything he might be made to regret and Edward refused his kind uncle's request. The Admiral, frustrated, took to prowling hungrily in the corridors of St James's Palace, throwing out hints that he wished the King were at home in his house and speculating on how easy it would be to steal him away. But even Thomas Seymour could see the folly of trying to kidnap Edward without the assurance of some very solid backing. He patched up his quarrel with the Protector and subsided – temporarily at least.

There was a Tudor family reunion that Christmas. Elizabeth came up to Court from Chelsea in December and apparently enjoyed herself so much that she asked to stay on over the holiday. Edward wrote inviting Mary to join the party and, for the first time since their father's death, these three survivors of Henry's long, desperate battle to beget an heir met under one roof. The relationship between brother and sisters had altered radically since they had last been together. The deference accorded to a Tudor king, even one just ten years old, was immense; nor were the formalities relaxed on the occasion of a family dinner party. Etiquette required that the King's sisters must not sit close enough to be overshadowed by the cloth of estate above his head, and a visiting Italian reported that he had seen the Princess Elizabeth drop on one knee five times before her brother before she took her place at table with him. Petruccio Ubaldini thought these elaborate ceremonies 'laughable', but both Mary and Elizabeth had been brought up to regard the person of the sovereign with the utmost reverence and neither would have found anything in the least laughable about kneeling to their little brother who was also their King.

In the spring of 1548 a storm was brewing in the Queen Dowager's household. After three childless marriages Katherine had fallen pregnant for the first time, and seems no longer to have been taking quite such a light-hearted view of her husband's playful attentions to her stepdaughter. Had she perhaps begun to suspect that they were no longer quite so playful? There had been an odd little incident at Hanworth, when the Queen told Mrs Ashley that the Admiral had looked in at the gallery window and seen the princess throw her arms round a man's neck. The princess denied the accusation tearfully but Mrs Ashley knew it could not be true, 'for there came no man but Grindal, the Lady Elizabeth's schoolmaster', and he was evidently quite unembraceable. All the same, the governess began to wonder rather uneasily if the Queen was becoming jealous and had invented the tale of a strange man as a warning that she should take better care of her charge, 'and be, as it were, in watch betwixt her and my Lord Admiral'. Mrs Ashley's husband also warned his wife more than once to be on her guard, as he had noticed that the Lady Elizabeth 'did bear some affection' for the Lord Admiral. Matters came to a head shortly before Whitsun when 'the Queen, suspecting the often access of the Admiral to the Lady Elizabeth's grace, came suddenly upon them, when they were all alone, he having her in his arms. Wherefore the Queen fell out both with the Lord Admiral and with her grace also' and hereupon 'there was much displeasure'.

Katherine's 'displeasure' is very understandable, but she could not afford the luxury of making scenes – gossip once started would be unstoppable and a public scandal would have disastrous consequences for all concerned. She did, though, take immediate steps to put as much distance as possible between the princess and the Admiral, sending Elizabeth away on an extended visit to Sir Anthony and Lady Denny, both old and trusted friends of the royal family, at their house at Cheshunt. The Queen and her stepdaughter parted affectionately. Katherine was determined to avoid any suggestion of hard feelings and a penitent Elizabeth recognized and appreciated the older woman's generosity. 'Although I could not be plentiful in giving thanks for the manifold kindness received at your highness's hands at my departure', she wrote from Cheshunt, 'yet I am something to be borne withal, for truly I was replete with sorrow to depart from your highness, especially leaving you undoubtful of health.' Fortunately everyone knew that the Queen Dowager, now in the sixth month of an uncomfortable pregnancy, was planning to spend the summer on her husband's estate at Sudeley in Gloucestershire, and in the general upheaval of the move it had been possible to contrive Elizabeth's departure without causing comment.

The Seymours left for the country on 13 June, accompanied by a princely retinue and taking Jane Grey with them. It was at Sudeley, on 30 August, that Katherine's baby was born, a girl christened Mary. At first all seemed to be well and the Protector sent a kind note congratulating his brother on becoming the father 'of so pretty a daughter'. But sadly the congratulations were premature. Katherine developed the dreaded symptoms of childbed fever and within a week she was dead. She was buried in the chapel at Sudeley Castle with all the pomp and ceremony due to a Queen Dowager of England; Miles Coverdale, the biblical translator, preached the sermon and Jane Grey, a diminutive figure in deepest black, acted as chief mourner for the only person ever to show her disinterested kindness.

Thomas Seymour had been sufficiently shaken by his wife's death to consider sending Lady Jane back to her parents, but this uncharacteristic attack of self-doubt soon passed and on 17 September, a fortnight after the funeral, he told Lord Dorset that he found he would not, after all, be obliged to break up his household. The Dorsets, though, were growing restive. More than a year had gone by with no sign of any of the Admiral's 'fair promises' being fulfilled, and while Lord Dorset assured Lord Seymour that he was still ready to be guided by him in the matter of his daughter's 'bestowing', he was plainly looking for an excuse to back out of his previous undertakings. Jane, he wrote, was too young to be left to rule herself and he feared lest, for want of a bridle she might take too much head and forget all the good behaviour she had learned from Queen Katherine. His lordship, therefore, felt strongly that she should be returned to the governance of her mother 'to be framed and ruled towards virtue'. Frances Dorset added her voice in a letter enclosed with her lord's, in which she thanked her 'good brother' the Admiral for all his gentleness, but begged him to trust her and to believe that a mother knew what was best for her child.

This sudden concern for their daughter's welfare imperfectly concealed the Dorsets' ruthless determination to sell her to the highest bidder and they were, in fact, beginning to wonder whether it might not be wiser to settle for a match with the Lord Protector's son, which had already been tentatively discussed. But Jane was too valuable an asset to lose without a struggle. Tom Seymour went to see the Dorsets and, according to the Marquis, was 'so earnestly in hand with me and my wife' over the custody of Lady Jane that in the end he would not take no for an answer. He renewed his promise that if only 'he might once get the King at liberty' he would ensure that his majesty married none but Jane and agreed to advance another £500 of the £2,000 he was 'lending' to her parents. No need for a bond, declared the Admiral expansively, the Lady Jane's presence in his house would be security enough. The Dorsets, greedy, foolish and chronically hard up, rose to the bait and Jane went back to Hanworth, where old Lady Seymour had been installed as chaperone.

Although the Admiral was now hardly bothering to conceal his eagerness to put an end to the Protectorate, dropping broad hints about his plans and boasting of his strength in the country to anyone who would listen to him, he was no nearer to getting his hands on Edward than he had ever been. Elizabeth also remained out of his reach. But in the princess's household, once more established at Hatfield, there was much excited speculation about his intentions. Katherine Ashley, who was already hearing wedding bells, told her charge that now 'her old husband' was free again, he would be sure to come wooing before long. To the romantic Mrs Ashley it looked like a happy ending. Thomas Seymour had, after all, been considered worthy to marry the Queen and was 'the noblest man unmarried in this land'. Such a fine figure of a man, too. What could be more suitable for her beloved princess?

The Admiral, in fact, still had just enough sense not to come wooing in person but he was taking a close, almost a proprietorial interest in Elizabeth's affairs, cross-examining her steward, Thomas Parry, about the state of her finances, the whereabouts of her landed property, the number of servants she kept and the details of her housekeeping expenses. Gossip soon began to link their names and it was being whispered that the Admiral had kept the late Queen's maids together to wait on the Princess Elizabeth after they were married.

In November, Lord Russell, the Lord Privy Seal, tried to warn Thomas

Princess Elizabeth by an unknown artist, c. 1542–7.

Seymour – pointing out that any Englishman who attempted to marry either of the princesses would 'undoubtedly procure unto himself the occasion of his utter undoing' and Thomas, who was so closely related to the King, would be particularly at risk. After all, observed old John Russell, it was a well-known fact that both Henry VII and Henry VIII, although wise and noble princes, had been famous for their suspicious natures. What, therefore, was more likely than that Edward would take after his father and grandfather in this respect? If one of his uncles married one of the heirs to his crown, he would inevitably think the worst, 'and, as often as he shall see you, think that you gape and wish for his death'.

But Thomas Seymour was past listening to advice. He continued to conduct his courtship of Elizabeth through the willing agency of Parry and Mrs Ashley. Like most adventurers, the Lord Admiral was extremely plausible and perhaps the steward and the governess can hardly be blamed for failing to realize just how flimsy was the flamboyant façade he presented to the world. But one person did realize it. Although the fifteen-year-old Elizabeth could not entirely conceal the 'good will' she still felt for the Admiral, her behaviour, compared with those who were supposed to be caring for her, was a model of discretion. She had not responded to Mrs Ashley's eager promptings and when Thomas Parry had the temerity to ask her outright whether, if the Council approved, she would marry the Admiral, she snubbed him sharply. The Tudor princess was fully alive to the dangers of being drawn into anything which might be construed as secret correspondence with a man committed to opposing the lawful government. Nor had she forgotten the clause in her father's will which laid down that if she or Mary married without the consent of their brother and his Council, they would forfeit their right of succession to the throne.

The New Year came in and the Lord Admiral's career approached its predestined climax. Tales of his various 'disloyal practices' had become too numerous and too circumstantial to be ignored any longer and in January 1549 the faction headed by John Dudley, Earl of Warwick, which had been waiting patiently for the Seymour brothers to destroy one another, decided that the time had come to start applying pressure on the Duke of Somerset. The Protector seems to have made a last minute effort to avert disaster by trying to send Thomas abroad, but it was too late – Lord Seymour of Sudeley had already tied a noose round his neck with the rope so generously paid out to him. He was arrested on 17 January and the Council started on the business of rounding up his associates. John Fowler of the Privy Chamber, Katherine Ashley and Thomas Parry were all taken away for questioning, while Sir Robert Tyrwhit was sent down to Hatfield to extract a confession from the Princess Elizabeth.

When Elizabeth was told that her governess and her steward had been arrested 'she was marvellous abashed and did weep very tenderly a long time', demanding to know whether they had confessed anything or not. This sounded promising and Robert Tyrwhit did not anticipate any difficulty in getting a useful statement out of her. All the same, their first interview was disappointing. The princess, it seemed, had nothing to tell him and Tyrwhit felt obliged to warn her 'to consider her honour and the peril that might ensue, for she was but a subject'. Having allowed Anne Boleyn's daughter to digest this scarcely veiled threat, Sir Robert went on to advise her to be frank with him. If she would 'open all things herself', then her youth would be taken into consideration by the Protector and the Council and the 'evil and shame' ascribed to Mrs Ashley and to Parry, who should have taken better care of her. But this was not the way to approach Elizabeth Tudor, always fiercely loyal to her friends. 'And yet', wrote Tyrwhit, 'I do see it in her face that she is guilty, and do perceive as yet she will abide more storms ere she accuse Mistress Ashley'.

At their next interview Elizabeth told Sir Robert how the Admiral had kindly offered her the use of Seymour Place when she came up to London to see the King (Durham House, where she usually stayed, being temporarily unavailable); how she had once written him a note asking some small favour for her chaplain; how there had been a suggestion that the Admiral might pay her a visit but Mrs Ashley had thought perhaps better not, knowing how people gossiped. It was all very innocent, very trivial and quite beside the point – just the ordinary friendly intercourse between two members of the same family. Still, it was a start and Tyrwhit hoped that more would follow now that he had begun 'to grow in credit' with the princess. At the same time, he told the Protector, 'I do assure your Grace she hath a very good wit, and nothing is gotten of her but by great policy.'

In her present predicament Elizabeth needed all the wit and self-control she could muster. Utterly alone, her household full of strangers and spies, she was being called upon to answer the kind of charge – based chiefly on tittle-tattle and innuendo – which is always most difficult to refute. She faced hours of skilled and relentless questioning, designed to trap her into admissions which would have ruined her good name and quite possibly cost her her place in the succession. Her liberty, her whole future might very well be at stake. And she was still only fifteen years old. Tyrwhit tried all the tricks of the interrogator's trade but on 28 January, after more than a week of unremitting effort, he was obliged to report: 'I have practised with my lady's grace by all means and policies to cause her to confess more than she has already done. But she does plainly deny that she knows any more than she has already opened to me.'

The Protector himself had now written to Elizabeth, counselling her 'as an earnest friend' to declare all she knew. This was the opportunity Elizabeth had been hoping for and she took it with both hands. Her reply to Somerset, polite but businesslike and written in the exquisitely legible Italic script she had learned from her best remembered tutor Roger Ascham, is by any standards a masterpiece of its kind. There had never at any time been any sort of secret understanding with the Admiral and neither Mrs Ashley nor Parry had ever advised her to marry anyone without the full consent of the King's Majesty, the Protector and the Council. Even if they had, she herself would never have agreed to such a thing. She had already told Robert Tyrwhit everything she knew about her own and her servants' contacts with Thomas Seymour since the Queen's death, but if she remembered anything further, she would either write it herself 'or cause Master Tyrwhit to write it'. Her letter ended with an indication of the sort of methods being used to break her resistance. 'Master Tyrwhit and others have told me that there goeth rumours abroad which be greatly against my honour and honesty (which above all other things I esteem) which be these; that I am in the

Tower and with child by my Lord Admiral. My lord, these are shameful slanders, for the which, besides the great desire I have to see the King's majesty, I shall most heartily desire your lordship that I may come to Court after your first determination, that I may show myself there as I am.'

Elizabeth Tudor had defended herself and her friends against the most unwarrantable accusations with courage and dignity, and had more than hinted that she would expect an official apology. Unfortunately, though, neither her much loved governess nor her steward possessed the stalwart qualities of their mistress. Under interrogation in the Tower, first Parry and then Katherine Ashley broke down and made long, verbose statements. These were rushed to Hatfield where, on 5 February, Robert Tyrwhit was able to confront the princess with her servants' 'confessions'. 'She was much abashed and half breathless' he reported and studied the signatures with particular attention, although as Tyrwhit remarked, she knew both Mrs Ashley's hand and the cofferer's 'with half a sight'. He went on, 'I will tomorrow travail all I can to frame her for her own surety and to utter the truth.'

But by the next day Elizabeth had recovered her poise. It was, of course, acutely humiliating to see the intimate details of those merry romps at Chelsea and Hanworth set down in writing for everyone to read. It was humiliating but it was not remotely treasonable. There was still no evidence whatever that Elizabeth, or Mrs Ashley, or Thomas Parry had been involved in any sort of plot. So, when Tyrwhit returned to the attack, the princess graciously allowed him to take down her own 'confession' which, apart from a few unimportant details, contained absolutely nothing new. 'They all sing the same song', wrote Tyrwhit in exasperation, 'and so I think they would not do, unless they had set the note before.'

The Council now appointed Sir Robert's wife to replace Mrs Ashley as the princess's governess, hoping that the princess would 'accept her service willingly'. The princess would not. She cried all that night and 'lowered' at Lady Tyrwhit all the next day – signs that prolonged strain was having its effect. 'She beginneth now a little to droop', Tyrwhit reported towards the end of February, 'by reason she heareth that my Lord Admiral's house be dispersed. And my wife telleth me now that she cannot bear to hear him discommended but she is ready to make answer therein; and so she hath not been accustomed to do, unless Mistress Ashley were touched, whereunto she was very ready to make answer vehemently.'

The Admiral had, of course, been doomed from the moment of his arrest. Although Elizabeth herself had turned out to be such a disappointing witness, there was no lack of evidence from other sources. Even the King obligingly recalled the details of certain conversations with his uncle, and those gifts of pocket money, once eagerly accepted, were now produced as evidence of treasonable intent. Since Parliament was still in session, the Council decided not to accord Thomas Seymour the courtesy of an open trial, but to proceed against him by means of an Act of Attainder – a cheap and convenient method of dealing with enemies of the State. First, though, the consent of the victim's two closest relatives must be obtained and on 24 February, 'after the King's majesty had dined', the full Council assembled in his presence. The Lord Chancellor 'declared forth the heinous facts and treasons of the Admiral', adding that the prisoner had obstinately refused to answer any of the charges except in open trial. Everyone then cast their votes in favour of remitting the matter to his Majesty's high court of Parliament. When it came to the Protector's turn, he said – and he had very little choice, after all – that deeply distressing though the case was to him, his first duty must be to the King's majesty and the crown of England, for he 'did weigh more his allegiance than his blood'. Now it was up to the King. Was he going to make any effort to help his kind uncle? He was not. 'We do perceive', announced the eleven-year-old Edward Tudor, 'there is great things which be objected and laid to my lord Admiral mine uncle, and they tend to treason; and we perceive that you require but justice to be done. We think it reasonable, and we will well that you proceed according to your request.' At these words, 'coming so suddenly from his Grace's mouth of his own motion', the assembled company, greatly relieved by his Grace's admirably unsentimental attitude, gave him 'most hearty praise and thanks'.

Thomas Seymour was executed on Tower Hill on 20 March but unlike that other Queen Dowager's widower who had suffered a similar fate in the market square at Hereford nearly ninety years ago, the Lord Admiral left no posterity to alter the course of history. Little Mary Seymour, stripped of her inheritance and abandoned to the reluctant care of the dowager Duchess of Suffolk – once one of Queen Katherine Parr's closest friends – disappeared from the record and is believed to have died in childhood.

The indifference which Edward had shown over the downfall of his uncle Thomas, had been noted by the Earl of Warwick and had encouraged that intelligent individual – now in the final stages of preparing his own bid for power – to hope that the King would be equally indifferent to the fate of his other Seymour uncle. Events soon began to play into Warwick's hands. The year 1549 was marked by a general and increasing popular discontent – due partly to economic hardship caused by rising prices and widespread unemployment, and partly to an angry reaction in the more backward rural areas against the sweeping religious changes introduced since King Henry's death. This discontent presently erupted into two quite serious revolts, one in the West Country and one in Norfolk, which caused considerable alarm among the propertied classes. Somerset's high-minded liberalism might earn him the title of 'the Good Duke' among the common people, but his merciful attitude towards rebellious common people did not endear him to the nobility and gentry, who turned thankfully to the Earl of Warwick – a capable soldier with no tiresome notions about the rights of the poor.

Meanwhile, the Protector's growing arrogance and intolerance of opposition were also alienating his colleagues on the Council and his friend William Paget, who had done so much to help him attain his elevated position, warned him bluntly that unless he showed more consideration in debate and allowed other people freedom to speak their minds, he would soon have cause to regret it. But Paget had no more success in trying to warn the elder Seymour than John Russell had once had with the younger. Somerset, increasingly harassed and worried by the failure of his policies at home and abroad, seems to have been no longer able to face the realities of the political scene and had taken refuge behind a smokescreen of irascibility. His public image, too, had been fatally damaged by his brother's death – just as the Earl of Warwick had known it would be. His outwardly cold-blooded reaction to the Admiral's attainder and execution had disgusted a lot of people who now, most unfairly, stigmatized him as a fratricide, 'a blood-sucker and a ravenous wolf'.

In mid-September Warwick returned triumphantly to London after suppressing the rebellion in East Anglia. As well as being the hero of the hour, he now had a well-armed and victorious body of troops ready at his command. This was clearly the moment for a move to dislodge the Lord Protector from his shaky throne. Towards the end of the month, the citizens of London were surprised to see those members of the Council who followed Warwick's lead going armed about the streets, 'their servants likewise weaponed, attending upon them in new liveries'. There was much coming and going at the Earl's house in Holborn and rumours were flying round the city that the confederates were planning to seize the Tower.

Somerset was with Edward at Hampton Court when he learnt that the London Lords, as Warwick's party had become known, intended to pay him a 'friendly' visit. Only two members of the Council had remained at his side and only about five hundred men – some of his own and some wearing the royal livery – were available to guard the palace. Realizing his danger somewhat late in the day, the Protector sent out anguished appeals for reinforcements and issued a proclamation in the King's name, commanding 'all his loving subjects with all haste to repair to his Highness at his Majesty's manor of Hampton Court, in most defensible array, with harness and weapons, to defend his most royal person and his most entirely beloved uncle the Lord Protector, against whom certain hath attempted a most dangerous conspiracy.'

On 6 October, Cardinal Wolsey's handsome Thames-side mansion bustled with activity. Weapons and harness were brought out of the armoury, guards were mounted at the gates, messengers rode to and fro and, as the King himself put it, 'people came abundantly to the house'. But although Archbishop Cranmer arrived with a force of sixty horsemen, it soon became clear that help was not going to be forthcoming in time. The local peasantry had come in obediently to defend their king, but they would be no match for Warwick and his professional force; nor, in spite of all those warlike preparations, was Hampton Court defensible against any sort of determined assault.

At nine o'clock that night the Protector brought Edward down to the main gate of the palace where a large puzzled crowd was waiting and there, in the flickering torchlight, the child, prompted by his uncle, made a brief, rather sulky appeal to his assembled subjects. 'Good people', he said, 'I pray you be good to us – and to our uncle.' Then Somerset spoke, exclaiming rather hysterically that he would not fall alone. If he was destroyed, the King would be destroyed – kingdom and commonwealth would all be destroyed together. Pushing Edward in front of him, he went on: 'It is not I that they shoot at – this is the mark that they shoot at.' Horses were waiting saddled in the courtyard and uncle and nephew with a small escort mounted and rode hurriedly away into the night for the greater security of Windsor Castle.

It looked uncomfortably like flight and was for Edward a thoroughly upsetting and frightening experience. When he and Somerset reached Windsor at about three o'clock in the morning, no one was expecting them and nothing had been prepared. To the helpless boy surrounded by grim-faced adults talking in lowered voices over his head the gloomy, medieval fortress must have seemed more like a prison than a refuge, the whole adventure something of a nightmare. Nobody, it seemed, thought of offering him any comfort or reassurance. On the contrary, the Protector, anxious for the King's support, had worked to impress him with a sense of his danger from their common enemies. Edward had never felt any particular affection or even liking for his austere uncle, but he had hitherto respected and, on the whole, trusted him. Now he saw only a panicky middle-aged man trying to save his own skin by hiding behind the sacred person of his sovereign lord. Trust and respect died, but fear did not. Edward was not yet twelve years old and still very much in his uncle's power.

But not for long. Somerset had not succeeded in saving himself. The London Lords, under Warwick's skilful and determined leadership, pursued him to Windsor and on 10 October he was taken away under guard to the Tower. The Lords then waited on the King and gave him a carefully edited account of their doings. Edward listened politely. He asked no awkward questions and thanked their lordships for the pains they had taken in safeguarding him and the realm. (He later entered in his Journal, an unrevealing document, a list of the Protector's crimes, which included ambition, vainglory, entering into rash wars in the King's youth, enriching himself with the King's treasure, following his own opinion and doing all by his own authority.) The King kept his private thoughts on the October crisis to himself. As he grew older, Edward kept his private thoughts more and more to himself.

A few days after Somerset's arrest, Edward returned to Hampton Court with a reconstituted entourage and the palace revolution was over. In fact, Somerset was to survive, in and out of the Tower, for another fifteen months – until 22 January 1552, when the King made another entry in his Journal: 'The Duke of Somerset had his head cut off upon Tower Hill between eight and nine o'clock in the morning.'

Edward's apparent lack of any human feelings on this occasion has earned him a reputation for callous cold-heartedness, but did he perhaps derive some secret satisfaction from the knowledge that he was surely the first child king so effectively to have turned the tables on uncles? That he might, in a manner of speaking, be said to have avenged the little Princes in the Tower?

CHAPTER 10

Gone is Our Treasure

Adieu pleasure!
Gone is our treasure,
Mourning may be our mirth:
For Edward our King
That rose and spring
Is faded and lyeth in earth.

Therefore, mourn we may
Both night and day,
And in heart we may be full sad;
Since Brute came in,
Or at any time since,
The like treasure we never had.

It was agreed that there should be no more Lord Protectors. England's new strong man had no intention of repeating his predecessor's mistakes and, in any case, was a great deal more interested in the realities of power than in its trappings. Now in his late forties, John Dudley's career to date had set a perfect pattern of the rise of the Tudor meritocracy. Descended from a cadet branch of a respectably old and well-connected baronial family, his father, a clever lawyer with a first-class financial brain, had served Henry VII as fiscal adviser rather too efficiently for his own good. One of Henry VIII's first acts as King had been to offer Edmund Dudley and his colleague Richard Empson as sacrifices on the altar of public opinion, and both men were executed on charges of treason blatantly contrived to appease the outraged taxpayers of England. Young John had therefore had to make his own way in the world. Darkly handsome, athletic, gifted and aggressively ambitious, he was clearly destined to be a high-flier and progressed steadily in the royal service as a soldier, diplomat and administrator.

Throughout his career, first as Lord Lisle and then as Earl of Warwick, John Dudley had made a careful study of Tudor psychology. He became a particular favourite of the old King – especially after Charles Brandon's death – and had been named as one of the trusted inner circle of executors of Henry's will. His plan now was to use the still impressionable Edward as a screen behind which to consolidate his own position and secure the future of his numerous sons. First, though, he would have to be assured of the King's trust, his unqualified support

*John Dudley, Duke of
Northumberland. Having
successfully deposed
Somerset, Dudley married
his own son to Lady Jane
Grey intending to make her
queen on Edward's death.*

and, if possible, his love. Warwick was a man of commanding presence and magnetic personality. In private life he was an affectionate family man with plenty of experience of bringing up boys, but he never made the mistake of treating Edward as a child. He treated him as a King, and as a King who should now be old enough to start taking an active part in the serious business of government. Edward naturally responded eagerly to this form of flattery. He began to attend regularly at Council meetings and not merely to rubber-stamp decisions already taken. So at least it appeared, and so Edward himself believed. Those who were surprised at his grasp of affairs were possibly not aware that Warwick was in the habit of visiting the King privately late in the evening to brief him on the next day's business. He would listen deferentially to the royal opinion but was careful to ensure that his own viewpoint should always be uppermost in Edward's mind before he slept.

It used to be said that Warwick took Edward out of the stuffy atmosphere of the schoolroom and brought him into the fresh air. In fact, Edward's timetable had always included provision for plenty of outdoor exercise and training in the sports and pastimes proper for kings. At the same time it was certainly a very important item of Warwick's strategy to bring Edward forward, to introduce him to the more glamorous aspects of kingship and generally to keep him happy and amused.

A special embassy came over from France in the early summer of 1550 to conclude a new Anglo-French treaty and the King was fully involved in the entertainment provided for the envoys. There was a state dinner, bull and bear baitings, a hunt and supper at Hampton Court and fireworks on the Thames. Several cheerful young Frenchmen were added to the royal entourage and on 19 June Edward took them down to Deptford, where Lord Clinton, the new Lord Admiral, put on an exciting display of tilting in which the contestants stood on boats and ran at one another until the loser fell into the water. This was followed after supper by a mock sea battle staged on the river – all exactly calculated to entrance a twelve-year-old boy. Edward was still keeping regular lesson hours, but under his new guardian's carefully unobtrusive guidance his horizons were widening every day and he was enjoying every moment of it.

In the autumn of 1551 he had his first experience of acting as host to foreign royalty, when Mary of Guise, Queen Dowager and Regent of Scotland, asked leave to pass through his realm on her way back to the North after visiting her daughter in France. The Dowager was storm-bound at Portsmouth and the English government immediately sent a welcoming deputation with friendly letters from the King and orders to escort the distinguished castaway to London, Edward adding a special message that he would be pleased to supply anything she needed for her comfort and that he looked forward to meeting her. The Court was at Westminster and the King received his guest with all the due ceremony in the Great Hall of the Palace. Later they dined together, the Queen Regent sitting on Edward's left under the cloth of estate and, so it was said, being much impressed by the maturity, wisdom and judgement of her youthful host.

Among those members of the royal family summoned to do honour to the Queen were the King's cousins Margaret, Countess of Lennox and Lady Jane Grey and her parents. Jane Grey's parents had recently taken a step up in the world. Following the sudden and tragic deaths from the sweating sickness of Charles Brandon's two sons by Katherine Willoughby, the dukedom of Suffolk had devolved on their half-sister Frances and her husband. In spite of the fact that Jane was no nearer to marrying the King – the present plan was for a betrothal between Edward and the French Princess Elisabeth – the Dorsets basked happily in the glory of their new honour. But Henry Grey was not the only new Duke at Court that autumn. John Dudley now felt sufficiently secure to petition the King on his own account and on 11 October he had been created Duke of Northumberland, the first Englishman with no blood tie with the royal house ever to bear a ducal title.

The King's sisters had not been invited to meet Mary of Guise. In fact the King's sisters played very little part in the life of the Court. In Mary's case this was due to a steadily widening rift over the religious question and by the early fifties the unfortunate princess was once again being hounded for her beliefs. Trouble had started in the spring of 1549 when Somerset's programme of reform had culminated in the establishment of Cranmer's English prayer book as the official order of service for the church in England. The Book of Common Prayer came into general use on Whitsunday, and it meant the end of the ancient Latin mass. Faced with the threatened extinction of the very foundations of her faith,

Mary appealed to the Emperor and Charles responded more energetically than usual, instructing his ambassador to obtain a written guarantee from the Duke of Somerset that his cousin would be allowed to continue to have mass unmolested in her own household. This guarantee was not forthcoming but, after a good deal of argument, François van der Delft did succeed in extracting a verbal promise from the Protector that the princess might do as she thought best in the privacy of her own house until the King came of age. There the matter might have rested. Somerset was a man of his word and Mary was an old friend of his wife's, who had once been one of her mother's maids. Then came the October *coup*. The Somersets were in eclipse and early in 1550 Mary had warning that the Council were planning further moves against her, that before long both she and her household would be forbidden to hear mass.

For the second time in her life Mary's thoughts turned to escape. It seemed as though she could not endure any more battles. She was older now and more tired, worn out by constant colds, toothache and headache. She yearned only to live at peace among her mother's kin in some quiet Catholic country and she begged the Emperor to give her sanctuary. The Emperor had his doubts. Whatever her private longings, Mary was still her brother's heiress. To connive at her escape would be a risky business, to harbour her would be expensive and embarrassing. On the other hand, she was potentially a very valuable property and Charles may have been touched by her despair. He may also have feared, as his ambassador certainly did, that if he, Mary's 'only hope and refuge in this world', failed her in this extremity, she would attempt to escape unaided and that 'the good lady through her own incompetence might fall into a worse evil'. At any rate, Charles gave his reluctant consent to a rescue attempt.

Speed and secrecy were essential. Van der Delft was recalled at the beginning of June and his replacement, a stolid Dutch merchant, kept in careful ignorance of what was going on. Mary had already moved to her manor at Woodham Walter, east of Chelmsford and only a couple of miles from Maldon on the tidal river Blackwater where, on the last day of the month, a smooth-talking Flemish merchant berthed his vessel at the quayside. Master Jehan Duboys was from Ostend with corn to sell in the Essex ports. Nothing unusual about that. Nothing unusual either in the Lady Mary's Comptroller, with a large household to feed, coming down to do business with him. The unusual thing about Master Duboys was his mission – somehow to smuggle the Lady Mary aboard that innocent-looking coaster and carry her downriver to a rendezvous with certain ships of the Imperial navy, currently lying off Harwich on the pretext of hunting pirates.

The plan was a bold and simple one and might very well have succeeded, but now the moment had arrived Mary's nerve failed her. She dithered in miserable indecision while those members of her household who disapproved of the whole project worked on her fears. Jehan Duboys was not unsympathetic but he could not hang about while the princess made up her mind. For Mary's sake as well as his own, he dared not delay. So the chance was lost and now Mary had to stay and face whatever her brother's Council had in store for her.

The secret of that aborted escape was soon out, of course, and the government took prompt steps to ensure that such a thing would not happen again, moving soldiers into all the likely east coast ports. No direct reprisals were taken against Mary, but the new line of attack being masterminded by John Dudley became apparent when a warrant was issued for the arrest of one of her chaplains who had unwisely celebrated mass in her absence. Previously the Council had aimed their warning shots at the princess herself and had been ignored. Now, and more effectively, they intended to penalize her servants.

By the autumn the battle of the Princess Mary's mass was fairly joined. Supported by the new Imperial ambassador, Jehan de Scheyfve, and by the Emperor, Mary based her defence on the promise made by the Duke of Somerset to Van der Delft. The Council blandly denied that such a promise had ever been given. In any case, they said, any promises made by Somerset were strictly temporary and provisional and applied only to Mary herself – certainly not to the fifty-odd members of her household, who could claim no privilege and must obey the King's laws or suffer the consequences.

It was not until January 1551 that the King himself took a hand in the affair, adding a personal postscript to one of the Council's hectoring letters. 'Truly, sister', he wrote, 'I will not say more and worse things, because my duty would compel me to use harsher and angrier words. But this I will say with certain intention, that I will see my laws strictly obeyed, and those who break them shall be watched and denounced, even as some are ready to trouble my subjects by their obstinate resistance.'

This unequivocal statement of the King's position came to Mary as a bitter revelation of the gulf which now yawned between them, causing her 'more suffering than any illness even unto death'. Previously she had been able to comfort herself with the thought that her brother was still a helpless puppet in the hands of men like John Dudley and his confederates; that it was they, not he, who were her enemies. But in Edward's letter the echo of their father's voice was too unmistakeable to be disregarded. Brother and sister had seen little of each other during the past two years. Mary had avoided the Court deliberately, keeping her occasional visits private and as brief as possible, for fear that she would in some way be forced or tricked into attending one of the new services and so seem to be giving public countenance to the hated new ways. Now there was the additional fear that Edward's mind was being poisoned against her and she realized that the dreaded confrontation could not be postponed any longer.

So, on 17 March she came to London in state, 'with fifty knights and gentlemen in velvet coats afore her, and after her four score gentlemen and ladies'. Her regular household had obviously been reinforced by other sympathizers and their wives. On the following day the princess made her way through Fleet Street and the Strand to Westminster, where Edward, supported by all twenty-five members of the Council, was waiting for her.

The proceedings began with another inconclusive wrangle about the Duke of Somerset's promise. Mary complained of the tone of the Council's letters, saying that contrary to previous undertakings she was now being prevented from practising her religion. Edward interposed at this point. He knew nothing about that, he said, for he had only taken a share in affairs during the past year. Mary saw her opening. In that case, she remarked, he had not drawn up the new ordinances about religion. There was no answer to this, but the councillors came back fighting with a warning that grave troubles might arise if she, sister to the King and heiress to the crown, continued to disobey his laws. The new ordinances applied to everyone, and although a measure of indulgence had been granted to Mary to please the Emperor and out of respect to her position, it would not be continued indefinitely.

Mary replied by turning to her brother. She was his humble subject and sister, she said, who would always pray for his prosperity and for the peace of the realm. Everyone praised the King's great knowledge and understanding and she had no wish to denigrate it, rather she would pray that God would increase his many virtues. Nevertheless, and she looked the thirteen-year-old Edward straight in the eye, riper age and experience would teach him much more yet. This was too much for the young Josiah, who promptly retorted that Mary might also have something still to learn, no one was too old for that. It would be very hard for her to change the religion in which the King her father had bred her, answered Mary sadly, not pretending to misunderstand. Here someone observed irresistibly that the late King had changed several points of religion and had he lived, he would no doubt have gone further. But Mary refused to be drawn on this point, merely sighing that she wished everything had remained as it was at the time of the King her father's death.

The bulky ghost of the King their father, who had bequeathed them their insoluble problem, was almost palpably present at this encounter between his son and daughter. The frail, indomitable woman and the fair, slender boy might physically be shadows of their tremendous sire, but no one could have mistaken those jutting chins, the stubbornly folded mouths, the unshakeable conviction of righteousness. Many of those standing by in the gallery at Westminster on that March morning must surely have heard the rumble of distant thunder.

The Council were now shifting the attack, trying to accuse Mary of disobedience to her father's will, but here they were on shaky ground. Mary, who knew the will as well as anybody, could reply with perfect truth that it bound her only in the matter of her marriage and, while they were on the subject, what about the two masses a day which her father had ordered for the repose of his soul? What about the four obsequies a year and the other ceremonies which were not being carried out? The provisions of the will *were* being carried out, was the rather feeble reply, but only insofar as they were not harmful to the present King. Her father had never ordered anything in the least harmful to the King, said Mary scornfully and, in any case, surely it was reasonable to suppose that he alone had cared more for the good of his son's kingdom than all the members of the Council put together? This defiance brought the Earl of Warwick into the fray. 'How now, my lady!' he exclaimed. 'It seems your Grace is trying to show us in a hateful light to the King our master without any cause whatsoever.' She had not meant to do so, answered Mary but they pressed her so hard that she would not dissemble or hide the truth. Then she turned back to Edward. She hoped that, remembering their nearness in blood, he would show her enough consideration to allow her to continue undisturbed in the observance of her religion. In the last resort, she went on, there were only two things – soul and body. Her soul she offered to God, her body to the King's service and she would rather he took away her life than the old religion in which she desired to live and die – and who then can have failed to hear echoes of the long-dead Catherine of Aragon? Edward, obviously embarrassed, said hastily that he had no desire for such a sacrifice and there the meeting ended. Mary, exhausted and shaking with nerves, asked permission to go home and permission was granted.

Edward is usually said to have been fond of his elder sister, although direct evidence of this is pretty slight. He may well have retained some affection and respect for the woman who had helped to mother him in his babyhood; but to the boy in his early teens, just beginning to feel his power, Mary and her awkward conscience (only Tudor kings were permitted the luxury of awkward consciences) and her elder sisterly habit of telling him he was too young to understand were becoming an irritation and a nuisance.

His own account of the matter is characteristically terse. 'The Lady Mary my sister came to me at Westminster', he wrote in his Journal, '. . . where it was declared how long I had suffered her mass *against my will* [he later crossed out these words] in hope of her reconciliation, and how now . . . except I saw some short amendment, I could not bear it. She answered that her soul was God's and her faith she would not change, nor dissemble her opinion with contrary doings. It was said I constrained not her faith, but willed her as a subject to obey.'

Edward took his responsibilities as the keeper of his people's conscience with great seriousness, but it seems likely that the question of his sister's conscience did not worry him too extremely at this time. Mary, by contemporary standards, was already middle-aged. To Edward she must have seemed already old – she was, after all, fully old enough to be his mother – and her poor health was notorious. The King, notably unsentimental in such matters, probably reflected that the problem would soon go away of its own accord and, left to himself, might have been prepared, however disapprovingly, to let his sister go her own way. But, unhappily for Mary, she was now once again the heiress presumptive and her actions and beliefs were of political importance. It had suited John Dudley to ally himself with the extreme radical wing of the religious reformers, men who stood well to the left of Cranmer. He knew that the conservative bulk of the population, the silent majority, disliked much of what he was doing and agreed with the Lady Mary when she wished that everything had remained as it was at the time of her father's death. Her example and her influence were important and so, as once before in her life, it was necessary to force her submission. And, as once before, Mary finally surrendered. By the autumn of 1551 mass was no longer being publicly celebrated in her chapel where, of course, any of her neighbours who wanted to come and worship in the old way, had always been welcome. Mary herself continued to seek the consolation of her religion, but in fear and secrecy behind the locked doors of her own apartments.

The King's relations with his younger sister were uncomplicated by religious differences, and, so it was said later, there was between them 'a concurrency and sympathy in their natures and affections, together with the celestial conformity in religion which made them one, and friends; for the King ever called her his sweetest and dearest sister, and was scarce his own man, she being absent.'

Protestant historians and propagandists writing in the seventeenth and eighteenth centuries were concerned to present an idealized picture of this brother and sister, both such notable champions of the faith, and undoubtedly a genuine bond of affection *did* exist. Born on the same side of the great divide, Henry VIII's two younger children shared the same sort of background, the same pattern of education, many of the same ideals. They corresponded fairly regularly and Edward always seemed pleased to see Elizabeth when she came to Court. But nevertheless, the depth of their relationship has undoubtedly been exaggerated. Apart from the barrier set up by Edward's accession, the intimacy of childhood faded as he grew towards manhood. He had more exciting things to think about now than either of his sisters and, in any case, he naturally preferred to spend his leisure in sporting activities than in feminine company.

Elizabeth had by this time pretty well succeeded in living down any unfortunate impression left behind by the Seymour scandal – at least among those people whose opinions mattered. She had adopted a severely plain style of dressing which suited her elegant figure admirably and won golden opinions from leading Protestant divines, who commented approvingly on her maidenly apparel – such a dramatic contrast to those society ladies who persisted in going about 'dressed and painted like peacocks'. The visit of Mary of Guise had awakened a new interest in French fashions but the Lady Elizabeth would alter nothing, keeping 'her old maiden shamefacedness'. She was, of course, setting a fashion herself, eagerly followed by such high-born Protestant maidens as her cousin Jane Grey.

Jane had recently received a present from Mary of a dress of 'tinsel cloth of gold and velvet, laid on with parchment lace of gold' and is said to have complained: 'What shall I do with it?' 'Marry, wear it', answered one of her ladies in surprise. 'Nay', said Jane, never noted for her tact, 'that were a shame to follow my Lady Mary against God's word, and leave my Lady Elizabeth, which followeth God's word.'

Elizabeth came up to London about once a year between 1549 and 1552. 'She was most honourably received by the Council', wrote Jehan de Scheyfve acidly, 'who acted thus in order to show the people how much glory belongs to her who has embraced the new religion and is become a very great lady.' But apart from her carefully spaced public appearances, Elizabeth was living quietly in the country, dividing her time between her Hertfordshire manors of Hatfield and Ashridge. One reason for this retired existence was her own indifferent health. As a little girl she had always been remarkably fit – there is no mention even of ordinary childish ailments – but ever since her separation from Katherine Parr in the spring of 1548 she had been poorly on and off, suffering from recurrent severe attacks of migraine and catarrh. Probably this was largely of nervous origin – the effect of shock and strain on an adolescent girl. But Elizabeth also found her symptoms provided a useful excuse on occasions. Her other, and perhaps more compelling reason for avoiding the limelight was her determination to avoid any involvement in any controversial issue while the political situation remained so fluid.

Elizabeth's innate good sense had saved her at the time of the Admiral's downfall, but that episode had left an indelible mark on her and had taught her some valuable lessons about discretion and caution and dissimulation – about the necessity of keeping one's mouth shut and one's feelings to oneself in a hard, unforgiving world. 'Her mind has no womanly weakness', wrote her ex-tutor, Roger Ascham, to his friend the Rector of Strasbourg University, 'her perseverance is equal to that of a man and her memory long keeps what it quickly picks up.' Ascham, of course, was referring with justifiable pride to the princess's wide knowledge of the classical authors, her ability to speak 'readily and well' in Latin and moderately in Greek, not to mention her fluency in modern languages, and certainly Elizabeth contributed her full share to the sudden intellectual flowering among the third and fourth generations of the house of Tudor. But that brilliant mind could also apply itself to the strictly practical problems of survival and the retentive memory long keep its hold on matters other than Greek grammar. Fortunately for herself and for posterity, Elizabeth remembered and profited by lessons learned outside the schoolroom before she was sixteen. She had her eighteenth birthday in September, 1551 – an age when it was unusual for such a princess to be still unspoken for – but she was content to wait, biding her time and keeping a low profile until she saw more clearly what the future might hold for her.

What the future held for Elizabeth and Mary Tudor, and for the people of England, depended entirely on Edward who was already becoming a factor to be reckoned with politically and who, if he survived, would soon be casting off the tutelage of his Council. If he survived. . . . Edward was not the big, strong boy his father had been and his fair colouring and slender physique promoted an impression of fragility, so that emissaries of Catholic powers – alarmed by evidence of his increasingly belligerent Protestantism – dropped hopeful hints in their letters home that the King of England was delicate and not likely to live long. In fact, at fourteen, the King seemed healthy enough. He was now showing every sign of developing the family passion for outdoor sports and spent every spare moment on the tennis court, in the tiltyard or shooting at the butts, and his Journal contains frequent references to various interesting sporting events. The Spanish ambassador reported that the King was beginning to exercise himself in the use of arms and enjoyed it heartily. The French ambassador complimented him on the dexterity of his swordplay, declaring that his Majesty 'had borne himself right well' and receiving the modest reply from Edward that it was a small beginning but as time passed he hoped to do his duty better.

Then, in April 1552, the King developed a high temperature and a rash. He himself later recorded, 'I fell sike of the mesels and the smallpokkes.' This would surely have been a lethal combination and Edward's illness was probably a sharp attack of measles. He made a good recovery and was able to attend a St George's Day service at Westminster Abbey, wearing his Garter robes. On the thirtieth the Court moved down to Greenwich and Edward held a review of his men-at-arms on Blackheath. On 27 June, apparently in his usual health and spirits, he set out on an extended progress through the south and west. The progress was a triumphant personal success for the King and Edward, who had never before travelled so far from London, thoroughly enjoyed himself. But the programme was an exhausting one and people noticed that he was looking pale and thin. In fact, that unlucky bout of measles, coming just at the most dangerous age for Tudor boys, and followed by a strenuous summer, had fatally weakened him and by the time he got back to Windsor, a few days after his fifteenth birthday, tuberculosis was already established. By Christmas it was obvious that he was far from well and a more than usually elaborate round of festivities was organized to distract attention from this disturbing fact. When Mary came to London at the beginning of February, Edward was running a temperature and it was three days before he was well enough to see her. Jehan de Scheyfve reported that the princess was received with noticeably more attention and courtesy than on previous occasions, the Duke of Northumberland himself going down to the outer gates of the Palace of Westminster to welcome her. Edward was still in bed and Mary sat beside him while they chatted amicably about safe subjects – the thorny topic of religion was not mentioned.

Edward stayed in his room for the rest of the month. He seemed, wrote de Scheyfve, 'to be sensitive to the slightest indisposition or change' and suffered a good deal when the fever was on him. In March he rallied temporarily and was able to open the new session of Parliament, although the Lords and Commons had to go to him and a much curtailed ceremony was performed within the precincts of the palace. The doctors, who remained in constant attendance, made reassuring noises but those courtiers who had not seen the King since Christmas were horrified by the change in him. He had become thin to the point of emaciation and his left shoulder seemed higher than his right. On 11 April 1553 Edward was moved out to the purer air of Greenwich, but de Scheyfve wrote that he was no better and the ambassador heard from 'a trustworthy source' that his sputum was 'sometimes coloured a greenish yellow and black, sometimes pink, like the colour of blood'. A month later, de Scheyfve had another grisly bulletin for the Emperor. 'The physicians are now all agreed that he is suffering from a suppurating tumour on the lung . . . He is beginning to break out in ulcers; he is vexed by a harsh, continuous cough, his body is dry and burning, his belly is swollen, he has a slow fever upon him that never leaves him.'

The government was making every effort to conceal the gravity of the King's condition, but it was impossible to stop the rumours spreading. Mary wrote anxious letters begging to be allowed to visit him and Elizabeth made a determined effort to reach her sick brother. Some time that spring she had actually started on the journey to London but was met on the way by a messenger purporting to come from the King, who 'advised' her to turn back. After this, there was nothing to be done but return to Hatfield and await developments. She continued to write to Edward but it is doubtful if any of her letters ever reached him. Having once faced the fearful fact that the King's illness was mortal, the Duke of Northumberland had gone to considerable pains to separate him from his sisters. He wanted no outside influence brought to bear on the dying boy and was anxious to prevent either of the princesses from hearing of certain plans for their future.

Northumberland's power would end with the King's death – the best he could expect from Mary and her friends was political extinction, the worst an early

Right: *Henry Grey, Duke of Suffolk, father of Jane, Katherine and Mary Grey; an engraving after a contemporary portrait.* Below: *Frances Brandon, Dowager Duchess of Suffolk, with her second husband, Adrian Stokes, her Master of Horse and sixteen years her junior, painted by Hans Eworth, 1559. There is now, however, some doubt about the identity of the couple in this portrait.*

appointment on Tower Hill – and since no one believed he would give up without a struggle, the Court and City seethed with nervous speculation. At the beginning of May John Dudley took the first steps towards securing his position by announcing the betrothal of Lady Jane Grey to his youngest and only remaining unmarried son, Guildford. Bearing in mind that Henry VIII had willed the crown to the so-called Suffolk line after his own children, the intention behind this move could hardly be mistaken.

At first the plan encountered some unexpected opposition from fifteen-year-old Lady Jane. After the arrest of Thomas Seymour, Jane had been reluctantly obliged to return home. Her only escape would be marriage but she disliked Guildford Dudley, a conceited, oafish youth and his mother's darling, and she considered herself already promised to the young Earl of Hertford, son of the late Protector. Her protests did her no good. Her deplorable parents set on her in unison and the marriage duly took place at Durham House on Whitsunday, 21 May. At the same ceremony, Jane's younger sister Katherine, now thirteen, was married to Lord Herbert, son and heir of the powerful Earl of Pembroke, and one of Northumberland's daughters, another Katherine, to Lord Hastings, heir of the Earl of Huntingdon. This triple wedding, designed by John Dudley to forge a triple-strength chain of alliances, was 'a very splendid and royal' occasion, attended by 'a great concourse of the principal persons of the kingdom'. It had been given out that the King himself would be there, but Edward was by now in no condition to leave his bed. According to de Scheyfve, writing on 11 June, he was now obliged to lie flat on his back all day. He could keep nothing on his stomach and was living 'entirely on restoratives and obtaining little or no repose'.

By this time, in fact, the wretched Edward, suffering as much, if not more, from the remedies being inflicted on him as from his disease, was very near his end. But there was to be no merciful oblivion for England's Treasure, or at any rate not yet. Somehow he must stay alive until he had completed his blueprint for the future as set out in his Device for the Succession, which disinherited Mary and Elizabeth as 'not lawfully begotten and related to him by half-blood only', passed over Frances Suffolk and bequeathed the crown directly to Jane Grey and her 'heirs male'.

While Northumberland must bear a considerable share of the blame, the prime mover in this patently illegal attempt to set aside the provisions of the 1544 Act of Succession was undoubtedly Edward himself. His motives appear to have been straightforwardly ideological. Trained in the school of advanced evangelical Protestantism, he believed, just as rigidly as Mary did, that his was the only way of salvation for himself and for his people, for whose salvation he had always been taught, he was personally responsible under God. Conviction of this kind overrode all considerations of earthly justice and as soon as he began to realize that he might not live to provide heirs of his own body, Edward knew that if he valued his immortal soul, he must take every possible precaution to safeguard the work of godly reform. Why he was so determined to rule out the Protestant Elizabeth as well as the Catholic Mary has never been fully explained, but it would obviously be difficult to justify the exclusion of one princess and not the other, and Elizabeth, however good her intentions, might well find herself obliged to marry a Catholic prince. For that matter, both the princesses were liable to acquire foreign husbands, who would gain control of affairs and 'tend to the utter subversion of the commonwealth'.

The Device went through several drafts, but by the middle of June it was ready in its final form and before the end of the month had been ratified, more or less reluctantly, by the Privy Council, the judiciary and the bishops. The most determined opposition had come from Sir Edward Montague, the Lord Chief Justice, who pointed out that, without another Act of Parliament, Edward had no power to alter his father's dispositions, and from Archbishop Cranmer, whose conscience troubled him deeply. Montague put up a spirited resistance, but he was an elderly man, frightened of Northumberland and conditioned to obeying royal commands, and in the end he surrendered. So too, in the end, did Cranmer, who wanted more than anything to see his pathetic, suffering godson die in peace – happy in the belief that he had ensured the survival of the true Protestant faith.

Edward had now taken no solid food for nearly three weeks; his sputum was black, fetid and stinking; his fingers and toes were becoming gangrenous and the boy, born in such joy and wondrous hope fifteen years and nine months ago, longed only for death. Release came during the afternoon of 6 July, when the last Tudor King died in the arms of his friend Henry Sidney.

Edward VI was the first committed Protestant King of England – a fact which unfortunately tended to overshadow everything else in the minds of his contemporaries – and the flood of eulogies on his godly wisdom and government, his zeal in abolishing 'the deformities of popish idolatry' and overthrowing 'the tyranny of Anti-Christ' have very largely succeeded in obscuring the reality of the living, breathing boy. Perhaps the most interesting, because disinterested, appreciation comes from an outsider, Girolamo Cardano, an Italian mathematician and physician, who saw and talked to the King in the autumn of 1552 when a trained observer could already discern 'the mark in his face of death that was to come too soon'. Cardano could report at first-hand on Edward's 'singularly perfect' knowledge of Latin and French and could easily believe that he was equally proficient in Greek, Italian and Spanish. 'Neither was he ignorant in logic, in the principles of natural philosophy, or in music. There was in him lacking neither humanity, the image of our mortality, a princely gravity and majesty, nor any kind of towardness beseeming a noble king. Briefly, it might seem a miracle of nature to behold the excellent wit and forwardness that appeared in him being yet a child.' And yet, Cardano insisted, he was not exaggerating. If anything 'the truth is more than I do utter'. They met several times and discussed, among other things, astronomy and the causes of comets. Cardano was deeply impressed by his grasp of and interest in the liberal arts and sciences, his sagacity and his 'amiable sweetness'. 'By this little trial', he wrote, 'a great guess may be given what was in this King.'

Even allowing for a measure of exaggeration in all the tributes to his virtue and wisdom, there is no reason to doubt that Edward did have great natural intelligence, a real eagerness to learn and an enormous capacity for concentrated hard work. Nor is there any reason to doubt the utter sincerity of his religious convictions, even if they do make him seem priggish to a materialistic age. The coldly uncommunicative front he presented, especially in the early years of his reign, was probably a defence mechanism as much as anything and where his suspicions had been aroused his hostility could be implacable – witness his attitude towards his unfortunate Seymour uncles. But Edward could both give and inspire affection. His personal attendants were all devoted to him and Edward himself had formed a close and lasting friendship with Barnaby Fitzpatrick, the Irish boy who shared his childhood.

In his obstinacy, his streak of ruthlessness, his personal charm, his love of music and pageantry, and his addiction to physical exercise Edward was a very recognizable Tudor. It seems more than possible that he might have grown up to combine his father's more attractive characteristics with his grandfather's longheadedness and made England a very great king. But he had been able to give 'a show or sight only of excellency' and now:

> Out of Greenwich he is gone,
> And lieth under a stone,
> That loveth both house and parke:
> Thou shalt see him no more,
> That set by thee such store,
> For death hath pearced his hart.
>
> Gone is our King,
> That would runne at the ringe,
> And oftentimes ryde on Black heath:
> Ye noblemen of chevalry,
> And ye men of artillerie,
> May all lament his death.
>
> That swete childe is deade,
> And lapped in leade,
> And in Westminster lyeth full colde:
> All hartes may rue,
> That ever they him knew,
> Or that swete childe did beholde.
>
> Farewell, diamonde deare!
> Farewell, christall cleare!
> Farewell, the flower of chevalry!
> The Lorde hath taken him,
> And for his people's sinne;
> A just plague for our iniquitie.

The plague, just or otherwise, which Edward's people now faced was that old recurring nightmare, a disputed succession, and in the summer of 1553 the outlook was particularly gloomy. With the royal house reduced to a handful of women and babies and the rightful heir a delicate ageing spinster, the way seemed wide open for the strong men to take over. Mary had been waiting out the last few months in 'sore perplexity' and increasing fear of the future. Northumberland sent her regular reports on Edward's condition and he even sent her a present, a blazon of her coat of arms as Princess of England, but Mary and de Scheyfve believed these attentions were intended to lull her suspicions, that the moment Edward was dead the Duke meant to seize power for himself by proclaiming his new daughter-in-law Queen, and that Mary would then be in deadly danger. All the same, when a summons to her dying brother's bedside reached her at Hunsdon, probably on 5 July, she obediently set out on the journey. She had not gone far – she was at Hoddesdon on the London road – before she received an anonymous warning, which can surely have come as no surprise, that Northumberland's message was a trap.

The crisis which had been lying in wait for Mary all her adult life was now upon her. Now, if ever, she must forget her megrims, her nervous headaches, her self-doubts and hesitations and fits of weeping. Now, if she was to save herself, let alone her chances of becoming Queen, she must act with speed and decision. With only one possible course of action before her, Mary showed that she could rise bravely to an occasion. After sending a brief word to the Imperial embassy, she turned aside and, with no more than half a dozen loyal companions, rode hard and straight down the Newmarket road for Kenninghall in Norfolk. She had friends in the eastern counties and there, if it came to the worst, she would be within reach of the coast and rescue.

In London the King's death was being kept a close secret, or as close as it was possible to keep a secret in any royal household, but when he heard that Mary had slipped through his fingers, Northumberland could wait no longer – for him, too, speed was of the essence. He despatched a party of three hundred horse under the command of his son Robert with orders to pursue and capture the Lady Mary and on Sunday, 9 July, he finally showed his hand. The Bishop of London, preaching at St Paul's Cross, referred to both the princesses as bastards and fulminated especially against Mary as a papist who would bring foreigners into the country. Also on that Sunday the Lady Jane was officially informed of her new status.

The six weeks since her marriage had not been happy ones for Jane. She seems to have feared and disliked the whole Dudley family, particularly her husband and his mother, to such an extent that even her own mother's company was preferable and immediately after the wedding she had gone back first to Suffolk Place and then to her parents' house by the river at Sheen. But the Duchess of Northumberland, who did not get on with the Duchess of Suffolk, soon became impatient. She told Jane that the King was dying and that she ought to be ready for a summons at any time, because he had made her his heir. According to Jane, this information, flung at her without warning, caused her the greatest stupefaction, but she put it down to 'boasting' and an excuse to separate her from her mother. She probably said so, for the result was a furious Tudor–Dudley quarrel – the Duchess of Northumberland accusing the Duchess of Suffolk of deliberately trying to keep the newly-weds apart and insisting that whatever happened, Jane's place was with her husband. This argument was unanswerable and, in the end, Jane was forced to join Guildford at Durham House where, apparently, the marriage was consummated. But the reluctant bride stayed only a few days with her in-laws. She had become ill – probably some form of summer complaint aggravated by nervous strain – and, with curious lack of logic, was convinced that the Dudleys were poisoning her. In fact, of course, her health and wellbeing were of vital concern to the Dudleys just then and they sent her out to Chelsea, with its happy memories of Katherine Parr, to recuperate. She was still there on the afternoon of 9 July when Northumberland's daughter, Mary Sidney, came to fetch her to Syon House – another of the Duke's residences. At Syon she found her parents, her husband, her mother-in-law, and the Lords of the Council headed by Northumberland himself. These distinguished personages greeted her with 'unwonted caresses and pleasantness' and, to Jane's acute embarrassment, proceeded to kneel before her and do her reverences which she considered most unsuitable to her state. Northumberland then broke the news of Edward's death and went on to disclose the terms of the King's 'Device'; how he had decided for good and sufficient reasons that neither of his sisters was worthy to succeed him and how – 'he being in every way able to disinherit them' – he had instead nominated his cousin Jane as heir to the crown of England.

Jane's partisans have always maintained that this was the first she knew of her deadly inheritance, but it is hard to believe that a girl of so much brilliant, highly-trained intelligence can have failed to grasp the significance of her hasty forced marriage to Guildford Dudley, or that she had not at least guessed what was being planned for her. Not that prior knowledge in any way affected the helplessness of her position. Half-fainting, she managed to gasp out something about her 'insufficiency' and a hasty prayer that if the crown *was* rightfully hers, God would help her govern the realm to His glory. In present circumstances, God looked like being her only friend.

On the following afternoon, the new Queen was taken in state by water from Syon to the Tower and a Genoese merchant, one Baptista Spinola, who was standing in a group of spectators outside the fortress to see the procession disembark, took the trouble to describe her appearance in detail. 'This Jane', he wrote, 'is very short and thin (all the Grey sisters were diminutive, Mary, the youngest, being almost a dwarf), but prettily shaped and graceful. She has small features and a well-made nose, the mouth flexible and the lips red. The eyebrows are arched and darker than her hair, which is nearly red. Her eyes are sparkling and reddish brown in colour.' Spinola was standing so close to Jane that he noticed her complexion was good but freckled and her teeth, when she smiled, white and sharp. She was wearing a gown of green velvet stamped with gold, while Guildford, 'a very tall strong boy with light hair' resplendent in white and silver, preened himself at her side and 'paid her much attention'.

Guildford was enjoying himself. He made no pretence of loving his wife, but he was quite prepared to be polite to her in public in return for the golden stream of social and material benefits which would flow from her. Unfortunately these happy expectations were about to receive a severe set-back. No sooner was Jane installed in the royal apartments at the Tower than she was visited by the Lord Treasurer, the Marquis of Winchester, bringing a selection of royal jewels for her inspection. He also brought the crown itself although, as Jane was later careful to stress, she had not asked for it. Either in an ill-judged attempt to please her, or (more likely) to force her into committing herself beyond any possibility of return, Winchester urged her to put it on to see if it suited her. Jane recoiled in horror. The crown was the ultimate symbol of sanctified earthly power – to treat it as a plaything, a sort of extra special head-dress, would be tantamount to blasphemy. Winchester failed to see the storm-signals. She could take it without fear, he told her and added kindly that another should be made to crown her husband.

This was the final straw. It was perhaps only now that Jane realized, 'with infinite grief and displeasure of heart', exactly how she had been tricked. No one cared a snap of their fingers about fulfilling her dead cousin's wishes, about maintaining the gospel and the Protestant faith, or whether the throne was rightfully hers. The plot was simply to use her and her royal blood to elevate a plebeian Dudley to a throne to which he had no shadow of right so that his father could continue to rule. Jane had her full share of Tudor family pride and now that pride was outraged. Small, stubborn, terrified and furious, she laid back her ears and dug in her heels. She would make her husband a duke but never, never would she consent to make him king. This naturally precipitated a full-scale family row. Guildford rushed off to fetch his mother and together they launched an all-out attack on their victim – he whining that he did not want to be a duke, he wanted to be King; she scolding like a fishwife. At last, finding Jane immovable, they stormed out of her presence, the Duchess of Northumberland swearing that her precious son should not stay another minute with his unnatural and ungrateful wife but would return immediately to Syon. Jane watched them go and then sent for the Earls of Arundel and Pembroke. Little though she wanted Guildford's company, she had no intention of allowing him to put such an open slight on her. She ordered Arundel and Pembroke to prevent him from leaving. Whether or not he continued to share her bed, his place was by her side and there he must stay. Guildford sulked but he did as he was told.

While these domestic storms were raging inside the Tower, the heralds were going round the city proclaiming Queen Jane but, noted the Greyfriars Chronicle ominously, 'few or none said God save her'. The sullenly silent crowds in Cheapside and Ludgate that summer evening set the pattern for the rest of the country. The English people knew nothing and cared less about Jane Grey; they had always had a soft spot for Mary Tudor and, even more to the point, they had come to loathe the whole tribe of Dudley for greedy, tyrannical upstarts. Richard Troughton, bailiff of South Walshen in Lincolnshire, hearing of Mary's plight from his friend James Pratt as they stood together by the cattle drinking-place called hedgedyke, was moved to exclaim: 'Then it is the Duke's doing and woe worth him that ever he was born, for he will go about to destroy all the noble blood of England.' John Dudley might control the capital, the Tower with its armoury, the treasury and the navy; he might have all the great lords in his pocket, meek as mice; but Richard Troughton spoke for England, and England had had more than enough of John Dudley and his like and was not prepared to stand idly by while King Harry's daughter, poor soul, was cheated of her rightful inheritance.

Meanwhile, King Harry's daughter had reached the comparative safety of Kenninghall and on 9 July had written defiantly to the Council, commanding them to proclaim her right and title in *her* City of London. Mary's challenge was delivered just as the new Court was sitting down to dinner on that eventful Monday, 10 July and caused the Duchesses of Suffolk and Northumberland to shed tears of alarm. The news that Mary was still at large and showing fight came as an unwelcome surprise to her enemies, 'astonished and troubled' as they read her letter, but not even the most optimistic of her friends dared to hope that she might stand a chance. At the Imperial embassy, where Jehan de Scheyfve had recently been reinforced by three envoys extraordinary, they were confidently expecting the worst and could only deplore my Lady's obstinate refusal to accept defeat.

But the Duke knew how slight were the foundations on which his power rested. Every day that Mary remained free would undermine them further and disquieting reports were beginning to come in about the support rallying to her. The Earl of Sussex and his son were on their way to Norfolk, while the Earl of Bath and men like Sir Thomas Wharton, Sir John Mordaunt, Sir Henry Bedingfield and Henry Jerningham, as well as other substantial gentlemen and their tenantry – not to mention 'innumerable small companies of the common people' – were already helping to swell the numbers at the little camp now established at Framlingham Castle, a stronger place than Kenninghall and nearer the coast. No cause yet perhaps for serious anxiety, but any hope of the swift, silent *coup* which John Dudley had been banking on was gone. He would have to mount a full-scale expedition 'to fetch in the Lady Mary' and ride out the consequent bad publicity as best he could.

Preparations began on the twelfth with a muster at Tothill Fields and that night wakeful citizens could hear carts laden with weapons and supplies 'for a great army towards Cambridge' rumbling eastward through the streets. Northumberland had intended to put the Duke of Suffolk in command of the army, but when this information was conveyed to Queen Jane, she burst into tears and begged that her father 'might tarry at home in her company' – the prospect of being left alone in a nest of Dudleys was altogether too much. The Lords of the Council looked uneasily at their weeping sovereign and then at each other, an idea beginning to form in their collective minds. This idea they presently propounded to Northumberland. It would be so much better, they suggested, if he took command himself. No other man was so well fitted for the task, especially seeing that he had already suppressed one rebellion in East Anglia and was therefore so feared in those parts that no one would dare offer him any resistance. Besides, was he not 'the best man of war in the realm'? Then there was the matter of the Queen's distress and the fact that she would 'in no wise grant that her father should take it on him'. So it was really up to the Duke, murmured someone, a note of steel audible under the persuasion, it was really up to the Duke 'to remedy the matter'. The Duke, sensing that control of events was beginning to slide out of his hands, gave way. 'Since ye think it good', he said, 'I and mine will go, not doubting of your fidelity to the Queen's majesty which I leave in your custody.'

The fidelity of his associates to anything but their own best interests was, of course, highly doubtful and it was the lively fear of what they might do as soon as his back was turned which lay behind John Dudley's reluctance to take the field himself. He knew that he was being manoeuvred into the role of scapegoat, but there was no going back now.

Next day, all his arrangements made, he addressed the assembled Council for the last time, in a last effort to impress them with the hypnotic force of his personality. He and his companions, he said, were going forth to adventure their bodies and lives trusting to the faith and truth of those they left behind. If anyone was thinking of violating that trust, let them remember treachery could be a two-handed game; let them also remember God's vengeance and the sacred oath of allegiance they had taken 'to this virtuous lady the Queen's highness', whom they had all helped to entice into a position she had never asked for or sought. 'My lord', said someone – it may have been Winchester, the eldest of the peers – 'if ye mistrust any of us in this matter, your grace is far deceived; for which of us can wipe his hands clean thereof?' While they were talking the servants had come in with the first course of dinner and were laying the table, but Winchester (if it were he) went on: 'If we should shrink from you as one that were culpable, which of us can excuse himself as guiltless? Therefore herein your doubt is too far cast.' 'I pray God it be so', answered the Duke abruptly. 'Let us go to dinner.'

After the lords had eaten, Northumberland went to take his leave of the Queen and receive from her his signed and sealed commission as Lieutenant of her army. Jane thanked him 'humbly' for allowing her father to stay at home and asked him to use all his diligence. 'I will do what in me lies', he said, looking down at the thin, red-haired slip of a girl to whom he had bound himself by the unbreakable kinship of mutual destruction. Early on the following morning, 14 July, he rode out of Durham Place in the Strand, his eldest son at his side, and took the road through Shoreditch – the way lined with silent, staring crowds.

During the next few days the faces of those left behind in the Tower grew steadily longer as word arrived that Mary had been proclaimed in Norwich and that the town had sent her men and weapons. Even more worrying were the reports of desertions and dissension in Northumberland's forces. Then came a shattering piece of news – the crews of the six royal ships sent to Yarmouth to cut off Mary's escape route had gone over to her in a body, taking their captains and their heavy guns with them. 'After once the submission of the ships was known in the Tower', wrote an eyewitness, 'each man then began to pluck in his horns.' It was now a question not of whether, but when they would follow the sailors' example. Already certain individuals were looking for ways of escaping from the stifling confines of the fortress 'to consult in London', and on the sixteenth there was a sudden alarm at about seven o'clock in the evening when the main gates of the Tower were locked and the keys carried up to Queen Jane. It was given out that there was a seal missing, but the same anonymous eyewitness believed the truth of the matter was that the Queen suspected the Lord Treasurer of some evil intent. Old Winchester had sneaked out to his own house and had to be fetched back at midnight.

Jane could not hope to stem the tide – she had neither the experience nor the authority – and two days later she was forced to allow Arundel, Pembroke and about a dozen others to leave on the excuse that they had urgent business to discuss with the French ambassador. But, on the following afternoon, it was the Imperial embassy which received a visit from a deputation of councillors. They had come to explain how reluctant they had been to subscribe to King Edward's 'Device', but really they had had no choice for they had been so bullied by the Duke and treated 'almost as if they were prisoners'. Of course they all believed in their hearts that Mary was the rightful Queen and they were going to proclaim her that very day.

And so they did, between five and six in the evening of 19 July at the Cross in Cheapside amid scenes of hysterical excitement. People with money in their purses flung it out of their windows into the cheering, yelling crowds – the Earl of Pembroke was seen to throw a whole capful of gold angels and no doubt regarded it as a good investment. Sober citizens wrenched off their gowns and capered in the streets like children. The church bells rocked and crashed in a forest of steeples. Bonfires were lit on every corner and all that night the people of London sang and danced and feasted, drinking the health of the rightful Queen and destruction to her enemies.

Faint echoes of the general rejoicing could be heard in the Tower where, so it was said, the Duke of Suffolk broke the news to his daughter and with his own hands helped to tear down the cloth of estate over her head. Then he went out on to Tower Hill and proclaimed the Lady Mary's grace to be Queen of England before scuttling away to Sheen. Jane was left alone in the stripped and silent rooms to listen to the distant pealing of the bells – for her there was no going home.

At Framlingham, Mary's first act as Queen had been to order the crucifix to be set up again in the parish church where a Te Deum was sung. To her friends, to all those conservative gentlemen who had risked their lives and fortunes to come to her aid, to the hundreds of thousands of ordinary people who believed in the rule of law because it was their only protection, her victory against all the odds seemed like a miracle. To Mary there was no question about it. She had been vouchsafed a clear and obvious sign that God was prepared to give her a second chance, a chance to expiate an old festering sin, a chance to lead her people back into the light.

CHAPTER 11

The Rule of the Proud Spaniards

The rose that chearfully doth showe,
  At midsomer her course hath shee;
The lilye white after doth growe,
  The columbine then see may yee;
The gillyflower, in fresh degree;
  With sundrie more then can be tolde,
Though they never so pleasaunt be,
  Yet I commende the Marigolde . . .

To Marie our queene, that flower so sweete,
  This Marigolde I doo apply:
For that the name doth serve so meete,
  And propertie in each partie.

One of the first people to congratulate the new Queen on her triumphant accession was her sister Elizabeth. Elizabeth had contrived to avoid becoming involved in John Dudley's machinations by the simple expedient of taking to her bed. She, like Mary, had received a summons to Edward's deathbed but had promptly given out that she was ill – much too ill to travel – and was prepared to send a doctor's certificate to prove it. She had, however, followed the course of events with anxious attention. If Northumberland won, her own future was likely to have been as problematical as Mary's and the news of his downfall can only have come as an enormous relief. Elizabeth had made no public gesture of solidarity with her sister while Mary stood alone – gestures of that kind were for those who could afford to commit themselves – but she wasted no time in sending a message of loyal good wishes on the occasion of this famous victory for the family. Nor did she lose any time in presenting herself in person. On 29 July she rode into London handsomely attended by a thousand horsemen in green and white Tudor liveries. She spent a couple of nights at Somerset House, the mansion built by the Lord Protector and now appropriated by Elizabeth as a town residence, before riding out again through Aldgate 'towards the Queen's highness'.

The sisters met at Wanstead. It was some time since they had seen one another – possibly not since they had last spent Christmas with Edward in 1547 – but they had continued to correspond and, on the surface at least, had remained good friends. Now Mary greeted Elizabeth affectionately and the two processions

Mary I, 1544; a portrait by Master John.

joined forces for the Queen's state entry into London. The royal party reached the village of Whitechapel at seven o'clock on the evening of 3 August and Mary paused only to change her dress before going on to take formal possession of her capital.

They made a poignant contrast, those two daughters of Henry VIII, as they rode together through streets decorated with banners and streamers, the trumpets sounding before them and the citizens cheering themselves hoarse on every side. Mary, wearing purple velvet and satin with a heavily jewelled collar round her neck, was thirty-seven years old and looked her age. As a girl she had been pretty – small and finely made, with a delicate pink and white complexion and the family's red-gold hair. Now she was painfully thin, and although dispassionate foreign observers still described her as 'fresh-coloured', the pink and gold had long since faded, leaving a small, sandy-haired, tightlipped woman with myopic grey eyes and a surprisingly deep gruff voice. Elizabeth would be twenty in a month's time. She was never, even in the full bloom of youth, considered strictly beautiful, but the Venetian ambassador thought her face and figure 'very handsome' and her bearing regally dignified. There can be little doubt that to very many people in those welcoming crowds of Londoners it was she who represented all England's future hope.

When the Queen's procession reached the Tower, the guns thundering a salute, she was greeted at the gate by three kneeling figures – the old Duke of Norfolk, still lying under sentence of death; Stephen Gardiner, 'Wily' Winchester, who had spent most of Edward's reign in prison for his reactionary opinions, and young Edward Courtenay, grandson of Katherine Courtenay née Plantagenet, who had spent most of his life in prison for that reason alone. Mary raised the suppliants and kissed them, saying smilingly 'these are my prisoners'. If she was remembering the time when Norfolk had taken the lead in trying to bully her into submitting to her father, she gave no sign of it. Perhaps, in her moment of triumph, she remembered only that it was his castle at Framlingham which had recently given her shelter.

While her brief, incredulous glow of happiness lasted, Mary was ready to call the whole world her friend, believing innocently that the country in general hated the new ways as much as she did, and that the great majority of the people were only waiting for a lead to return thankfully to the fold of the true Church. Living for so many years in rural retreat, surrounded by her Catholic household, she had completely failed to realize how strongly a nationalistic form of Protestantism had taken root, especially in London and the south-east, during the past decade; and she had completely misinterpreted the true nature of the rapturous welcome she had received. The people were thankful to be rid of the Dudleys and genuinely pleased to see the triumph of the rightful heir, but this did not mean they were prepared to submit once more to the authority of the Bishop of Rome and within a month of the Queen's accession there had been a number of violent anti-Catholic demonstrations on the streets of London.

For a time Mary clung to her hopes of a peaceful reconciliation. She told the Council on 12 August that she did not mean to 'compel or constrain other men's consciences', but trusted that God would put a persuasion of the truth into their hearts. Soon afterwards a proclamation was issued in which the Queen expressed her desire that the religion which she herself had professed from infancy would now be quietly and charitably embraced by all her subjects. But while Mary was prepared to be patient and to listen to the advice of those who warned her to be cautious at first in matters of religion, there were some things over which her own conscience would not allow her to be cautious. She had, for example, worried a good deal about Edward's burial, feeling it would be wrong to let her unhappy, misguided brother go to his grave unhallowed by the rites of Holy Church. In the end, she was persuaded to compromise. Archbishop Cranmer read the new English funeral service over his godson in Westminster Abbey, while the Queen attended a solemn Requiem Mass in the ancient Norman chapel in the White Tower. Mass, although still officially illegal, was being publicly celebrated at Court – not once, as the Emperor was informed at the end of August, but six or seven times a day, with the councillors (whose consciences were conveniently elastic) assisting in force. There was, however, one notable absentee, for the Queen's sister and heir had not as yet put in an appearance.

In the first two or three weeks of her reign Mary had shown Elizabeth a flattering degree of attention, holding her by the hand whenever they appeared in public together and always giving her sister the place of honour at her side. This

An illustration from the plea roll of the Court of the King's Bench, Michaelmas 1553, records the defeat of the rebels leading to Mary's accession.

happy state of affairs was inevitably shortlived. Mary had inherited all her mother's inflexibility and stubborn rectitude – none of her father's magnetism and political acumen. A 'good' woman, narrow in outlook, limited in intelligence, embittered by long years of loneliness and unhappiness, and still carrying that terrible burden of guilt, she was to prove a dangerous person to deal with – and especially so for Elizabeth. Mary had never borne malice to the child who had been the innocent cause of so much of her suffering, but it was rapidly becoming clear that she could not bring herself to like or trust the cool, self-confident young woman – the past and its ghosts lay too heavily between the daughters of Catherine of Aragon and Anne Boleyn. A past for which Elizabeth bore no direct responsibility could scarcely be acknowledged as a reasonable cause for present disfavour but the matter of her religious observance was something else altogether and could, indeed must, be brought into the open without delay.

The religious problem was a particularly tricky one for Elizabeth. Now that Edward was gone and Jane Grey hopelessly discredited, the Protestant party was already turning to her as their figurehead and white hope for the future, and, so far as it is possible to tell, her own private inclinations lay with the Protestant right wing. Elizabeth was never one to make an issue over her religion but it would not do to alienate her friends – a time might well be coming when she would need them all. Apart from this, if she seemed to apostatize too eagerly, she would be tacitly admitting her own illegitimacy. On the other hand, she dared not offend the Catholics too deeply and Mary's attitude was beginning to show that she would soon have to make some placatory gesture. Early in September the gesture was made, an event which, as Simon Renard of the Imperial embassy reported sardonically, 'did not take place without a certain amount of stir'.

The Court had now moved out to Richmond and Elizabeth, alarmed by her sister's sudden coldness, asked for a private audience which took place in one of the galleries of the palace, a half-door separating the participants. The princess fell on her knees and shed tears. She could see only too clearly that the Queen was not well-disposed towards her and could think of no other cause but religion. However, she might surely be excused on this point, as she had been brought up in the way she held and had never been taught the doctrine of the old faith. She asked Mary to send her books 'contrary to those she had always read and known hitherto' so that she might see whether her conscience would allow her to be persuaded; 'or that a learned man might be sent to her to instruct her in the truth.' Mary had never felt any need to read books about her faith but she granted these requests and Elizabeth apparently found her conscience easily persuadable, for on 8 September, the day after her twentieth birthday, she accompanied the Queen to mass. Simon Renard had no illusions about the worth of Elizabeth's 'conversion' and Antoine de Noailles, the French ambassador, told the King of France on 22 September, 'everyone believes that she is acting rather from fear of danger and peril from those around her than from real devotion.'

The religious difficulty was only one of the perils surrounding Elizabeth at this time. Mary, accustomed all her adult life to rely on her mother's relations for advice and support, was now turning as naturally and trustfully to Simon Renard as once she had turned to Eustace Chapuys; and Renard, the shrewd, skilful diplomat who had taken over from Jehan de Scheyfve as the Emperor's resident ambassador, was dedicated to re-building the Anglo-Imperial alliance. But although the inexperienced Queen listened eagerly to the sage counsel passed on by her cousin's representative, he soon discovered she was quite unlike any ruler he had ever had to do with before. The Emperor had sent instructions that Mary must be dissuaded from taking too harsh a revenge on her enemies, but it seemed that she had no appetite for vengeance and only three of the Northumberland conspirators – the Duke himself and two of his most notorious henchmen, Thomas Palmer and John Gates, actually went to the block. In Renard's opinion a number of others, including, naturally, Jane Grey, should properly have gone with them. But over this Mary proved unexpectedly intractable. 'As to Jane of Suffolk, whom they tried to make Queen', he wrote, 'she could not be induced to consent that she should die.' Jane had written a long letter to Mary, freely admitting that she had done wrong in accepting the crown but denying that she had either consented or been a party to Northumberland's plot. Mary believed her. She had always been fond of her little cousin in spite of her regrettable heresy – at least you always knew exactly where you were with Jane and the child could not help the way she had been brought up. She told Renard that although Jane must, of course, stand trial and be 'cast' as a traitor, her conscience would not permit her to have an innocent young creature put to death. Appalled, the ambassador pointed out that in affairs of state power and tyranny sometimes brought better results than right or justice. Mary was apologetic but immovable. Nevertheless, she did promise to be careful and take all necessary precautions before setting Lady Jane free! Renard could only hope, without much conviction, that the Queen would not have cause to regret her astonishing clemency. But however much he deplored Jane's continued existence, he regarded Elizabeth as potentially even more dangerous. The Queen's heretical heir would be an obvious focal point for all discontent, both religious and political, and her name recurs in his despatches with relentless iteration. He told the Emperor that she had a spirit full of enchantment and was greatly to be feared. He told the Queen at every opportunity not to trust her sister 'who might, out of ambition, or being persuaded thereto, conceive some dangerous design and put it to execution, by means which it would be difficult to prevent, as she was clever and sly.'

The open hostility of Simon Renard was bad enough, but Elizabeth knew she had as much, if not more to fear from his rival, Antoine de Noailles, who professed to be her friend. De Noailles' business was to prevent too close an alliance between England and Spain. Such an alliance could only be a threat to France and, as rumours began to circulate that the Queen of England was contemplating marriage with the Emperor's son, Philip, French alarm increased. The King of France also had close personal reasons for his interest in English affairs. The young Queen of Scots, now nearing her eleventh birthday, would soon be ready for her long-planned marriage to the Dauphin and, her great-uncle's will notwithstanding, she still possessed, by all the accepted laws of inheritance, a strong claim to the reversion of the English crown. The King of France was naturally much attracted by the idea of seeing his future daughter-in-law as queen of both the island kingdoms and, if only a sufficiently lethal form of mischief could be made between the Tudor sisters, he was not unhopeful of the outcome.

Relations between the Tudor sisters were, in fact, already deteriorating. Mary entertained serious doubts as to the purity of Elizabeth's motives in going to mass, and before the end of September had asked her if she really believed as the Catholics did concerning the holy sacrament. Elizabeth replied that she was considering making a public statement 'that she went to mass and did as she did because her conscience prompted and moved her to it; that she went of her own free will and without fear, hypocrisy or dissimulation'. Mary could not believe her and the suspicion that Elizabeth was deliberately using the religious faith which the Queen held sacred as a political weapon did nothing to improve her opinion of the girl.

All the same, by using these rather doubtful methods, Elizabeth was able to maintain a foothold at Court and to secure her proper place at Mary's coronation, which was scheduled for 1 October. She was partnered by that old friend of the family, Anne of Cleves, still living in England in comfortable retirement. They rode together in a chariot draped with cloth of silver in the procession through the city from the Tower, and later they both dined at the Queen's table at the banquet in Westminster Hall. But even during the coronation festivities Renard was watching Elizabeth closely and reported that she appeared to be conspiring with the French ambassador. Apparently the princess had complained about the weight of her coronet and de Noailles had answered brightly that she must have patience, for soon this crown would bring her a better one.

Not everyone was so sure of this. Mary's first Parliament met on 5 October and at once proceeded to repeal the divorce of Henry VIII and Catherine of Aragon, pronouncing their marriage to have been good and lawful. Mary can scarcely be blamed for wanting to vindicate her mother's memory and doing what she could to right that old wrong, but it was embarrassing for the heiress presumptive to have her bastard state thus emphasized. In fact, and contrary to Renard's expectations, the re-establishing of Mary's legitimacy did not affect Elizabeth's position in the succession. Under the peculiar powers granted to Henry VIII, as long as the 1544 Act of Succession remained in force she was still next in line for the throne if Mary died childless. So far, Parliament, though willing to oblige the Queen up to a point, had shown no inclination to alter this arrangement, but Elizabeth had no illusions about what her sister might do if the opportunity presented itself. In one hysterical outburst that autumn, Mary had cried out that it would be a scandal and a disgrace to the kingdom to allow Elizabeth to succeed, for she was a heretic, a hypocrite and a bastard. On another occasion the Queen went so far as to say that she could not even be sure that Elizabeth was King Henry's bastard. Her mother had been an infamous woman and Elizabeth herself 'had the face and countenance' of Mark Smeaton, the lute-player. No doubt all this was faithfully passed on to the princess and on 25 October de Noailles reported that Madame Elizabeth was very discontented and had asked permission to withdraw from the Court.

Certainly Elizabeth had some reason for annoyance. In November, the Queen was foolish enough to insult the heir presumptive by giving precedence to the

Countess of Lennox and the Duchess of Suffolk at public functions. To be obliged to walk out of a room behind Margaret Lennox, the daughter of her aunt's second marriage, and Frances Suffolk, mother of the convicted traitor Jane Grey, was too much for Elizabeth's temper. Nor, indeed, could she afford to ignore such a deliberate slight. She showed her feelings by sulking in her own apartments and although Mary's friends cut her, the younger element at Court – especially the younger male element – sided openly with the princess.

Simon Renard, who smelt heretical plots behind every bush and saw Elizabeth's hand in all of them, heard rumours that she was entertaining the French ambassador in private. Elizabeth denied the accusation indignantly and renewed her demands to be allowed to retire into the country. This time leave was granted, and at the beginning of December the sisters met to say goodbye.

Mary had previously been given a good talking-to by Renard, who told her that she must make up her mind what to do about Elizabeth. Either she would have to regard her as an enemy and put her under some form of restraint (Renard himself favoured the Tower as a suitable residence for the princess), or else, for reasons of policy, she must treat her sister with at least outward civility. His words had some effect, for although he wrote 'I had much trouble in persuading the Queen to dissemble', Mary made a heroic effort and gave Elizabeth an expensive parting present of a sable hood. Her dislike of her young half-sister had grown by now into a near obsession and Renard observed 'she still resents the injuries inflicted on Queen Catherine, her lady mother, by the machinations of Anne Boleyn, mother of Elizabeth'. All the courtesies were, however, observed at their leave-taking. De Noailles heard that there had been a complete reconciliation and, according to Renard, Elizabeth had begged the Queen not to believe anyone who spread evil reports of her without at least letting her know and giving her a chance to prove 'the false and malicious nature of such slanders'.

Relieved of the strain imposed by her sister's presence, the Queen should now have been free to concentrate on pleasanter matters – the matter of her own approaching marriage in particular. But here, too, the way ahead was stormy. Early in November, when it became generally known that Mary intended to marry Philip of Spain, rumbles of disapproval, ominous as distant thunder, were immediately audible. Many people, indeed, began to wonder if John Dudley was going to be proved right after all, for Philip was not merely a foreigner and a Catholic, he represented the most formidable Catholic power bloc in Europe. The Houses of Parliament sent a joint deputation to the Queen to beg her to marry an Englishman and there were grave misgivings within the Privy Council itself.

No one, of course, questioned that the Queen should marry and the sooner the better. Obviously she must have a husband to support and guide her and undertake, as Simon Renard tactfully put it, 'those duties which were not the province of ladies'; but, in the opinion of the vast majority of her subjects, her wisest choice of consort would have been Edward Courtenay, 'the last sprig of the White Rose'. Courtenay, now in his mid-twenties, had good looks, high birth, charm and education (he had had plenty of leisure for study) to recommend him, but he inevitably lacked experience in the ways of the world and was an essentially shallow, rather commonplace youth. Mary had released him from the Tower and was prepared to be kind to him – his only crime, after all, lay in being the great-grandson of Edward IV and his parents had been among her mother's most influential supporters. She made him Earl of Devon and arranged that he should be given special opportunities to make up for the time he had wasted in prison – rumour had it that young Courtenay was making up for lost time on his own account in an intensive tour of the London brothels – but, and the Queen made this very clear, she had no intention of marrying him or any other Englishman. Tragically, nothing in Mary's experience had ever given her cause to love or trust her fellow countrymen and her desire for Philip, politically and personally disastrous as it was to prove, was natural enough in the circumstances. The fact that the Prince of Spain happened to be the most brilliant match in Europe weighed far less with her than the fact that he was one of her mother's kin.

Simon Renard's primary concern on taking up his post had been to put the Queen into 'a marrying humour'. This in itself was not difficult. Her smiles and sidelong looks when the subject was raised made it abundantly clear how agreeable it was, and when Renard first dropped Philip's name into the conversation he felt reasonably certain of a successful outcome. It was not all plain sailing, though. Mary worried that Philip would be too young for her (there was ten years' difference in their ages) or that she would be too old for him and that she would not be able to satisfy him. This fear could scarcely be admitted even to such a close confidant as Renard but had to be hinted at in a confession of ignorance of 'that which was called love'. Over three months of private interviews, slipping in and out through back entries and up the privy stairs escorted by confidential servants, Renard had patiently and dexterously piloted the nervous Queen through the shoals of her maidenly shrinking, self-doubt and vacillation. It was not the way he was accustomed to conduct such negotiations, but as Mary's trust in him deepened and he began to understand her better, he saw with growing satisfaction that she would be like putty in his master's hands; that physical love would overwhelm this simple but passionate woman who had so far schooled herself to an almost nun-like renunciation of the flesh.

One of the reasons officially advanced in favour of the Queen's marriage was to secure an heir to safeguard the succession but, although nobody actually said so publicly, few people believed that Mary would ever be able to bear a child. Mary herself was not so sure. After all, God had already worked one miracle for her. Might he not work another and give her a son to ensure the future success of her mission? For, with Philip at her side and all the might of the Holy Roman Empire behind her, surely nothing could stop her bringing England back to Rome. She did not reach her decision lightly and when, on 29 October, after weeks of agonized heart-searching, tears and prayer, Mary finally gave her word to Renard in the presence of the Holy Sacrament that she would marry Philip and love him perfectly, it was done with desperate sincerity and in the conviction that her answer had been divinely inspired.

Stephen Gardiner, now Lord Chancellor, was the only Englishman with sufficient prestige to try and make the Queen understand the sort of trouble she was storing up, but unhappily there was little confidence between them. Mary could not forget that Gardiner had once been one of her father's ablest instruments in the struggle for the divorce, and he was hampered by his known personal fondness for Courtenay. As Mary snappishly remarked, was it reasonable to expect her to marry someone just because a bishop had made friends with him in prison? Gardiner could only repeat, rather feebly, that the people would never stomach a foreigner who would make promises he would not keep. The Queen retorted that if her Chancellor preferred the will of the people to her wishes, then he was not keeping *his* promises. The Chancellor, with his long experience of Tudor temperament, gave up, saying it was too dangerous to meddle with the marriages of princes. Mary took an even higher tone with the parliamentary delegation. It was no business of theirs, she told them, to try and dictate to her on such a personal matter and added, in a burst of schoolgirlish petulance, that if they forced her to marry against her will, she would not live three months and they would only be defeating their own ends.

On the other side of the Channel, the French, seeing themselves threatened with encirclement, were full of gloomy forebodings, despite Mary's assurances that she intended to continue in peace and amity with them, no matter whom she married. Henri II was not convinced. 'It is to be considered', he observed to Mary's ambassador, Nicholas Wotton, 'that a husband may do much with his wife; and it shall be very hard for any wife to refuse her husband any thing that he shall earnestly require of her.' Indeed, the fear that England would be dragged into war with France was one of the most serious objections to the Spanish marriage – an objection which, as it turned out, was to prove only too well-founded. But de Noailles in London had still not given up hope of preventing the marriage from taking place.

The Emperor was bending over backwards in his efforts not to offend the delicate susceptibilities of the English – an alliance which would give him command of the sea route between Spain and the Netherlands was worth any amount of diplomacy – but the English, in the grip of one of their periodic attacks of xenophobia, preferred to believe the rumours currently being spread by various interested parties: that a horde of Spaniards, all armed to the teeth, would shortly be landing on their coasts; that England would become a province of the Empire and the Pope's authority be reimposed by force. The undergrowth of alarm, suspicion and a general restless dissatisfaction over the way things were going was rapidly becoming tinder-dry and the French ambassador thought he knew the best way of setting a match to it. The Queen might have refused young Courtenay, but there was always Elizabeth. 'From what I hear', he wrote in December, 'it only requires that my Lord Courtenay should marry her, and that they should go together to the counties of Devonshire and Cornwall. Here it can easily be believed that they would find many adherents, and they could then make a strong claim to the crown.' Certainly the combination of Edward Courtenay and Elizabeth Tudor, both of them young, handsome, English and royal, should have been irresistibly appealing to a sentimental public, but de Noailles, who was no fool, could see at least one snag. 'This misfortune', he went on, 'is that the said Courtenay is of such a fearful and timid disposition that he dare not make the venture.' It was exasperating when there were so many influential people ready and willing to help the wretched youth.

Nevertheless, detailed plans for resisting the threatened Spanish invasion were now being drawn up. They were still being discussed when, on 2 January 1554, the Emperor's envoys, led by Count Egmont, arrived 'for the knitting up of the marriage' between the Queen and the Prince of Spain. Egmont and his colleagues landed at Tower Wharf to the salute of 'a great peal of guns' from the Tower batteries. On Tower Hill a reception committee, headed by Courtenay, was waiting to conduct them ceremoniously through the City but they got no welcome from the watching crowds, for 'the people, nothing rejoicing, held down their heads sorrowfully'.

The next couple of weeks were probably the happiest of Mary's life. She had got her own way and could now legitimately dream of wedded bliss. Her councillors, their palms sticky with the Emperor's gold, were growing noticeably less hostile and the Queen, as bride-to-be, came in for some arch teasing which made her laugh and change colour. Well before the end of the month her shiny, insubstantial bubble had burst. The marriage treaty, signed on 12 January, should have been generous enough to satisfy the most exacting Englishman, but unfortunately the rising tide of panic and prejudice which was sweeping the country could no longer be stemmed by reason. The mindless rallying-cry 'We will have no foreigner for our King' had driven out common-sense, and within a week word had reached London that Sir Peter Carew was up in Devonshire 'resisting of the King of Spain's coming'. Almost simultaneously news came in that Sir Thomas Wyatt, son of the poet, was up in Kent 'for the said quarrel in resisting the said King of Spain'; that Sir James Crofts had departed for Wales, 'as it is thought to raise his power there', and that the Duke of Suffolk had mysteriously vanished from Sheen.

The fourfold rising had been timed for March – to coincide with the date of Philip's expected arrival – but someone had leaked information. It was generally believed that Courtenay, always a weak link, had lost what little nerve he possessed and blabbed to Gardiner, or else that the Chancellor had become suspicious and wormed a confession out of his protégé. The other conspirators, uncertain to what extent they had been betrayed and too deeply committed now to draw back, were scrambled into premature action. The movement in the West Country was virtually still-born. It had always depended very largely on Courtenay's presence and the prestige of his name. Without him it rapidly collapsed and Peter Carew fled to France. But in Kent things looked serious. By 26 January Thomas Wyatt had taken Rochester and the crews of the royal ships lying in the Medway had gone over to him with their guns and ammunition.

A hastily mustered force, consisting of men of the Queen's guard and the City militia, under the command of that old war horse the Duke of Norfolk, was sent to meet the threat; but the Londoners and a fair proportion of the guard promptly defected to the rebels amid rousing cries of 'We are all Englishmen'. In the words of one Alexander Brett, they preferred to spend their blood in the quarrel of 'this worthy captain Master Wyatt' and prevent at all costs the approach of 'the proud Spaniards' who, as every right-thinking Englishman knew, would treat them like slaves, despoil them of their goods and lands, ravish their wives before their faces and deflower their daughters in their presence.

Sir Thomas Wyatt, leader of the unsuccessful rebellion against Mary which began in January 1554. The rebels intended to make Elizabeth queen; their defeat led to her arrest and imprisonment.
Below: *The Tower of London; after a plan drawn in 1597.*

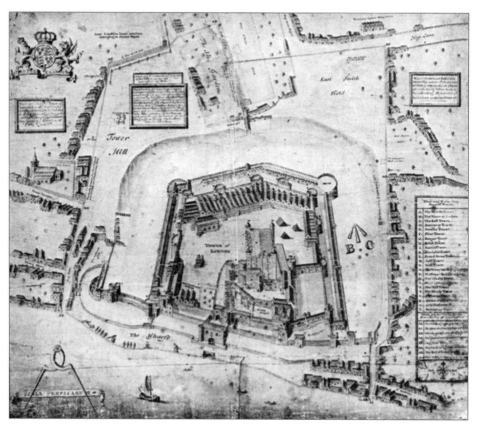

Thus encouraged, Wyatt pressed on towards the capital and on the thirtieth he was camped around Blackheath and Greenwich. From there he announced his terms: the custody of the Tower with the Queen in it, the removal of certain councillors and their replacements to be chosen by him. London was in an uproar of alarm and confusion, and for a couple of tensely anxious days the loyalty of the citizens hung in the balance. It was Mary herself who saved a potentially very ugly situation. Like every Tudor, she showed to her best advantage in a crisis demanding a display of physical and moral courage. Ignoring advice that she should seek her own safety, she marched into the City and made a fighting speech in the crowded Guildhall that not even Elizabeth could have bettered. Her audience rose to her, and when Wyatt reached Southwark on 3 February he found the bridge closed and heavily defended.

It was a long time since London had been besieged and 'much noise and tumult was everywhere' as shops were shuttered, market stalls hastily dismantled and weapons, rusty from long disuse, unearthed from store. Children gazed wide-eyed at the Lord Mayor and his aldermen riding about the streets in unaccustomed battle array, 'aged men were astonished' and many women wept for fear. The Queen had refused to allow the Tower guns to be turned on the rebels in case the innocent inhabitants of Southwark might suffer and after three days' uneasy stalemate Wyatt withdrew his army from 'the bridge foot'. They marched up-river to Kingston, where they crossed to the northern bank and turned eastward again. But the steam had gone out of them. They were tired and hungry, and too much time had been wasted. Still they came trudging on through the western suburbs, and by eleven o'clock on the morning of Ash Wednesday, 7 February they had reached Knightsbridge. There followed some rather indecisive skirmishing with the royalist forces, commanded by the Earl of Pembroke, around St James's and Charing Cross and some panic at Whitehall when, in the general turmoil, a cry of treason was raised within the precincts of the palace as a rumour spread that Pembroke had gone over to the enemy. 'There', remarked one observer, 'should ye have seen running and crying of ladies and gentlewomen, shutting of doors, and such a screeching and noise as it was wonderful to hear.' But although her very presence chamber was full of armed men, the Queen stood fast. Earlier in the day her barge had been ordered for a hasty retreat to the Tower, but Mary had changed her mind, sending word that 'she would tarry to see the uttermost'. Now, with the gunfire from Charing Cross clearly audible and 'divers timorous and cold-hearted soldiers' begging her to escape while she could, her grace would not stir a foot out of the house. She asked for the Earl of Pembroke and was told he was in the field. 'Well then', answered the Queen, 'fall to prayer, and I warrant you we shall hear better news anon; for my lord will not deceive me I know well.'

On this occasion at least, her confidence was not misplaced. Wyatt and a handful of followers got through Temple Bar and on down Fleet Street, but found Ludgate barred and strongly held by Lord William Howard, the Lord Admiral. It was the end for Wyatt. He himself had 'kept touch', as he said, but his friends in the city had failed him. He sat for a while in the rain on a bench outside the Belle Sauvage Inn and then, realizing it was hopeless, turned back towards

Charing Cross. Fighting flared again briefly as Pembroke's forces came up and the men round Wyatt prepared to sell their lives dearly, but the bloodshed was stopped by Norroy herald who approached Wyatt and begged him to surrender, pointing out that further resistance was useless. Wyatt, exhausted and confused, hesitated a moment and then yielded.

The immediate danger was over, but the Queen's troubles were only just beginning. Either she must bow to the will of the people violently expressed and abandon her marriage plans, or she must stand firm. Mary, hurt, angry and bewildered, chose to stand firm and this meant that she could no longer afford the luxury of showing mercy. The first victim of the new hard-line policy was inevitably Lady Jane Grey. Innocent she might have been of complicity in Northumberland's treason, innocent she undoubtedly was of complicity in Wyatt's rebellion – none of this altered the fact that her continued existence now represented an unacceptable danger to the state. Her own father's behaviour had made this abundantly clear. The Duke of Suffolk, who owed his life and liberty entirely to the Queen's generosity, had shown his gratitude by attempting to raise the Midlands and had been deeply involved with Wyatt. Jane had actually worn the crown, she had been named as heir by the late King (who now wore a Protestant halo), and had been publicly proclaimed. What was more likely than that she might be used again as the figurehead of a Protestant plot? Few people urged this view more strongly than men like Arundel, Winchester and Pembroke, themselves so recently prominent Protestant plotters and now increasingly anxious that the living reminder of their past indiscretions should be obliterated. Reluctantly Mary was forced to agree that Jane would have to die, but though she had not been able to save her cousin's life, the Queen was determined to make a last minute effort to save her soul and sent Dr Feckenham, Abbot of Westminster, to see what he could do with this obdurate heretic.

The six months since her brief 'reign' had passed quietly for Jane. She had been living in the house of Partridge, the Gentleman Gaoler, with pleasant enough quarters fronting on to Tower Green. She was allowed three women servants and a page to wait on her and had been treated with respectful consideration by Partridge and his wife. Nobody was bullying her. She was free of the oppressive demands of her husband, her parents and her in-laws. She had her books and leisure for study and the Queen's promise that one day she would be released. Now all that was over and she had only a few days left to prepare for eternity. Nevertheless, she received Feckenham graciously and they enjoyed several stimulating debates on such topics as the dogma of transubstantiation and the scriptural number of sacraments. But when it was hinted that she could, even now, save her life if she would embrace the Catholic religion, the offer was flatly rejected. Jane had poured indignant scorn on the Duke of Northumberland's abject apostasy before his execution – 'I pray God I, nor no friend of mine die so.' She would never forsake her faith for love of life; that would be the ultimate shame for this brilliant, vital sixteen-year-old with everything to live for. All the same, she accepted Feckenham's offer to accompany her to the scaffold and parted from him with some regret, since they plainly could not look forward to resuming their discussions in the hereafter. Unless, of course, he repented and turned to God. She would, she told him, 'pray God in the bowels of his mercy to send you his Holy Spirit; for he hath given you his great gift of utterance, if it pleased him also to open the eyes of your heart.' Jane seems to have been rather disturbed by the realization that she had come dangerously close to liking a Catholic priest, that she had found him sympathetic, intelligent and cultivated. Perhaps it was just as well for her peace of mind that she had so little time to brood on the worrying implications of this discovery.

The last two days of her life were taken up with the macabre preparations that had to be made by all highly placed victims of judicial execution. The Lady Jane must choose a suitable dress for her final public appearance and nominate two members of her household to witness her death and afterwards to 'decently dispose' of her body. The speech that she would make from the scaffold must be drafted, polished and copied out for subsequent circulation among her friends. There were farewell letters to be written, too, and farewell gifts to be made. Her sister Katherine got her Greek testament – 'it will teach you to live and learn you to die' – plus a long-winded letter of spiritual exhortation, wasted on feather-brained Katherine. To her father, now awaiting his own execution, Jane sent a message of comfort, though her outraged sense of justice impelled her to remind him that her death was being hastened by one 'by whom my life should rather have been lengthened'. There was no letter for her husband, who was to die with her. It is said that the Queen had sent word that the young couple might be allowed to meet to say goodbye, but Jane refused the proffered indulgence. Guildford was an irrelevance now and in any case they would soon be meeting 'in a better place'. She might find him more congenial there.

The executions were to take place on 12 February. Guildford's on Tower Hill, Jane's, as befitted a princess of the blood, privately on the Green – from Partridge's house she would have had an excellent view of her scaffold being erected 'over against the White Tower'. At about ten o'clock in the morning Guildford was brought out of his prison in the Beauchamp Tower and Jane, who had stationed herself at her window, saw the procession leave. She waited obstinately for its return, and presently the cart with the decapitated carcase of that tall, strong boy who had wanted her to make him a king lying on the bloodstained straw, the head wrapped roughly in a cloth, rattled past below her on its way to St Peter's. The sight moved her perhaps more than she had expected, and those standing by heard her murmur Guildford's name and something about 'the bitterness of death'. Now it was her turn, and she emerged on the arm of the Lieutenant, Sir John Brydges. Her two attendants, Nurse Ellen and Mrs Tilney, were in tears but Jane herself was dry-eyed and perfectly composed, her prayer book open in her hand. She climbed the steps of the scaffold and turned to make her speech to the invited audience that had gathered to see her die.

Jane did not waste words. She admitted again that she had done wrong in accepting the crown but again declared her innocence 'touching the procurement and desire thereof'. She begged those present to witness that she died a good Christian woman and that she looked to be saved 'by none other mean, but only by the mercy of God in the merits of the blood of his only son Jesus Christ. . . . And now, good people', she ended, 'while I am alive, I pray you to assist me with

Lady Jane Grey, the unfortunate victim of Northumberland's plotting.

The Lady Jane, Proclaimed Queen

The Lady Jane Beheaded in y^e Tower

The reign of Queen Jane; contemporary woodcuts.

your prayers.' Kneeling, she turned to John Feckenham, saying: 'Shall I say this psalm?' and then repeated the fifty-first psalm, the Miserere, in English, Feckenham beside her following her in Latin.

Now there were just the final formalities to be gone through. She got to her feet, handed her gloves and handkerchief to Mrs Tilney and her prayer book to John Brydges' brother and began to untie the fastenings of her gown. The executioner, that nightmare masked figure, stepped forward and Jane, not understanding perhaps that his victim's outer garments were the hangman's perquisite, shrank back and 'desired him to leave her alone'. Nurse Ellen and Mrs Tilney helped her to undress and gave her 'a fair handkercher to knit about her eyes'. Now the executioner was kneeling for the ritual asking and receiving of forgiveness. He told her to stand upon the straw and in so doing she saw the block for the first time. There was nothing left to do but make an end. Whispering 'I pray you despatch me quickly', she tied the blindfold over her eyes. The world vanished and she was alone and groping in the darkness, crying 'What shall I do? Where is it?' Someone came forward to guide her and 'she laid her down upon the block and stretched forth her body and said: "Lord, into thy hands I commend my spirit."' The axe swung and blood spouted obscenely over the scaffold, soaking the straw and spattering the bystanders.

Some time later that day the butchered corpse of Henry VIII's great-niece was thrust unceremoniously under the stones of St Peter ad Vincula, to lie between the remains of Anne Boleyn and Catherine Howard. The judicial murder of Jane Grey – and no one, even at the time, ever pretended it was anything else – caused no particular stir, not even among the aggressively Protestant Londoners. Public opinion, which played such a significant part in saving her cousin Elizabeth, was not mobilized to help Jane, whose name, so far as it was remembered at all, remained too closely associated with the hated Dudleys to rouse much sympathy. There is a tradition that the oak trees at her family home, Bradgate Park, were pollarded in a gesture of mourning and defiance when news of Lady Jane's beheading reached Leicestershire, and a story that the judge who had sentenced her died in a raving delirium, crying 'Take the Lady Jane from me! Take away the Lady Jane!' But although Roger Ascham remembered her, as did her tutor John Aylmer, who became Bishop of London under Queen Elizabeth, and John Foxe included her in his gallery of Protestant martyrs, for reasons both personal and political it became increasingly tactless to mention the Suffolk family in polite Elizabethan circles.

CHAPTER 12

In Honour of Worthy Philip

Then he [Philip] addressed the Spanish lords who were about him, and told them they must at once forget all the customs of Spain, and live in all respects after the English fashion, in which he was determined to begin and show them the way; so he ordered some beer to be brought to him, and drank of it.

Simon Renard could reflect with satisfaction on the virtual extinction of the house of Suffolk, but he would not feel quite easy in his mind until two more heads had rolled, those of 'the two persons most able to cause trouble in the realm' – Courtenay and Elizabeth. Not that the ambassador anticipated any difficulty over this. As he told the Emperor, 'at present there is no other occupation than the cutting off of heads', and now that the Queen had at last realized the folly of showing mercy to her enemies, she was 'absolutely determined to have strict justice done'. Courtenay was already back in the Tower and Elizabeth would soon be joining him.

Throughout the recent crisis Elizabeth had remained holed up at Ashridge, suffering, so she said, from such a cold and headache as she had never felt before. On 26 January, the day after Wyatt entered Rochester, the Council had written summoning the princess to Court for her own safety, in case 'any sudden tumult' should arise in the neighbourhood of Ashridge. But Elizabeth had replied that she was far too ill to travel. All the same, rumours were flying about that she was planning to move further away from London, to Donnington Castle, a semi-fortified house near Newbury; that Ashridge was being provisioned for a siege and that Elizabeth was gathering troops – her household, it was said, was now eating in a week what normally lasted a month. Stephen Gardiner, convinced that the French ambassador was heavily involved with Wyatt, had resorted to highway robbery on one of de Noailles' couriers and the resultant haul had included a copy of Elizabeth's last letter to the Queen on its way to France by diplomatic bag. It therefore seemed reasonable to deduce that the Queen's heir was in secret correspondence with the emissaries of a foreign power. Just how important a part she had played in Wyatt's conspiracy remained to be seen. Her name had never been openly invoked but there could be no doubt that she, if anyone, stood to gain from its success. Now it had failed, she had some explaining to do.

Mary, already deeply suspicious of her sister's convenient 'illness', sent two of her own physicians to examine the patient and report on her condition, and on 10 February the medical team was reinforced by a commission headed by Lord

William Howard, Elizabeth's maternal great-uncle. The doctors having pronounced her fit to travel, the commissioners felt justified in requiring her, in the Queen's name and all excuses set apart, to be ready to leave with them on the following day. The invalid herself was found to be 'very willing and conformable', but afraid that her weakness was so great that she would not be able to endure the journey without peril of life. Elizabeth, aware that the peril lay not in the journey but its destination, begged for a further respite – 'until she had better recovered her strength'. But when it was politely but firmly made clear that the time for such delaying tactics was over, she gave in with becoming meekness.

Although, for obvious reasons, she was making the most of it, there is no doubt that her illness on this occasion was perfectly genuine. From the description of her symptoms – her face and limbs were so distended that she was 'a sad sight to see' – Elizabeth appears to have been suffering from acute nephritis and it has been suggested that she may have had an attack of scarlet fever, of which inflammation of the kidneys is sometimes a complication. But however great her physical discomfort, it can scarcely have compared with her mental anguish. The situation she had been dreading ever since Mary's accession had become a reality and there could be no disguising the fact that she stood in mortal danger.

In deference to his charge's fragile state of health, William Howard had planned the thirty-mile journey from Ashridge in very easy stages, expecting it to take five days; but he had reckoned without Elizabeth's talent for procrastination and it was getting on for a fortnight before the cavalcade began the descent of Highgate Hill into the city. Simon Renard reported that Elizabeth, who was dressed all in white, had the curtains of her litter drawn back 'to show herself to the people'. According to Renard, she 'kept a proud, haughty expression' which, in his opinion, was assumed to hid her 'vexation'. It may also have masked fear and revulsion – certainly the sights which greeted her as she was carried through Smithfield and on down Fleet Street towards Westminster can have done little to raise her spirits. Gallows had been erected all over London, from Bermondsey and Southwark in the east to Charing Cross and Hyde Park Corner in the west, and the city gates were decorated with severed heads and dismembered corpses – an intentionally grim reminder of the consequences of unsuccessful rebellion.

When Elizabeth reached Whitehall the portents were not encouraging. Mary refused to see her and she was lodged in a part of the palace from which, said Renard, neither she nor her servants could go out without passing the guard. There she remained for nearly a month, a prisoner in fact if not in name. Renard could not understand the delay in sending her to the Tower, since, he wrote, 'she has been accused by Wyatt, mentioned by name in the French ambassador's letters, suspected by her own councillors, and it is certain that the enterprise was undertaken for her sake.'

But evidence linking the princess with the insurrection was proving disappointingly hard to come by. Wyatt, who was being rigorously interrogated, admitted having sent her two letters; one advising her to retreat to Donnington, the other informing her of his arrival at Southwark. Francis Russell, the Earl of Bedford's son, confessed to acting as postman, but the replies, if any, had been verbal and non-committal. Sir James Crofts, another of the conspirators now in custody, had been to see Elizabeth at Ashridge and had apparently incriminated William Saintlow, one of the gentlemen of her household. But Saintlow denied knowing anything about Wyatt's plans, 'protesting that he was a true man, both to God and his prince'. Crofts, too, although 'marvellously tossed', failed to reveal any really useful information. Even the discovery of that letter in de Noailles' post-bag was not in itself evidence against Elizabeth. There was nothing in her handwriting; nothing to show that she herself had given it to de Noailles or had instructed anyone else to do so.

On 15 March Wyatt was at last brought to trial and convicted. Next day, it was the Friday before Palm Sunday, Elizabeth received a visit from Stephen Gardiner and nineteen other members of the Council, who 'burdened her with Wyatt's conspiracy' as well as with 'the business made by Sir Peter Carew and the rest of the gentlemen of the West Country'. It was the Queen's pleasure, they told her, that she should now go to the Tower while the matter was further tried and examined. Elizabeth was appalled. She denied all the charges made against her, adding desperately that she trusted the Queen's majesty would be a more gracious lady unto her than to send her to 'so notorious and doleful a place'. But it seemed the Queen was 'fully determined'. Elizabeth's own servants were removed and six of the Queen's people appointed to wait on her and ensure that 'none should have access to her grace'. A hundred soldiers from the north in white coats watched and warded in the palace gardens all that night, and a great fire was lit in the hall, where 'two certain lords' kept guard with their company.

The twenty-year-old Elizabeth, lying awake in the darkness listening to the tramp of feet beneath her window, knew that the net was closing around her. Within a very few hours, failing some miracle, she would be in that doleful place from which so few prisoners of the blood royal ever emerged alive. But when the two lords, Sussex and Winchester, came for her in the morning, she made it clear that she was not going to go quietly. She did not believe, she said, that the Queen knew anything about the plan to send her to the Tower. It was the Council's doing and especially the Lord Chancellor's, who hated her. She begged again for an interview with her sister and, when this was refused, at least to be allowed to write to her. Winchester would have refused this, too, but the Earl of Sussex suddenly relented. Kneeling to the prisoner, he exclaimed that her grace should have liberty to write and, as he was a true man, he would deliver the letter to the Queen and bring an answer, 'whatsoever came thereof'.

It might well be the most important letter of Elizabeth's life, it might be the last letter she would ever write and she must write quickly, while her escort hovered impatiently in the background. Her pen flowed smoothly over the first page, in sentences polished during a sleepless night. 'If any ever did try this old saying', she began, 'that a king's word was more than another man's oath, I most humbly beseech your Majesty to verify it in me, and to remember your last promise and my last demand, that I be not condemned without answer and due proof, which it seems that now I am; for that without cause proved I am by your Council from you commanded to go into the Tower, a place more wonted for a false traitor than a true subject'. Elizabeth had never 'practised, counselled nor consented' anything that might be prejudicial to the Queen's person or dangerous to the state, and she beseeched Mary to hear her answer in person 'and not suffer me to trust to your councillors'.

It might be dangerous to remind the Queen of Thomas Seymour. Mary would know all about that old scandal and probably believed the worst about it, but Elizabeth decided to risk it. 'I have heard in my time', she went on, 'of many cast away for want of coming to the presence of their prince; and in late days I heard my lord of Somerset say that if his brother had been suffered to speak with him, he had never suffered; but the persuasions were made to him too great, that he was brought in belief that he could not live safely if the Admiral lived, and that made him give his consent to his death . . . I pray God as evil persuasions persuade not one sister against the other.'

So far so good, but as she turned over the page mistakes and corrections began to come thick and fast. Perhaps Sussex was at her elbow now, urging her to make haste. 'I humbly crave to speak with your Highness', scribbled Elizabeth, 'which I would not be so bold to desire if I knew not myself most clear as I know myself most true. And as for the traitor Wyatt, he might peradventure write me a letter, but on my faith I never received any from him. And for the copy of my letter sent to the French king, I pray God confound me eternally if ever I sent him word, message, token or letter by any means. And to this my truth I will stand to my death.' There was nothing more to be said, but more than half her second sheet was left blank – plenty of space for someone to add a forged confession or damaging admission – so Elizabeth scored the page with diagonal lines before adding a final appeal at the very end. 'I humbly crave but only one word of answer from yourself. Your Highness's most faithful subject that hath been from the beginning and will be to my end, Elizabeth.'

As it turned out, she might have saved herself the trouble. When her sister's letter was brought to her, Mary flew into a royal Tudor rage. She roared at Sussex that he would never have dared to do such a thing in her father's time and wished, in a triumph of illogicality, that he were alive again if only for a month. Even so, Elizabeth had won a brief respite, for she had managed to miss the tide. The starlings which supported the piers of London Bridge restricted the flow of the river and turned the water beneath it into a mill-race. 'Shooting the bridge' was always a hazardous business but when the tide was flooding it became impossible – there could be a difference of as much as five feet in the level of the water. The Council were not going to risk taking the princess through the streets, so it was decided to wait until the following morning. When Sussex and Winchester arrived at nine o'clock there was no question of further delay, but as Elizabeth was hurried through the gardens to the landing-stage, she looked up at the windows of the palace as if hoping to catch a glimpse of the Queen. There was no sign. Mary was in church on Palm Sunday morning. The party embarked at the privy stairs, the barge was cast off and rowed away downstream – down towards the grey, ghost-ridden bulk of the Tower. There her mother had died and her mother's cousin, poor wanton Catherine Howard; her own cousin Jane, with whom Elizabeth had once shared lessons and gone to children's parties, and so many others – the Seymour brothers, John Dudley, 'that great devil' and Suffolk, the weak fool. Behind them rose the wraiths of all those shadowy Plantagenet cousins, sacrificed to make England safe for the Tudors. This had been journey's end for them all. Was it to be the end of her journey, too?

The boatmen were shipping their oars and tying up at the Water Gate – Traitor's Gate. At first Elizabeth refused to land. She was no traitor, besides she would get her feet wet. Winchester told her brutally that she had no choice. He offered her his cloak – it was raining hard – but the princess rejected it 'with a good dash' and then, with one foot on the stairs, cried out: 'Here landeth as true a subject being prisoner, as ever landed at these stairs; and before thee, O God, I speak it, having none other friends but thee alone!' A company of soldiers and Tower warders were drawn up on the landing stage and Elizabeth immediately appealed to them to bear witness to her innocence and loyalty. She was rewarded by several voices crying from the ranks 'God preserve your grace!' and, turning to the Lord Chamberlain, Sir John Gage, asked if all these harnessed men were for her. 'No madam', came the reply and someone else explained that it was the custom for the reception of any prisoner. But Elizabeth would not have her effect spoilt. 'Yes', she insisted mournfully, 'I know it is so. It needed not for me, being, alas! but a weak woman.' And, to emphasize this point, she sank down exhaustedly on a convenient stone. 'Madam, you were best to come out of the rain', said the Lieutenant of the Tower, 'for you sit unwholesomely.' 'Better sitting here than in a worse place', answered Elizabeth, 'for God knoweth, I know not, whither you will bring me.' This was too much for her gentleman usher, who burst into tears and was promptly rounded on by his mistress demanding to know what he meant 'so uncomfortably to use her'. She knew her truth to be such that no man had cause to weep for her. Then, her courage restored, or satisfied perhaps that she had wrung every drop out of the situation, she got up from her wet stone and allowed herself to be escorted into the fortress.

She was lodged in a room in the Bell Tower, and Winchester and Sir John Gage began to lock the doors 'very straitly' and to discuss further security arrangements. But the Earl of Sussex, who all along had shown himself more compassionate, or more far-sighted, intervened. They would be wise, he remarked, to remember that 'this was the King our master's daughter' as well as the Queen's sister. 'Therefore', said Sussex, 'let us use such dealing that we may answer it hereafter, if it shall so happen; for just dealing is always answerable.' This shrewd reminder that their prisoner might yet become their Queen went home, and the others departed rather subdued.

Elizabeth might have been cheered if she had known just how deeply the government was divided on the question of her future, and that it was only after long and heated debate and because nobody would accept responsibility for her safekeeping, that the decision to send her to the Tower had been taken. Sussex told her that several members of the Council were sorry for her trouble and he himself was sorry he had lived to see this day; but now, abandoned in the prison that seemed only too likely soon to become her grave, there was not much comfort to be gained by mere sympathy. Years later she was to tell a foreign ambassador how, having no hope of life, she had planned to beg the Queen as a last favour to have a French swordsman brought over for her execution, as had been done for her mother – anything rather than suffer the hideous butchery of the axe.

*Simon Renard, an able diplomat and
one of Mary's closest advisers.*

All this time preparations for the Queen's marriage had been going forward and the only thing lacking now was the presence of the bridegroom, but Simon Renard, only too conscious of his heavy responsibilities, felt serious doubts as to the wisdom of allowing Philip to hazard his precious person in such an ungrateful and heresy-ridden land – at least while it continued to harbour Elizabeth Tudor and Edward Courtenay. In Renard's opinion a more than suspicious negligence was being shown over bringing these two 'great persons' to trial, and he could only conclude that delay was being deliberately created in the hope that something would crop up to save them. The ambassador saw the Queen on Easter Saturday and took the opportunity of expressing some of his misgivings, adding that until 'every necessary step' had been taken he would not feel able to recommend the prince's coming to England. The threat was implicit and Mary replied, with tears in her eyes, that 'she would rather never have been born than that any harm should be done to his Highness.' She promised to see to it that Elizabeth's and Courtenay's trials were over before his arrival.

This was all very well but, although Renard continued to press the matter, it seemed there was still not enough evidence against either of the suspects even to begin proceedings. As far as Courtenay was concerned, the circumstances were certainly suggestive, but the fact remained that he had not actually *done* anything. He had not gone down to the West Country. He had not, at any time, taken up arms against the Queen. He had not attempted to escape. The plan to marry him to Elizabeth had been openly raised by William Paget the previous autumn, but

Courtenay had rejected it on the grounds that such a match would be unworthy of his unblemished lineage. As for Elizabeth, Renard was obliged to report that the laws of England did not provide penalties applicable to her 'because those with whom she plotted are fugitives'. 'Nevertheless', he went on, 'the Queen tells me that fresh proof is coming up against her every day, and there were several witnesses to assert that she had gathered together stores and weapons in order to rise with the rest and fortify a house in the country whither she had been sending her provisions.' The house in the country was, presumably, Donnington, but this promising line of enquiry had turned into a blind alley and Elizabeth swore that any defensive preparations made at Ashridge were simply as a protection against the Duke of Suffolk who had been in the neighbourhood at the time. Frustrating though it might be for those like Renard and Stephen Gardiner, who believed that as long as Elizabeth lived there would be no peace in England, the government was no nearer to making out a case against her than it had been two months earlier.

On 11 April Thomas Wyatt, who had been kept alive in the hope that he might yet be induced to incriminate his fellow prisoners, was executed at last and on the scaffold he explicitly exonerated both Elizabeth and Courtenay from any guilty knowledge of the rebellion. Although the authorities tried to suppress it, this news spread rapidly and joyfully through the city and it was now clear that there would be very little chance of ever securing a conviction against the princess. A mere detail like lack of proof might not have mattered in the days of the Queen's father or grandfather, but Mary possessed none of the ruthless self-confidence which had characterized her progenitors. Already, to Simon Renard's barely suppressed annoyance, she was beginning to pardon her rebels and this despite the fact that open opposition to her policies, her religion and her marriage was already beginning to reappear. Violent incidents in churches and physical attacks on priests saying mass were on the increase; and inflammatory pamphlets had begun to circulate in the capital – one urging all Englishmen to stand firm and keep out the Prince of Spain, another 'as seditious as possible and in favour of the Lady Elizabeth'. Even the children were joining in rough games where the 'Spaniards' were always heavily defeated.

To make matters worse, the Council, an unwieldy and cantankerous body, was split from top to bottom. 'Quarrels, jealousy and ill-will have increased among the councillors', wrote Renard on 22 April, 'becoming so public that several of them, out of spite, no longer attend the meetings. What one does, another undoes; what one advises, another opposes; one strives to save Courtenay, another Elizabeth; and such is the confusion that one can only expect the upshot to be arms and tumult.' Renard believed that the Queen would soon be persuaded to release Courtenay altogether while, as for Elizabeth, it had now been officially admitted that the lawyers could not find sufficient evidence to condemn her and she was already being allowed out to walk in the Tower gardens, so it looked as if her release, too, was only a matter of time.

Elizabeth owed her preservation to a number of factors – her own impenetrable discretion, the strength of public opinion, government weakness and lack of direction – but most of all she owed it to her sister. Mary's opinion of her had not changed – early in March she told Renard sourly that 'Elizabeth's character was just what she had always believed it to be' – but, in spite of her deep-rooted personal dislike and distrust of the girl and in spite of the pressure being exerted on her most vulnerable flank, the Queen had stuck stubbornly to her principles. Her conscience had forced her to insist on a thorough and painstaking enquiry, thus creating the very delay which Renard knew would be fatal, and as long as the case remained 'not proven' Elizabeth would continue to get the benefit of the doubt.

The problem now arose of what was to be done with the princess. She could not be left in the Tower indefinitely; neither would it be politic to set her free, and the Queen could scarcely be expected to receive her at Court – nor yet at any rate. Some sort of face-saving formula would have to be found and Mary eventually fell back on the time-honoured expedient of sending her sister to live under restraint in a remote country house. After a good deal of indecision, the manor of Woodstock, a hunting-lodge once much favoured by the Plantagenets, was selected, although Renard would have preferred some more secure northern castle. Elizabeth had now been consigned to the custody of Sir Henry Bedingfield, a stolid, staunchly Catholic gentleman from Oxborough in Norfolk, whose loyalty to the Queen could not be questioned, and on 19 May she left the Tower under his escort to a salute of guns from the merchants of the Steelyard and the cheers of the Londoners, who believed she had been released. The journey to Woodstock, although accomplished in a warped and broken litter, rapidly developed into something suspiciously like a triumphal progress. At Windsor the townsfolk turned out *en masse* to see her pass; at Eton she was nearly mobbed by the scholars and church bells were rung defiantly in many villages along the route, while everywhere the country people crowded to the roadside to cry blessings on her, to throw cakes and flowers into her lap and wish her Godspeed.

At the end of the month Mary also left London, thankful to escape from that insolent, irreligious city where she spent her days struggling with the Council, surrounded by an almost tangible miasma of treachery and deceit which she was yet powerless to disperse. No wonder she longed for a husband who would relieve her of the burden of government – a burden she was beginning to find insupportable. The Queen's destination was Richmond, from where she was expecting soon to ride south to meet her bridegroom. It had been agreed that Philip should land at Southampton and the wedding take place in Winchester Cathedral – no one felt like risking a ceremony in London – but May turned into June and Philip was still in Spain paying a leisurely round of farewell visits. By the beginning of July the delay was becoming embarrassing. Mary told Renard that it was painful to her because it encouraged the heretics, but there was deeper pain in the sense of rejection.

All the same, Philip can scarcely be blamed for his dilatoriness. It was not only that his bride was a delicate, middle-aged woman to whom he referred in a letter to his friend Ruy Gomez as 'our dear and well-beloved aunt' – that was just the luck of the draw in the lottery of royal marriage. Far more off-putting were the prospects of humiliation in a strange land. By the terms of the marriage treaty he was debarred from taking any independent part in the government; he could appoint no officials, send no English money abroad. He was forbidden to bring any Spanish troops with him – he would in fact be a mere cipher, his wife's husband and nothing more. This was bad enough, but even more galling to a young man like Philip, who hid his shyness under a stiff public manner, was the anxious, constantly repeated advice from his father, from his father's ministers and from Simon Renard, to sink his pride and strain every nerve to conciliate the ungrateful, heretical islanders. He must be affable and show himself to the people. He must be lavish with presents as well as smiles. He must bring as few as possible of his own friends and servants and resign himself to being served by clumsy, suspicious strangers – all the harder since he spoke no English. Those Spaniards who did accompany him must on no account bring their wives, for they were more likely to cause trouble even than soldiers. For the sake of the alliance, he and his retinue must be prepared to put up with insult and anything else the English might choose to throw at them. Small wonder then that Philip lingered, finding excuses of 'business' to keep him in Spain, until at last the iron sense of duty which drove him throughout his life would let him delay no longer. He sailed from Corunna on 13 July and six days later, on the anniversary of Mary's accession, his fleet was dropping anchor in Southampton Water.

The prince came ashore on the afternoon of 20 July to be greeted not by insult or hostile crowds but, in far more typically English fashion, by a persistent downpour of fine summer rain. He rested in Southampton over the weekend and on Monday set out on the ten-mile ride to Winchester. The rain which had been falling steadily for three days managed to penetrate even the thick red felt cloak he wore over his black velvet and white satin finery, so that he was obliged to stop at the Hospital of St Cross to change. The laggard bridegroom was still, it seemed, in no hurry. On arriving at Winchester he went first to the cathedral, where there was such a crowd of sightseers eager to catch a glimpse of him that several people were nearly suffocated in the crush, and it was past ten o'clock before he made his way by torchlight through the gardens to the Bishop's Palace where the Queen was waiting.

They met in the long gallery, he kissing her on the mouth in 'English fashion' and then, she taking him by the hand, they sat together under the cloth of estate talking in a mixture of French and Spanish. That first meeting was short and informal but Philip, who was doing his utmost to ingratiate himself (even to the extent of forcing himself to drink beer), insisted on kissing all the Queen's ladies 'so as not to break the custom of the country, which is a good one'. He asked Mary to teach him what he should say to the lords in English at his departing and she told him to say 'good night my lords all' – a formula which he carefully repeated before leaving for his lodgings in the Dean's house. Next day he came to see his fiancée again, with more ceremony this time, although they had another quarter of an hour's private talk 'each of them merrily smiling on the other, to the great comfort and rejoicing of the beholders'.

No one was in any doubt as to what the Queen thought of Philip and in general he was making a good impression. His appearance was in his favour, for he was a small, slender man with reassuringly un-foreign blue eyes and fair complexion.

Philip II of Spain.

Some people thought his yellow hair and beard made him look like a Fleming and the Flemings had always been popular in England. What Philip thought of his bride he kept to himself but in their letters home the other Spaniards were less discreet. The Queen was a dear, good creature but older than they had been led to expect. She was a perfect saint but dressed badly. She was certainly not beautiful and had no eyebrows. Ruy Gomez thought she might look better and less flabby if she adopted Spanish fashions but, he went on, it was just as well Philip understood that the marriage had been arranged for political and not fleshly considerations, for this elderly virgin would obviously give him no satisfaction in bed.

The Queen of England and the Prince of Spain were married in Winchester Cathedral on 25 July with all the solemn ritual, all the pomp and splendour proper to the occasion. The flickering tapers glinted on the gorgeous clothes of the wedding guests and the rich vestments of the officiating clergy – six bishops, coped and mitred – on the sumptuous velvet and satin, on the jewels and the gleaming altar plate; but Mary's wedding ring was, by her own request, a plain gold band with no stone in it 'because maidens were so married in old times'. After high mass, during which the Queen remained wrapt and motionless, her eyes never leaving the sacrament, the heralds announced in Latin, French and English, the impressive list of the newly married couple's styles and titles: Philip

Winchester Cathedral where Mary and Philip were married on 25 July 1554.

and Marie, by the grace of God King and Queen of England, France, Naples, Jerusalem and Ireland, Defenders of the Faith, Princes of Spain and Sicily, Archdukes of Austria, Dukes of Milan, Burgundy and Brabant, Counts of Hapsburg, Flanders and Tyrol. But to Mary only two things mattered – that at last she was married and was already helplessly in love.

The King and Queen walked hand-in-hand under the canopy of state back to the Bishop's Palace for the wedding feast with its quantities of elaborate food and displays of gold plate, the musicians playing in the background and the heralds crying largesse. There was dancing afterwards and then, when darkness had fallen, the Bishop of Winchester blessed the marriage bed and the newly-weds were left alone. 'What happened that night only they know', observed one of the Spaniards eagerly, but 'if they give us a son our joy will be complete.'

The Court stayed at Winchester till the end of the month, the Queen, according to custom, not appearing in public. The Spaniards amused themselves sightseeing and lounging in the antechamber, talking or dancing or playing cards with the Queen's ladies. None were beautiful by Spanish standards, although some were better than others and at least it helped to pass the time. On the thirty-first the household was on the move towards London, going by way of Basing, Reading and Windsor, where Philip was installed as a Garter knight. 'Their majesties are the happiest couple in the world', wrote someone enthusiastically to a friend in Salamanca, 'and more in love than words can say'. Certainly Philip was unfailingly polite and considerate, riding at Mary's side, always at hand to help her mount and dismount, attentive, said someone else with perhaps unconscious cruelty, as a son. By 11 August they were at Richmond and a week later the Queen brought her husband to the capital. London had been swept and garnished, the gibbets and blackened heads removed and decorations more suitable to the occasion substituted. The citizens, well primed with free drink, were in a benevolent mood and although there was plenty of jealousy and backbiting at Court and the Spaniards complained they were being charged twenty-five times the proper price for everything in the shops, on the surface things were going reasonably well.

Philip was determined that they should continue to do so. The whole point of his marriage (and the only reason why he was enduring it) was to enable him to gain control of the government, to bring England permanently within the Imperial Hapsburg orbit, and to achieve this it was essential to avoid serious friction. Mary, lost in her fool's paradise of love, was only too happy to leave everything in his hands; to trust prudent, pious, Catholic Philip to be wise for both of them.

While Mary was giving herself up to the delights of married life, Elizabeth was still languishing at Woodstock. The Queen had given orders that her sister was to be treated 'in such good and honourable sort as may be agreeable to our honour and her estate and degree', and Elizabeth had a respectable number of servants to wait on her, was allowed to walk in the gardens and orchard and to have any books, within reason, to help pass the time. But time passed with agonizing slowness and the princess, who was becoming increasingly bored and resentful, did not hesitate to tease her custodian with demands for all sorts of additional concessions and to complain that she was being worse treated than any prisoner in the Tower or, on second thoughts, worse than the worst prisoner in Newgate. The unhappy Henry Bedingfield, acutely conscious of his heavy responsibilities and never quite sure if 'this great lady', as he always described Elizabeth, was in earnest or not, found himself in a constant state of marvellous perplexity 'whether to grant her desires or to say her nay'. Like a good civil servant, he took refuge in tenacious adherence to his instructions and insisted on referring every detail to London, although, as he apologetically admitted, he realized this meant that he was having to trouble the Council 'with more letters than be contentful to mine own opinion'.

This was precisely what Elizabeth intended he should do, for while she undoubtedly got a certain amount of amusement out of baiting Bedingfield, she had another and more serious purpose. The public memory was short and buried in the country she could all too easily be forgotten. Her enemies might then seize the opportunity to have her shipped abroad – the Emperor had a scheme to send her to his sister in Brussels – and once there she might be married off to some obscure Hapsburg dependant or perhaps even more permanently disposed of. So she nagged persistently to have her case re-opened and in June had got permission to write to the Queen. But Mary had not deigned to reply, merely sending Bedingfield a curt message that she did not want to be bothered with any more of her sister's 'disguised and colourable' letters. A month later, though, she did agree to allow Elizabeth to 'write her mind' to the Council and the princess begged their lordships 'upon very pity, considering her long imprisonment and restraint of liberty', to persuade the Queen either to have her charged 'with special matter to be answered unto and tried, or to grant her liberty to come unto her highness's presence, which . . . she would not desire were it not that she knoweth herself to be clear even before God, for her allegiance.' Elizabeth addressed her appeal specifically to those members of the Council who had been executors 'of the Will of the King's majesty her father' – a shrewd reminder that, outcast and disgraced though she might be, she was still heir presumptive to the throne.

Elizabeth may have hoped that now Mary was married and had presumably got everything she wanted, she would be in a more amenable frame of mind. But Mary made no sign and the Council remained deaf to Elizabeth's complaints. The Queen, it appeared, was determined to wring some admission of guilt or contrition out of her sister before she would consider setting her free. The winter closed in and the household at Woodstock gloomily resigned itself to waiting for an indefinite contest of Tudor stubbornness.

In London that winter events were taking place which, temporarily at least, had pushed the problem of Elizabeth's fate into the background. Mary believed herself to be pregnant, and on 12 November she and Philip together opened the third Parliament of the reign – a Parliament which, if all went well, would re-establish Rome's authority over the church in England. Two weeks later Cardinal Pole, the first papal legate to set foot on English soil since the far-off days of the King's Great Matter, travelled up-river to Westminster bringing with him the Pope's absolution for his schismatic and excommunicated countrymen. Reginald Pole, an exile for more than twenty years, was the son of Margaret Plantagenet, the butchered Countess of Salisbury, and for Mary Tudor he brought back precious memories of happy childhood days as well as being the living symbol of so many of her future hopes. As she stood waiting to greet this long-lost kinsman and prince of the Church, the Queen felt a joyous conviction that 'the babe had quickened and leapt in her womb'.

A few days later the reconciliation with Rome had been accomplished. The three estates of the realm knelt together in the Great Chamber of the Court at Westminster to receive the absolution pronounced by the Bishop of Winchester and England was once again a Roman Catholic country. The negotiations leading up to this remarkable moment had been going on throughout the autumn under the personal supervision of Philip of Spain and had been primarily concerned with devising unbreakable safeguards for the property rights of all holders of church lands. Once these had been hammered out to everyone's satisfaction, the

Cardinal Reginald Pole, Papal
Legate to England.

Commons, a body carefully chosen from 'the wise, grave and Catholic sort', was ready to complete the work of undoing the Reformation, of repealing all the religious and ecclesiastical legislation passed during the last two reigns, of abrogating the Royal Supremacy and restoring the ancient laws and penalties against heresy.

So far, it seemed, so good. But as the expected date of Mary's delivery approached, the question of the future in general and of Elizabeth's future in particular was once more exercising men's minds. Stephen Gardiner was openly of the opinion that all attempts to eradicate Protestantism in England would amount to no more than stripping the leaves and lopping the branches as long as the root of the evil – the heretical heiress herself – remained untouched. Now if ever was the time, urged the Lord Chancellor, to push a bill through Parliament disinheriting her once and for all. But there was strangely little enthusiasm for this project. Even the Spaniards were lukewarm, reflecting that if Elizabeth was passed over, it would be very difficult to resist the claims of the Catholic but half-French Mary Stuart.

Philip, in consultation with Simon Renard, was now giving the problem his serious attention. He was assured of the regency if Mary died in childbed and her child survived. But supposing, as seemed probable enough, neither mother nor child survived? Suppose, even, as was being whispered in some quarters, Mary was not pregnant at all? Philip was a tidy-minded man and he wanted to see the whole matter of the English succession put on a regular basis. Elizabeth would have to be released sooner or later and, according to Bedingfield's reports, she was conducting herself like a good Catholic these days. It would, therefore, surely be more sensible to try and establish friendly relations with her now, at a time when she was likely to be grateful for her brother-in-law's support and was still young enough to be influenced. A Catholic husband could then be found for her – that useful Hapsburg pensioner Emmanuel Philibert, Prince of Piedmont, would do as well as any, or there might be a suitable German prince available – and the future of the alliance would be secured. Philip's reasoning was politically sound but he may also have been motivated by purely human curiosity in his evident desire to make the acquaintance of this enigmatic, dangerous young woman he had heard so much about.

At the beginning of April 1555, the Queen moved to Hampton Court to 'take her chamber' in preparation for her lying-in and towards the end of the month Bedingfield received a summons to bring his charge to the palace. The journey from Woodstock was made in typical blustery spring weather and the party encountered violent squalls and gusts of wind which got under the ladies' skirts and blew the princess's hood from her head. She wanted to take shelter in a nearby gentleman's house but Bedingfield, inflexible to the end, refused to allow even this slight deviation from the itinerary, and Elizabeth had to do up her hair under a hedge as best she could.

She was brought to Hampton Court by a back entrance, still under close guard. According to a French source, Philip came to see her privately three days later, but it was nearly a fortnight before any official notice was taken of her arrival. Then she received a visit from a deputation headed by the Lord Chancellor himself, who urged her to submit herself to the Queen. If she did so, he had no doubt that her Majesty would be disposed to be merciful. Elizabeth answered sharply that she wanted justice not mercy. She was not going to ask pardon for crimes she had not committed. Besides, if once she yielded and confessed herself to be an offender, the Queen would never trust her again. It would be better for her to lie in prison for the truth, than to be abroad and suspected of her prince.

There was silence for another week and then, suddenly, at ten o'clock one night, a summons came for Elizabeth to go at once to the Queen. She had been agitating for a personal interview for more than a year, but now the moment had come and as she was walking with her escort through the darkness she must have wondered what the outcome would be. At the foot of the staircase leading to the Queen's lodging, the little procession halted. Bedingfield waited outside while Elizabeth, accompanied by one of the Queen's ladies and one of her own, went up to her sister's bedroom. Without giving Mary a chance to speak, she fell on her knees and once again proclaimed her innocence. 'You will not confess your offence', said Mary out of the shadows, 'but stand stoutly to your truth. I pray God it may so fall out.' 'If it doth not', answered Elizabeth, 'I request neither favour nor pardon at your Majesty's hands.' 'Well', came the somewhat ungracious response, 'you stiffly still persevere in your truth. Belike you will not confess but that you have been wrongfully punished.' 'I must not say so, if it please your Majesty, to you.' 'Why then', persisted the Queen, 'belike you will to others.' 'No', said Elizabeth, 'no, if it please your Majesty, I have borne the burden and must bear it. I humbly beseech your Majesty to have a good opinion of me, and to think me to be your true subject, not only from the beginning, but for ever, as long as life lasteth.'

As she stared at the supple figure of her sister, kneeling before her in the candlelight, Mary knew that she had lost the battle of wills. She must accept, however reluctantly, Elizabeth's assurances of loyalty and make her peace with Anne Boleyn's daughter.

Elizabeth was now relieved of Sir Henry Bedingfield and his departure marked the end of a period of detention which had lasted just over fifteen months. She remained at Court and, although not yet fully restored to favour, had regained a limited freedom of action. A freedom which she wisely used with caution for Elizabeth, like everyone else that summer, was in a state of suspended animation while the uncertainty surrounding the Queen's impending confinement hung like a fog blotting out the future. If, against all the odds, Mary did succeed in bearing a healthy child – and Mary had already once succeeded against all the odds – then the political scene would be transformed, perhaps for generations to come. As Simon Renard observed, 'everything in this kingdom depends on the Queen's safe deliverance'.

By mid-April all was ready. The palace was crowded with noble ladies summoned to assist at the Queen's delivery. Midwives, nurses and rockers were in attendance, and the empty cradle waited. Here, nearly eighteen years before, Edward Tudor had been born. Was another Tudor prince about to draw his first breath in Cardinal Wolsey's fine red-brick mansion? Everything possible was being done to encourage the Queen. The Venetian ambassador reported on 2 April that to comfort her and give her heart and courage 'three most beautiful infants were brought for her Majesty to see; they having been born a few days previously at one birth, of a woman of low stature and great age like the Queen, who after delivery found herself strong and out of danger.'

At daybreak on 30 April a rumour reached London that Mary had given birth to a son just after midnight 'with little pain and no danger'. So circumstantial was this report that it was generally believed and bonfires were lit, church bells rung and 'in divers places Te Deum Laudamus was sung', while loyal citizens set up trestles before their doors and began dispensing free food and drink to their neighbours. It was late afternoon before the messengers returning from Hampton Court brought the dispiriting news that there was no son or daughter either and that the birth was not even imminent. As the days of waiting lengthened into weeks, the doctors announced that their calculations had been wrong, that the Queen would not now be delivered until the end of May, possibly not until the first week of June, although her Majesty's belly had greatly declined, a sign, it was said, of the nearer approach of the term.

June turned into July and the doctors and midwives were still talking about miscalculation, still promising the wretched Queen that she was carrying a child, but saying the birth might be delayed until August or even September. By this time, though, everyone knew that no baby would ever fill that 'very sumptuously and gorgeously trimmed' cradle. The amenorrhoea and digestive troubles to which Mary had always been subject, perhaps, too, cancer of the womb, had combined with her desperate longing which – according to the omniscient diplomatic corps – even produced 'swelling of the paps and their emission of milk' to create that tragic, long-drawn-out self-deception.

By the end of July the situation at Hampton Court was becoming too embarrassing to be allowed to continue any longer. Something had to be done to silence the ribald ale-house gossip and all those inevitable rumours about humble mothers being begged to give up their new-born babies to emissaries from the palace. The daily processions and prayers for the Queen's delivery were stopped and on 3 August the Court moved away to Oatlands in a tacit admission that Mary had at last given up hope. But as she struggled to come to terms with her bitter disappointment and humiliation, she had another sorrow to face – for the adored husband, on whom she had lavished all the love so long denied an outlet, was planning to leave her. Philip had now spent thirteen months in a country he disliked, being affable to people he despised and distrusted, being kind to a demanding, physically unattractive and unfruitful wife. He considered he had done everything that could reasonably be expected of him.

He was to embark at Dover as soon as the escorting fleet could be made ready and on 26 August the Court moved down to Greenwich to see him off. Three days later he was gone, after punctiliously kissing all the ladies, just as he had done that first evening in Winchester, and Mary stood in tears at a window overlooking the river watching until the barge taking him away to Gravesend had passed out of her sight. It was the end of her brief happiness.

The Queen planned to stay at Greenwich during Philip's absence and Reginald Pole was given apartments in the palace, so that he might 'comfort and keep her company, her Majesty delighting greatly in the sight and presence of him'. Elizabeth was also at Greenwich, though it is doubtful if her presence gave Mary any particular pleasure. However, Elizabeth was now in a privileged position. She had used those weeks of waiting at Hampton Court to good purpose and, at least according to the Venetian ambassador, had 'contrived so to ingratiate herself with all the Spaniards and especially the King, that ever since no one has favoured her more than he does.' Years later a report circulated that Philip had been heard to admit that whatever he suffered from Queen Elizabeth was no more than the just judgement of God, because 'being married to Queen Mary, whom he thought a most virtuous and good lady, yet in the fancy of love he could not affect her; but as for the Lady Elizabeth, he was enamoured of her, being a fair and beautiful woman.' Whether Philip was really smitten by his sister-in-law's charms remains a matter for conjecture but he had clearly made up his mind that notwithstanding her dubious birth and heretical tendencies, she would make an infinitely preferable successor to the English throne than Mary Queen of Scots. Before he left England, therefore, he had particularly commended Elizabeth to Mary's good will and (this time according to the French ambassador) was soon writing from the Low Countries to repeat what was virtually an order to the Queen to handle her sister with courtesy and care. Since Philip's lightest wish was Mary's command, she obediently choked down her instinctive antipathy, treating the princess graciously in public and only conversing with her about 'agreeable subjects'.

September turned into October with no sign of Philip's return and Mary was obliged to abandon her vigil and go back to London for the opening of Parliament. Elizabeth did not accompany her. She had been given permission to leave the Court and on 18 October she passed through the City on her way to Hatfield. Settled once more in her favourite residence after an absence of over two years, she began to take up the threads of her old life and to gather her old friends round her again. Things, in fact, were looking up for Elizabeth. She had made a powerful ally in Philip. Simon Renard had been recalled to Brussels and was no longer dropping poison into Mary's ear, and in November another old enemy disappeared with the death of Stephen Gardiner. The princess knew that time was now on her side. She had only to wait – and she was good at waiting – steer clear of politics and, above all, avoid any matrimonial entanglements, and sooner or later the prize would fall into her lap.

CHAPTER 13

England's Eliza

After the stormy, tempestuous and blustering windy weather of Queen Mary was overblown, the darksome clouds of discomfort dispersed and the dashing showers of persecution overpast; it pleased God to send England a calm and quiet season, a clear and lovely sunshine, a quietus from former broils, and a world of blessings by good Queen Elizabeth.

The last three years of Mary's life were for the Queen years of increasing ill-health, unhappiness and disillusion. For the English people they were a time of economic depression and political uncertainty, while the religious persecution that has left such an indelible stain on Mary's memory helped to thicken the general atmosphere of gloom and discontent. The first heretics had been burnt in February 1555, and altogether some three hundred men and women were condemned to suffer this particularly horrible form of death. It was not, by contemporary standards, an especially harsh campaign and affected only a small section of the population, but it remains a thoroughly unpleasant episode; one of its least attractive features being the fact that the great majority of its victims were humble people – poor widows, journeymen and apprentices, agricultural labourers, weavers, clothworkers, artisans and tradesmen – who died in agony for the sake of what they believed to be God's truth. The better-to-do either conformed just sufficiently to keep out of trouble, or else took their consciences abroad more or less unhindered.

From the point of view of what it hoped to achieve, the Marian persecution was monumentally counter-productive and the fires that consumed the bishops Hooper, Latimer and Ridley, who, with Thomas Cranmer, were virtually the only sufferers of note, did indeed light such a candle in England as, with God's grace, never was put out. Perhaps the most inept act, both psychologically and politically, of an inept administration was the degradation and martyrdom of Thomas Cranmer. Having once recanted, the former archbishop, that gentle, kindly, diffident man, was driven at last beyond fear or doubt and died publicly proclaiming his Protestant faith. Had his life been spared, he would surely have been one of the most notable apostates in history and worth more to the Catholic cause than all the Protestant martyrs put together. But to Mary, Cranmer was the false shepherd who had deliberately led the silly, credulous sheep into the fires of hell. To the Queen, heresy was a plague of the deadliest kind, destroying the immortal soul rather than the body, and to her it would have been an unforgivable

Thomas Cranmer, the former
Archbishop of Canterbury, who
was burned at the stake in March
1556, painted by Gerlach Flicke.

dereliction of the duty so clearly laid upon her by the Almighty if she had not striven by all the means at her disposal to save her poor deluded subjects from certain damnation.

Mary yearned for Philip, but the months passed and there was still no sign of his return. The old Emperor, preparing to bow off the stage and end his days in a monastery, had now handed over all his burdens, save the Empire and Burgundy, to his son and in future Philip would have less time than ever to spare for England. He sent only promises – promises repeatedly and cynically broken – in reply to her self-abasing pleas that he would come back to her. Mary's last birthday had been her fortieth and she could only rage and despair by turn as her stubborn, unquenchable hopes of bearing children were mocked by her husband's absence.

Then, at the end of March 1557, Philip did come back. It was for a short visit only, with only one objective – to drag England into the everlasting Franco-Spanish quarrel, just as the King of France had always predicted he would. By July he was gone and this time, as if she guessed she would never see him again, Mary went with him to Dover, down to the water's edge. But Philip had left a piece of unfinished business behind which continued to nag at him. He had long since resigned himself to the fact that Elizabeth would succeed her sister and

Elizabeth, at twenty-three, was still unmarried, still unfettered to the Spanish interest.

The previous September Providence had thoughtfully removed her most dangerous suitor from the scene. Edward Courtenay had been released from the Tower at about the time Elizabeth was sent down to Woodstock (however doubtful his guilt, he would not have been so fortunate under Henry VIII) and, after a period of detention in Fotheringay Castle, had been allowed to go abroad. He had wandered across Europe as far as Venice, where he caught a chill, and about a fortnight later the great-grandson of Edward IV died of fever in lodgings at Padua. Peter Vannes, Queen Mary's agent in Venice, took the precaution of obtaining sworn statements from Courtenay's servants and the Italian doctors who had attended him, but even so rumours that he had been poisoned soon got about and his death appears to have been the signal for Philip to renew his efforts to get Elizabeth suitably betrothed.

The princess came to Court that December and, so the King of France told the Venetian ambassador, the Queen had made a strong effort to persuade her sister to accept the Prince of Piedmont. But Elizabeth had burst into tears and declared she would rather die. In the summer of 1557 Philip returned to the attack, sending his confessor, Francisco de Fresnada, to urge the Queen to have the marriage arranged without further delay and, if necessary, without consulting Parliament. Fresnada had instructions to impress on Mary how important this was for considerations of religion, the safety of the realm and to prevent Elizabeth from making some quite unsuitable choice of her own. This time, though, opposition was by no means all on Elizabeth's side, for Philip now wanted Mary not only to get her sister married off to Emmanuel Philibert but publicly to recognize her as her heiress. The Venetian ambassador heard that de Fresnada found the Queen 'utterly averse to giving the Lady Elizabeth any hope of the succession, obstinately maintaining that she was neither her sister nor the daughter of the Queen's father, King Henry. Nor would she hear of favouring her, as she was born of an infamous woman, who had so greatly outraged the Queen her mother and herself.'

Philip, naturally exasperated by the unreasonableness of his wife's behaviour, made his annoyance plain; but Mary, although miserable in the knowledge that she was displeasing him, could not be blackmailed. Old wrongs cast long shadows and for the sad, sick woman, now facing the ruin of all her hopes, the bitter past was as real, perhaps more real than the bitter present. Once she had acknowledged Elizabeth's right to succeed her, she would have acknowledged that Anne Boleyn and her daughter had won. Not even for Philip, not even for the Catholic church could Catherine of Aragon's daughter bring herself to admit that ultimate defeat.

The year 1558 opened with a military disaster. The war in France had begun promisingly with the Anglo-Spanish victory of St Quentin, then things went less well and finally very badly indeed, culminating in the news that Calais had fallen to the French – 'the heaviest tidings to London and to England that ever was heard of'. The town of Calais and its surrounding Pale might no longer be of much strategic value but, as the last outpost of England's once great Continental empire, it possessed considerable sentimental value. Its loss was a national humiliation. For Mary it was followed by yet another personal grief. During the Christmas holidays Reginald Pole had written to tell Philip that the Queen once again believed she was pregnant. This time she had kept the news to herself for nearly seven months 'in order to be quite sure of the fact'. Can she really have believed it, or was it just a pathetic, last-ditch attempt to bring her husband back to her? It did not bring him, but Count de Feria was sent over to England, ostensibly bearing congratulations but with instructions to find out if such a thing could possibly be true. It could not, of course, and by April Mary had once again given up hope.

The gloomy spring gave place to a restless, uneasy summer. The Queen was obviously gravely ill, dying most probably of cancer, and a sense of great changes impending rumbled in the air like distant thunder. By October the news reaching Philip in Flanders was sufficiently disturbing for him to send de Feria back to London 'to serve the Queen during her illness'. He arrived on 9 November only to find there was nothing now that he or anyone else could do for Mary. Three days earlier, the Council, taking advantage of a brief lucid interval, had gathered at the Queen's bedside with a request that she would 'make certain declarations in favour of the Lady Elizabeth' and Mary had given in. She was too tired to struggle any longer and perhaps it no longer seemed to matter very much. A deputation had gone straight down to Hatfield to tell Elizabeth that the Queen was willing she should succeed but asked two things of her – that she would maintain the old religion as Mary had restored it and pay her sister's debts.

After this Mary was left alone. The road to Hatfield was crowded with courtiers and place-seekers eager to stake an early claim, while at St James's Palace the Queen lay waiting for release from the world in which she had known little but sorrow, anxiety and humiliation. She was unconscious for long periods during those last weeks but once, when she drifted to the surface and saw her ladies weeping round her, she is said to have comforted them by telling them what good dreams she had, seeing many little children playing and singing before her. Mary had loved little children, loved christenings and babies (always, tragically, other people's babies); had revelled in weddings and new clothes, and taken a passionate interest in those small domestic concerns which fill the lives of ordinary women – for Mary Tudor was at heart a very ordinary woman, made to be a busy, devoted, pious wife and mother. She was hopelessly at sea in the world of high politics, where she could only do what she believed to be her duty, what she believed to be right, with predictably disastrous results. Poor Mary, there was so much that was good in her. She had not deserved to be the most unhappy lady in Christendom.

The end came at six o'clock in the morning of 17 November and later that same day, as if to emphasize the ending of a chapter, Reginald Pole, the Cardinal of England, died too, just across the river in his palace at Lambeth. There was little pretence of public mourning. As the news spread the church bells were rung and presently the November dusk was being illuminated by bonfires, while the Londoners set tables in the streets and 'did eat and drink and make merry for the new Queen Elizabeth'.

Mary exercises her mystic royal power: praying for blessing on rings for curing cramp.

Despite Mary's views on the subject, Elizabeth had long been accepted as the heir to the throne and over the last couple of years she had attracted an increasing amount of interest from the outside world. In 1557 the retiring Venetian ambassador had included a detailed description of the princess in his report to the Senate, and from the evidence of Giovanni Michiel and other contemporaries a picture emerges of a slim, active young woman, slightly above average height. Michiel considered her narrow, sharp-featured face to be 'comely' rather than handsome, though she had a good complexion, if a little sallow. He also remarked on her fine eyes, which were probably grey, and on her beautiful hands which she took care to display. Elizabeth had the family colouring. Her hair was more red than yellow and curled naturally, at least in her twenties. Michiel noted, with a faint air of disapproval, that although she knew she was born of 'such a mother', she did not consider herself of inferior degree to the Queen. She did not, apparently, even consider herself illegitimate, since her parents' marriage had had the blessing of the Archbishop of Canterbury. 'She prides herself on her father and glories in him', remarked the ambassador, 'everybody saying that she also resembles him more than the Queen does.' In view of Mary's freely expressed opinion about her origins, this must have given Elizabeth a very understandable satisfaction, but in appearance she seems to have resembled her paternal grandfather more than any other member of the family.

About her mental powers no one was in any doubt. 'Her intellect and understanding are wonderful', wrote Michiel, 'as she showed very plainly by her conduct when in danger and under suspicion' and he went on to praise her proficiency as a linguist, noting that her Latin was better than the Queen's. Her Italian, too, was fluent and she liked to show it off in front of the Venetians. Roger Ascham, who had recently been renewing his acquaintance with his former pupil, told Dr Sturm in Strasbourg that they had been reading together in Greek the orations of Aeschines and Demosthenes on the crown and that the Lady Elizabeth 'at first sight understands everything . . . in a way to strike you with astonishment'.

The Lady Elizabeth had already proved the quality of her trained and formidable intelligence, and demonstrated that she had inherited her grandfather's shrewd, cautious, subtle brain. Now, in the first weeks of her reign, she was to show that she had also inherited all her father's ability to charm the birds off the trees. 'If ever any person had either the gift or the style to win the hearts of people', wrote the historian John Hayward, 'it was this Queen.'

When Elizabeth made her official entry into London, riding through Barbican and Cripplegate and on to Leadenhall and Gracechurch Street to the Tower, the City literally exploded with joy around her. But beneath all the cheering and pealing bells and crashing salutes from the Tower guns there was a rather desperate optimism. For Elizabeth was the last of King Harry's children and in that winter of 1558 she looked like being England's last hope of peace and good government. Certainly a quick glance round the other members of the royal house would not have encouraged anyone seeking an alternative – or a successor.

If King Henry's will was to be followed, then of course the new Queen's heir must be sought among the descendants of Mary Brandon. Mary's elder daughter,

'The Succession of Henry VIII', painted in Elizabeth's reign, shows Henry handing his sword to Edward while Philip and Mary lead in Mars, the god of war, and Elizabeth leads in peace and plenty.

the widowed Duchess of Suffolk, was now past forty and had, in any case, already renounced her claim in favour of her daughters. Just as well, perhaps, since Frances Suffolk had wasted no time in mourning and within a month of her husband's execution in 1554 she had married one Master Adrian Stokes, a flashy, red-haired young gentleman of her household. Her two surviving daughters, Katherine and Mary, became maids of honour to Queen Mary, who had gone out of her way to be kind to them. Katherine Grey's marriage to the Earl of Pembroke's son had been hastily dissolved after Northumberland's disaster and in November 1558, the two girls, now aged eighteen and thirteen, were still at Court and still unmarried – their future, especially Katherine's future, the subject of some speculation. The other child of that long-ago Tudor–Brandon marriage, Eleanor Clifford, was more than ten years dead and *her* daughter, Margaret, had been married in 1555, with Queen Mary's blessing, to Lord Strange, the Earl of Derby's heir. Some people, including young Lady Strange herself, believed her claim to be purer than Katherine Grey's – there was, after all, no 'reproach' of treason on her side of the family – but although Margaret lived on into the 1590s,

The young Queen Elizabeth, by an unknown artist.

her life was to be chiefly remarkable for an unhappy marriage, perpetual quarrels with her in-laws and an unfortunate interest in necromancy.

For those who were of the opinion that the natural laws of inheritance should take precedence over royal, even over royal Tudor testamentary provisions, the next heir could only be the descendant of Margaret Tudor's marriage to James IV of Scotland and that meant Mary Queen of Scots, now rising sixteen and married seven months previously to the French King's heir. There were those who believed that by rights Mary Stuart and not Elizabeth Tudor should now be wearing the English crown. The King of France certainly did – or said he did – underlining his point by having his daughter-in-law referred to as Queen of England in official documents and causing her to quarter the English royal arms with her own. But although the pretensions of her Scottish cousin were to create increasingly serious problems for Elizabeth as time went by, very few Englishmen – even those Englishmen whose religion obliged them to regard Henry VIII's second daughter as a bastard – wished to see Mary displace her. Then there was another body of opinion which, although preferring the senior line, regarded Mary Stuart as a foreigner and therefore automatically disabled. For those who held this view, the alternative was Margaret Tudor's daughter, the Countess of Lennox, who, thanks to her mother's precipitate flight from Edinburgh forty-three years ago, had at least been born on the right side of the Border. There were also Margaret Lennox's two hopeful sons, Henry Lord Darnley and Charles Stuart, now being brought up on the family estates at Temple Newsam in Yorkshire.

It was a varied field and offered plenty of scope for argument, perhaps bloody argument, but everyone devoutly hoped the question would never arise. Elizabeth was a young, healthy woman and in 1558 there seemed no reason why she should not be able to provide her country with a Prince of Wales. It was perfectly true that she had steadily refused all the suitors offered for her consideration during the past five years, saying at regular intervals that she did not want to marry; but naturally no sensible person had believed a word of such nonsense and in January 1559 the Speaker of the House of Commons, with a few selected companions, waited on the Queen to deliver an earnest petition that she would by marriage bring forth children – this being 'the single, the only, the all-comprehending prayer of all Englishmen'. The petitioners got little satisfaction from their sovereign lady who reminded them sharply that she had already joined herself in marriage to a husband, 'namely, the Kingdom of England', and taking the coronation ring from her finger, she flourished 'the pledge of this my wedlock' (which she marvelled they could have forgotten) under their perplexed noses. As for children: 'Do not', snapped Elizabeth Tudor, 'upbraid me with miserable lack of children; for every one of you, and as many as are Englishmen, are children and kinsmen to me.' After this, the Queen relented sufficiently to give an assurance that if she ever were to consider taking a more conventional husband, it would be someone who would have as great a care of the commonwealth as herself. If, on the other hand, she continued in the course of life she had begun, she had no doubt that, in the fullness of time, God would provide a suitable successor; while she would be more than content to have engraved on her tombstone: 'Here lieth Elizabeth which reigned a virgin and died a virgin'.

This was only the first of many similar exchanges between an increasingly anxious and importunate Parliament and an obstinately virgin Queen – only the first of many 'answers answerless'. The reasons for Elizabeth's determination to remain single have been exhaustively discussed over the centuries but, psychological speculation set aside, it seems that at twenty-five she had already faced and accepted the fact that, in the sixteenth-century world, marriage and a career could not be combined. Mary had always needed a man to lean on, but Elizabeth had learned to rely on herself by the time she was fifteen and was not now going to entrust her body or her soul to any man. This did not mean that she was not fully alive to all the advantages, both personal and political, of being the best match in her parish. She certainly exploited them for all they were worth with every appearance of keen enjoyment – giving her various swains just enough encouragement to keep them hopeful for just as long as it happened to suit her.

One proposal she did reject out of hand – the one which came from, of all people, her former brother-in-law. Philip might be prepared to sacrifice himself a second time for the sake of the Catholic religion and the English alliance, but Elizabeth was quite definitely not going to repeat her sister's mistakes. She was, though, very interested in Philip's friendship and she allowed him to suggest his

Elizabeth proceeding to Westminster on the day before her coronation, 14 January 1559. The Queen is accompanied by Lord Ambrose Dudley and Lord Giles Paulet and followed by her Master of Horse, Lord Robert Dudley.

Austrian arch-ducal cousins, Ferdinand and Charles von Hapsburg, as possible alternatives. Ferdinand's uncompromising Catholicism soon put him out of the running, for by Easter 1559 England had once more become a Protestant country with a national church. The more amenable and long-suffering Charles remained a useful stand-by, to be brought out and reconsidered whenever the marriage question was being pressed, and kept dangling for nearly ten years.

Much as she always delighted in the ritual dance of courtship, Elizabeth had very little leisure to spare for dalliance during the first six months of her reign. She had inherited enough problems to keep her fully occupied with more prosaic matters, and it was not until the late spring of 1559 that she was able to give some attention to her private life – by which time a religious settlement had been hammered out at home, a peace treaty negotiated with France and a loan raised in the money-market at Antwerp to replenish a virtually empty Treasury. It was then, significantly, that the first whispers linking her name with Lord Robert Dudley began to circulate and by the autumn everyone was asking the same question – was Elizabeth, whose marriage was of such vital importance for the country, wasting her time and ruining her chances by having an affair with a married man?

Robert Dudley, the younger of the Duke of Northumberland's two surviving sons, was, like all his family, immensely ambitious and none too scrupulous about the methods he used to advance himself. He was intensely unpopular – an unpopularity which cannot entirely be accounted for by jealousy – and his contemporaries, almost without exception, loathed and detested him. The most notable exception, of course, was the Queen herself and the relationship, often stormy and in some ways totally mysterious, which existed between Elizabeth Tudor and Robert Dudley was to endure for very nearly thirty years.

No one at the time could begin to understand what the Queen, who could have taken her pick of the bachelors of Christendom, saw in Robert, the son and grandson of convicted traitors, a man who had only narrowly avoided the penalty of treason himself. The historian William Camden, who knew them both, could only hazard a guess that perhaps he gave some shadowed tokens of virtue, visible to the Queen alone, or else that the hidden content of the stars at the hour of his birth had led to 'a most straight conjunction of their minds'. What did the Queen see in Robert Dudley? He was very good-looking certainly – 'comely of body and limbs' – everybody agreed about that and looks were always important to Elizabeth. But Robert was more than just a pretty face. He was a fine athlete and a superb horseman (he held the position of Master of the Horse from the first week of the Queen's reign until his death), and Elizabeth, like her father, loved a man who *was* a man and not, as she scornfully remarked of one unfortunate suitor, one who would sit at home all day among the cinders. He was a good dancer – also very important. He was amusing company, witty, sophisticated, accustomed all his life to moving in the highest social and political circles. He had a fine, commanding presence and made a first rate ornament for the Court. But probably what mattered most was the fact that he was already one of the Queen's oldest friends. They were almost exactly the same age and had known one another from childhood. They had grown up together and been prisoners in the Tower together. They talked the same language, shared the same jokes, the same background. With Robert Elizabeth could relax, unwind and be herself, and she who lived so much of her life at concert pitch needed someone she could relax with, someone to be the companion of her off-duty hours.

Were they lovers in the accepted sense? The answer is almost certainly no – although there was a strong element of sexual attraction in the relationship. Elizabeth always insisted vehemently that they were just good friends and, with the best will in the world, no one was ever able to produce a scrap of evidence to the contrary. Caspar von Breuner, an agent of the Hapsburg family in London to promote the marriage with Archduke Charles, made the most searching enquiries but came to the conclusion that, while the Queen showed her affection to Lord Robert more markedly than was consistent with her dignity, there was no reason to suppose she had ever been forgetful of her honour.

But lack of evidence did nothing to silence gossip, and rumours about the Queen's intentions proliferated. As early as April 1559 Count de Feria had told King Philip that Lord Robert's wife was suffering from 'a malady in one of her breasts' and Elizabeth was only waiting for her to die to marry the widower. The new Spanish ambassador, Bishop de Quadra, who arrived in London during the summer, soon heard from a reliable source that Lord Robert was planning to poison his wife. In March 1560 the bishop was reporting that Robert was assuming every day a more masterful part in affairs and added 'they say that he thinks of divorcing his wife'.

Considering that she had become one of the central figures in an international scandal, remarkably little is known about Amy Dudley, born Amy Robsart, the daughter of a wealthy Norfolk landowner. She and Robert had been married nearly ten years and it seems probable that theirs was originally a love match. But

Robert Dudley, Earl of Leicester;
artist unknown.

country-bred Amy had not been able to keep pace with her brilliant, rapacious husband. Physical passion was soon spent and now she was simply an encumbrance to be kept out of sight and as far as possible out of mind. The Dudleys had no settled home and while Robert remained in constant attendance on the Queen, Amy spent her time moving about from one country house to another, taking her own servants and living as a kind of superior paying guest, usually with friends or connections of her husband's. During the summer of 1560 she moved into Cumnor Hall near Abingdon and the Dudley affair began to build towards crisis point.

William Cecil, the Queen's sober Secretary of State, had gone on a diplomatic mission to Scotland and while he was away people noticed that Elizabeth was not 'coming abroad' nearly as much as usual. It was said that Robert was keeping her shut up with him and old Annie Dow of Brentwood got into trouble with the magistrates for telling a neighbour that Lord Robert had given the Queen a child. In fact, the Queen and Lord Robert were spending most of their time out riding, and Robert wrote to the Earl of Sussex in Ireland for some hobbys for the royal saddle – 'especially for strong, good gallopers'. Elizabeth was enjoying herself, but when Cecil got back from the North at the end of July he was seriously worried by the situation which seemed to be developing. The Queen was in her most tiresome mood, refusing to attend to business or, perhaps more accurately, refusing to attend to William Cecil, and Robert was peacocking about the Court in a manner which irritated the Secretary of State profoundly. He told the Spanish ambassador in a burst of calculated indiscretion that he fully expected the ruin of the realm unless someone could bring Elizabeth to her senses. He was very much afraid, he added, that she meant to marry Lord Robert, who was thinking of killing his wife.

Cecil saw de Quadra during the weekend of 7–8 September. On Monday the Court was thrumming with the news that Amy Dudley had been found lying at the foot of a flight of stairs at Cumnor Hall with a broken neck. This was a stunning climax to eighteen months of scandalmongering and it looked as if William Cecil had been quite right in his gloomy forebodings. Certainly things looked black for Robert Dudley and the Queen sent him away to his house at Kew, with orders to stay there until the matter had been investigated. Most people, of course, had already made up their minds and, in the circumstances, it is hardly surprising that no one believed such a remarkably convenient death could possibly have been coincidence. The fact that a coroner's jury, drawn from the leaders of the local community, could find no 'presumption of evil' and, albeit reluctantly, presently returned a verdict of death by misadventure in no way altered the general conviction of Robert's guilt. Officially, though, he had been exonerated and the world at large held its breath to see what would happen next.

Bishop de Quadra did not know what to make of the situation. He was always disposed to think the worst of the heretical Queen of England and her subjects and told Philip: 'The cry is that they do not want any more women rulers and this woman may find herself and her favourite in prison any day.' The bishop very properly considered the whole business most shameful and scandalous but, at the same time, he was not sure whether Elizabeth meant to marry Robert or even whether she meant to marry at all, as he did not think she had her mind sufficiently fixed.

In France no one was in any doubt about what to think and Queen Elizabeth's ambassador, that sturdy Protestant Nicholas Throckmorton, was being driven to distraction. 'I wish I were either dead or hence', he wrote from Paris on 10 October, 'that I might not hear the dishonourable and naughty reports that are made of the Queen . . . One laugheth at us, another threateneth, another revileth the Queen. Some let not to say: What religion is this that a subject shall kill his wife and the Prince not only bear withal but marry with him? If these slanderous bruits be not slaked, or if they prove true, our reputation is gone forever, war follows and utter subversion of the Queen and country.'

At home, one man was prepared to disregard gossip and slander and all those rude, low-minded foreigners. The Earl of Sussex could not stand Robert Dudley and could hardly bring himself to be civil to him in public, but, as he reminded William Cecil, the one thing that really mattered was for Elizabeth to have a child. Therefore, she should be left to 'follow so much her own affection as by the looking upon him whom she should choose, her whole being may be moved to desire.' For that, as Sussex pointed out, 'shall be the readiest way, with the help of God, to bring us a blessed prince.' If the Queen really loved and desired Robert

Dudley, then let her marry him and Sussex, for his part, would be prepared to sink his personal prejudices, and love, honour and serve his enemy to the uttermost. But the Earl found few supporters in this humane and generous attitude. When young Mary Queen of Scots exclaimed merrily – 'So, the Queen of England is to marry her horsekeeper who has killed his wife to make room for her', she pretty well summed-up foreign and Catholic opinion; while Caspar von Breuner in London believed that if such a marriage took place, the Queen would incur so much enmity that 'she may one evening lay herself down as Queen of England and rise the next morning plain Mistress Elizabeth.' Not even for the sake of a blessed prince would the English stomach an upstart and wife-murderer as their king.

How did Amy Dudley die? Had she been murdered by Robert's hired assassins and her body arranged at the foot of that fatal staircase to make the death look like an accident? Had she killed herself, driven to despair by the knowledge of her own mortal disease and her husband's callous neglect? Or was the jury's verdict a true one after all? It has been suggested that if Amy was suffering from advanced breast cancer, secondary deposits may have been present in the bones. The effect of such deposits in the spine is to make it so brittle that the slightest stumble, even the act of walking downstairs, could have caused a spontaneous fracture. The question marks remain, but for Elizabeth Tudor they were scarcely relevant. What mattered was that Robert's wife had died violently and mysteriously, and that alone made marriage with Robert impossible.

By the late autumn of 1560 the crisis had begun to go off the boil and by the end of the year William Cecil was able to assure Nicholas Throckmorton that whatever the reports and opinions might be, he knew for certain 'that Lord Robert himself hath more fear than hope and so doth the Queen give him cause'. Lord Robert was back at Court and apparently restored to high favour, but when the Letters Patent for his creation as Earl of Leicester – an honour he greatly coveted – were drawn up, the Queen slashed the document through with her penknife instead of signing it. The Dudleys had been traitors three descents, she exclaimed unkindly, and she would not confer a title on the present generation. Robert sulked and Elizabeth seemed to relent. She patted his cheek and said, with a reference to the Dudley coat of arms, 'No, no, the bear and ragged staff are not so soon overthrown.' But when some of Robert's friends tried to urge his suit, she would only 'pup with her mouth' and say she would never marry a subject. She would then be no better than the Duchess of Norfolk and people would come asking for my lord's grace. Well then, argued Robert's supporters, let her make him King. No, the Queen would not hear of such a thing.

She would not make him King and nor would she allow him to presume too far on his present somewhat ambiguous position. When, on one occasion, Robert attempted to take a high hand with one of the royal servants, he received a devastating royal snub. Rapping out 'her wonted oath', Elizabeth turned on him in a fury. 'God's death, my lord, I have wished you well, but my favour is not so locked up for you that others may not participate thereof . . . And if you think to rule here, I will take a course to see you forthcoming. For I will have here but one mistress and no master!' This, of course, was the nub of the matter. Robert was a masterful man, that was one of the reasons Elizabeth loved him; but it was also another of the reasons why she would never marry him.

Robert was too intelligent not to take the warning, but he had by no means given up hope of winning the greatest matrimonial prize in Europe and continued to intrigue actively towards that end. Even Elizabeth had not yet entirely abandoned the idea, for in February 1561 she was putting out feelers to Bishop de Quadra as to what the King of Spain would say if she married one of her servitors. In March it was reported that 'the great matters whereof the world was wont to talk were now asleep', but in June they woke up again. De Quadra had been invited to a grand water-party and firework display on the Thames given by Lord Robert and he told Philip that 'in the afternoon we went on board a vessel from which we were to see the rejoicings, and the Queen, Robert and I being alone in the gallery, they began joking, which she likes to do much better than talking about business. They went so far with their jokes that Lord Robert told her that, if she liked, I could be the minister to perform the act of marriage. She, nothing loath to hear it, said she was not sure whether I knew enough English.' De Quadra let them have their fun and then tried to make them see sense. If Elizabeth would only reinstate the Catholic religion and put herself under King Philip's protection, she could marry Robert when she pleased and de Quadra would be delighted to perform the ceremony.

And so it went on – and on. The possibility of the marriage continued to be canvassed from time to time. Rumours that it had actually taken place were circulated on more than one occasion, but the cataclysm which everyone had been dreading never materialized. Fortunately for England and for herself, Elizabeth did not suffer from that disastrous lack of emotional control which was to bring Mary Stuart to ruin and she had been able to face and overcome the first and, as it turned out, the only serious conflict between her desires as a woman and her responsibilities as Queen. All the same, the past few months had been a strain and when she left London in July for a summer progress to East Anglia, it was noticed that she looked as pale as a woman who had lately come out of childbed. There were plenty of people ready enough to suggest that this might be literally true, but Bishop de Quadra had seen no sign of such a thing and did not believe it. He had heard other gossip to the effect that the Queen, because of 'certain physical infirmities', would never be able to have children. This gossip was to persist and probably originated in the fact that at one time Elizabeth's monthly periods were very irregular.

The Queen, irritable and in low spirits, seems to have been suffering from a revulsion of feeling on the subject of men in general and marriage in particular. In a burst of bad temper she told the Archbishop of Canterbury that she wished she had never appointed any married clergy, and when Dr Parker reminded her that the idea of a celibate priesthood was Roman Catholic rather than Anglican, Elizabeth, so Parker told William Cecil, 'took occasion to speak in that bitterness of the holy estate of matrimony that I was in a horror to hear her.' In the circumstances, therefore, it was particularly unfortunate that Katherine Grey should have chosen this moment out of all others to get married without the Queen's consent.

As one of Elizabeth's closest relatives and leading contender for the position of heir presumptive, Katherine had now become a figure of considerable political importance; but unhappily she possessed none of the qualities of tact, discretion or even basic common-sense which might have helped her to survive in the political jungle. To make matters worse, she did not get on with the Queen. Elizabeth had never cared for any of her Grey cousins – there is nothing to suggest that there had ever been any sort of intimacy between her and Jane, in spite of the months they had spent together under Katherine Parr's roof, and she had no opinion at all of Jane's younger sister. Katherine, for her part, seems to have regarded Elizabeth, on whom her whole future depended, with an unhealthy mixture of fear and resentment. She knew the Queen despised her and took offence because she was no longer admitted to the Privy Chamber.

The fact that Elizabeth and Katherine Grey were on bad terms was soon being noted with interest in certain circles, and during the second half of 1559 Sir Thomas Challoner, the English ambassador in Brussels, warned the Queen about rumours that the Spaniards were planning to kidnap Lady Katherine. Apparently the idea was to marry her to Don Carlos, Philip's imbecile son, 'or with some other person of less degree if less depended on her', and then to keep her as a possible counter-claimant to France's Mary Stuart should the occasion arise. Since Katherine was known to be 'of discontented mind' and not regarded or esteemed by the Queen, it was thought there would be no difficulty in enticing her away. Elizabeth reacted characteristically by reinstating her cousin as a lady of the Privy Chamber and telling a puzzled de Quadra that she regarded the Lady Katherine as her daughter and was thinking of formally adopting her.

In fact, Katherine was not in the least interested in Spanish intrigues or in the ramifications of the European political scene. She was interested only in her own plans to marry Edward Seymour, Earl of Hertford, son of the former Protector Somerset. She must have known Edward Seymour since she was a child – he had been suggested as a bridegroom for her sister Jane – but it was during Queen Mary's reign, when Katherine had been staying with the Duchess of Somerset at Hanworth, that the two young people had first begun 'to accompany together' and to think about marriage. The idea of the match had been discussed in the Seymour and Grey families, and in the spring of 1559 Katherine's mother had agreed to approach the Queen for her consent. But unfortunately the approach was never made. Frances Suffolk, or Frances Stokes as she now was, became ill that summer and by November she was dead. The lovers now had no one to speak for them and the whole affair might well have died a natural death if Hertford's sister, Lady Jane Seymour had not decided to take a hand.

Jane Seymour was one of Katherine's fellow maids of honour, an ambitious, energetic young woman determined that her brother should not lose the chance of making such a brilliant match. It was Jane who brought the couple together again (they had quarrelled when Hertford began to take an interest in another, quite inferior, girl); and it was almost certainly she who put the disastrous idea of a secret marriage into their hands. The three of them met in Lady Jane's private closet at Whitehall some time in October 1560 and there Katherine and Edward Seymour plighted their troth. It was agreed that the wedding should take place at the Earl's house in Cannon Row 'the next time that the Queen's highness should take any journey', and Jane undertook to have a clergyman standing by.

Opportunity came early in December, when the Queen decided to go down to Eltham for a few days' hunting. Katherine pleaded toothache and Jane, who was already consumptive, was often ailing. As soon as Elizabeth was safely out of the way, at about eight o'clock in the morning, the two girls slipped out of the palace by the stairs in the orchard and walked along the sands by the river to Cannon Row. The marriage ceremony was performed in Hertford's bedroom and afterwards, while Lady Jane kept guard in another room, the newly married couple went to bed and had 'carnal copulation'. They did not have long together – awkward questions would be asked if Katherine failed to appear at dinner with the Controller of the Household – and after about an hour and a half they had to start scrambling back into their clothes. This was a point on which they were later to be closely questioned. The authorities found it hard to believe that such gently nurtured young people could have performed the complicated feat of getting dressed unaided. They must, it was felt, have had assistance – and accomplices.

Katherine had achieved her immediate ambition, but her altered status made little practical difference to her circumstances. She and Hertford still had to be content with furtive meetings at Westminster, Greenwich or Cannon Row – a few odd hours snatched whenever they could manage it. How long they intended to try and keep their secret, it is impossible to say. Neither of them appears to have given any serious thought to the problem of how they were going to break the news, but it was not long before events began to catch up with them. Jane Seymour died in March 1561 and without her help it became more difficult for them to meet. Then the Queen decided to send the Earl of Hertford abroad as a companion to William Cecil's son, who was going to France to finish his education. This was an unexpected complication, to be followed by another, not so unexpected. Katherine thought she might be pregnant but could not, or would not, say for certain. Her husband finally went off to France in April, probably rather relieved to escape, at least temporarily, from a situation which was rapidly getting out of control, but promising to return if she wrote to tell him she was definitely with child.

Left alone, Katherine seems at last to have begun to realize the enormity of what she had done. The reality of her pregnancy could no longer be ignored and already the matrons of the Court were casting suspicious glances at her shape. She wrote to Hertford, begging him to come back and support her, but could not be sure that her letters were reaching him. In July she had to accompany the Queen on the East Anglian progress and at the beginning of August, while the Court was at Ipswich, the secret finally came out.

The Queen, understandably, was furious. She had never liked Katherine but had always treated her fairly. Now the girl had repaid her with ingratitude, deceit and perhaps worse. Anything which touched on the succession touched Elizabeth on her most sensitive spot. She was never to forget her own experiences as a 'second person' during Mary's reign and of the intrigues which inevitably surrounded an heir presumptive. In the activities of Katherine Grey she had caught a sulphurous whiff of treason. Katherine's choice of husband was also unfortunate. The Seymours had a reputation for being politically ambitious and

Lady Katherine Grey and Edward, her elder
son by Edward Seymour, Earl of Hertford,
born in the Tower on 24 September 1561.

their connection with the royal family was too close for comfort. If Katherine and
Edward Seymour were now to produce a son, it would complicate still further an
already complicated dynastic situation. The new Countess of Hertford was
therefore promptly committed to the Tower, where her husband soon joined her,
and the government's investigators proceeded to extract from them every detail of
that hole-and-corner marriage in the house at Cannon Row.

On 24 September Katherine duly gave birth to a healthy son, who was
christened after his father in the chapel of St Peter-ad-Vincula and in close
proximity to the headless remains of both his grandfathers, two of his great-
uncles and his aunt Jane Grey. The most exhaustive enquiries had failed to
uncover any evidence of a plot involving the baby's parents, although the Queen
was still not entirely convinced. But the Hertfords resolutely denied that anyone,
apart from the strong-minded Jane Seymour, had ever 'advised, counselled or
exhorted them to marry', and since it was no longer a treasonable act to marry a
member of the royal family without the sovereign's consent, the sovereign was
obliged to fall back on the expedient of attacking the validity of the marriage.

As the only witness to the ceremony was now dead and the officiating
clergyman had disappeared without trace, this did not present much difficulty –
especially as Katherine was predictably unable to produce the one piece of
documentary evidence she had possessed. Before he left for France, her husband
had given her a deed, signed and sealed with his own hand, assuring her of an
income of a thousand pounds a year in the event of his death. This deed,
Katherine tearfully informed her interrogators, she had put away in a safe place,

but 'with removing from place to place at progress time, it is lost and she cannot tell where it is become.' The Queen put the whole matter in the hands of the ecclesiastical authorities and on 10 May 1562 the Archbishop of Canterbury gave judgement that there had been no marriage between the Earl of Hertford and Lady Katherine Grey. He censured them for having committed fornication and recommended a heavy fine and imprisonment during the Queen's pleasure.

The culprits remained in the Tower, but there were some compensations. The Lieutenant, Sir Edward Warner, was a kindly man. He allowed Katherine to keep her pet monkeys and dogs, in spite of the damage these quite un-housetrained creatures were doing to government property, and he also allowed her to see her husband, turning a discreetly blind eye to unlocked doors. Warner later justified himself by explaining that having once been overpersuaded, he thought there was no point in continuing to keep his prisoners apart and during the summer of 1562 the young Hertfords enjoyed the nearest approach to a normal married life they were ever to know. Then, in February 1563 came the inevitable sequel – Katherine had another baby, another healthy son.

This time the Queen was really angry. She found it very difficult to forgive her cousin for her apparently cynical disregard for the authority and prestige of the crown; for the fact that instead of showing contrition, or even any understanding of the nature of her offence, she had gone and done it again. To one of Elizabeth's highly disciplined intelligence and acute political awareness, it naturally seemed incredible that Katherine's behaviour stemmed rather from sheer thoughtlessness, a complete inability to grasp the realities of her position, than from deliberate contempt. At all events, the Queen was now determined that both the Hertfords should be made to realize, beyond possibility of mistake, just what it meant to have 'so arrogantly and contemptuously' offended their prince. There were no more stolen meetings and during the summer an outbreak of plague in the capital provided an opportunity to separate the little family more completely. The Earl and the elder child were released into the custody of the Duchess of Somerset, while Katherine and the baby Thomas were sent down to Pirgo in Essex to her uncle Lord John Grey.

There was no question now about Katherine's contrition. John Grey reported that 'the thought and care she taketh for the want of her Majesty's favour, pines her away'. She was eating hardly anything and was so permanently dissolved in tears that her uncle became seriously worried about her health. Katherine's troubles were aggravated by the fact that she appears to have been virtually destitute. She had no money, no plate and, according to John Grey, was so poorly furnished that he was ashamed to let William Cecil have an inventory of her possessions. Lord John reluctantly supplied the deficiencies but he baulked at paying for his charge's keep and the Queen was soon complaining about his expenses. Lord John retaliated by sending a detailed account to Cecil. The weekly rate for 'my lady of Hertford's board, her child and her folks' amounted to £6 16s 8d. As this included eight servants and even five shillings for the widow who washed the baby's clothes, it seems reasonable enough but Elizabeth, who was never averse to having things both ways, decided that henceforward the Earl of Hertford should be made responsible for Katherine's maintenance and he was ordered to pay a sum of over a hundred pounds to the Greys.

The Queen was not normally vindictive and once she felt satisfied that the Hertfords had thoroughly learnt their lesson, she might have responded to their frequent tear-stained appeals for mercy – indeed, hints to this effect had already been dropped. Unfortunately, though, in the spring of 1564 John Hales, a clerk in the Lord Chancellor's office, was tactless enough to publish a treatise supporting Katherine Grey's claims to be recognized as heir presumptive and maintaining that her marriage was a valid one. 'This dealing of his', remarked William Cecil (who also privately supported Katherine Grey), 'offendeth the Queen's majesty very much.' The succession was a matter which Elizabeth regarded as being entirely her own business and over which she would not tolerate outside interference on any pretext. She was not in the least appeased by Hales's assurance that his only thought had been to promote the Protestant Tudor line against the Catholic Mary Stuart; nor was her temper improved by the knowledge that there was widespread public sympathy for the imprisoned Katherine and considerable public support for her dynastic claims. She was, after all, an Englishwoman, a staunch Protestant and had already only too effectively proved her ability to bear sons.

In the summer of 1565 an element of black comedy entered the story. On 21 August William Cecil wrote tersely to his friend Sir Thomas Smith: 'Here is an unhappy chance and monstrous. The sergeant-porter, being the biggest gentleman in this court, hath married secretly the Lady Mary Grey, the least of all the court. They are committed to separate prisons. The offence is very great.' The current Spanish ambassador, Guzman de Silva, passing on the news to King Philip, recorded that Mary Grey, who was little, crookbacked and very ugly, had married a gentleman named Keys, sergeant-porter at the palace. 'They say', he added, 'the Queen is very much annoyed and grieved thereat.'

In fact, this grotesquely pathetic attachment between dwarfish, nineteen-year-old Mary Grey and the enormous gate-keeper, a middle-aged widower with several children, was the last straw as far as Elizabeth was concerned. Both the Grey sisters were now under strict house arrest and Katherine had given up all hope of release. She died in January 1568 at the age of twenty-seven of a mixture of tuberculosis and a broken heart. Two years later Hertford was at last allowed to go free, although the Queen never really forgave him. The Earl remained faithful to Katherine's memory for nearly thirty years, eventually marrying again to a daughter of the powerful Howard clan. But he never gave up the fight to have his first marriage recognized and his sons' legitimacy established – a fight he finally won in 1606. He lived on until 1621 and was to see his grandson maintain the family tradition by trying to elope with Lady Arbella Stuart, another member of the royal house.

Mary Grey – or rather Mary Keys, for the legality of her improbable marriage never seems to have been challenged – spent about six years as the involuntary house-guest of various unwilling hosts, but was released after her husband's death; she at least had never compounded her offence by having children. The last sad little remnant of the once great house of Suffolk died in poverty and obscurity in the summer of 1578; but outcast though she had become, under the terms of her great-uncle's will Mary Keys died heiress to the throne of England – that deadly legacy which had ruined the lives of the descendants of Mary Brandon, born Mary Tudor.

CHAPTER 14

When Hempe is Spun

The trivial prophecy which I heard when I was a child, and Queen Elizabeth was in the flower of her years, was,

> *'When hempe is sponne*
> *England's done'*

whereby it was generally conceived, that after the princes had reigned which had the principal letters of that word hempe (which were Henry, Edward, Mary, Philip, and Elizabeth), England should come to utter confusion; which, thanks be to God, is verified only in the change of name; for that the king's style is now no more of England but of Britain.

FRANCIS BACON

By 1568, after ten years on the English throne, Elizabeth Tudor had matured into a vigorous, elegant, self-confident woman in her mid-thirties who, by intelligent statecraft and good housekeeping, had lifted her country out of its mid-century doldrums and won the respect, if not always the approval, of her fellow monarchs. Any misgivings which her subjects may once have felt about embarking on another experience of petticoat government had long since vanished and the love affair between Queen and people – foundation and cornerstone of the whole astonishing Elizabethan epic – was already a vital part of the national ethos. As a relationship it is something unique in history and, like most love affairs, defies too close an analysis. Probably it was best and most succinctly described in two verses of the popular ballad – *A Song Between the Queen's Majestie and Englande* – first printed in 1571, but written quite early in the reign.

> I am thy lover fair,
> Hath chosen thee to mine heir;
> And my name is merry Englande;
> Therefore, come away,
> And make no more delay,
> Sweet Bessie! give me thy hand.

Here is my hand,
My dear lover Englande,
I am thine both with mind and heart,
For ever to endure,
Thou mayest be sure,
Until death us two do part.

'Until death us two do part' . . . The fear that Elizabeth might die with the succession still unsettled haunted all politically conscious Englishmen, who were only too well aware that their present peace and prosperity depended, quite literally, on the slender thread of the Queen's life. The terrifying ease with which that thread might be cut was demonstrated in the autumn of 1562, when Elizabeth caught a virulent strain of smallpox and did very nearly die. Not surprisingly, this scare led to a renewed onslaught on the Queen to name her successor and to get married. When Parliament met in January 1563, the Speaker of the Commons wasted no time in presenting a petition referring to 'the great terror and dreadful warning' of the Queen's illness. He went on to paint a gloomy picture of the 'unspeakable miseries' of civil war, foreign interference, bloodshed and destruction of lives, property and liberty which lay in wait for the country if she were to die without a known heir. A few days later, the House of Lords presented another, similar petition which begged the Queen to dispose herself to marry 'where it shall please you, to whom it shall please you, and as soon as it shall please you'.

The Queen received these impassioned pleas graciously enough, but she would not be stampeded into action she might later regret. She knew she was mortal, she told the Commons, and asked them to believe that she, who had always been so careful of her subjects' welfare in other matters, would not be careless in this, which concerned them all so nearly. But, because it was a matter of such importance, she would not make any hasty answer. In fact, she would defer making any answer at all until she had been able to consider it further. 'And so I assure you all', she ended, 'that, though after my death you may have many stepdames, yet shall you never have a more natural mother than I mean to be unto you all.'

Elizabeth succeeded in stalling Parliament – although there were some rebellious mutterings in the Commons about withholding subsidies if she continued to be obstinate – but the problem refused to go away. It was, after all, the same problem which had overshadowed English political life ever since the death of Prince Arthur in 1502. Elizabeth was fully alive to the dangers of the situation. On the other hand, she was even more acutely aware of the danger of having a named heir. She knew, none better, that the heir inevitably became the focal point for discontent of every kind and was utterly determined never to risk being 'buried alive' like her sister.

As far as marriage, with its necessarily uncertain corollary of childbearing, was concerned, the Queen, quite apart from her personal inclinations and her reluctance to lose her most valuable card in the game of international diplomacy, could see the practical difficulties involved far more clearly than her faithful

Mary Queen of Scots; artist unknown.

Lords and Commons. Since the death of Edward Courtenay, there was no available Englishman of sufficiently high rank to make him acceptable to his fellows and if Elizabeth were to marry a subject, she would arouse violent jealousies and animosities – the uproar over Robert Dudley had already proved that. If she chose a foreigner, the problems would have been as great, if not greater. Nationalistic feeling would once again have run high and, to make matters worse, pretty well every eligible European prince was a Roman Catholic. The consort of a sixteenth-century queen regnant could not remain a cipher; he would have expected, and been expected, to take an active part in the government. But to attempt to introduce a Catholic king into an increasingly fervent Protestant country would have been asking for the most alarming variety of trouble.

Elizabeth's instinct was to do nothing and go on gambling on her own survival. 'So long as I live', she once remarked, 'I shall be Queen of England. When I am dead, they shall succeed that have most right.' But she was a reasonable woman. She could understand and sympathize with her subjects' natural anxiety about their own and their children's future, and during the early sixties she did cautiously explore the possibility of finding a way out of the *impasse*. It was, however, perfectly plain that, her father's will and the Protestant preferences of her people regardless, Elizabeth never for one moment contemplated recognizing the claims of English and Protestant Katherine Grey. If a solution acceptable to the Queen of England were to be found, it would have to involve the Queen of Scotland.

During the first decade of her cousin's reign, the fortunes of Mary Stuart had fluctuated wildly. In 1558 she had apparently stood on the threshold of a career of unexampled brilliance. In the summer of 1559 the freakish death of her father-in-law, Henri II, in a tiltyard accident had brought her to the throne of France beside her youthful husband – a Queen twice over at the age of sixteen-and-a-half. Then, in December 1560 the sickly François II was also dead and Mary had become a widow three days before her eighteenth birthday. 'The thoughts of widowhood at so early an age', commented a sympathetic Venetian, Michel Surian, 'and of the loss of a consort who was so great a King and who so dearly loved her . . . so afflict her that she will not receive any consolation, but, brooding over her disasters with constant tears and passionate and doleful lamentations, she universally inspires great pity.'

All the same, Mary soon began to cheer up and take stock of her altered situation. Her ten-year-old brother-in-law was now King of France and power had passed into the hands of the Queen Mother, that formidable matriarch Catherine de Medici, who was making no particular secret of the fact that she would prefer the Queen of Scots' room to her company. Mary Stuart had been brought up to regard her Scottish kingdom as a mere appanage of France but now, in the spring of 1561, Scotland appeared in a rather different light. To a full-blooded, optimistic teenager with little taste for taking a back seat, it offered a challenge and a promise of adventure with, perhaps, more glittering triumphs to come. The question was, would Scotland have her back, for there, too, things had changed.

Two years before, the Protestant nobility, banded together under the title of the Lords of the Congregation and assisted, albeit somewhat reluctantly, by the Queen of England, had risen in revolt against the Catholic and alien government of Mary's mother, the Queen Regent Mary of Guise. In June 1560 the Regent died and French influence in Scotland reached its lowest ebb for a generation. William Cecil had hurried up to Edinburgh to attend the peace talks and during the course of a fortnight's hard bargaining succeeded in extracting a number of important concessions from the French commissioners acting on behalf of the young Queen and her husband. The religious question was tactfully left in abeyance but when the Scots Parliament met in August, they at once proceeded of their own authority to adopt the Calvinistic form of Protestantism as their national religion. In the circumstances, therefore, it was scarcely surprising that the Lords of the Congregation should have been less than enthusiastic over the projected return of their Catholic sovereign.

Mary, as Queen of France, had refused to ratify the Treaty of Edinburgh and in the autumn of 1560 had expressed strong disapproval of the proceedings in the Scottish Parliament. 'My subjects of Scotland do their duty in nothing, nor have they performed one point that belongeth to them', she told Nicholas Throckmorton. 'I am their sovereign, but they take me not so. They must be taught to know their duties.' By the spring of 1561 she was no longer in a position to take such a high tone and instead set herself out to charm the English and Scottish envoys who came to France to look her over. She repeatedly declared her earnest desire to live in peace and friendship with Elizabeth, 'her good sister and tender cousin', and also declared her willingness to accept the new status quo in Scotland. Not, of course, that she could have done otherwise but she did it gracefully, insisting only that she must be given the right to practise her own religion in private, and as it dawned on the Protestant lords that their Queen's dynastic potentialities would now work in favour of Scotland rather than France, they began to take a more optimistic view of the future.

Young Mary Stuart was, in fact, winning golden opinions all round and Nicholas Throckmorton's dispatches were full of her virtue and discretion, her good judgement, her modesty and her readiness to be ruled by good counsel. It may not have been very tactful to praise one Queen to another in quite such glowing terms, but Throckmorton had not yet forgiven his mistress for the acute embarrassment she had caused him over the Dudley affair. Elizabeth, for her part, was clearly disconcerted by the seductive qualities being exhibited by her eighteen-year-old cousin. If Mary could so captivate Nicholas Throckmorton, a hard-headed diplomat and a strict Protestant, who could tell what havoc the pretty creature might create among the excitable and boisterous Scottish warlords? Who could tell how many simple men might be 'carried away with vain hope, and brought abed with fair words'?

As it turned out Mary Stuart's first three years in her northern kingdom were by no means unsuccessful. Her subjects, with the exception of that archetypal male chauvinist John Knox, were ready to be pleased with her and Mary, although never approaching the political acumen of Elizabeth Tudor, had had the sense to make friends with her bastard half-brother, the influential James Stuart, Earl of Moray. With Moray's efficient and tough-minded support, she was able to manage reasonably well at home. Abroad, all her efforts were directed towards ingratiating herself with the Queen of England and persuading Elizabeth to recognize her as heir presumptive to the English throne.

Elizabeth seemed prepared to be friendly. She was even ready to admit, in private conversation with the Scottish envoy William Maitland of Lethington, that she personally considered Mary to be her natural and lawful successor; but further than that she would not go. She would not make her good sister and cousin her heir 'by order of Parliament', which was what Mary was after. Unless . . . and there was just one possible solution. The widowed Queen of Scotland was very nearly as eligible a match as the spinster Queen of England. Everything would depend on the identity of Mary's second husband and it was during the spring of 1563, when Elizabeth was desperately looking for some way of relieving the almost intolerable pressure being exerted on her to settle the succession, that she first proposed Robert Dudley as a bridegroom for Mary Stuart. On the face of it, it seemed such an eccentric suggestion that William Maitland thought the Queen must be joking. But no, she was apparently quite serious. That autumn, Thomas Randolph, the English agent in Edinburgh, was instructed to drop broad hints on the subject to Mary herself and finally, in the spring of 1564, Elizabeth authorized Randolph to make the matter official.

Mary's public reaction was non-committal. Privately she regarded the whole idea with the utmost scepticism. If, as was implicit, Elizabeth really meant to recognize her right to the reversion of the English crown in return for accepting Elizabeth's choice of husband, the Queen of Scots might have swallowed her understandable umbrage over the choice of the notorious Lord Robert. But she could not rid herself of the suspicion that she was being hoaxed; that by offering her cousin her own discarded lover, Elizabeth was planning to turn her into a laughing-stock and perhaps prevent her from making some more advantageous marriage. Mary was not alone in her opinion and many people since have found it hard to credit that Elizabeth could ever have genuinely intended to part with her favourite – and not merely part with him but give him up to a younger, prettier woman and her most dangerous rival. But in the last resort, what mattered to Elizabeth Tudor was the peace and security of her realm. If she had felt satisfied that her peculiar plan would have achieved this end, there seems little reason to doubt that she would have gone through with it.

Perhaps the most curious feature of the whole curious incident is the apparently unlimited degree of trust that the Queen was prepared to repose in Robert Dudley. She told James Melville that she would have married Lord Robert herself, had she ever been minded to take a husband. But being determined to end her life a maid, she wanted Mary to have him. For this, she explained, 'would best remove out of her heart all fear and suspicion to be offended by usurpation before her death; being assured that he was so loving and trusty that he would never give his consent nor suffer such thing to be attempted during her time.'

Melville spent about ten days in London as Mary's special envoy during September 1564 and saw Elizabeth every day. She displayed an insatiable curiosity about the cousin she had never seen and wished repeatedly that they might meet. When Melville jokingly offered to smuggle her into Scotland disguised as a page, so that she might see his Queen, Elizabeth smiled and said, 'Alas! that I might do it.' But she told him she wanted a closer friendship with Mary in the future and that 'she was minded to put away all jealousies and suspicions between them.' Unhappily, though, the Queen of Scots found herself unable to conquer her aversion to the idea of marriage to the horse-keeper, in spite of the fact that he had now at last been elevated to the dignity of Earl of Leicester. In any case, by the following spring, her actions had ceased to be governed by policy, for Mary had fallen head over heels in love with another of her cousins, Henry Stuart, Lord Darnley, now a graceful 'lady-faced' youth of nineteen, and was no longer willing 'to be ruled by good counsel'. She quarrelled fatally with Moray and the Protestant party and had apparently ceased to care if she offended Queen Elizabeth. Her old admirer, Nicholas Throckmorton, was shocked at the change in her and William Cecil, as usual, feared the worst.

Mary and Darnley were married in July 1565 and from then on the home life of the Queen of Scotland became different indeed from that of most well-regulated royal households. Darnley soon revealed himself to be a bully and a drunkard – weak, cowardly and vicious – and an easy dupe in the hands of the jealous, ruthless, power-hungry men pressing round the Scottish throne. Darnley was of the party which burst into that little supper room at Holyrood in March 1566 and

Lord Darnley by Hans Eworth.

forced the Queen – she was six months pregnant – to witness the brutal murder of her Italian secretary. Darnley had been in the plot to seize and imprison the Queen, instal himself as a puppet king and bring back the exiled Earl of Moray. Mary survived the ordeal, outwitting her enemies and regaining her freedom of action in a brilliant display of courage and resourcefulness, but she did not forgive her husband.

In spite of everything, her baby was born safely that June and James Melville came south again to bring the news to London and ask the Queen of England to stand godmother to the infant Prince James. As far as Elizabeth was concerned, the arrival of Mary's son was the best thing to have come out of the whole messy business. For if the child survived (and that was a biggish 'if', given the current state of affairs in Scotland), who better than this double great-great-grandson of the first Henry Tudor to succeed to the Tudor throne? But that was for the future. In the meantime, what was to be done about the baby's parents?

It was now an open secret that Mary was urgently looking for a way to get rid of Darnley. 'It is heartbreaking for her to think he should be her husband, and how to be free of him she sees no outgait', wrote William Maitland on 24 October. But it was obvious that some 'outgait' *would* be found and no one was unbearably surprised when the miserable Darnley met his Grand Guignol end at the house of

Kirk o'Field in January 1567. His widow's subsequent career, culminating four months later in marriage to the uncouth and charmless Earl of Bothwell, was, however, followed with horrified astonishment by the outside world.

In London, Darnley's mother was crying out for vengeance on her murdered son, and Margaret Lennox, who had been in the Tower and Queen Elizabeth's black books for having allegedly schemed to bring about the Scottish match in the first place, was let out of gaol by her sympathetic sovereign. In Edinburgh, increasingly outspoken placards were appearing on the streets, naming Bothwell as the King's murderer and accusing the Queen of having been his accomplice. Elizabeth, with her own experience after the death of Amy Robsart still fresh in her mind, wrote vehemently to Mary: 'I should not do the office of a faithful cousin and friend, if I did not urge you to preserve your honour, rather than look through your fingers at revenge on those who have done you "such pleasure" as most people say.' And from Mary's friends abroad came anxious appeals to bring her husband's murderers to justice and clear her own name.

But Mary, having apparently cast all considerations of prudence and even elementary commonsense to the winds, paid no attention to the repeated warnings and remonstrances of her well-wishers. Instead of taking steps to bring Bothwell to justice, she continued to show every sign of pleasure in his company and by May she had married him, a divorced man, according to the rites of the Protestant church. It has been suggested that she was suffering from a complete mental breakdown and that she may have been a victim of porphyria, the mysterious hereditary ailment which afflicted her descendant George III. Certainly this is the most charitable explanation, but her contemporaries could only suppose that the Queen of Scotland had allowed her illicit passion to run away with her. Whatever the real reasons behind Mary's self-destructive rampage during the first half of 1567, nemesis was not long in catching up with her. If her second marriage had been a tragic mistake, her third was an unmitigated disaster. By June Bothwell had fled for his life and Mary was a prisoner in the hands of her outraged nobility. By July she had been forced to abdicate in favour of her year-old son.

Elizabeth Tudor may not have felt much personal sympathy for the cousin who was making such a spectacular hash of her life, but she held strong views about subjects who, whatever the provocation, insulted, threatened and imprisoned an anointed Queen. She fired volleys of explosive warnings into Scotland about what would happen if the lords took any further action against Mary, and she sent Nicholas Throckmorton north to make the situation crystal clear to the new Scottish government. William Cecil and Throckmorton himself were strongly opposed to this policy. They, and the majority of the Privy Council, were eager to support the Scots lords and terrified that Elizabeth's violent hostility would have the effect of driving Scotland once again into the arms of France. But the Queen was not to be deflected and gave Cecil several anxious moments. He told Throckmorton early in August that she had sent for him in great haste and made him 'a great offensive speech that nothing was thought of for her to do to revenge the Queen of Scots' imprisonment and deliver her.' 'I answered her as warily as I could', wrote Cecil, 'but she increased so in anger against these lords that in good earnest she began to devise revenge by war.'

Although Mary remained in prison and Elizabeth did not fulfil her threats to go to war on her behalf, there can be no doubt that the Queen of England's intervention had saved the Queen of Scots' life. Then, less than a year later, the inevitable happened. Mary, resourceful, brave and optimistic as ever, escaped from Lochleven Castle. On 13 May she and her supporters were routed at the battle of Langside and three days later, on 16 May 1568, she landed on the coast of Cumberland, a refugee with nothing but the clothes she stood up in. 'I fear', wrote Archbishop Parker prophetically, 'that our good Queen hath the wolf by the ears.'

According to the French and Spanish ambassadors, Elizabeth's first, generous impulse was to send for Mary and welcome her as an honoured guest, but the Council quickly overruled their mistress's instinctive desire to show solidarity with her sister Queen. 'Although these people are glad enough to have her in their hands', wrote the Spanish ambassador, 'they have many things to consider. If they keep her as in prison, it will probably scandalize all neighbouring princes, and if she remain free and able to communicate with her friends, great suspicions will be aroused. In any case', added Guzman de Silva with studied understatement, 'it is certain that two women will not agree very long.'

The English Council, painfully aware of the many things they had to consider, at once 'entered into serious deliberation' as to what should be done with the Queen of Scots. 'If she were detained in England', says William Camden, 'they reasoned lest she (who was as it were the very pith and marrow of sweet eloquence) might draw many daily to her part which favoured her title to the crown of England, who would kindle the coals of her ambition and leave nothing unassayed whereby they might set the crown upon her head.' If she were allowed to return to France, her powerful kinsmen there would inevitably stir up a hornets' nest of faction in both Scotland and England. For Elizabeth to attempt to restore the Queen of Scots to her throne by force would be to invite civil war in Scotland, a rupture of the precious and still none too secure 'amity' with that country, and an almost certain revival in some form of the old Franco-Scottish alliance which had been the cause of so much trouble and bloodshed in the past. On the other hand, it had to be remembered that Mary was one of Elizabeth's closest relatives and that she had sought refuge in England trusting in her cousin's promises of protection and support. To hand her back to men who would not hesitate to kill her, was equally unthinkable.

At first sight the problem looked insoluble – especially as Mary's attitude made it plain that she was unlikely to agree to any sort of compromise. Elizabeth's old and trusted friend, Francis Knollys, who had been sent up to take charge of the situation at Carlisle, where the Queen of Scots was now holding court, found her full of an articulate sense of grievance. 'She showeth a great desire to be avenged of her enemies', he wrote on 11 June. 'The thing that most she thirsteth after is victory, and it seemeth to be indifferent to her to have her enemies diminished either by the sword of her friends, or by the liberal promises and rewards of her purse, or by division and quarrels raised among themselves: so that for victory's sake pain and peril seemeth pleasant to her: and in respect of victory, wealth and all things seemeth to her contemptible and vile. Now what is to be done with such a lady and princess?' enquired Francis Knollys, with a certain rhetorical flourish, of his friend William Cecil.

What indeed? Mary was told that Elizabeth could not receive her while she remained under suspicion of having been an accessory before the fact of Darnley's murder. Mary demanded to be allowed to justify herself before Elizabeth in person, and Elizabeth wrote: 'O Madam, there is no creature living who wishes to hear such a declaration more than I, or will more readily lend her ears to any answer that will acquit your honour.' The Queen of England offered to mediate in the dispute between the Queen of Scots and her rebellious subjects, but since neither side would budge an inch from their previously entrenched positions the enquiry, held at York and Westminster, got nowhere. In the end, the Earl of Moray went back to Scotland as regent for the infant King James and Mary stayed in England. She was placed in the custody of the Earl of Shrewsbury and was to spend the next sixteen years in one or other of that much-tried nobleman's mansions in the North Midlands. It was, of course, a thoroughly unsatisfactory situation – expensive and embarrassing for the Queen of England, frustrating and humiliating for the Queen of Scots. Elizabeth continued with patient pertinacity to try and find some formula by which Mary could be restored peacefully to her own throne, but negotiations always foundered on the ineradicable distrust between the cousins, on the impossibility of devising adequate safeguards against Mary's subsequent repudiation of any undertakings given under duress.

For England the consequences of nourishing that 'bosom serpent', the *de facto* Catholic heir presumptive, soon became only too apparent, as Mary's restless energy found its outlet in an endless series of dangerous and futile intrigues. 'Alas, poor fool!' exclaimed the King of France, 'she will never cease until they cut off her head.' By the mid-1580s the revelations of the Ridolfi Plot, the Throckmorton Plot (Francis not Nicholas), the Parry Plot and the Babington Plot, together with an ever-darkening international scene and the increasing bitterness of the ideological conflict between Catholic and Protestant had all combined to bring the problem of the Queen of Scots to a festering head. As Francis Walsingham had put it, more than ten years earlier – 'So long as that devilish woman lives, neither her Majesty must make account to continue in quiet possession of her crown, nor her faithful servants assure themselves of safety of their lives.'

By 1586, Mary's guilt or innocence of complicity in the various Catholic conspiracies to depose the heretical Queen of England no longer had any real relevance. Guilty or innocent, the Protestant state, feeling itself threatened from within and without, could no longer contain her. It was as simple as that. Elizabeth had fought desperately to postpone the inevitable decision and when at last it had to be made, it caused her real and acute distress. Her extreme, apparently perverse reluctance to authorize the execution of her deadliest enemy – even after she had been presented with enough evidence to convince any reasonable person that Mary was not only prepared to seize her throne but to connive at her own assassination – is, on the face of it, difficult to understand. So difficult, in fact, that it has often been dismissed as mere play-acting. Perhaps there was some play-acting. Elizabeth always was a consummate actress, 'a princess who can act any part she pleases', and, of course, she knew she would be presenting the Catholic world with a first-rate propaganda weapon. 'What will they not now say', she exclaimed, 'when it shall be spread that for the safety of her life a maiden Queen could be content to spill the blood even of her own kinswoman!'

Elizabeth had always suffered from a most un-Tudor-like squeamishness when it came to spilling the blood of her kinsfolk, but she told Parliament in November 1586: 'I am not so void of judgement as not to see mine own peril, nor yet so ignorant as not to know it were in nature a foolish course to cherish a sword to cut mine own throat.' And yet, if she could have found a way of keeping Mary alive, even at that eleventh hour, she would undoubtedly have done so. If it had not been for Elizabeth, Mary would almost certainly have died at the hands of her own subjects in 1567. If it had not been for Elizabeth, she would quite certainly have gone to the scaffold with the Duke of Norfolk in 1572. So why was the Queen of England, that most practical of rulers, so anxious to preserve the woman she had herself recently described as a 'wicked murderess'?

There were sound practical reasons. For although Mary had come to represent such an intolerable threat to England's internal security, she also, ironically enough, remained England's best protection against attack from abroad. While she lived, Philip of Spain was likely to go on hesitating before launching his much-heralded Sacred Enterprise against the Protestant island and its anathematized Queen. The success of the Enterprise might well store up treasure in heaven for the King of Spain, but he would still be lavishing earthly treasure (always in painfully short supply) on elevating the half-French Mary Stuart to the English throne – and that elevation would sooner or later inevitably result in the close Anglo-French alliance which for generations the Hapsburgs had laboured to prevent. Once Mary was dead, the situation would look different to a King who could, after all, prove his own remote descent from John of Gaunt.

But more than the political considerations, more than her inherent dread of committing herself to any irreversible course of action, more than natural compassion for her close kinswoman and sister Queen, that aspect of Mary's end which upset Elizabeth most and which surely lay beneath her violent, hysterical reaction after the deed had been done, was the superstitious revulsion of one who has violated a sacred mystery. To one of Elizabeth's heredity and upbringing, there was something unspeakably atrocious in the act of subjecting God's anointed to the process of earthly trial and judicial execution. It was the ultimate taboo. It was also setting a grimly dangerous precedent.

Once Mary had gone, the problem of the English succession finally lost its urgency. The Suffolk line had withered away. Margaret Lennox was dead and so was her younger son, Charles; although he had left a daughter, Arbella, the last of those forlorn female descendants of Henry VII whose fate, in the next century, was closely to mirror that of the unfortunate Katherine Grey. Mary Stuart's son, James, was a man of twenty when his mother died and while Elizabeth, sticking rigidly to her principles, never openly acknowledged him as her heir, it was now generally and tacitly recognized that he would in due time succeed the ageing Queen of England. For Elizabeth, incredibly, was beginning to grow old. In the

Elizabeth riding in procession to Tilbury to address her troops in 1588; a contemporary painting on wood.

climactic year of 1588 she celebrated her fifty-fifth birthday and the thirtieth anniversary of her accession. Not that the Queen was prepared to make any concessions to the passage of time, and it would have been as much as anyone's place was worth to have reminded her of it. Her health remained excellent and she was as energetic as ever, dancing six or seven galliards in a morning and still riding and hunting tirelessly. But, all the same, time *was* passing and 1588 brought Elizabeth private sorrow as well as public triumph.

Robert Dudley, Earl of Leicester, had been given command of the citizen army hastily recruited to resist the threatened Spanish invasion and it was he who walked bare-headed at the Queen's bridle hand when she reviewed her troops during the famous visit to Tilbury. It was to be the last time he escorted her in public, so it was fitting that it should have been the most glorious occasion of all. In the middle of August, while the Invincible Armada was being beaten up the North Sea, Robert broke camp and returned to London – a stout, balding, red-faced man in his mid-fifties. He was not at all well, the past few months had been an appalling strain, and he had promised himself a short holiday. He spent a few quiet days with the Queen, dining with her every day, and then left for the country, intending to take the waters at Buxton. On the way he sent Elizabeth an affectionate little note from Rycote Manor, home of her old friends the Norris family, where they had often stayed together in the past. He wanted to know how his gracious lady was – she had been suffering a few twinges lately – 'it being the chiefest thing in this world I do pray for, that she should have good health and long life.' As for his own poor case, he wrote, 'I continue still your medicine and find it amends much better than with any other thing that hath been given me. Thus hoping to find a perfect cure at the bath, I humbly kiss your foot. From your old lodging at Rycott this Thursday morning, ready to take my journey. . . .' He got as far as Cornbury, a few miles from Oxford, and there, on 4 September, he died, possibly from cancer of the stomach.

In the general excitement which followed the defeat of the Armada, the disappearance of this great landmark of the Elizabethan scene passed unmourned and almost unnoticed. At a time when her people expected to see her bathed in the radiance of victory, the Queen could not afford the luxury of giving way to her grief, but she took that note scribbled at Rycote and put it away in a little coffer which she kept by her bed. Across the back she had written 'His last letter'. Although her relations with Robert had never been quite the same since his second marriage to the widowed Countess of Essex, he was still her 'brother and best friend', the man who had been an essential part of her life for almost as long as she could remember. His death, too, tore the first real gap in the ranks of that hand-picked coterie of intimates whom the Queen honoured with pet names and who ruled England under her supervision.

Robert had been her 'Eyes'. Francis Walsingham, who died in 1590, was 'the Moor' – a reference to his dark colouring. Elizabeth had never really liked Walsingham, he was too much of a left-wing Puritan for her taste, but he had been a faithful and valued servant and he, too, had been around for a long time. Christopher Hatton, 'Mutton' or 'Bellwether', went in 1591 and Francis Knollys in 1597, but the most irreparable loss came in August 1598 with the death of old William Cecil, Lord Burghley. The Queen missed her 'Spirit' bitterly. She would often speak of him with tears and turn her face aside when his name was mentioned. Their partnership had lasted for forty years and to Elizabeth its ending meant a break with the past more complete than anything that had gone before. So many of her old friends had vanished now – even her old enemy, Philip of Spain, died that autumn – and the Queen found the new generation growing up around her difficult to understand and to work with. It is true she had Robert Cecil, carefully groomed by his father to take his father's place, but it was not the same thing. There was never quite the same trust and confidence between them. Elizabeth had problems, too, with Robert Dudley's step-son, the young Earl of Essex, whom she was trying hard to train up to take Robert's place at Court. But Essex proved untameable and early in 1601 he paid the price of his paranoia to the executioner on Tower Hill. The Queen sorrowed for the death of a brilliant and beautiful young man, but she never hesitated over its necessity. Essex had committed the unforgivable sin of attempting to challenge the authority of the crown by violence; and when, nearly forty years before, the young Elizabeth Tudor had told William Maitland that as long as she lived she would be Queen of England, she had meant exactly what she said.

William Cecil, Lord Burghley, with his son Robert.

The last decade of the Queen's reign was overshadowed by the troubles in Ireland, by the protracted and inconclusive war with Spain, by faction within the government and by increasing monetary problems. But although the Queen might be growing old – she was well into her sixties now – she remained in full possession of her faculties and in full command of the political situation both at home and abroad. In December 1597 a French diplomat, André de Maisse, came over to London on a special mission from Henri IV and has left an unforgettable picture of Elizabeth as she was.

At his first audience, de Maisse found the Queen *en déshabillé*. A boil on her face had made her feel wretched she told him and, although she apologized for receiving him in her nightgown, the ambassador evidently got the impression of a somewhat outlandish old lady, perpetually fidgeting about and with a disconcerting habit of opening the front of her robe 'as if she was too hot', so that he could see the whole of her bosom. Elizabeth was very affable and ordered a stool to be brought for de Maisse but, he wrote, 'all the time she spoke she would often rise from her chair and appear to be very impatient with what I was saying. She would complain that the fire was hurting her eyes, though there was a great screen before it and she six or seven feet away; yet did she give orders to have it extinguished, making them bring water to pour upon it.'

*Robert Devereux, Earl of Essex,
succeeded his step-father,
Leicester, for a time as the
Queen's favourite.*

When de Maisse saw the Queen again a week later, she was feeling better and was rather more conventionally dressed. All the same, he noticed that 'when she raises her head, she has a trick of putting both hands on her gown and opening it so that all her belly can be seen.' In the course of conversation Elizabeth often referred to herself as 'foolish and old', saying she was sorry de Maisse, who had met so many wise men and great princes, should at length come to see a poor woman and foolish. The ambassador was not deceived by this kind of talk and remarked that the Queen liked to speak slightingly of her intelligence 'so that she may give occasion to commend her'. She was pleased when he praised her judgement and prudence, but said modestly 'that it was but natural that she should have some knowledge of the affairs of the world, being called thereto so young, and having worn that crown these forty years.' 'When anyone speaks of her beauty', wrote de Maisse, 'she says that she was never beautiful, although she had that reputation thirty years ago. Nevertheless, she speaks of her beauty as often as she can.'

Altogether Elizabeth and de Maisse had about half a dozen interviews. On Christmas Eve the Queen was 'in very good humour and gay'. De Maisse presented one of his entourage, 'the secretary Phillips', and describes how, when Phillips knelt before her, the Queen began to take him by the hair and made him rise and pretended to give him a box on the ears. 'It is a strange thing', wrote the ambassador, 'to see how lively she is in body and mind and nimble in everything she does.' Elizabeth had obviously taken to de Maisse and talked to him freely on a wide range of subjects, reminiscing and telling him 'tales of many kinds'. 'Whilst I was treating with her in the matter of my charge', he recorded in his journal, 'she would often make such digressions, either expressly to gain time . . . or because it is her natural way. Then would she excuse herself, saying, "Master Ambassador, you will say of the tales that I am telling you that they are mere gullery. See what it is to have to do with old women such as I am."' But de Maisse thought that apart from her face, which looked 'very aged', and her teeth, which were bad, it would not be possible 'to see a woman of so fine and vigorous disposition both in mind and body.' She knew all the ancient histories, he wrote, and 'one can say nothing to her on which she will not make some apt comment.' In fact, despite her various little oddities, the ambassador had come to feel an enormous respect for the Queen. 'She is a very great princess who knows everything' was his considered judgement.

André de Maisse was far from being alone in his opinion of this phenomenal woman. Even Pope Sixtus, who was not normally to be counted among Elizabeth Tudor's admirers, had been moved to declare shortly after the Armada sailed: 'She certainly is a great Queen and were she only a Catholic she would be our dearly beloved. Just look how well she governs! She is only a woman, only mistress of half an island, and yet she makes herself feared by Spain, by France, by all.' At the time of the highly successful descent on Cadiz in 1596, the Venetians were exclaiming: 'Great is the Queen of England! Oh, what a woman, if she were but a Christian!' After the unfortunate Essex affair, the King of France remarked: 'She only is a king. She only knows how to rule.'

To her own people, Elizabeth had come to embody every goddess of classical mythology they had ever heard of, every heroine from their favourite reading, the Bible. But she also remained their own much loved and familiar queen. A young Londoner, living in the Strand, near St Clement's Church, was always to remember how, at about five o'clock one dark December evening in the Armada year, he and his friends heard that the Queen had just gone to a Council meeting at Somerset House and were told, 'if you will see the Queen, you must come quickly'. 'Then we all ran', he wrote, 'when the court gates were set open and no man hindered us from coming in. There we stayed an hour and a half and the yard was full, there being a great number of torches, when the Queen came out in great state. Then we cried, "God save your Majesty." And the Queen turned to us and said, "God bless you all, my good people." Then we cried again, "God save your Majesty." And the Queen said again to us, "Ye may well have a greater prince, but ye shall never have a more loving prince." And so the Queen and the crowd there, looking upon one another a while, her Majesty departed. This wrought such an impression upon us, for shows and pageants are best seen by torchlight, that all the way long we did nothing but talk of what an admirable Queen she was, and how we would all adventure our lives in her service.'

It cannot be said that the Queen's temper mellowed with age. She was still quite capable of filling the air with good round oaths and was subject 'to be vehemently transported with anger'. Elizabeth in a rage could be heard several

'Queen Elizabeth I confounding Juno, Minerva and Venus' by Hans Eworth, 1569; such courtly allegories enhanced the mythical image of the virgin Queen which gave her a unique hold on the imagination of her subjects.

rooms away and she was not above throwing things – there is a story that she once threw her slipper at Francis Walsingham – or boxing the ears of some unfortunate who had irritated her. Tantrums of this kind, though, were always confined to the family atmosphere of the Court and council chamber, and, more often than not, the Queen's bark was worse than her bite. 'When she smiled', wrote her godson, John Harington, who frankly adored her, 'it was a pure sunshine.' Elizabeth could be tricky, exacting and infuriating, and not infrequently drove her long-suffering councillors to the point of nervous breakdown – strong men would totter from her presence in tears and babbling of resignation – but her methods undoubtedly got results and her fascination remained irresistible. Harington remembered that Christopher Hatton was wont to say 'the Queen did fish for men's souls, and had so sweet a bait that no one could escape her network.'

Elizabeth kept all her old aversion to the idea of marriage – her own and other people's – but she did, on one occasion, show some curiosity on the subject. John Harington records that 'the Queen did once ask my wife in merry sort, how she kept my good will and love.'

> My Mall, in wise and discreet manner, told her Highness she had confidence in her husband's understanding and courage, well-founded on her own steadfastness not to offend or thwart, but to cherish and obey. Hereby she did persuade her husband of her own affection, and in so doing did command his. 'Go to, go to, mistress', saith the Queen, 'you are wisely bent, I find. After such sort do I keep the good will of all my husbands, my good people; for if they did not rest assured of some special love toward them, they would not readily yield me such good obedience.'

Harington thought this anecdote deserved noting, 'as being both wise and pleasant'. In fact, of course, it reveals much of the secret of Elizabeth's success. Her loving relationship with her good people, which enabled one woman to rule a tough, independent-minded, quarrelsome nation virtually by the force of her personality, was no accident. Like all relationships it had to be worked for, and all her long reign Elizabeth Tudor never once forgot that – never took the goodwill of all her husbands for granted. In that one simple fact lay the essence of her genius.

Elizabeth remained astonishingly fit and active almost to the very end. In August 1602 Robert Cecil noted that she had not been in better health for twelve years and was still riding every day and hunting. In September the Earl of Worcester wrote to the Earl of Shrewsbury. 'We are frolic here at court; much dancing in the Privy Chamber of country dances before the Queen's majesty who is exceedingly pleased therewith'. Later in the month, another correspondent was telling the Countess of Shrewsbury, 'The best news I can yet write your ladyship is of the Queen's health and disposition of body, which I assure you is excellent good. And I have not seen her every way better disposed these many years.' Elizabeth had been fortunate in inheriting her father's splendid constitution and, unlike him, had never abused it. She always been extremely fastidious in matters of personal hygiene; had always taken plenty of fresh air and exercise and been notably abstemious over food and drink. She had also, wisely, avoided the ministrations of the royal physicians whenever possible. Perhaps, though, the real reason for her continued physical well-being was that she had been lucky enough to spend her life doing something she thoroughly enjoyed and was supremely good at.

But not even Elizabeth was immortal – though to James of Scotland it sometimes seemed as if she might be. She was now in her seventieth year, a great age for her times, and had lived considerably longer than any other member of her house, but when John Harington came to Court in December he was shocked at the change he saw in her. 'Our dear Queen, my royal godmother and this state's most natural mother, doth now bear show of human infirmity', he wrote to his wife. Elizabeth seemed very depressed and when Harington, in an attempt to

'Elizabeth I with Time and Death', by an unknown artist.

cheer her up, read her some of his witty verses, she smiled but said, 'When thou dost feel creeping time at thy gate, these fooleries will please thee less. I am past my relish for such matters.' She was eating hardly anything now and, for the first time, there were signs that her memory was beginning to fail. 'But who', wrote her godson sadly, 'shall say that "your Highness hath forgotten"?'

Harington must have seen her on a bad day, for she rallied again. Christmas was spent with all the usual gaieties and in January the Queen was said to be in excellent health. On the twenty-first the Court moved down to Richmond. The weather had turned very cold, but Elizabeth insisted on wearing 'summer-like garments'. On 6 February she received the new Venetian ambassador, dressed in white and silver, her hair 'of a light colour never made by nature' and apparently in good spirits. She addressed Scaramelli in his own language and said at the end of the audience – 'I do not know if I have spoken Italian well; still I think so, for I learnt it when a child and believe I have not forgotten it.' Elizabeth was still in harness, busy with Irish affairs but finding her daily routine more and more of a strain. Towards the end of February her closest woman friend, the Countess of Nottingham, died. The Queen's mood of depression returned and this time she did not recover.

Early in March her young relative, Robert Carey, grandson of her aunt Mary Boleyn, came down to Richmond to see her and found her in one of her withdrawing chambers 'sitting low upon her cushions'. 'She took me by the hand', he wrote, 'and wrung it hard and said, "No, Robin, I am not well"; and then discoursed with me of her indisposition, and that her heart had been sad and heavy for ten or twelve days, and in her discourse she fetched forty or fifty great sighs. I was grieved at the first to see her in this plight, for in all my lifetime before I never knew her fetch a sigh, but when the Queen of Scots was beheaded.' Carey did his best 'to persuade her from this melancholy humour', but found 'it was too deep-rooted in her heart and hardly to be removed.' This was on a Saturday evening. Next day the Queen was unable to go to church as usual and instead heard the service lying on cushions in her privy chamber. 'From that day forwards', says Robert Carey, 'she grew worse and worse. She remained upon her cushions four days and nights at the least. All about her could not persuade her to take any sustenance or go to bed.'

Elizabeth had always said that she did not desire to live longer than would be for her subjects' good. Now it seemed as if she felt her task was done. She had outlived her century, outlived nearly all her friends and her usefulness to her beloved country, and she wanted to make an end. Recently the coronation ring, the outward and visible token of her symbolic marriage to the kingdom of England which, for nearly forty-five years, had never left her finger, had grown into the flesh and had to be cut away. It was an omen. 'The Queen grew worse and worse,' said Robert Carey significantly, 'because she would be so.' Still no one could persuade her to go to bed. Eventually her cousin, the Lord Admiral, was sent for and partly by persuasion, partly by force, he succeeded in getting her off her cushions and into bed. There, temporarily, she felt a little better and was able to take some broth. But 'there was no hope of her recovery, because she refused all remedies.'

The immediate physical cause of Elizabeth's last illness seems to have been a streptococcal throat infection, possibly connected with dental sepsis, but soon pneumonia set in and she lay speechless and semi-conscious, her eyes open, one finger in her mouth. The story which had begun so long ago in blood and battle under the fiery banner of the red dragon was ending now in the great, richly furnished bedchamber at Richmond Palace where a tired old woman waited for her release.

Elizabeth died in the small hours of Thursday, 24 March 1603 – 'mildly like a lamb, easily like a ripe apple from the tree' – and Robert Carey, who had been standing by with a horse ready saddled, dashed away through the night on the first stage of his wild ride north to tell Margaret Tudor's great-grandson that the waiting was over. Hempe was spun and England done and the last English sovereign of the English nation lay at peace.

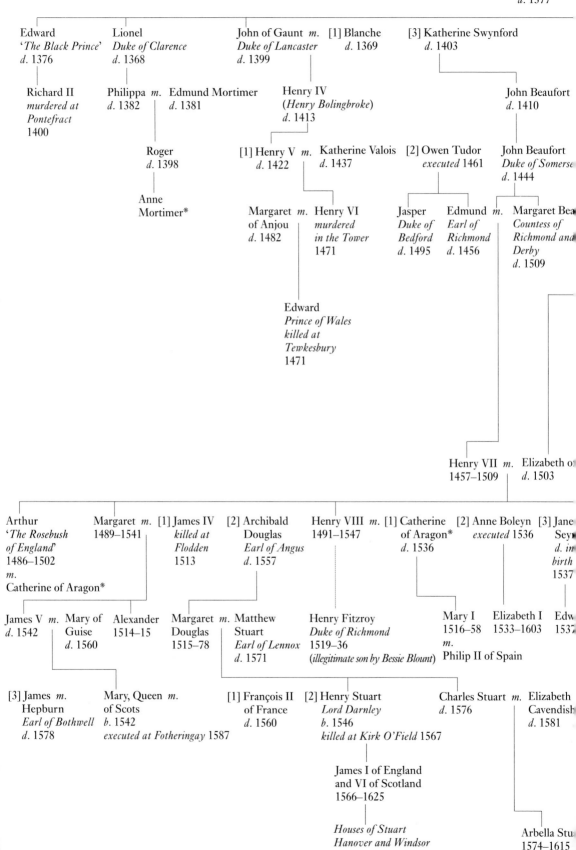

Edward III
d. 1377

Edward
'*The Black Prince*'
d. 1376

Lionel
Duke of Clarence
d. 1368

John of Gaunt *m.* [1] Blanche
Duke of Lancaster   *d.* 1369
d. 1399

[3] Katherine Swynford
d. 1403

Richard II
murdered at
Pontefract
1400

Philippa *m.* Edmund Mortimer
d. 1382   *d.* 1381

Henry IV
(*Henry Bolingbroke*)
d. 1413

John Beaufort
d. 1410

Roger
d. 1398

[1] Henry V *m.* Katherine Valois
d. 1422   *d.* 1437

[2] Owen Tudor
executed 1461

John Beaufort
Duke of Somerse
d. 1444

Anne
Mortimer*

Margaret *m.* Henry VI
of Anjou   *murdered*
d. 1482   *in the Tower*
                 1471

Jasper
Duke of
Bedford
d. 1495

Edmund *m.* Margaret Bea
Earl of   *Countess of*
Richmond   *Richmond and*
d. 1456   *Derby*
                 d. 1509

Edward
Prince of Wales
killed at
Tewkesbury
1471

Henry VII *m.* Elizabeth o
1457–1509   *d.* 1503

Arthur
'*The Rosebush*
of England'
1486–1502
m.
Catherine of Aragon*

Margaret *m.* [1] James IV
1489–1541   *killed at*
                Flodden
                1513

[2] Archibald
Douglas
Earl of Angus
d. 1557

Henry VIII *m.* [1] Catherine
1491–1547   of Aragon*
                 d. 1536

[2] Anne Boleyn [3] Jane
executed 1536   Sey▶
                  d. in
                  birth
                  1537

James V *m.* Mary of
d. 1542   Guise
               d. 1560

Alexander
1514–15

Margaret *m.* Matthew
Douglas   Stuart
1515–78   *Earl of Lennox*
                d. 1571

Henry Fitzroy
Duke of Richmond
1519–36
(*illegitimate son by Bessie Blount*)

Mary I   Elizabeth I   Edw
1516–58   1533–1603   1537
m.
Philip II of Spain

[3] James *m.*
Hepburn
Earl of Bothwell
d. 1578

Mary, Queen *m.*
of Scots
b. 1542
executed at Fotheringay 1587

[1] François II
of France
d. 1560

[2] Henry Stuart
Lord Darnley
b. 1546
killed at Kirk O'Field 1567

Charles Stuart *m.* Elizabeth
d. 1576   Cavendish
                     d. 1581

James I of England
and VI of Scotland
1566–1625

Houses of Stuart
Hanover and Windsor

Arbella Stu▶
1574–1615

opa of Hainault
.9

The House of Plantagenet

mund
ke of York
1402

Thomas of Woodstock
d. 1397

hard *m.* Anne
cuted | Mortimer*
5

Dukes of Buckingham

Richard
Duke of York
killed at Wakefield 1460

V *m.* Elizabeth Woodville	George	Richard III	Elizabeth *m.* John de la Pole	Margaret
d. 1492	*Duke of Clarence*	*killed at Bosworth* *d.* 1503	*Earl of Suffolk*	*d.* 1503
	d. 1478	1485	*d.* 1491	*m.*
				Charles the Bold
				Duke of Burgundy
				d. 1477

V	Richard	Katherine	Edward	Margaret	John	Edmund	Richard
d in	*Duke of York*	*d.* 1527	*Earl of Warwick*	*Countess of*	*killed at*	*'The White*	*killed at*
er	*murdered in*	*m.*	*executed* 1499	*Salisbury*	*Stoke* 1487	*Rose'*	*Pavia* 1525
	the Tower	William Courtenay		*executed* 1541		*executed* 1513	
	1483	*Earl of Devon*		*m.*			
		d. 1511		Sir Richard Pole			
				d. 1505			

Henry
Marquis of Exeter
executed 1538

Henry Pole
Lord Montague
executed 1538

Reginald Pole
Cardinal of
England
d. 1558

Edward Courtenay
Earl of Devon
d. at Padua 1556

The House of Tudor

e of	[5] Catherine	[6] Katherine	Elizabeth	Mary *m.*	[1] Louis XII	[2] Charles Brandon	Edmund	Katherine
es	Howard	Parr	1492–95	1495–1533	of France	*Duke of Suffolk*	1499–1500	*d. at birth*
57	*executed* 1542	*d.* 1548			*d.* 1515	*d.* 1545		1503

Henry	Frances *m.* [1] Henry Grey	[2] Adrian Stokes	Eleanor *m.* Henry Clifford
Earl of Lincoln	*d.* 1559	*Duke of Suffolk*	*d.* 1581	1519–47	*Earl of Cumberland*
1516–34	*executed* 1554		*d.* 1569

d Dudley *m.* Jane	Katherine *m.* Edward Seymour	Mary *m.* Thomas Keys	Margaret *m.* Henry Stanley
1554	*'The Nine*	1539–68	*Earl of Hertford*	1545–78 *d.* 1571	1540–96	*Earl of Derby*
Duke of	*Days Queen'*	*d.* 1621		*d.* 1593
nberland)	*b.* 1537	*(son of Protector Somerset)*	
	executed 1554		

Earls of Derby

Edward
b. in the Tower 1561

Thomas
b. in the Tower 1563

am

A Note on Sources

Chapter 1. A Bull of Anglesey

J. Williams, 'Penmynydd and the Tudors', *Archaeologia Cambrensis*, 3rd series, XV, 1869

Glyn Roberts, 'Wyrion Eden: the Anglesey descendants of Ednyfed Fychan in the 14th century', *Transactions of the Anglesey Antiquarian Society and Field Club* (1951), pp. 34–72

Ralph A. Griffiths and Roger S. Thomas, *The Making of the Tudor Dynasty*, Stroud, Alan Sutton, 1985

Three Fifteenth Century Chronicles, ed. J. Gairdner, Camden Society, 3rd series, XXVIII, 1880

C.H. Cooper, *Memoir of Margaret, Countess of Richmond and Derby*, Cambridge, 1874

M.K. Jones and M.G. Underwood, *The King's Mother: Lady Margaret Beaufort*, Cambridge, 1992

Chronicles of London, ed. C.L. Kingsford, Oxford, 1905

Polydore Vergil, *Anglica Historia*, ed. D. Hay, Camden Society, n.s. 74 (1950)

Andre, Bernard, 'Vita Henrici Septimi' in *Memorials of King Henry VII*, ed. J. Gairdner, Rolls Series, London, 1858

Chapter 2. The Rose of England

Michael Bennett, *The Battle of Bosworth*, Alan Sutton, 1985

Polydore Vergil, *Anglica Historia*

The Song of Lady Bessy, ed. J.O. Halliwell, Percy Society, 20 (1877)

Privy Purse Expenses of Elizabeth of York, ed. N.H. Nicolas, London, 1830

S.B. Chrimes, *Henry VII*, London, 1977

Materials for a History of the Reign of Henry VII, ed. W. Campbell, 2 vols, Rolls Series, London, 1873–7

The Reign of Henry VII from Contemporary Sources, ed. A.F. Pollard, 3 vols, London, 1913–14

Hall's Chronicle, ed. H. Ellis, London, 1809

Francis Bacon, *History of the Reign of King Henry the Seventh*, ed. Roger Lockyer, Folio Society, London, 1971

Chapter 3.
A Wonder for Wise Men

John Leland, *De Rebus Britannicis Collectanea*, ed. Thomas Hearne, Vol. IV, Oxford, 1715 (contains Margaret Beaufort's Ordinances)

Calendar of State Papers, Spanish, Henry VII, ed. G.A. Bergenroth, London, 1862

Letters and Papers Illustrative of the Reigns of Richard III and Henry VII, ed. J. Gairdner, Rolls Series, London, 1861–3

Hall's Chronicle, ed. Ellis

Francis Bacon, *History*, ed. Lockyer

The Fiancels of Margaret Tudor, Leland's *Collectanea*, Vol. V

Polydore Vergil, *Anglica Historia*

Chapter 4.
The Renaissance Prince

J.J. Scarisbrick, *Henry VIII*, London, 1968

Hall's Chronicle, ed. Ellis

Calendar of State Papers, Spanish, ed. G.A. Bergenroth, Vol. 2

Calendar of State Papers, Venetian, ed. Rawdon Brown, London, 1864, Vol. II

Letters and Papers, Foreign and Domestic, of Henry VIII, ed. J.S. Brewer, J. Gairdner and R.H. Brodie, London, 1862–1910). This is a monumental work in 21 vols in 33 parts and is the basic source for the whole reign.

S.J. Gunn, *Charles Brandon, Duke of Suffolk*, Oxford, 1988

Chapter 5. Tudor Sisters

M.A.E. Green, *Lives of the Princesses of England*, London, 1849, Vol. 5
Agnes Strickland, *Lives of the Tudor Princesses*, London, 1868
Hester Chapman, *The Sisters of Henry VIII*, London, 1969
W.C. Richardson, *Mary Tudor, the White Queen*, London, 1970
Hall's Chronicle, ed. Ellis
Letters and Papers of Henry VIII, ed. Brewer *et al.*
Cal. of State Papers, Venetian, Vol. II, ed. Brown

Chapter 6.
The King's Secret Matter

Antonia Fraser, *The Six Wives of Henry VIII*, London, 1992
Garrett Mattingly, *Catherine of Aragon*, 1942
J.E. Paul, *Catherine of Aragon and her Friends*, 1966
Hester Chapman, *Anne Boleyn*, 1974
E.W. Ives, *Anne Boleyn*, Oxford, 1986
Cal. of State Papers, Spanish, Vol. 2, ed. Bergenroth
Hall's Chronicle, ed. Ellis
George Cavendish, *The Life and Death of Cardinal Wolsey*, ed. R.S. Sylvester, Early English Text Society, 1959
The Letters of King Henry VIII, ed. M. St. Clare Byrne, ne edn, London, 1968
Charles Wriothesley, *Chronicle of England*, ed. W.D. Hamilton, 2 vols, Camden Society, n.s. XI, 1875–7

Chapter 7. England's Treasure

Agnes Strickland, *Lives of the Queens of England*, reprinted 1972
Letters and Papers of Henry VIII, ed. Brewer *et al.*
Cal. of State Papers, Spanish, Vol. 10,
H.F.M. Prescott, *Mary Tudor*, revised edition, 1952
David Loades, *Mary Tudor: a Life*, Oxford, 1989
Hester Chapman, *The Last Tudor King*, 1958

Chapter 8. The Old Fox

Lacey Baldwin Smith, *A Tudor Tragedy: The Life and Times of Catherine Howard*, London, 1961

John Foxe, *Acts and Monuments* [aka *The Book of Martyrs*], ed. S.R.T. Cattley and G. Townsend, London, 1837
Strickland, *Lives of the Queens of England*
Lacey Baldwin Smith, *Henry VIII: The Mask of Royalty*, 1971

Chapter 9.
A Boy of Wondrous Hope

P.F. Tytler, *England under the Reigns of Edward VI and Mary*, 1839
W.K. Jordan, *Edward VI: The Young King*, London, 1968
Literary Remains of King Edward VI, ed. J.G. Nichols, 2 Vols, Roxburghe Club, 1857
John Hayward, *The Life of Edward VI*, in White Kennett, *Complete History of England*, Vol. II, 1706
F.A. Mumby, *The Girlhood of Queen Elizabeth*, 1906
State Papers of William Cecil, Lord Burghley, ed. Samuel Haynes, 1740 (contains the depositions, letters, etc., concerning Elizabeth and Thomas Seymour)
Strickland, *Lives of the Tudor Princesses*
Hester Chapman, *Lady Jane Grey*, London, 1962

Chapter 10.
Gone is Our Treasure

W.K. Jordan, *Edward VI: The Threshold of Power*, 1970
——, *The Chronicle and Political Papers of Edward VI*, New York, 1966
Cal. of State Papers, Spanish, Vols 10 and 11
Diary of Henry Machyn, ed. J.G. Nichols, Camden Society, 42, 1848
F. Madden, *Privy Purse Expenses of the Princess Mary*, 1831
Chronicle of Queen Jane and Two Years of Queen Mary, ed. J.G. Nichols, Camden Society, 48, 1850

Chapter 11. The Rule of the Proud Spaniards

Prescott, *Mary Tudor*
Chronicle of the Greyfriars, ed. J.G. Nichols, Camden Society, 53, 1852
Chronicle of Queen Jane
Cal. of State Papers, Spanish, Vols 11 and 12

E.H. Harbison, *Rival Ambassadors at the Court of Queen Mary*, Princeton UP, 1940
Literary Remains of Lady Jane Grey, N.H. Nicolas, London, 1825

Chapter 12. In Honour of Worthy Philip

Cal. of State Papers, Spanish, Vol. 12
Cal. of State Papers, Venetian, Vols 5 and 6
Bedingfield Papers, ed. C.R. Manning, Norfolk and Norwich Archaeological Society, Vol. IV, 1855
Foxe, *Acts and Monuments*

Chapter 13. England's Eliza

Holinshed's Chronicle, ed. H. Ellis, London, 1807
Cal. of State Papers, Spanish, Elizabeth, ed. M.A.S. Hume, 1892–9, Vol. 1
Cal. of State Papers, Foreign, Elizabeth, ed. J. Stevenson, 1863, Vol. 2
John Hayward, *Annals of the first four years of the reign of Elizabeth*, ed. John Bruce, Camden Society, 7, 1840
J.E. Neale, *Queen Elizabeth I*, new edn, 1952
Elizabeth Jenkins, *Elizabeth and Leicester*, 1961
George Adlard, *Amye Robsart and the Earl of Leycester*, 1870
Strickland, *Lives of the Tudor Princesses*
Hester Chapman, *Two Tudor Portraits*, 1960 (for a modern study of Lady Catherine Grey)

Chapter 14. When Hempe is Spun

Cal. of State Papers, Spanish, Elizabeth, ed. Hume, Vols 1 and 2
Cal. of State Papers, Foreign, Elizabeth, Vols 3 and 4
F.A. Mumby, *Elizabeth and Mary Stuart: the Beginning of the Feud*, Boston, 1914
Antonia Fraser, *Mary Queen of Scots*, 1969
James Melville's Memoirs, ed. Frances Steuart, 1929
Andre de Maisse, *Journal*, trans. G.B. Harrison, 1931

ndex